BLADE
OF THE IMMORTAL

Last Blood

publisher
Mike Richardson

series editor
Philip Simon

collection editor
Chris Warner

collection designer
Debra Bailey

art director
Lia Ribacchi

**English-language version produced by
Studio Proteus for Dark Horse Comics, Inc.**

This volume collects issues ninety through ninety-eight
of the Dark Horse comic-book series
Blade of the Immortal.

Dark Horse Manga
A division of Dark Horse Comics, Inc.
10956 SE Main Street
Milwaukie, OR 97222

darkhorse.com

To find a comics shop in your area, call the
Comic Shop Locator Service toll-free at 1-888-266-4226

First edition: June 2005
ISBN-10: 1-59307-321-6
ISBN-13: 978-1-59307-321-3

3 5 7 9 10 8 6 4 2

Printed in the United States of America

BLADE
OF THE IMMORTAL

art and story
HIROAKI SAMURA

translation
Dana Lewis & Toren Smith

lettering and retouch
Tomoko Saito

Last Blood

DARK HORSE MANGA™

ABOUT THE TRANSLATION

The Swastika

The main character in *Blade of the Immortal*, Manji, has taken the "crux gammata" as both his name and his personal symbol. This symbol is also known as the *swastika*, a name derived from the Sanskrit *svastika* (meaning "welfare," from *su* — "well" + *asti* "he is"). As a symbol of prosperity and good fortune, the swastika was widely used throughout the ancient world (for example, appearing often on Mesopotamian coinage), including North and South America and has been used in Japan as a symbol of Buddhism since ancient times. To be precise, the symbol generally used by Japanese Buddhists is the *sauvastika*, which moves in a counterclockwise direction and is called the *manji* in Japanese. The arms of the *swastika*, which point in a clockwise direction, are generally considered a solar symbol. It was this version (the *hakenkreuz*) that was perverted by the Nazis. The *sauvastika* generally stands for night, and often for magical practices. It is important that readers understand that the swastika has ancient and honorable origins, and it is those that apply to this story, which takes place in the 18th century [ca. 1782–3]. *There is no anti-Semitic or pro-Nazi meaning behind the use of the symbol in this story. Those meanings did not exist until after 1910.*

The Artwork

The creator of *Blade of the Immortal* requested that we make an effort to avoid mirror-imaging his artwork. Normally, Westernized manga are first copied in a mirror-image in order to facilitate the left-to-right reading of the pages. However, Mr. Samura decided that he would rather see his pages reversed via the technique of cutting up the panels and re-pasting them in reverse order. While we feel that this often leads to problems in panel-to-panel continuity, we place primary importance on the wishes of the creator. Therefore, most of *Blade of the Immortal* has been produced using the "cut and paste" technique. There are, of course, some sequences where it was impossible to do this, and mirror-imaged panels or pages were used.

The Sound Effects & Dialogue

Since some of Mr. Samura's sound effects are integral parts of the illustrations, we decided to leave those in their original Japanese. We hope readers will view the unretouched sound effects as essential portions of Mr. Samura's extraordinary artwork. In addition, Mr. Samura's treatment of dialogue is quite different from that featured in typical samurai manga and is considered to be one of the features that has made *Blade* such a hit in Japan. Mr. Samura has mixed a variety of linguistic styles in this fantasy story, with some characters speaking in the mannered style of old Japan while others speak as if they were street-corner punks from a bad area of modern-day Tokyo. The anachronistic slang used by some of the characters in the English translation reflects the unusual mix of speech patterns from the original Japanese text.

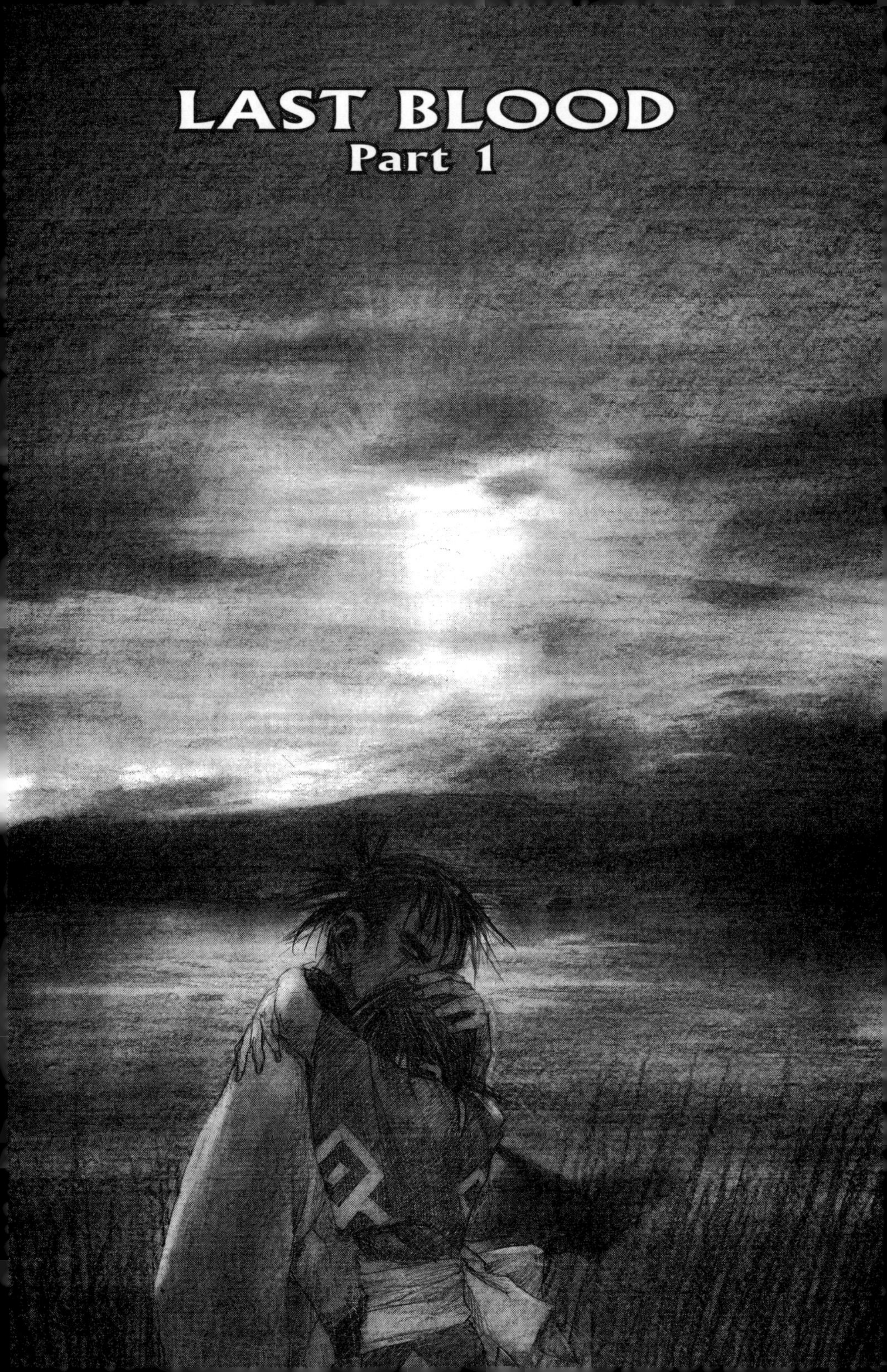
LAST BLOOD
Part 1

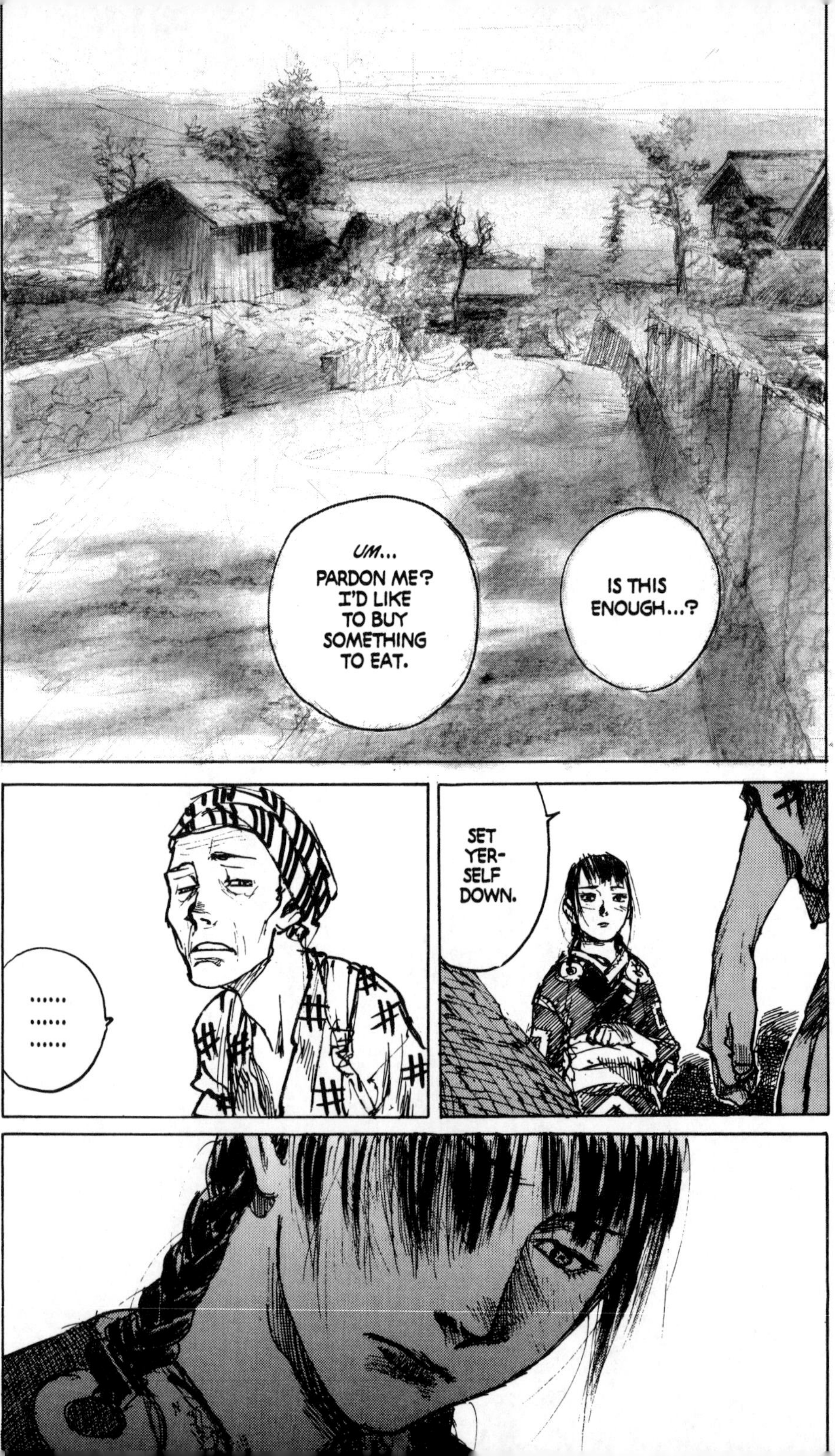
UM... PARDON ME? I'D LIKE TO BUY SOMETHING TO EAT.
IS THIS ENOUGH...?
....
SET YER-SELF DOWN.

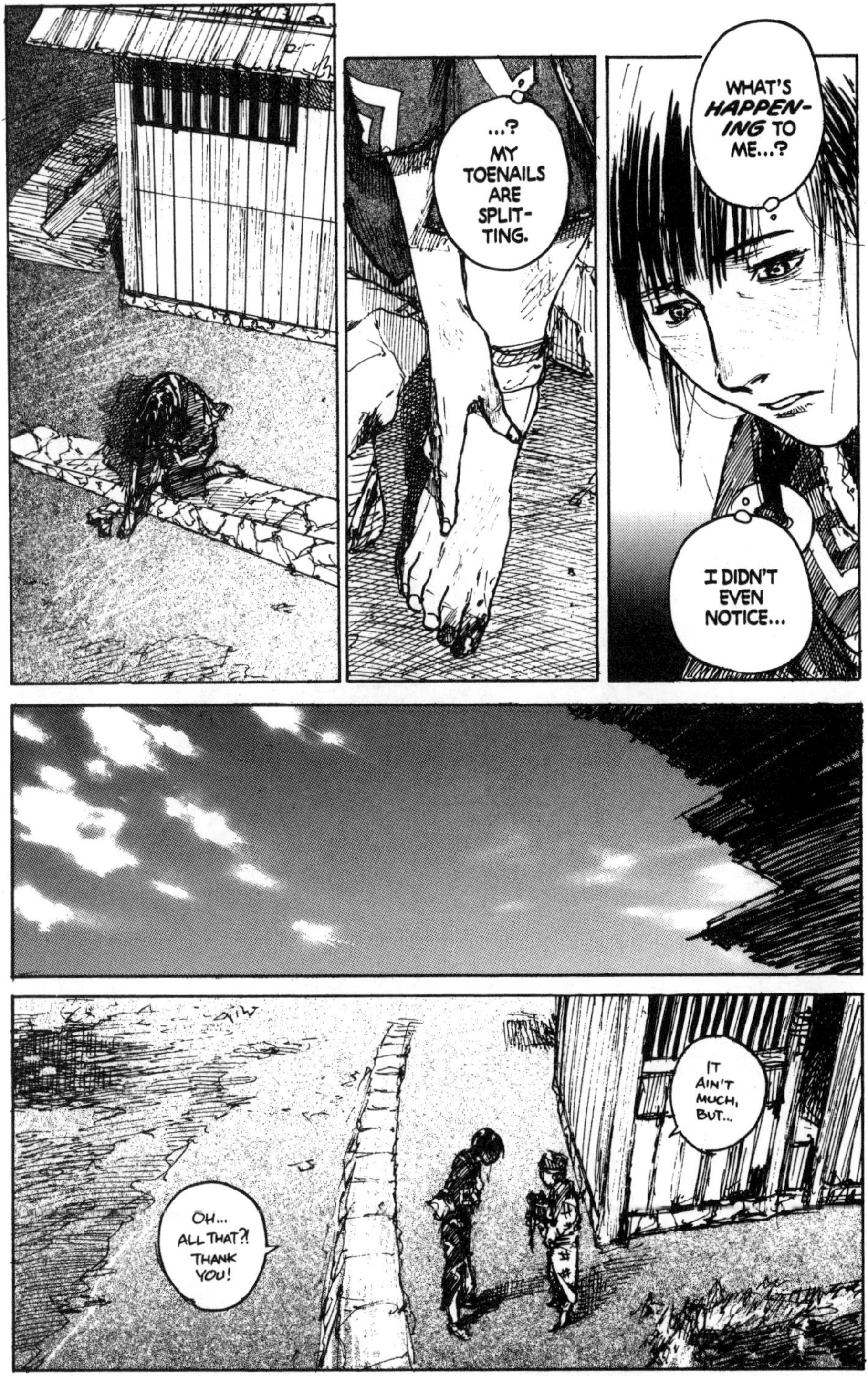
...? MY TOENAILS ARE SPLIT-TING.
WHAT'S HAPPEN-ING TO ME...?
I DIDN'T EVEN NOTICE...
IT AIN'T MUCH, BUT...
OH... ALL THAT?! THANK YOU!

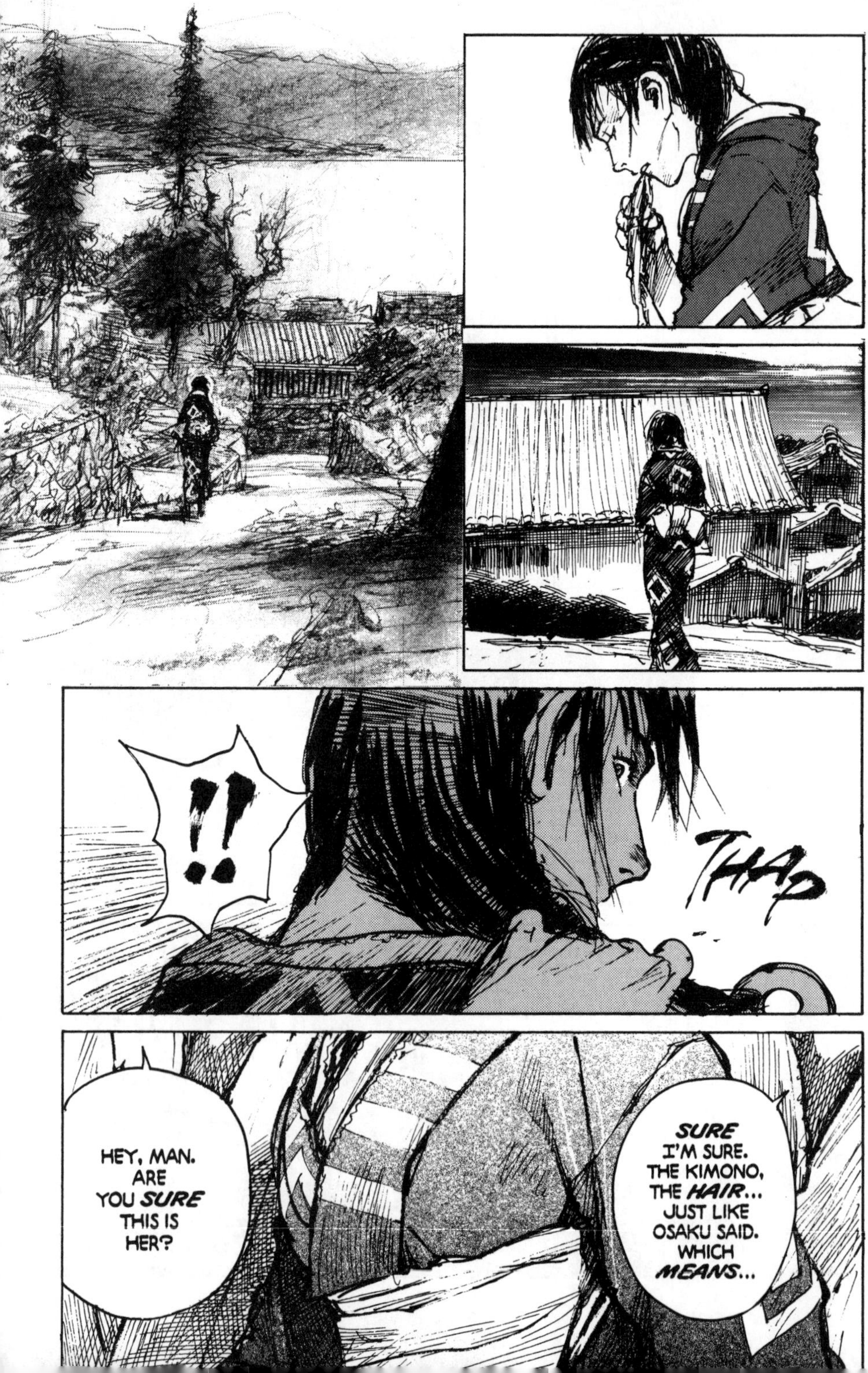
!!
THAP
HEY, MAN. ARE YOU *SURE* THIS IS HER?
SURE I'M SURE. THE KIMONO, THE *HAIR*... JUST LIKE OSAKU SAID. WHICH *MEANS*...

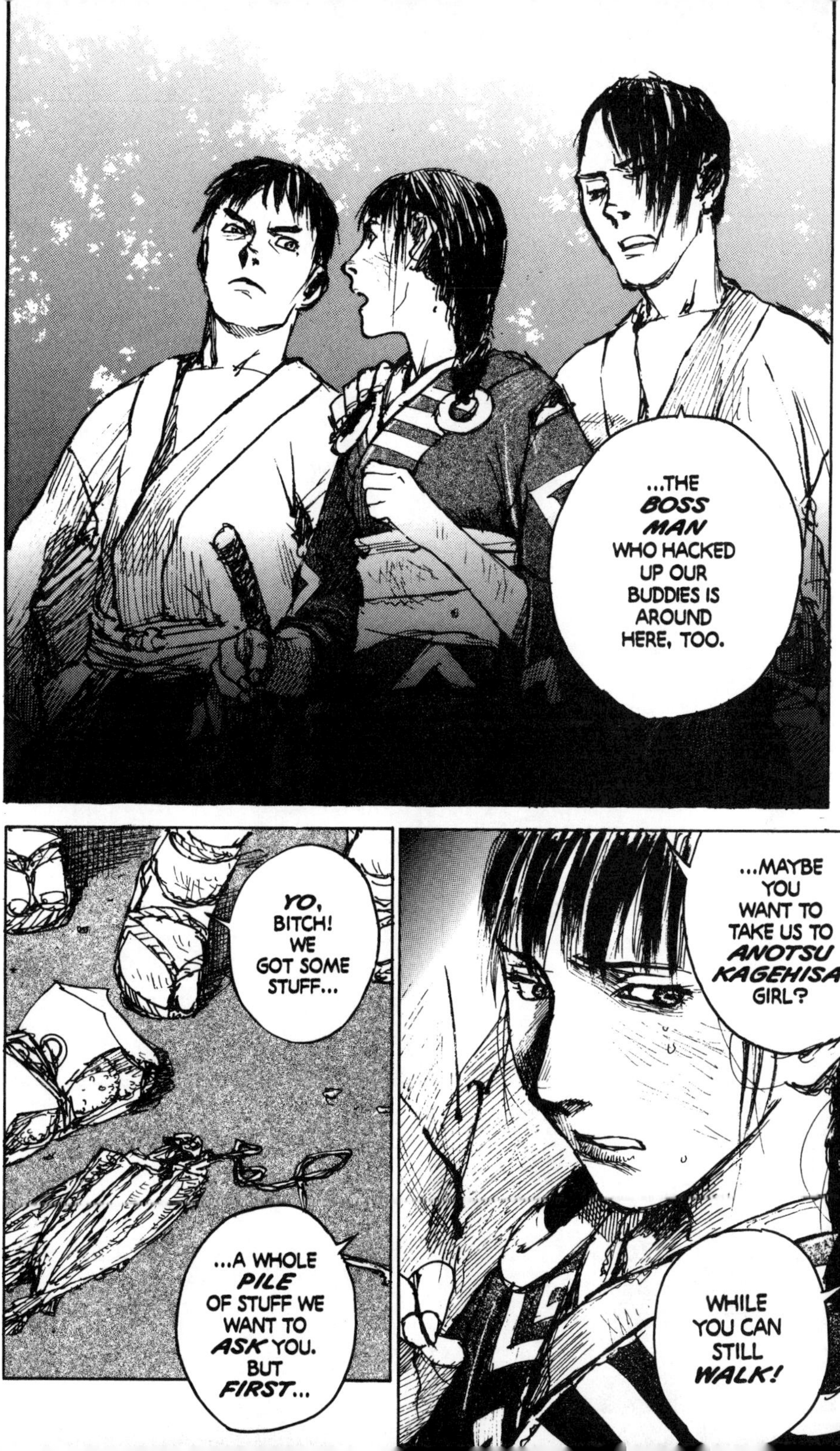
...THE *BOSS MAN* WHO HACKED UP OUR BUDDIES IS AROUND HERE, TOO.
YO, BITCH! WE GOT SOME STUFF...
...A WHOLE *PILE* OF STUFF WE WANT TO *ASK* YOU. BUT *FIRST*...
...MAYBE YOU WANT TO TAKE US TO *ANOTSU KAGEHISA*, GIRL?
WHILE YOU CAN STILL *WALK!*

ANOTSU
KAGEHISA!

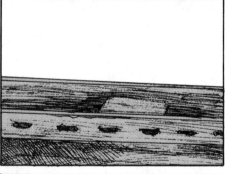

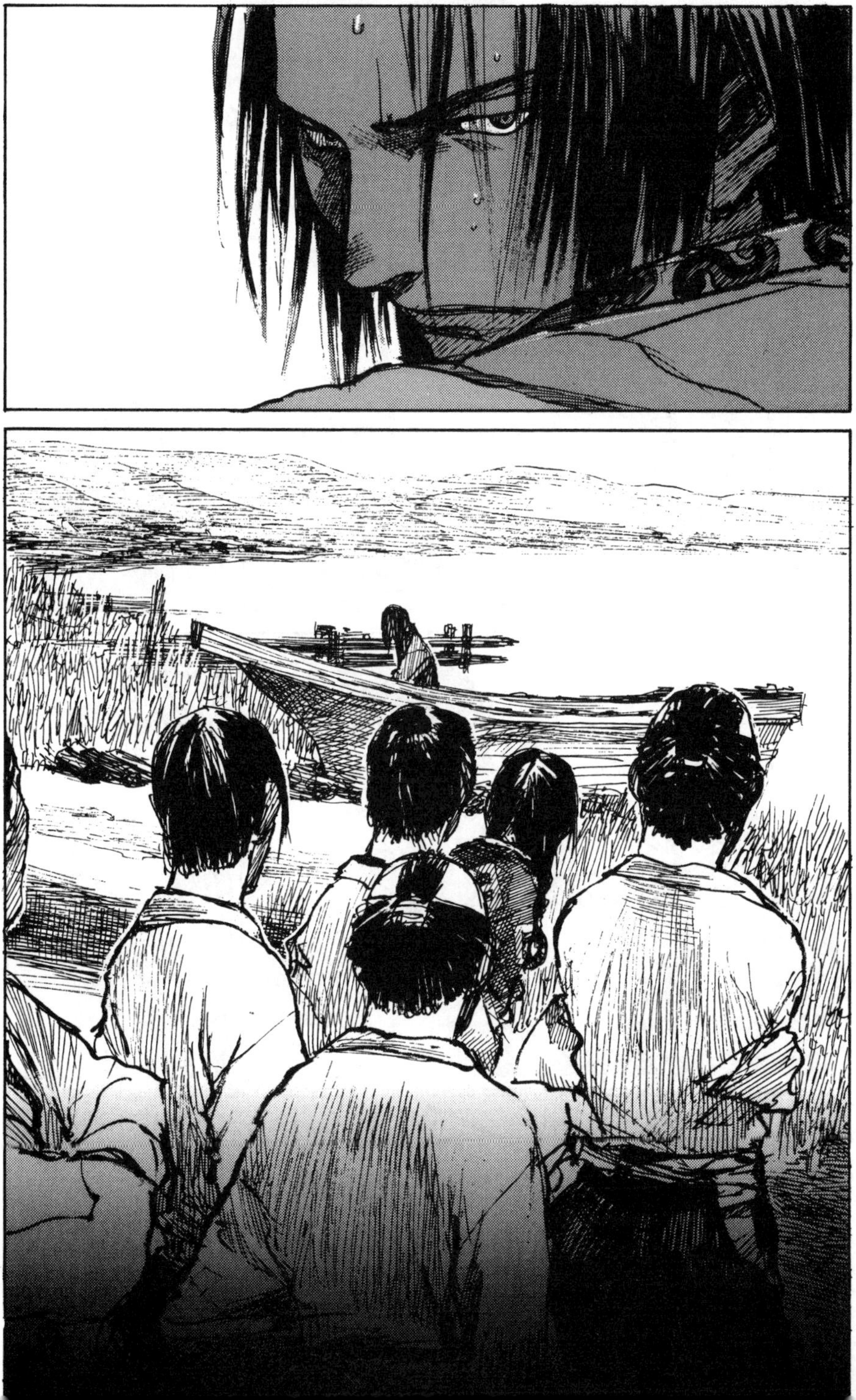

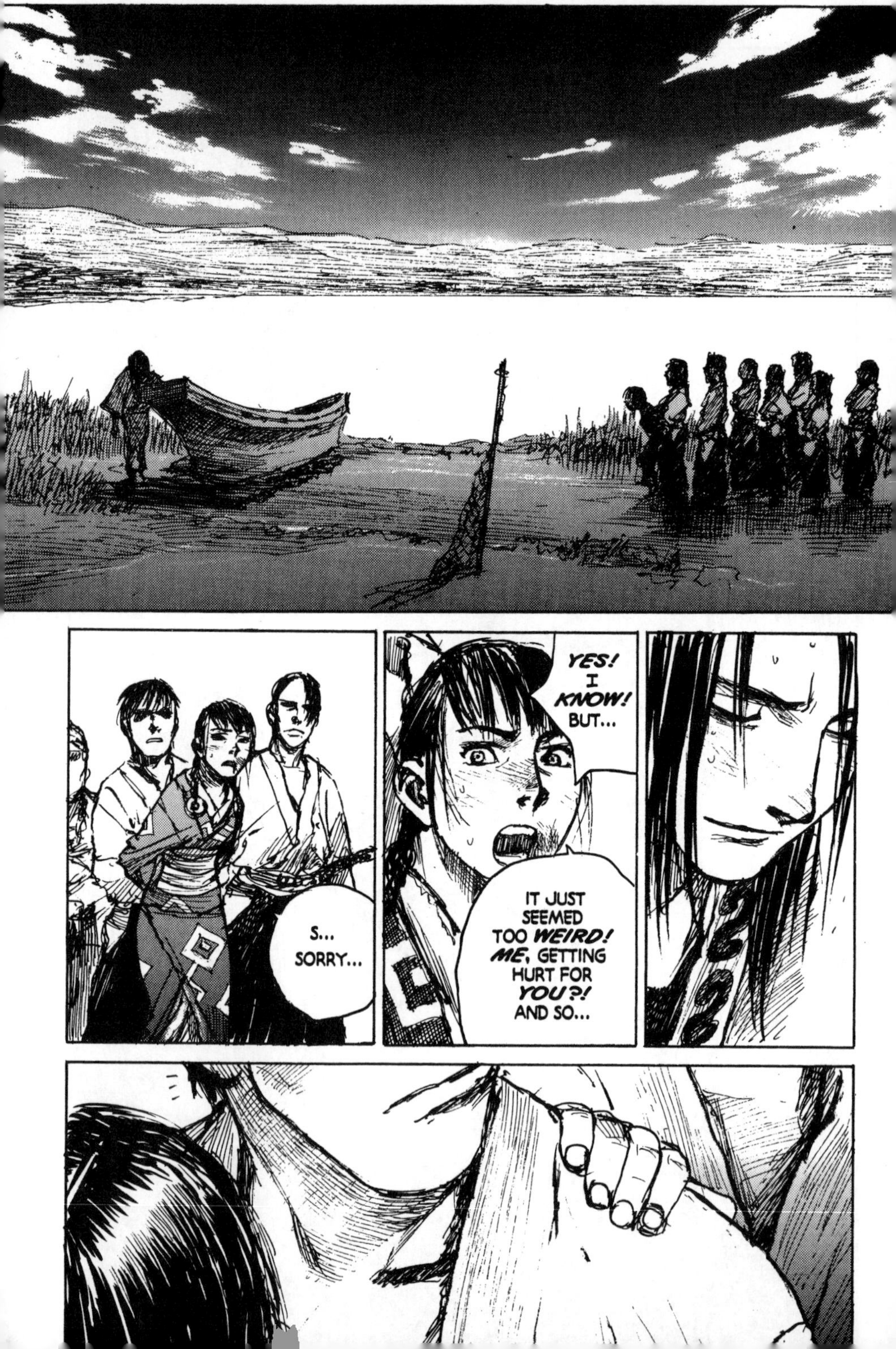
YES! I KNOW! BUT...
IT JUST SEEMED TOO WEIRD! ME, GETTING HURT FOR YOU?! AND SO...
S... SORRY...

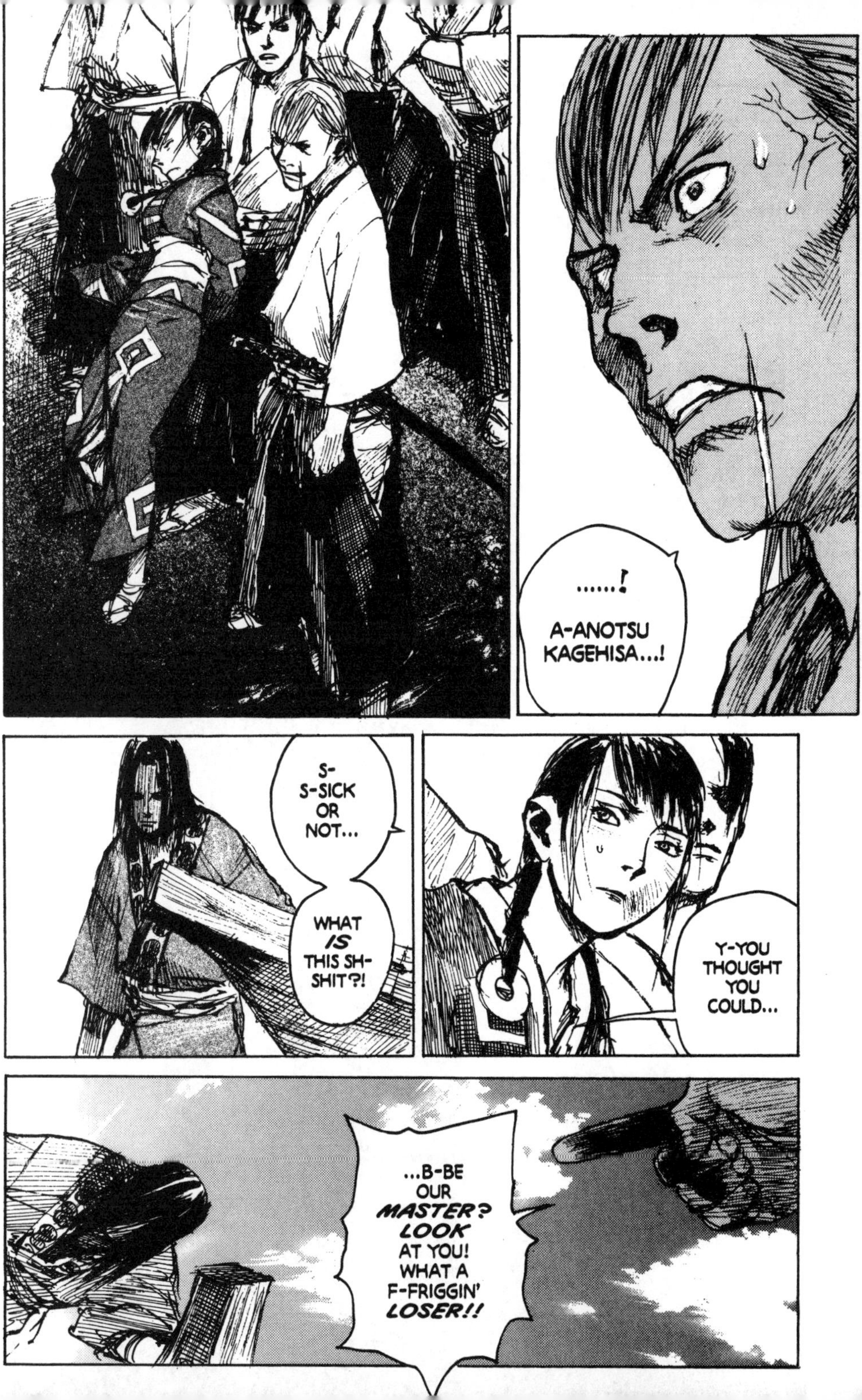
......!
A-ANOTSU KAGEHISA...!
Y-YOU THOUGHT YOU COULD...
S- S-SICK OR NOT...
WHAT IS THIS SH-SHIT?!
...B-BE OUR MASTER? LOOK AT YOU! WHAT A F-FRIGGIN' LOSER!!

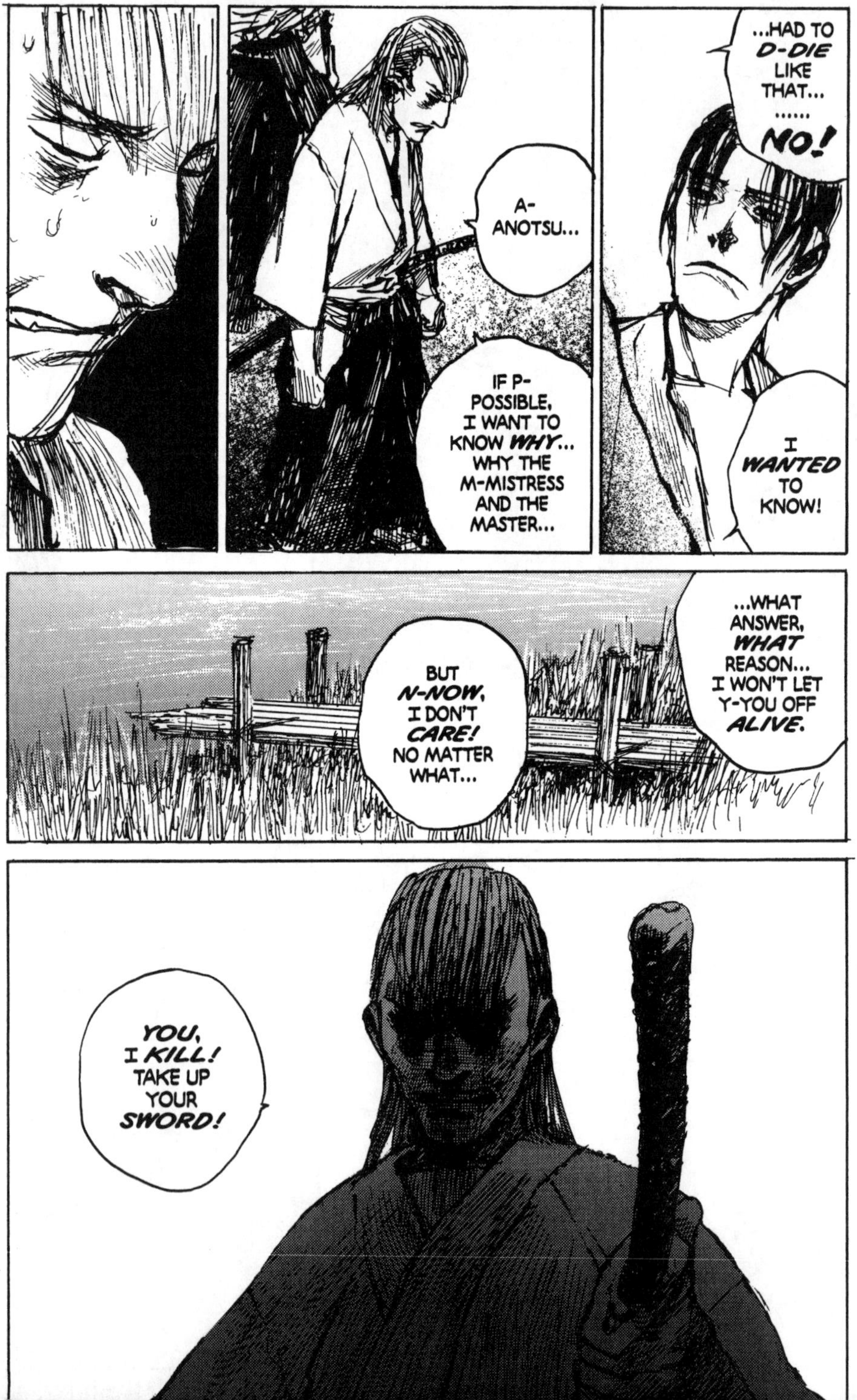
A-ANOTSU...
IF P-POSSIBLE, I WANT TO KNOW *WHY*... WHY THE M-MISTRESS AND THE MASTER...
...HAD TO *D-DIE* LIKE THAT... ...... *NO!*
I *WANTED* TO KNOW!
BUT *N-NOW*, I DON'T *CARE!* NO MATTER WHAT...
...WHAT ANSWER, *WHAT* REASON... I WON'T LET Y-YOU OFF *ALIVE*.
YOU, I *KILL!* TAKE UP YOUR *SWORD!*

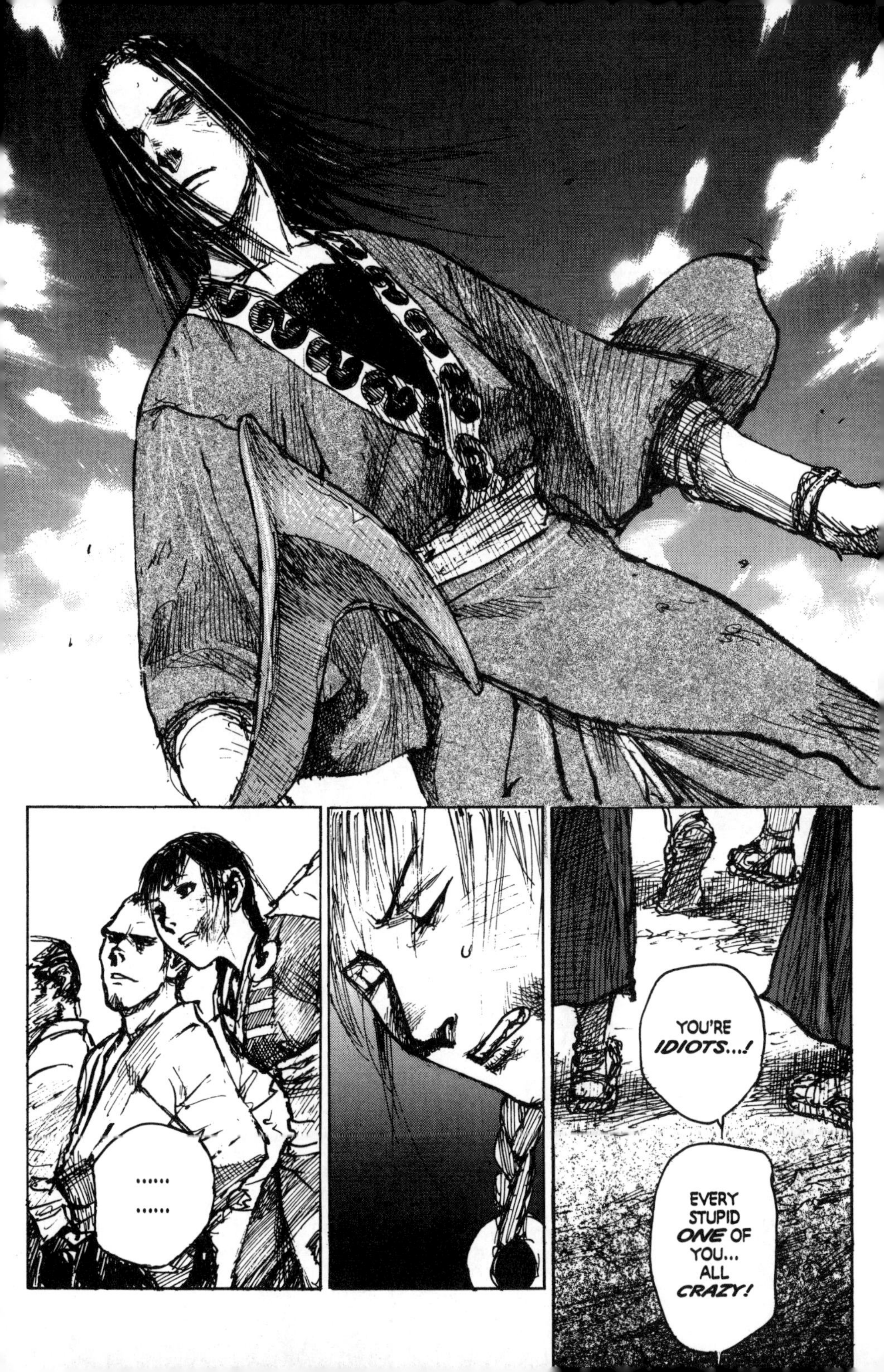
YOU'RE *IDIOTS*...!
EVERY STUPID *ONE* OF YOU... ALL *CRAZY*!
......
......

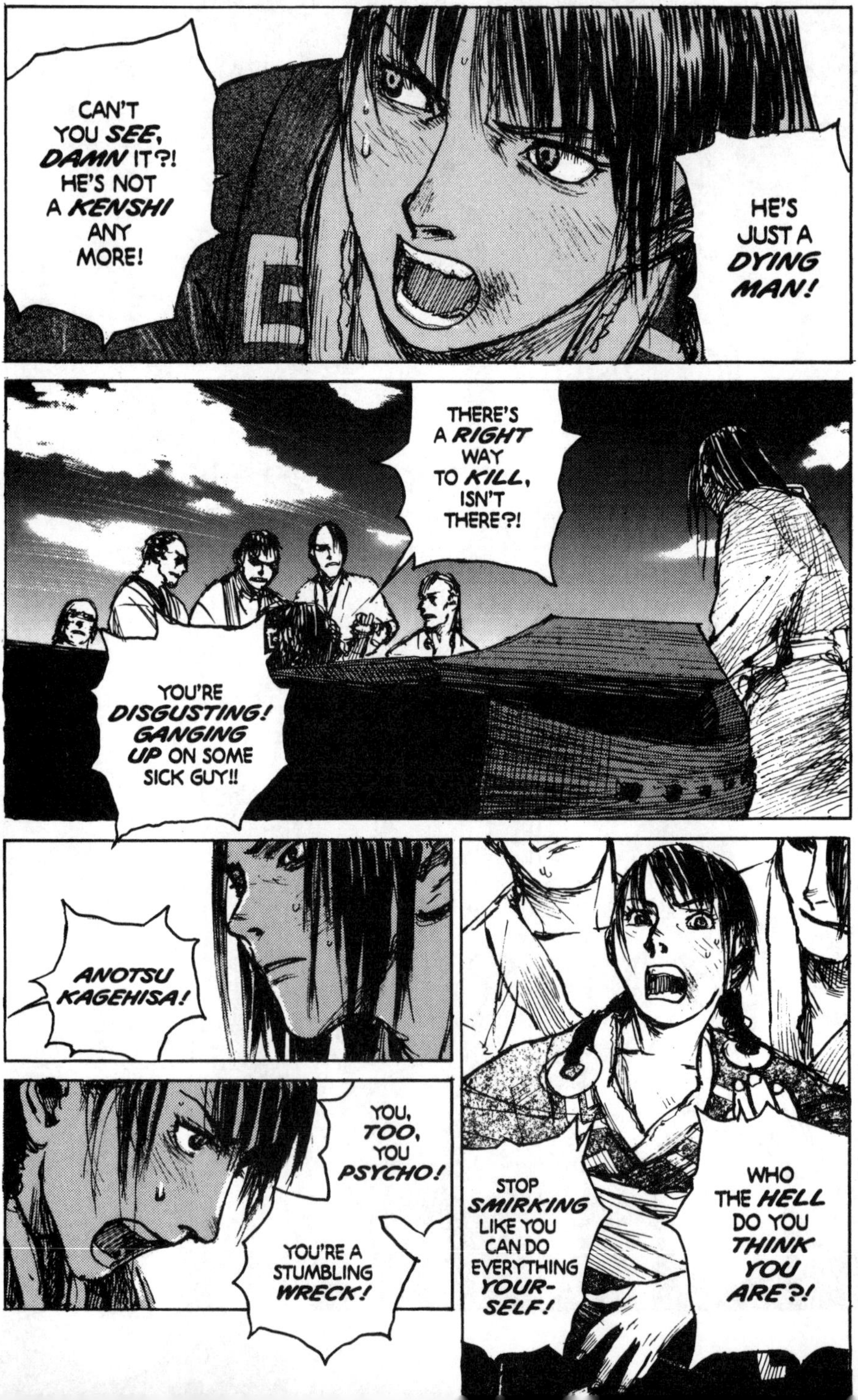
CAN'T YOU *SEE, DAMN* IT?! HE'S NOT A *KENSHI* ANY MORE!
HE'S JUST A *DYING MAN!*
THERE'S A *RIGHT* WAY TO *KILL,* ISN'T THERE?!
YOU'RE *DISGUSTING! GANGING UP* ON SOME SICK GUY!!
ANOTSU KAGEHISA!
YOU, *TOO,* YOU *PSYCHO!*
YOU'RE A STUMBLING *WRECK!*
WHO THE *HELL* DO YOU *THINK YOU ARE?!*
STOP *SMIRKING* LIKE YOU CAN DO EVERYTHING *YOUR-SELF!*

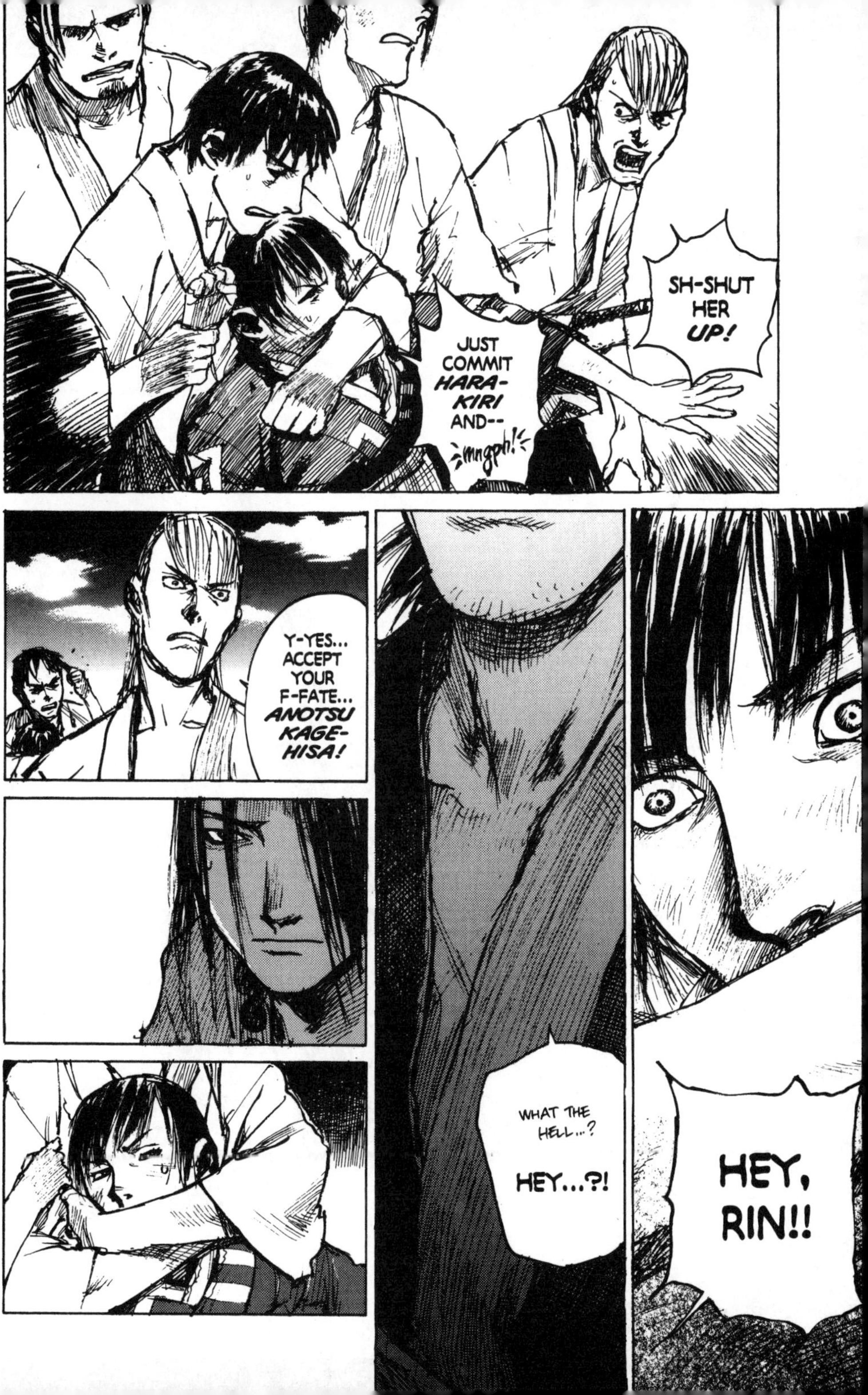
JUST COMMIT HARA-KIRI AND--
mngph!
SH-SHUT HER UP!
Y-YES... ACCEPT YOUR F-FATE... ANOTSU KAGE-HISA!
WHAT THE HELL...?
HEY...?!
HEY, RIN!!

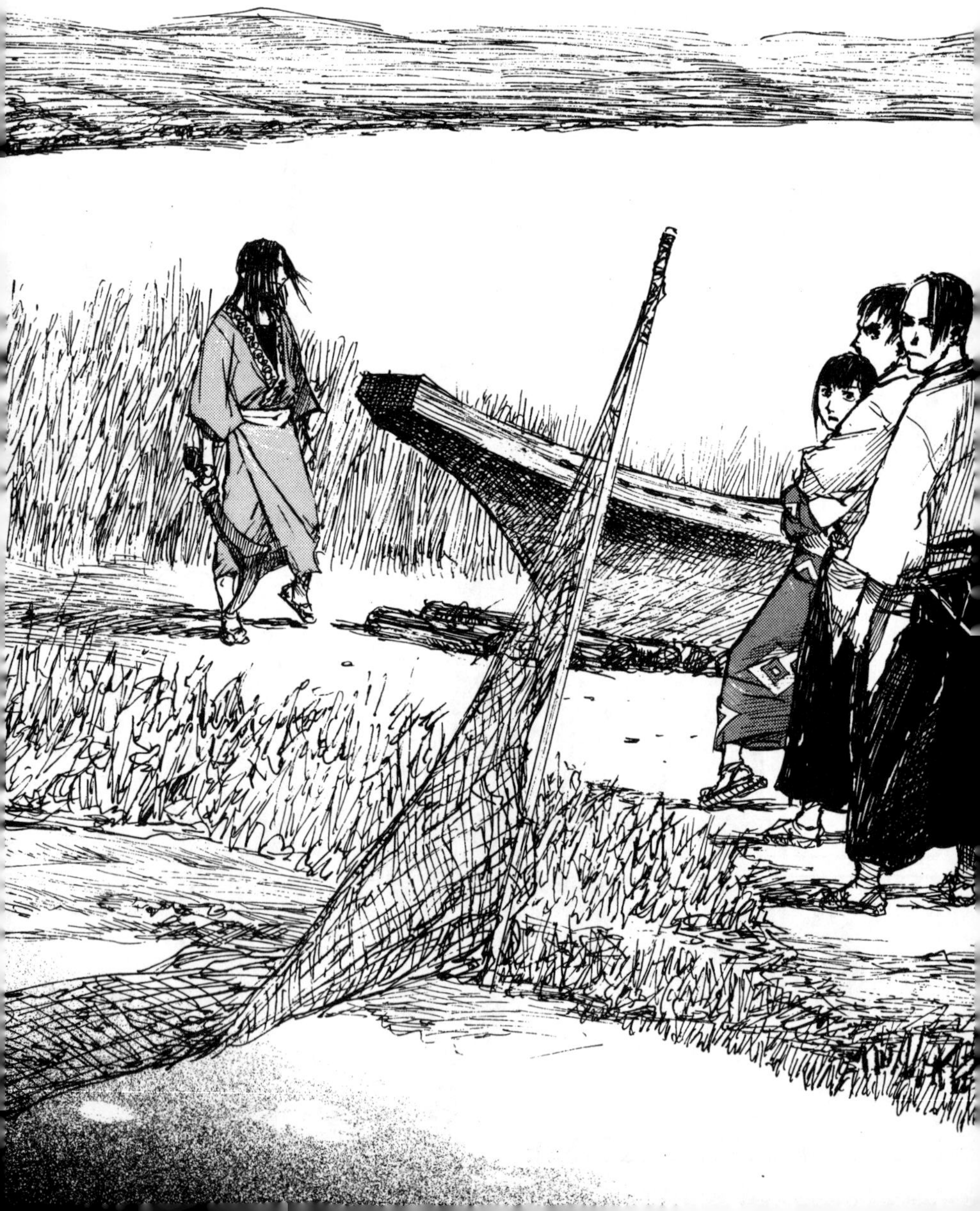

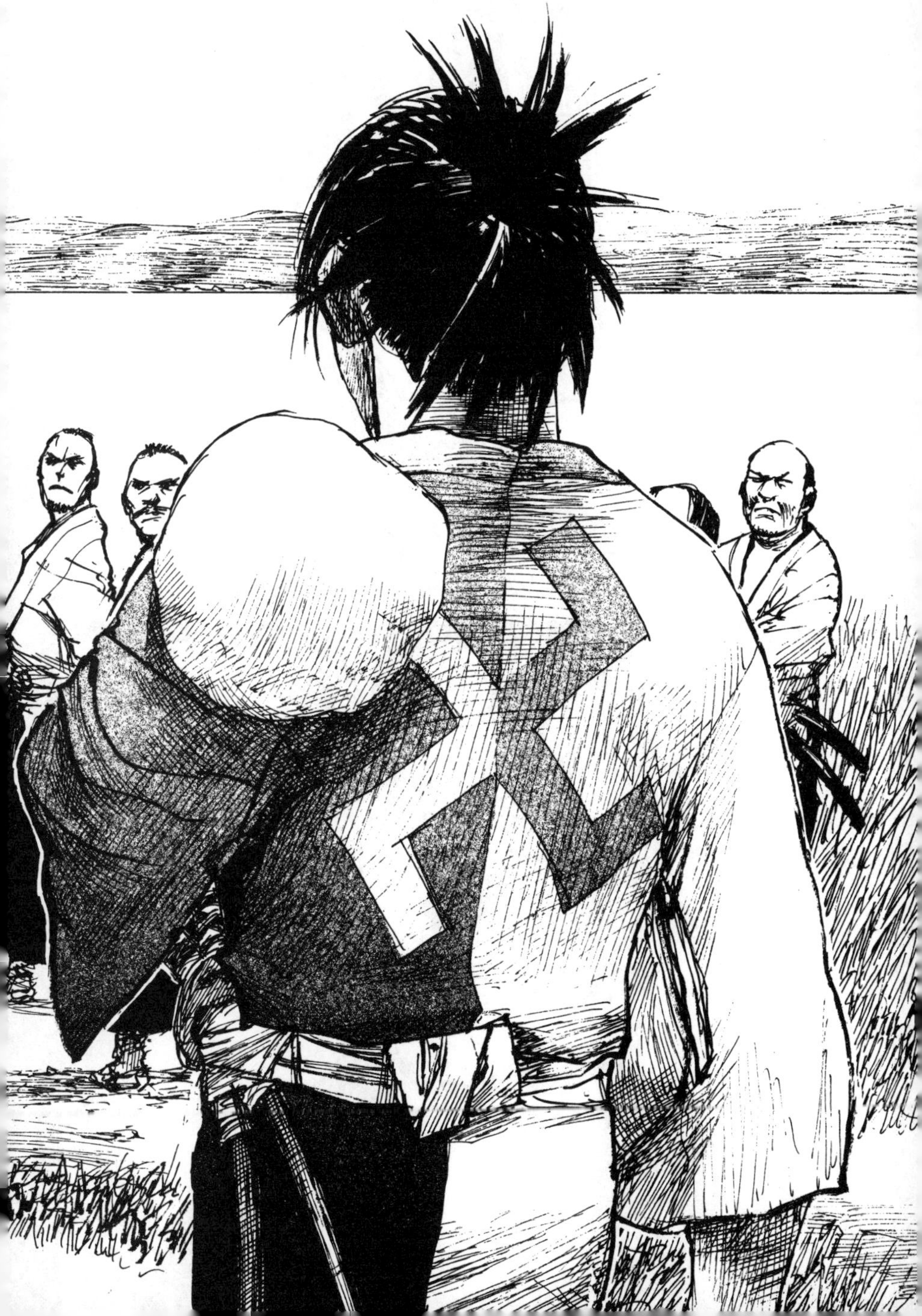

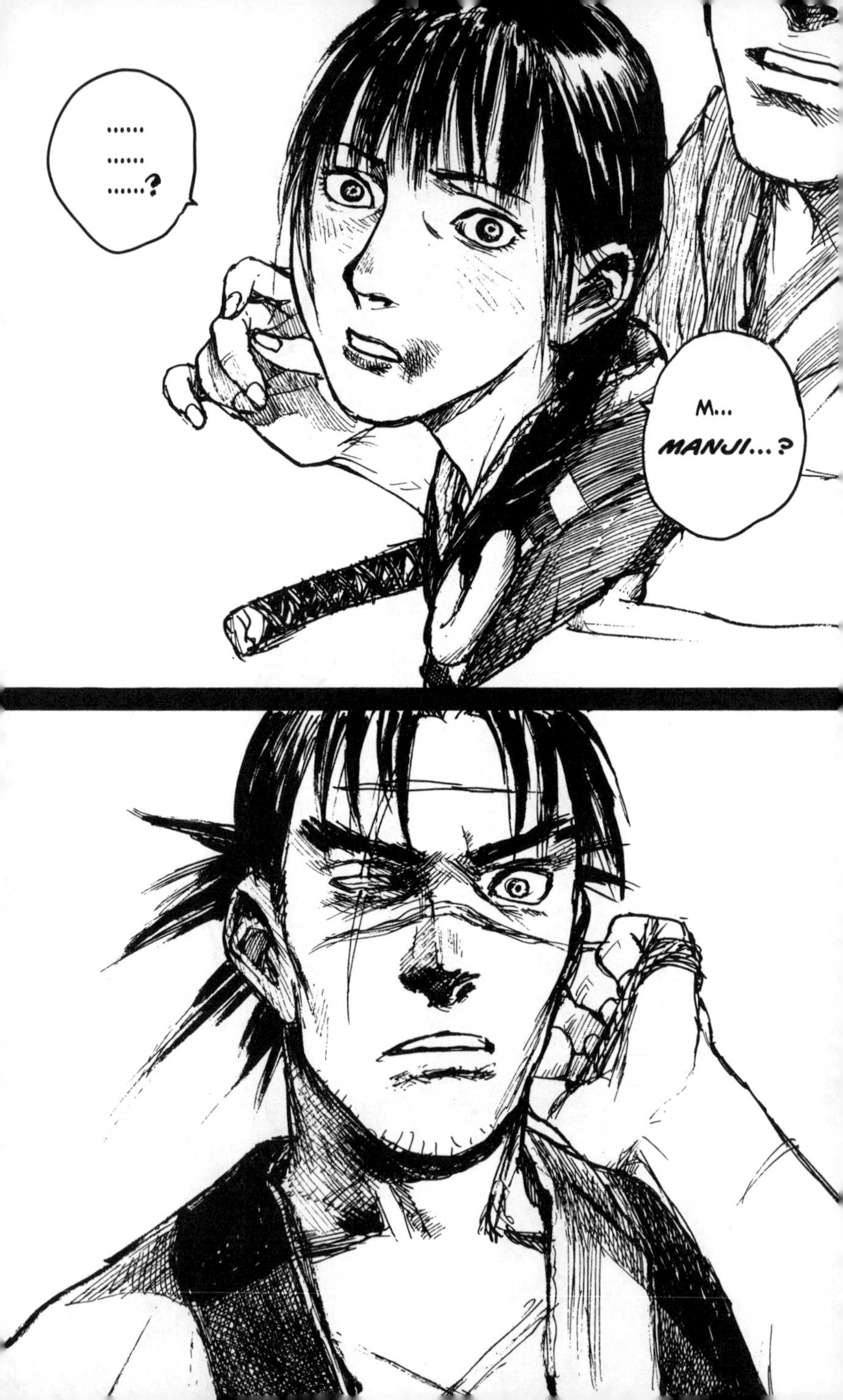
M... MANJI...?
......
......
......?

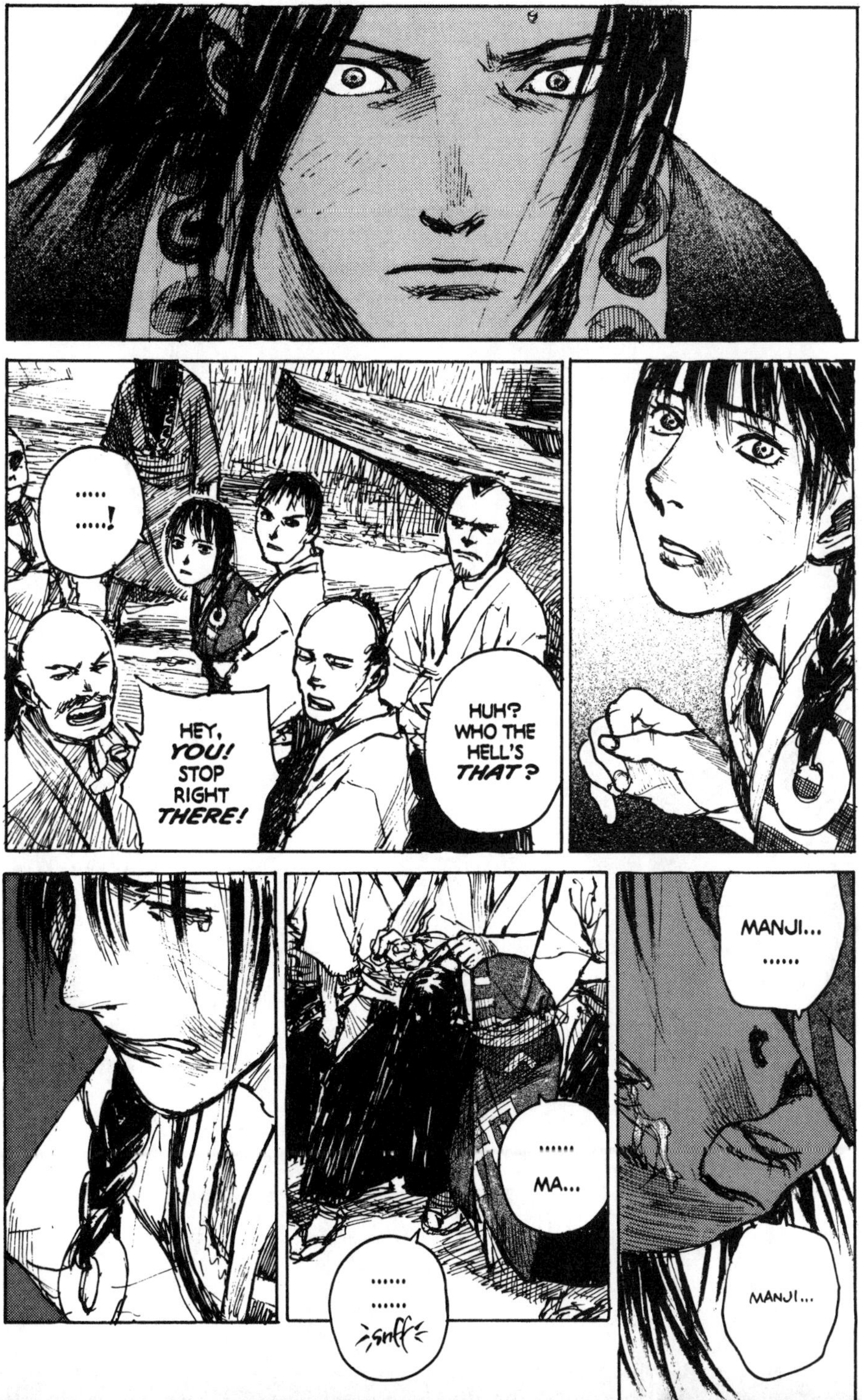
.....
.....!
HUH? WHO THE HELL'S *THAT*?
HEY, *YOU!* STOP RIGHT *THERE!*
MANJI... ......
MANJI...
...... MA...
.... snff

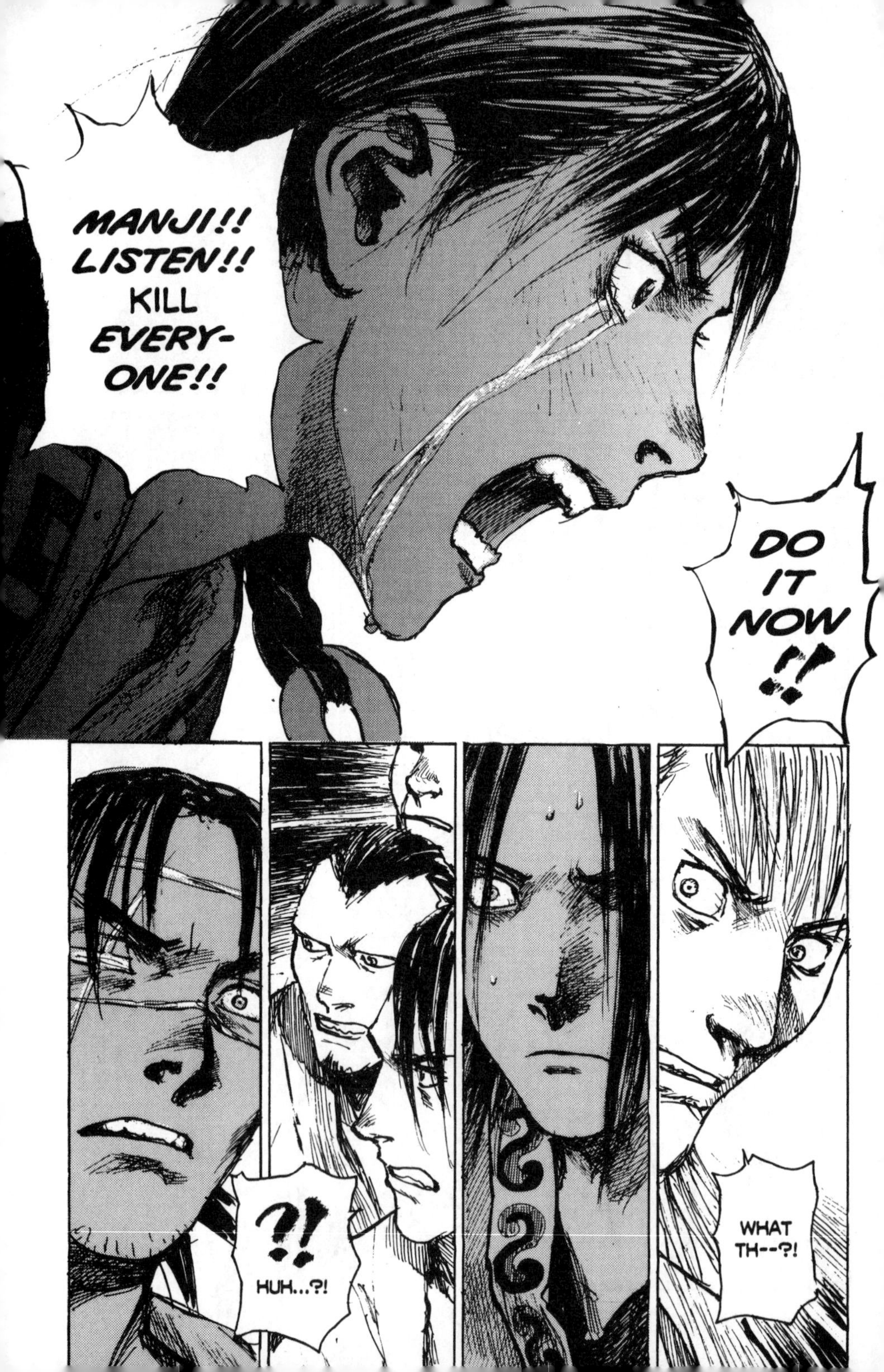
MANJI!! LISTEN!! KILL EVERY-ONE!!
DO IT NOW!!
WHAT TH--?!
?!
HUH...?!

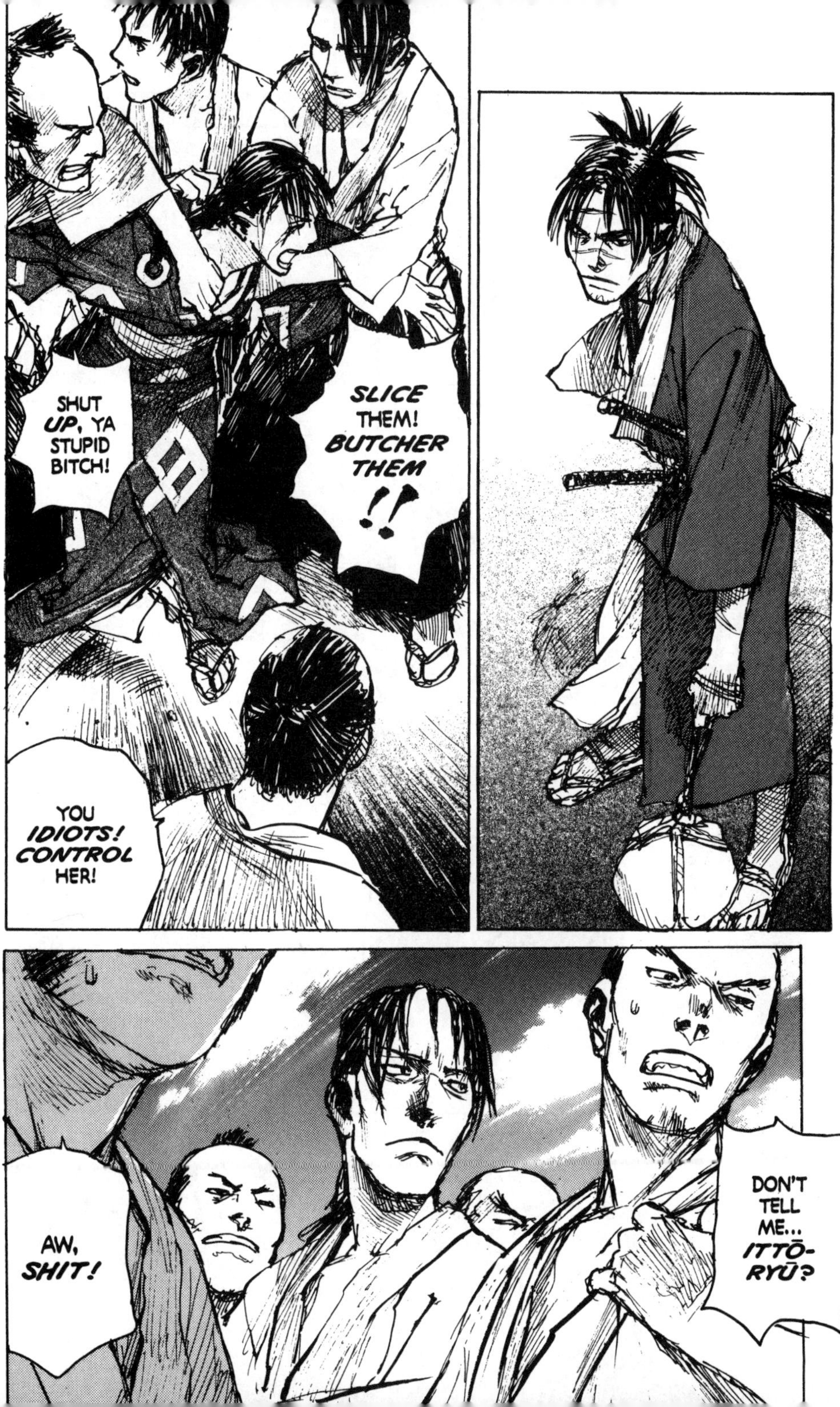
SLICE THEM! BUTCHER THEM!!
SHUT UP, YA STUPID BITCH!
YOU IDIOTS! CONTROL HER!
DON'T TELL ME... ITTŌ-RYŪ?
AW, SHIT!

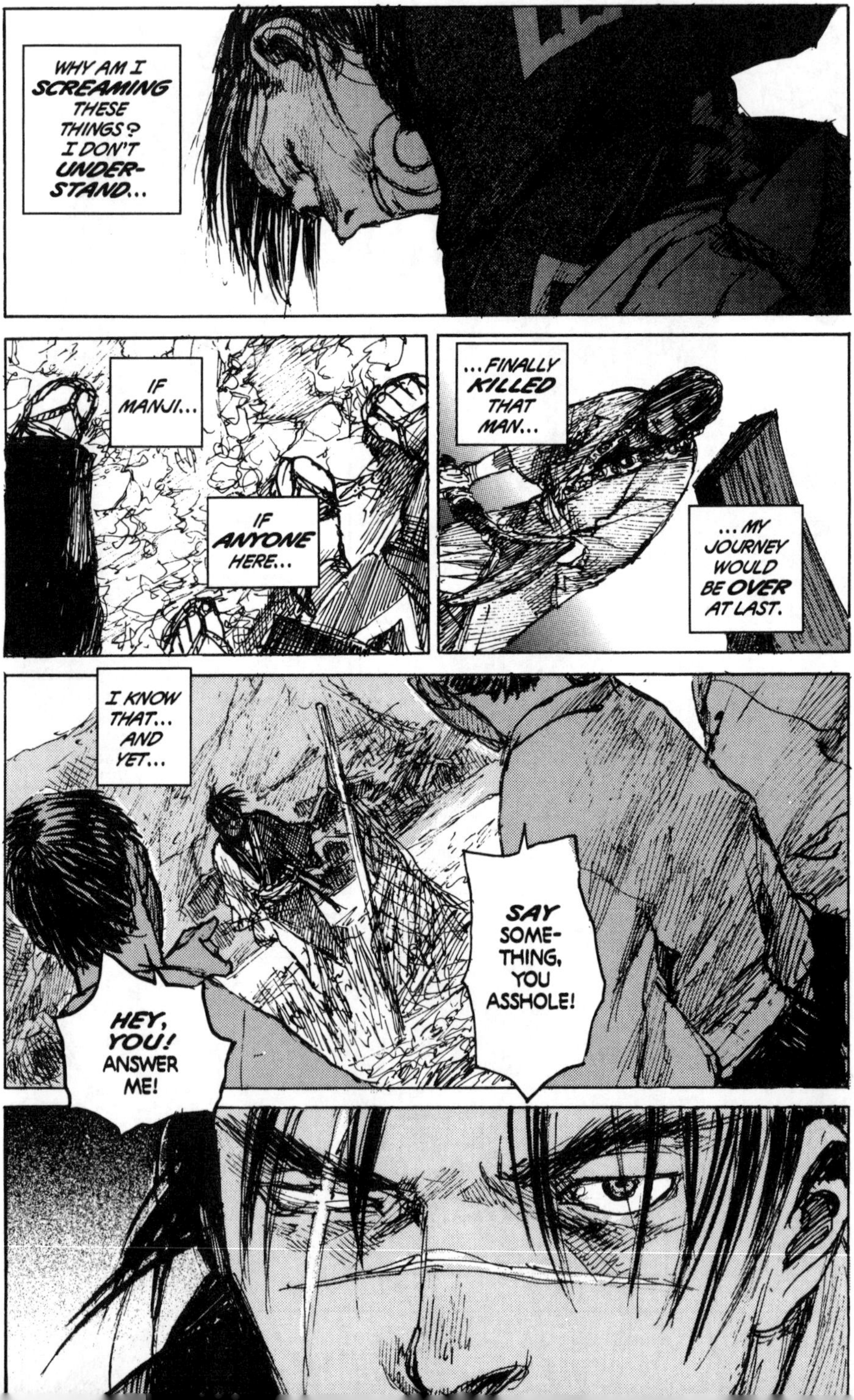
WHY AM I SCREAMING THESE THINGS? I DON'T UNDERSTAND...
IF MANJI...
IF ANYONE HERE...
...FINALLY KILLED THAT MAN...
...MY JOURNEY WOULD BE OVER AT LAST.
I KNOW THAT... AND YET...
HEY, YOU! ANSWER ME!
SAY SOMETHING, YOU ASSHOLE!

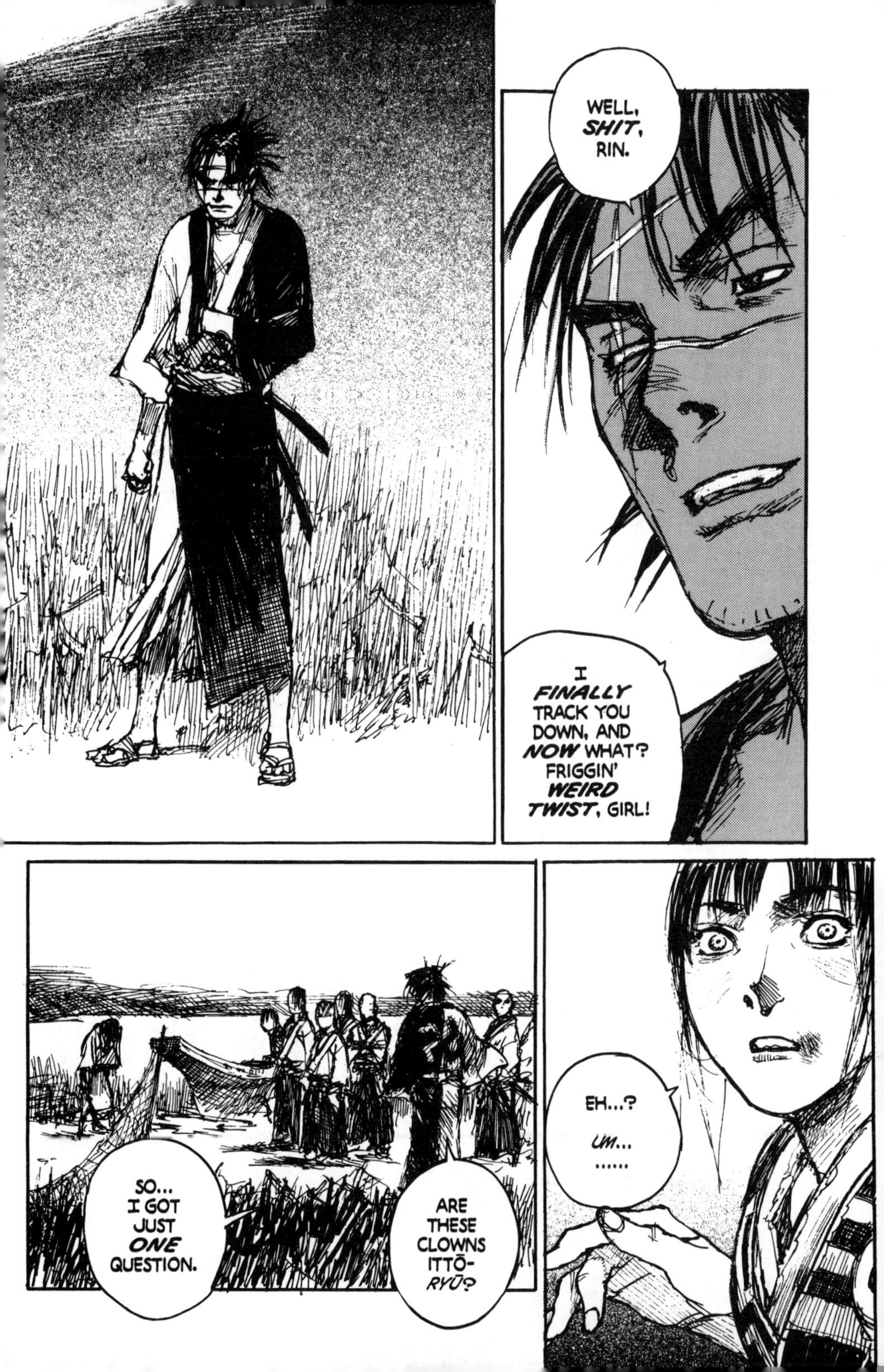
WELL, *SHIT*, RIN.
I *FINALLY* TRACK YOU DOWN, AND *NOW* WHAT? FRIGGIN' *WEIRD TWIST*, GIRL!
SO... I GOT JUST *ONE* QUESTION.
ARE THESE CLOWNS ITTŌ-*RYŪ*?
EH...? *UM*... ......

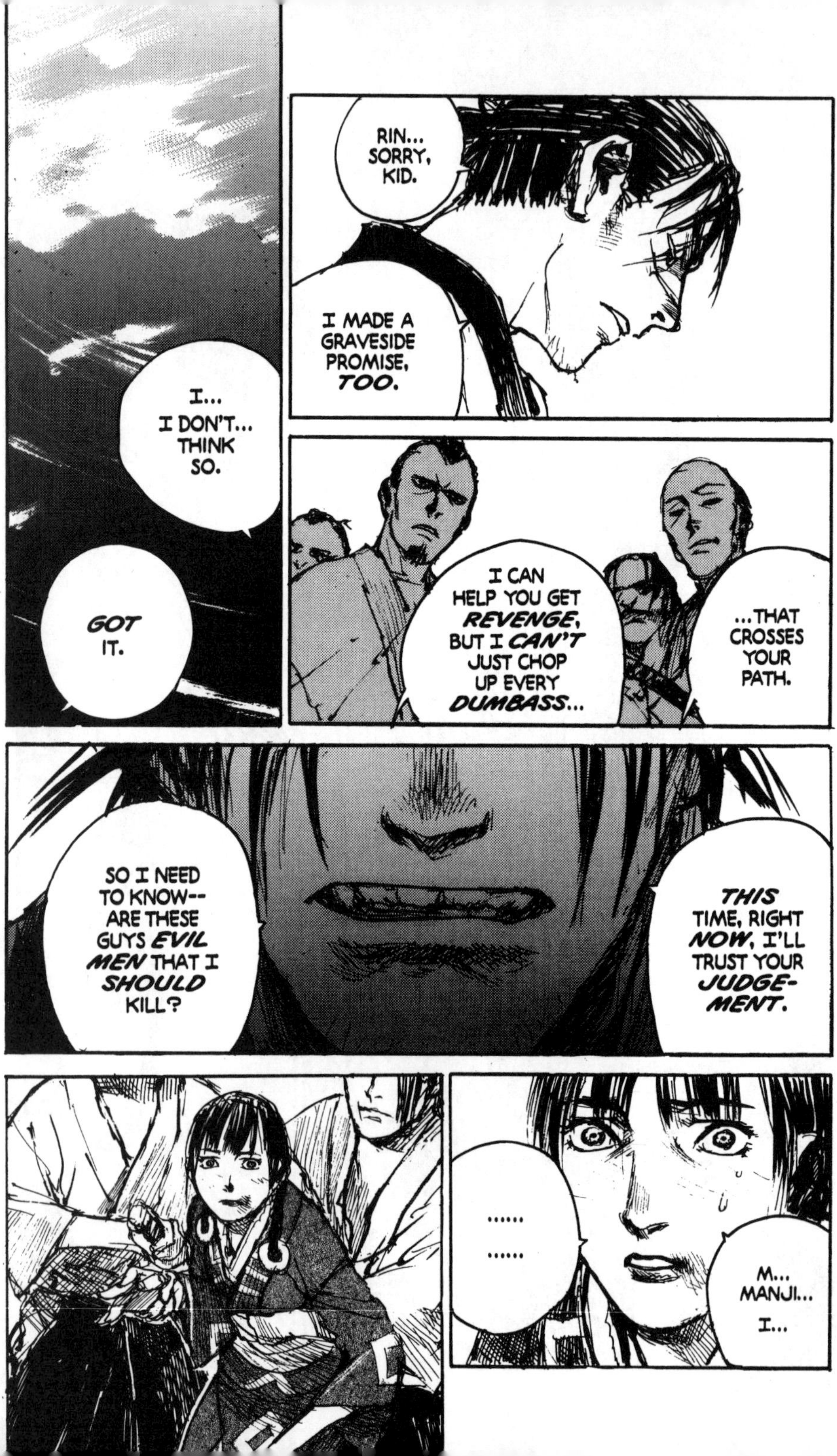
I... I DON'T... THINK SO.
GOT IT.
RIN... SORRY, KID.
I MADE A GRAVESIDE PROMISE, *TOO*.
I CAN HELP YOU GET *REVENGE*, BUT I *CAN'T* JUST CHOP UP EVERY *DUMBASS*...
...THAT CROSSES YOUR PATH.
SO I NEED TO KNOW-- ARE THESE GUYS *EVIL MEN* THAT I *SHOULD* KILL?
THIS TIME, RIGHT *NOW*, I'LL TRUST YOUR *JUDGEMENT*.
....
M... MANJI... I...

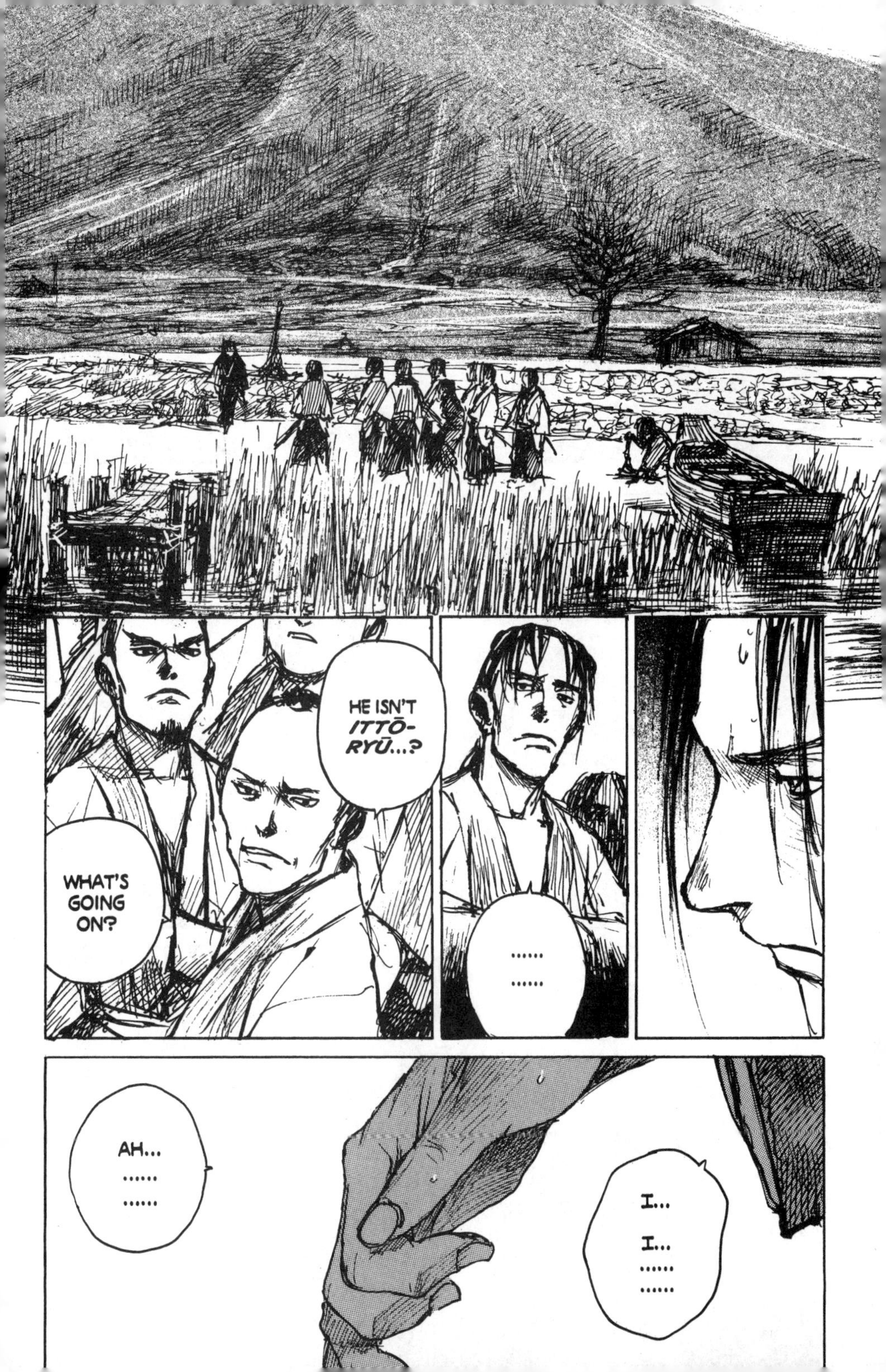

…… ……
HE ISN'T ITTŌ-RYŪ…?
WHAT'S GOING ON?
I… I… …… ……
AH… …… ……

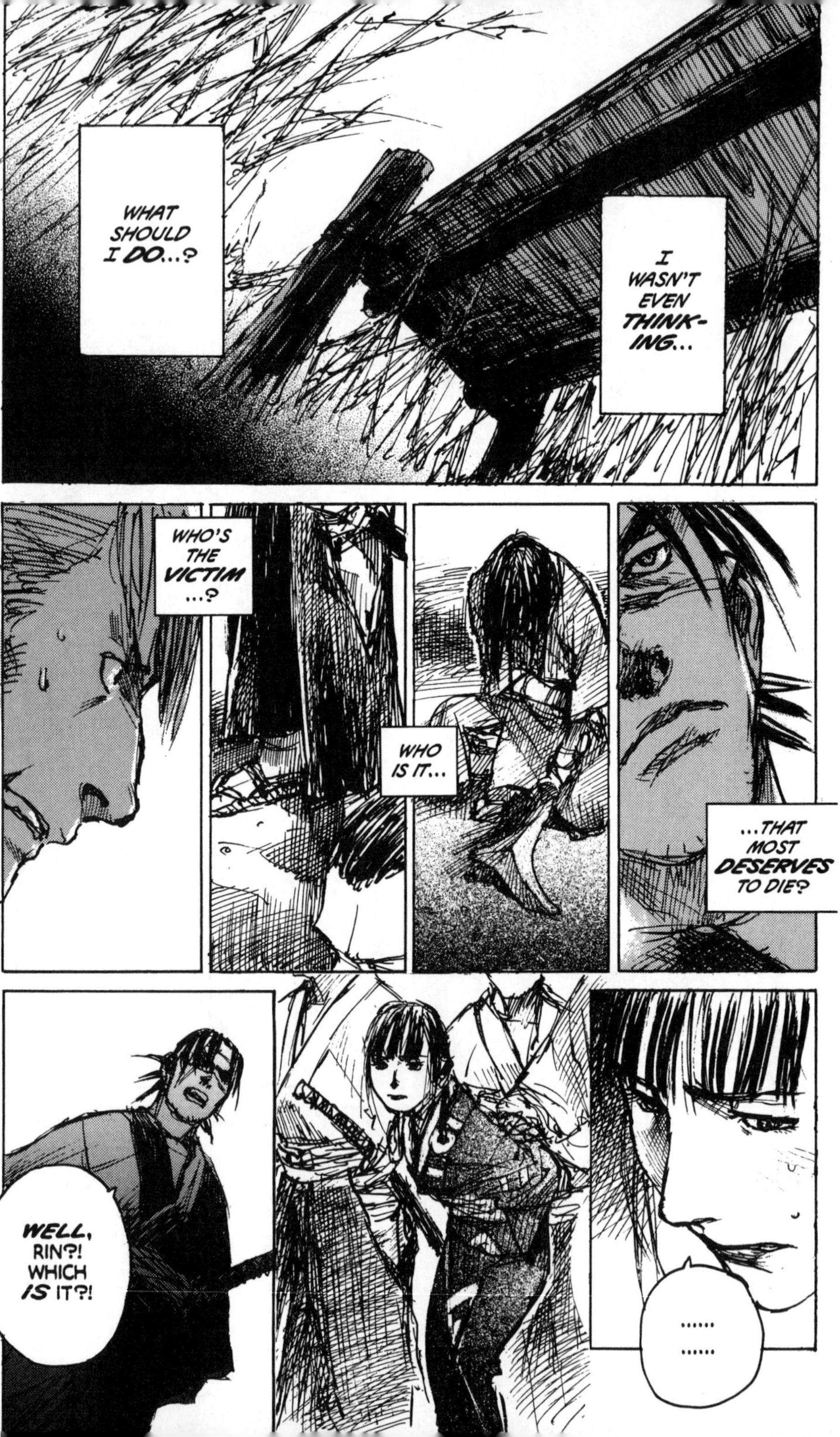
WHAT SHOULD I DO...?
I WASN'T EVEN THINKING...
WHO'S THE VICTIM ...?
WHO IS IT...
...THAT MOST DESERVES TO DIE?
WELL, RIN?! WHICH IS IT?!
......
......

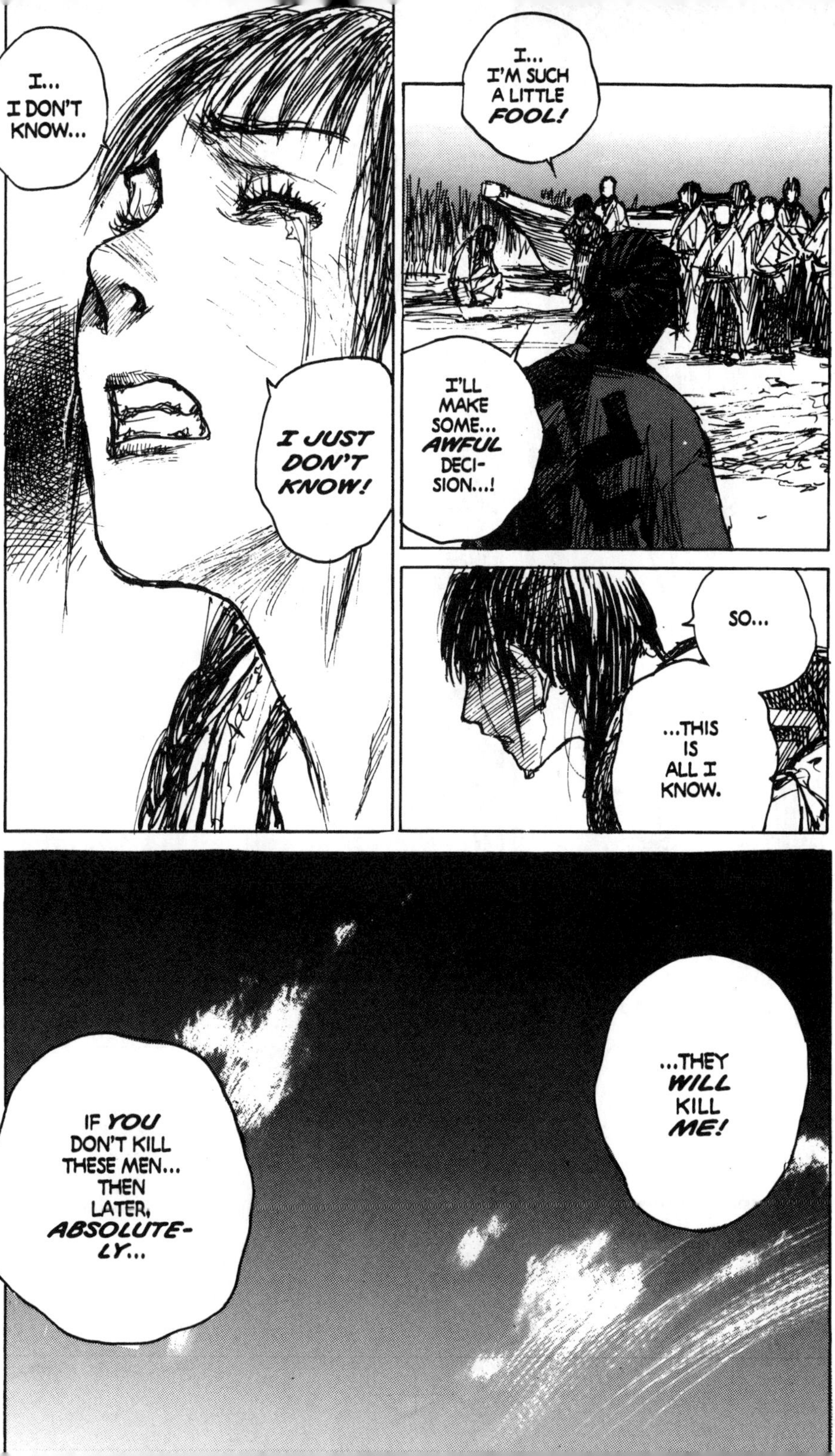
I... I DON'T KNOW...
I JUST DON'T KNOW!
I... I'M SUCH A LITTLE FOOL!
I'LL MAKE SOME... AWFUL DECISION...!
SO...
...THIS IS ALL I KNOW.
IF YOU DON'T KILL THESE MEN... THEN LATER, ABSOLUTE-LY...
...THEY WILL KILL ME!

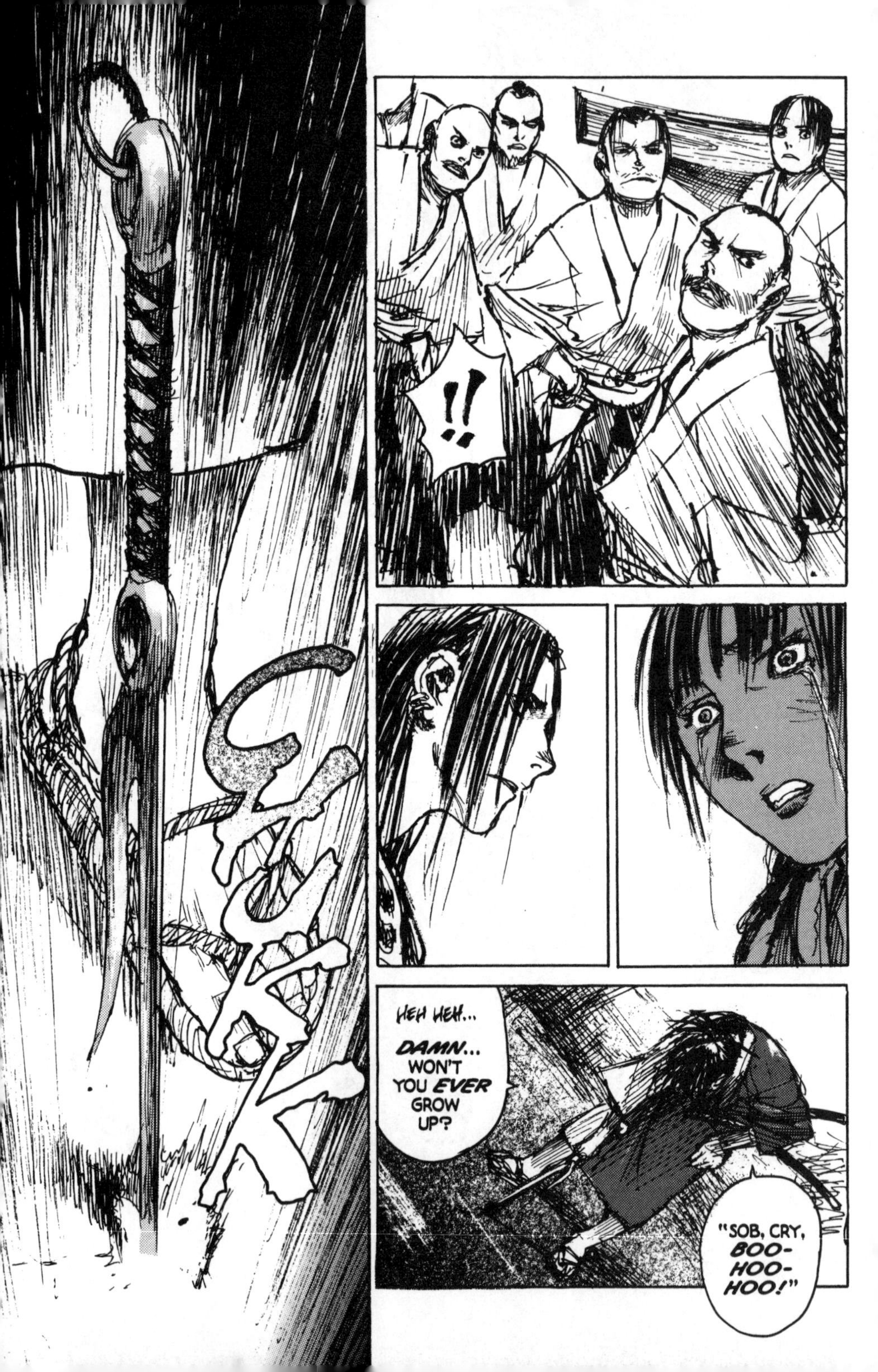
!!
HEH HEH...
DAMN... WON'T YOU EVER GROW UP?
"SOB, CRY, BOO-HOO-HOO!"

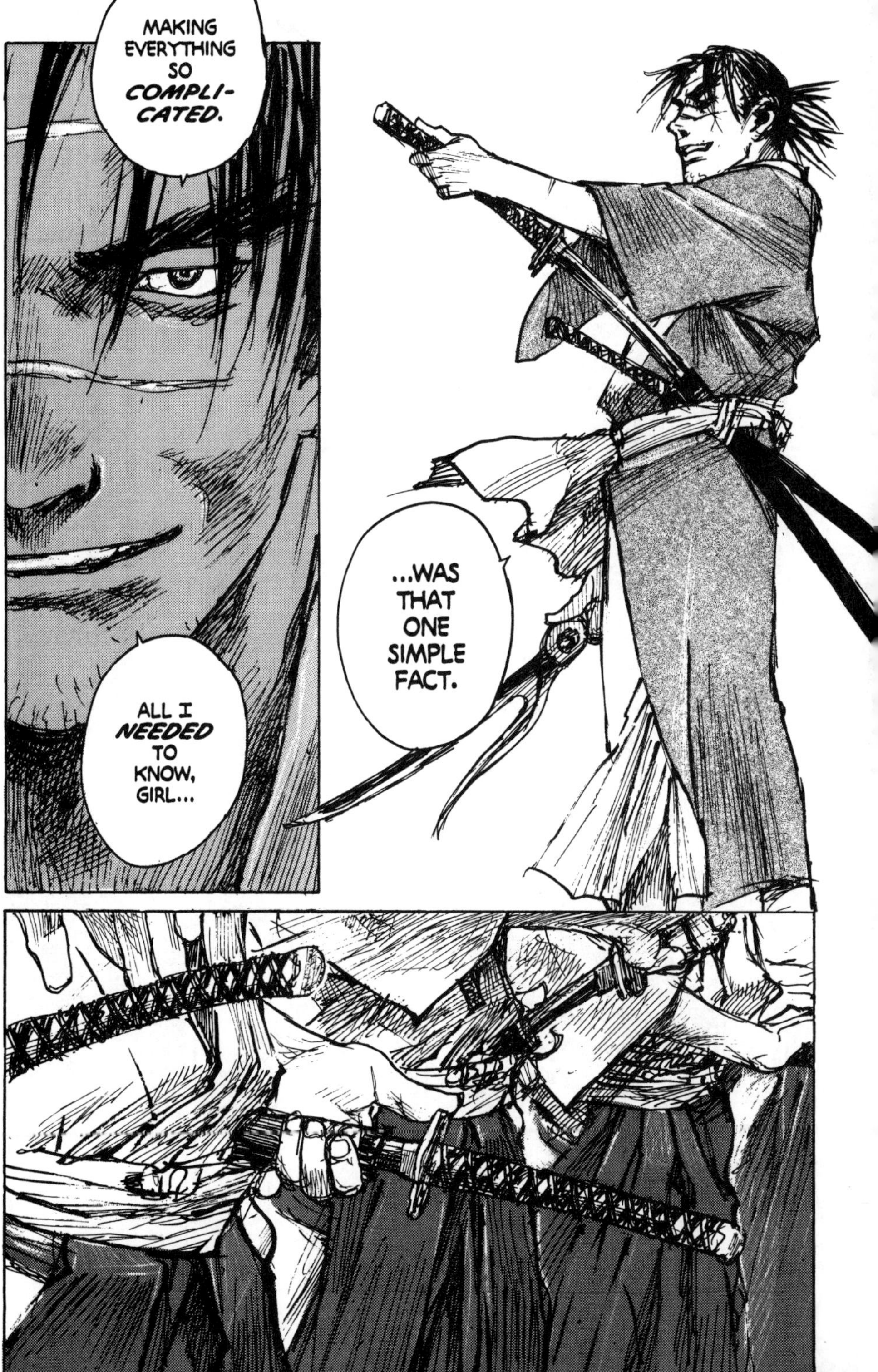
MAKING EVERYTHING SO *COMPLI-CATED.*
ALL I *NEEDED* TO KNOW, GIRL...
...WAS THAT ONE SIMPLE FACT.

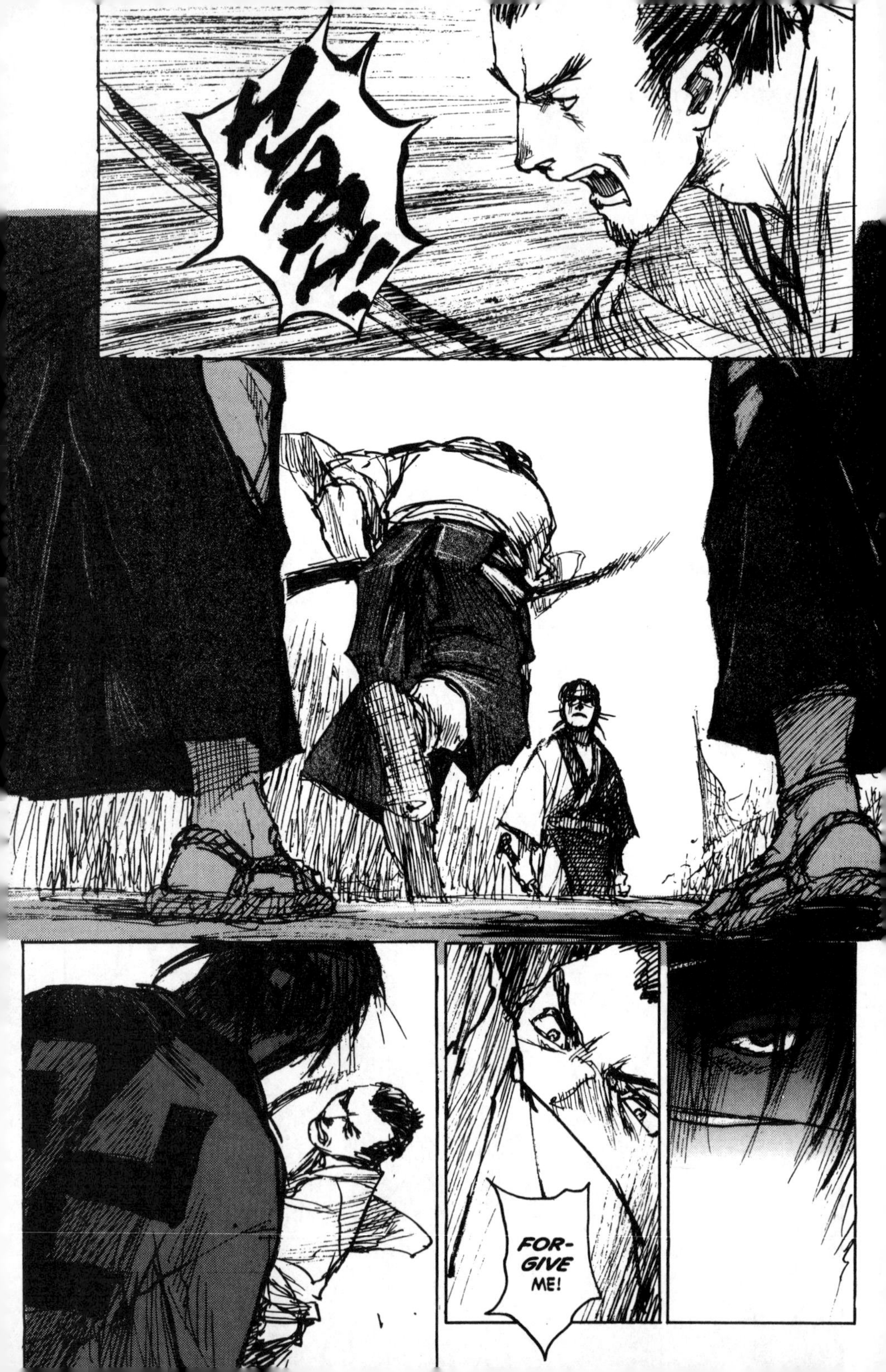
FOR-
GIVE
ME!

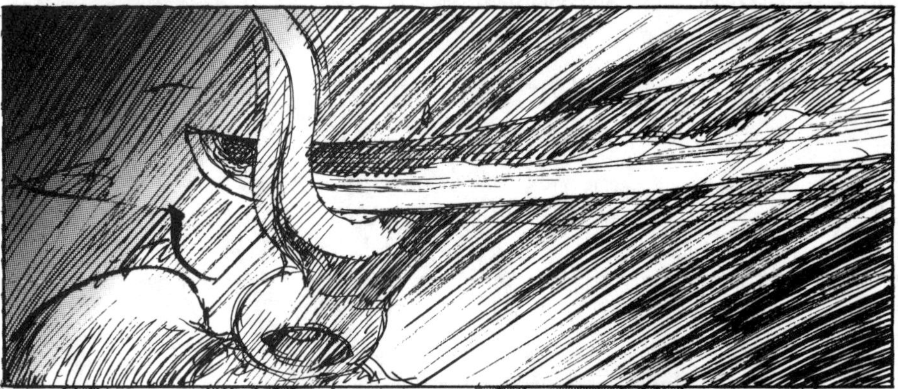
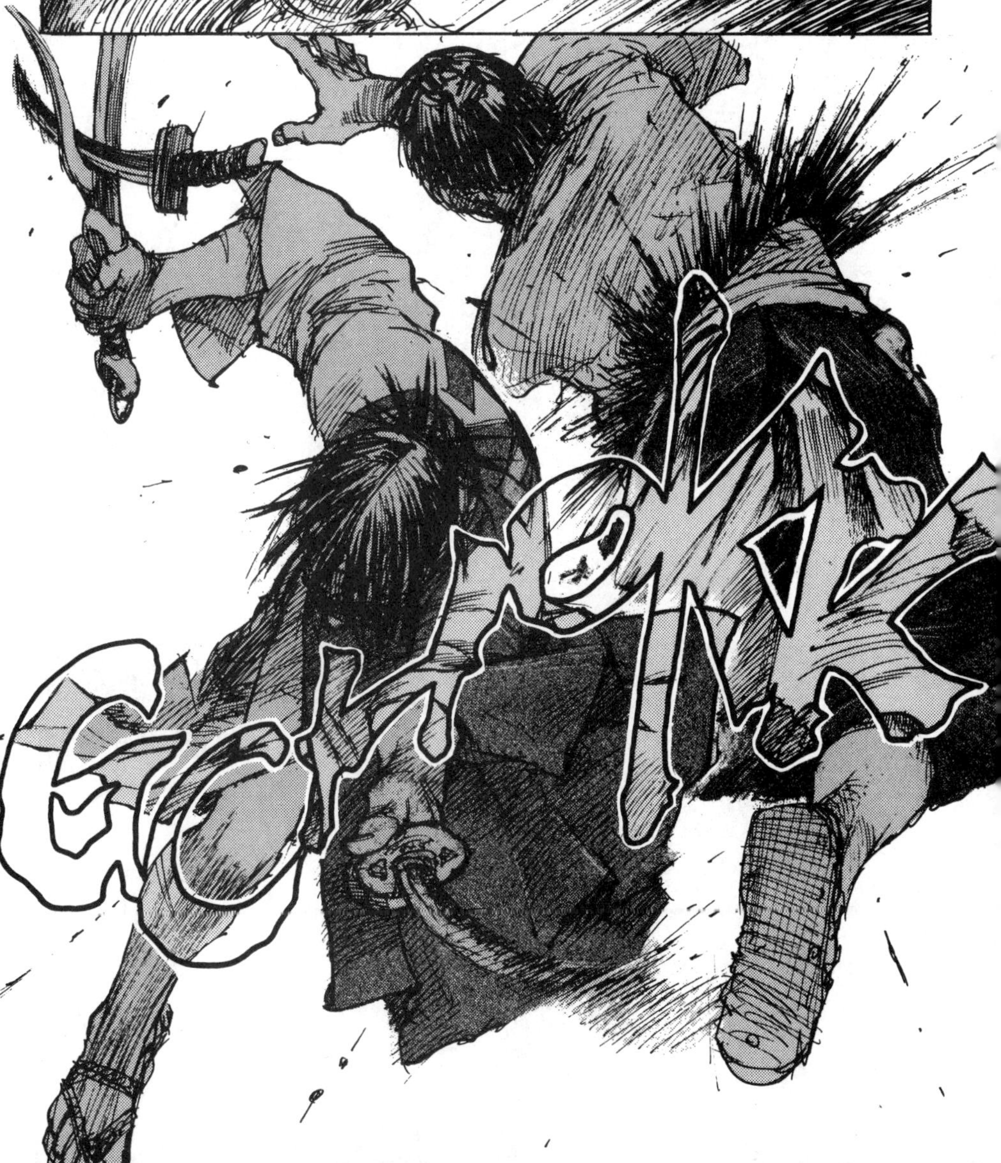

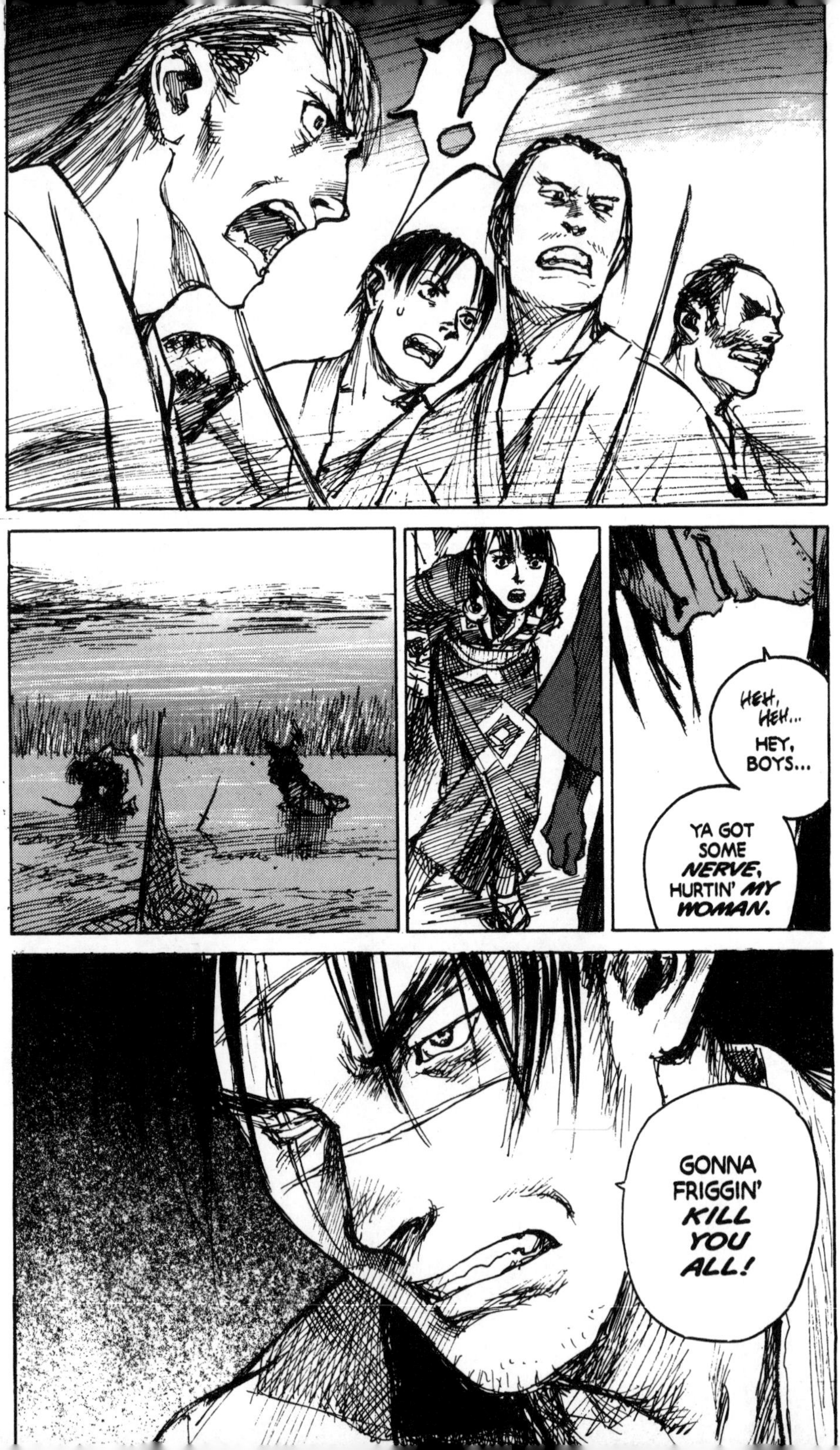
HEH, HEH...
HEY, BOYS...
YA GOT SOME *NERVE*, HURTIN' *MY WOMAN*.
GONNA FRIGGIN' *KILL YOU ALL!*

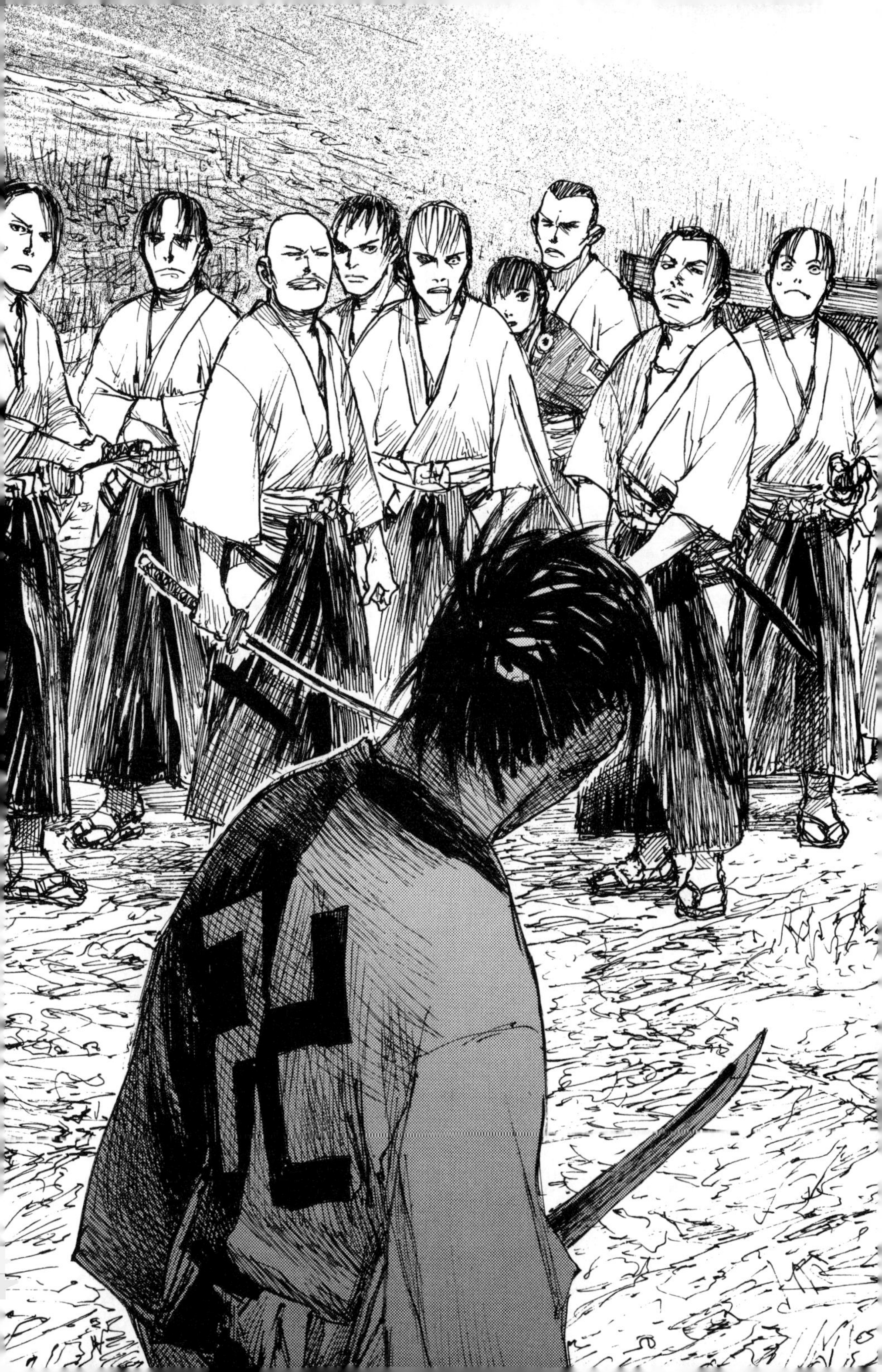

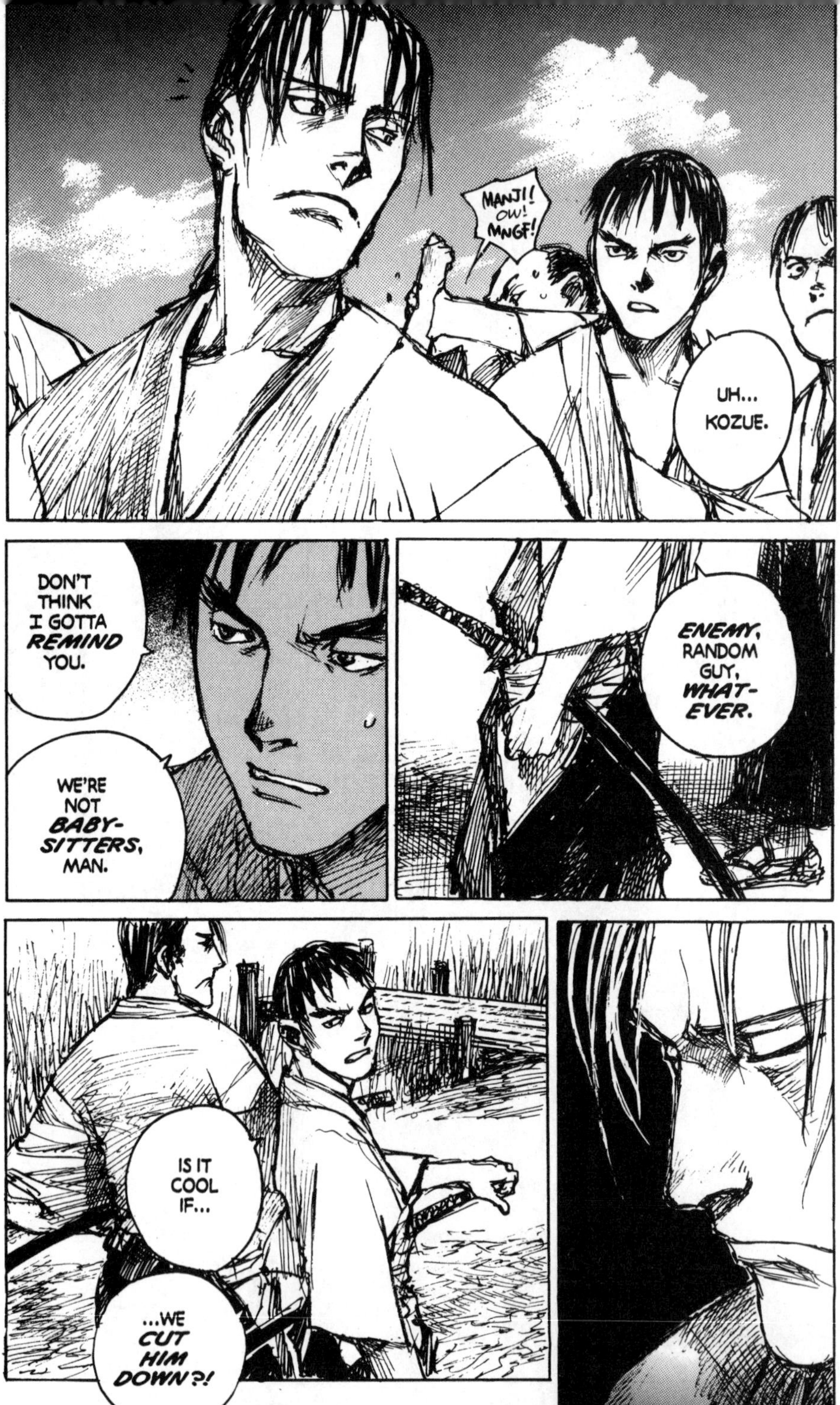
MANJI!! OW! MNGF!
UH... KOZUE.
ENEMY, RANDOM GUY, WHATEVER.
DON'T THINK I GOTTA REMIND YOU.
WE'RE NOT BABY-SITTERS, MAN.
IS IT COOL IF...
...WE CUT HIM DOWN?!

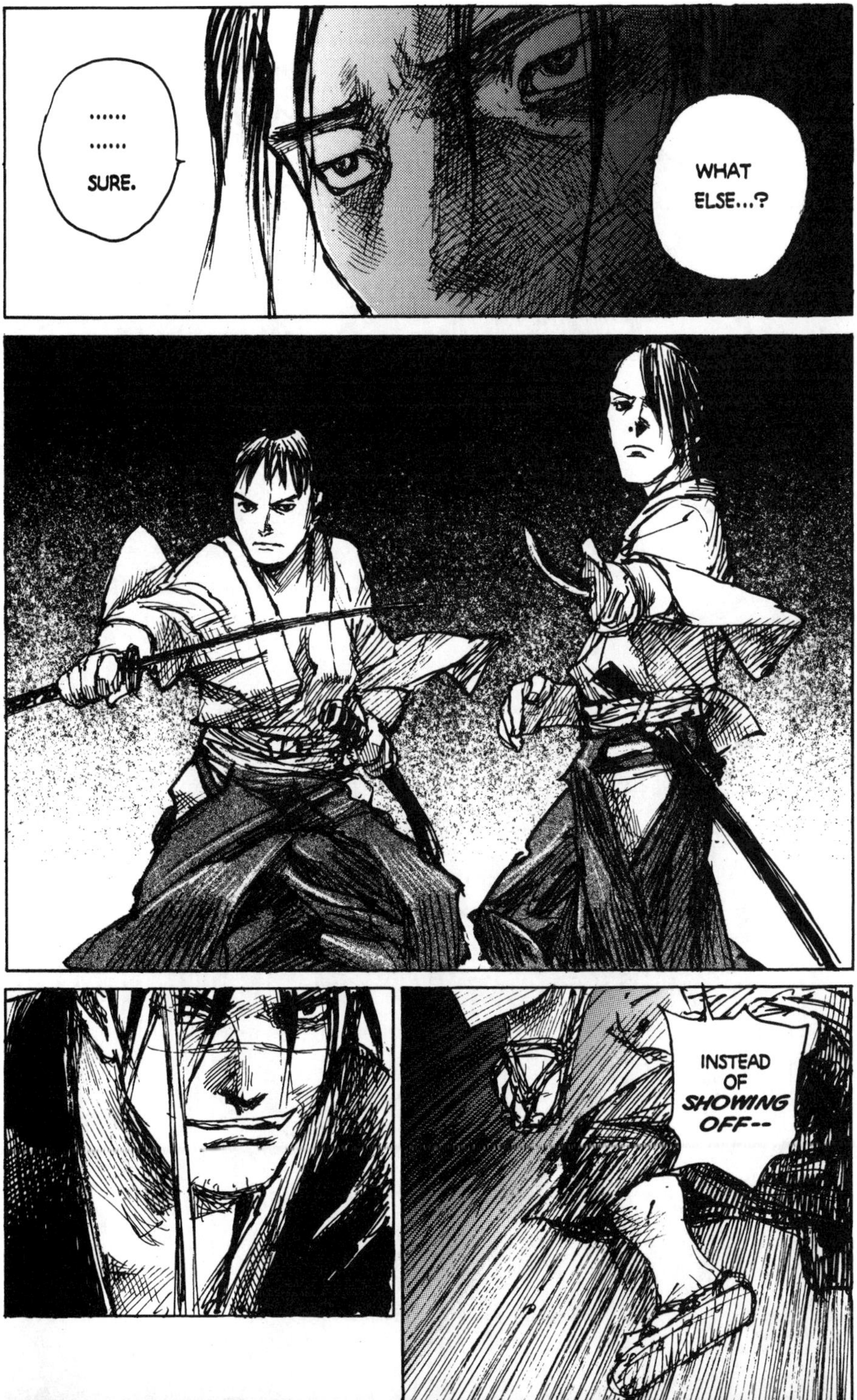
WHAT ELSE...?
......
......
SURE.
INSTEAD OF *SHOWING OFF--*

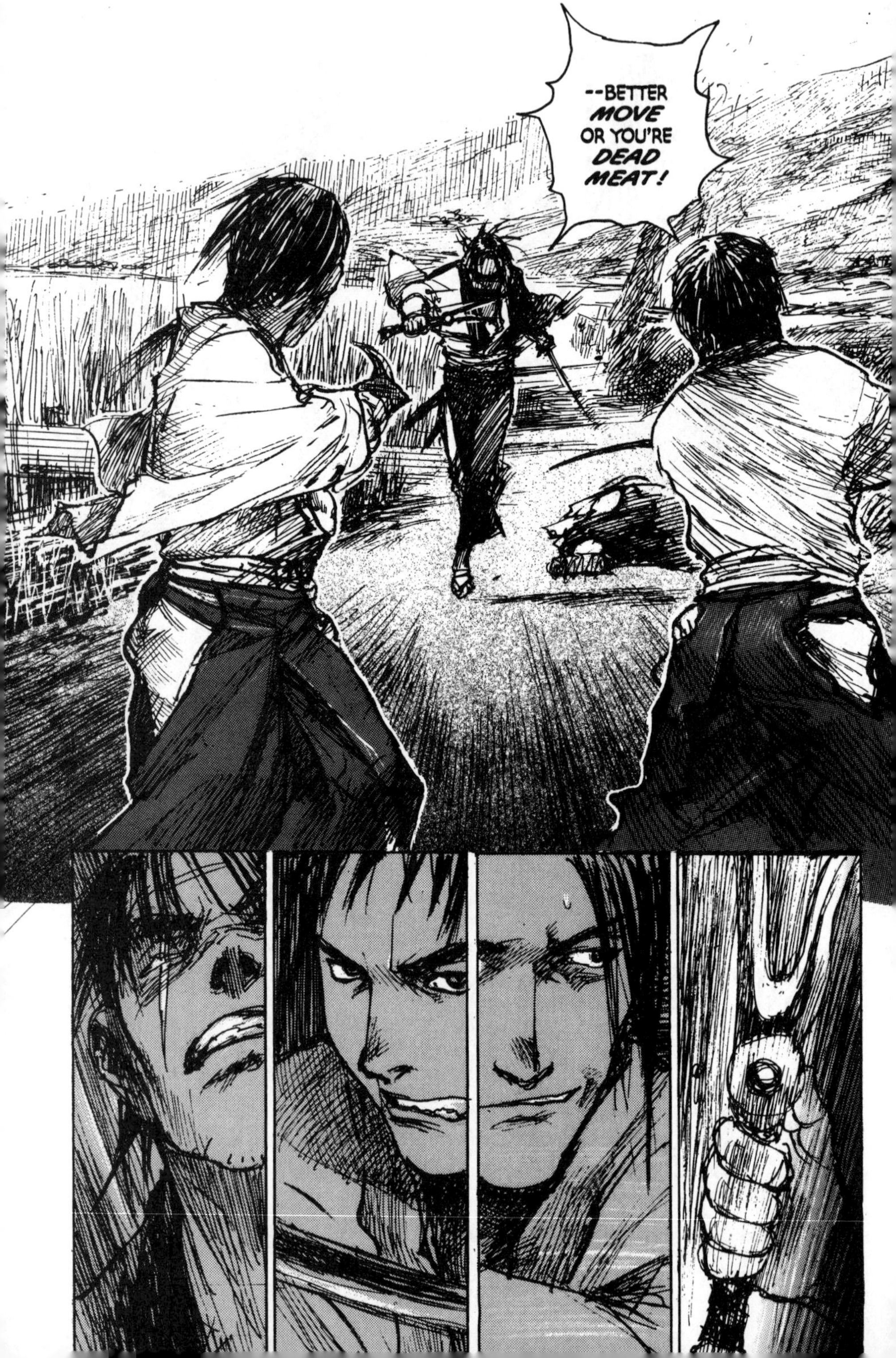
--BETTER MOVE OR YOU'RE DEAD MEAT!

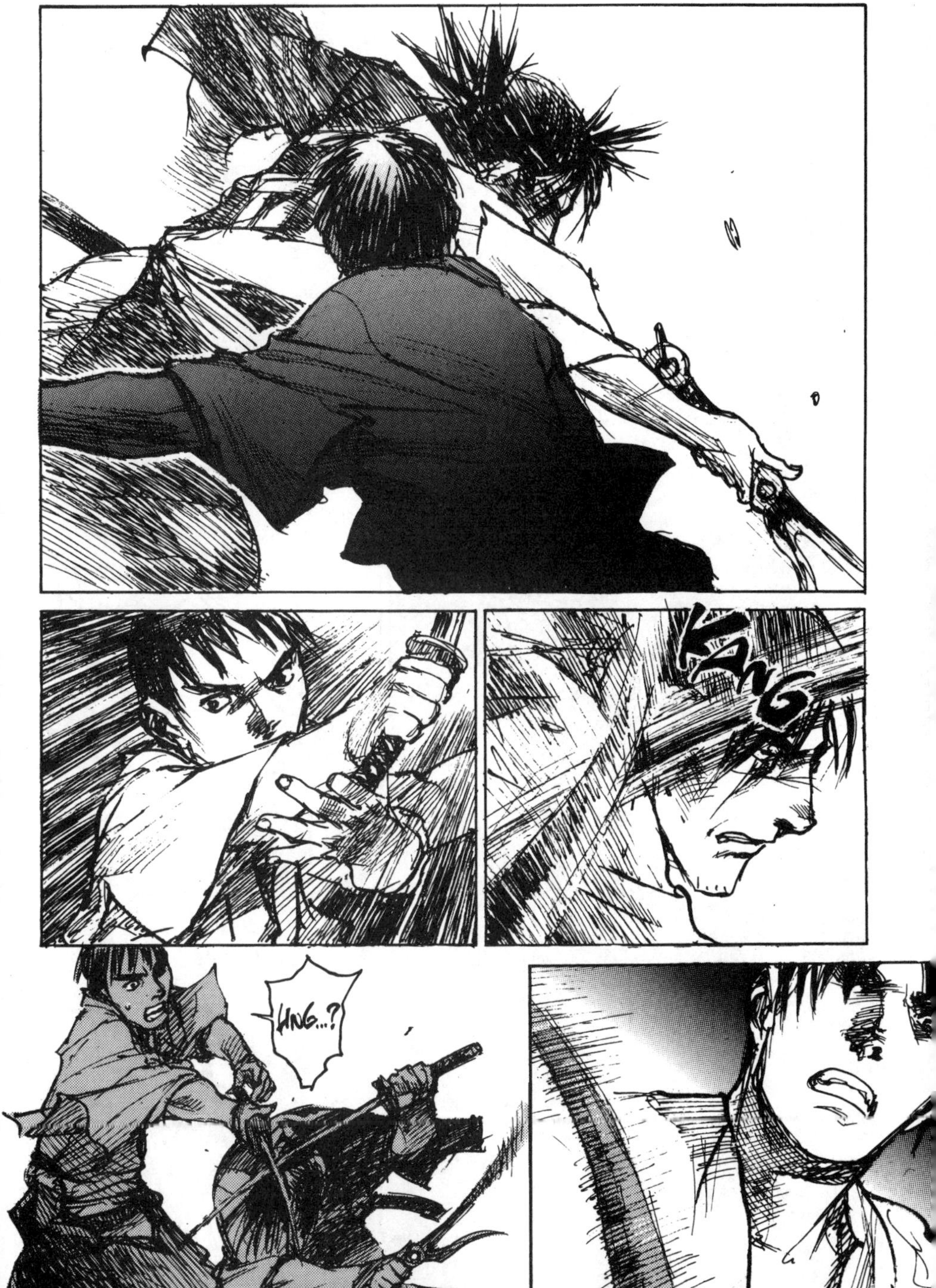
KANG
HNG...?

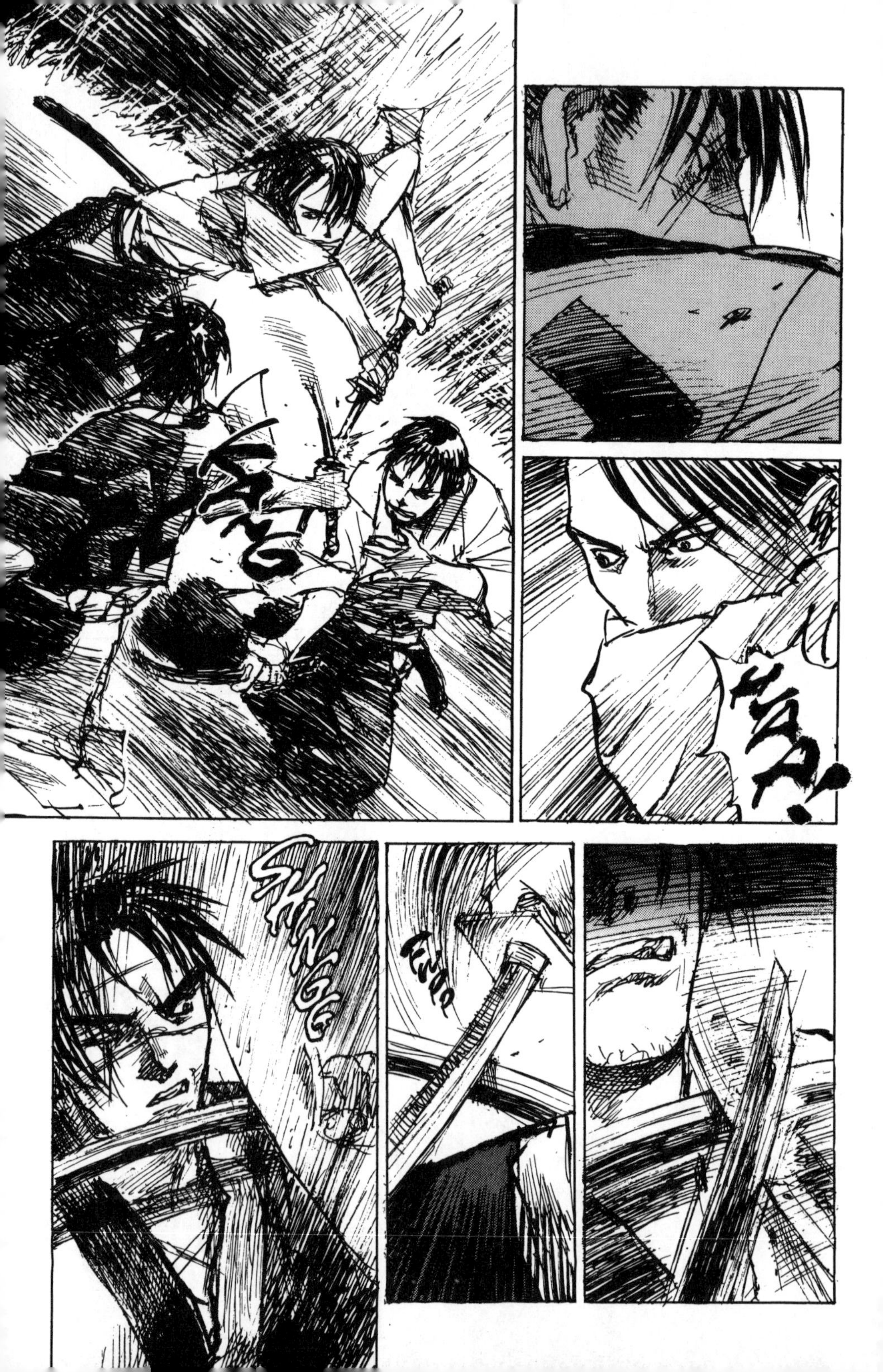
HYA!
SHINGG

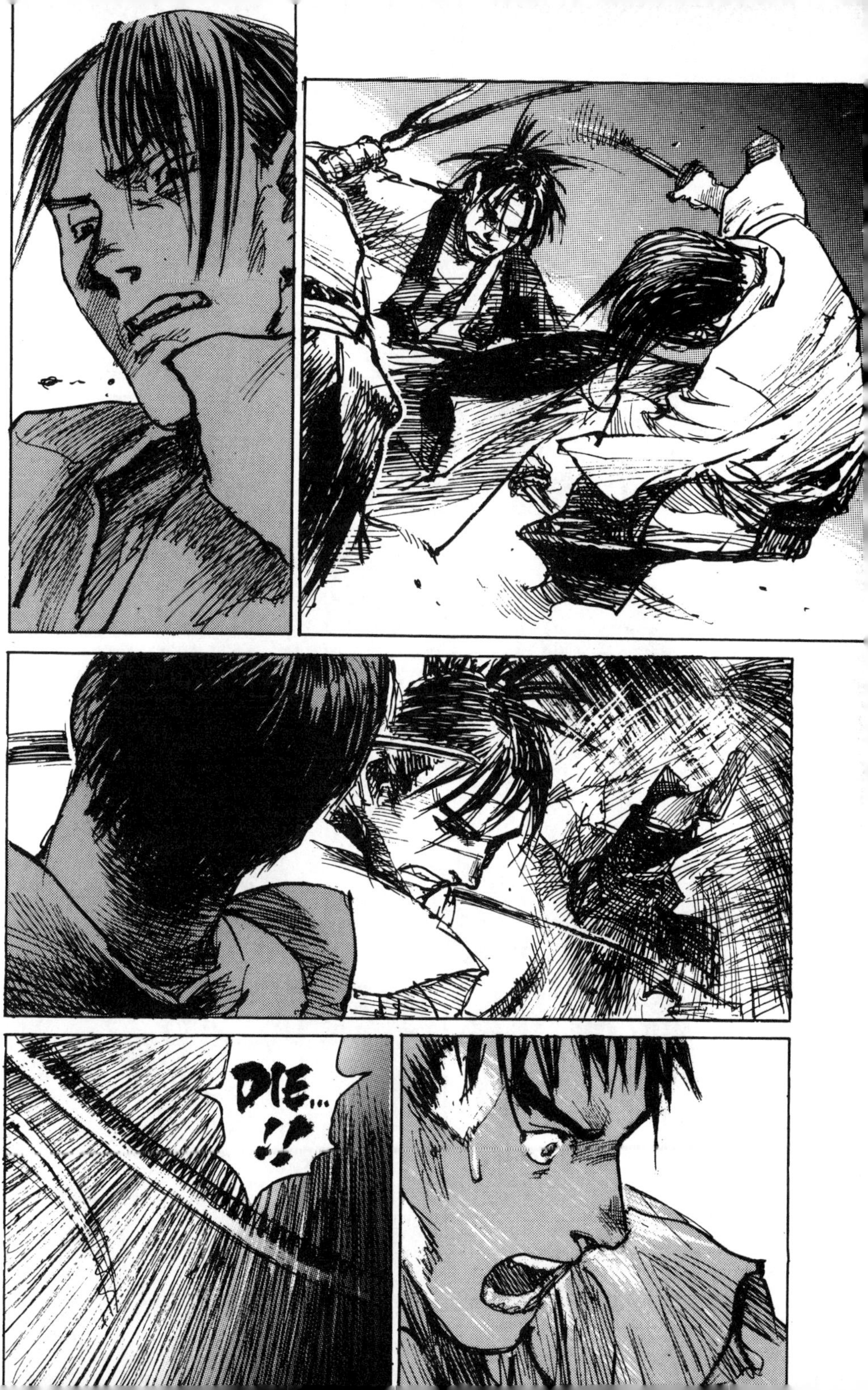
DIE...
!!

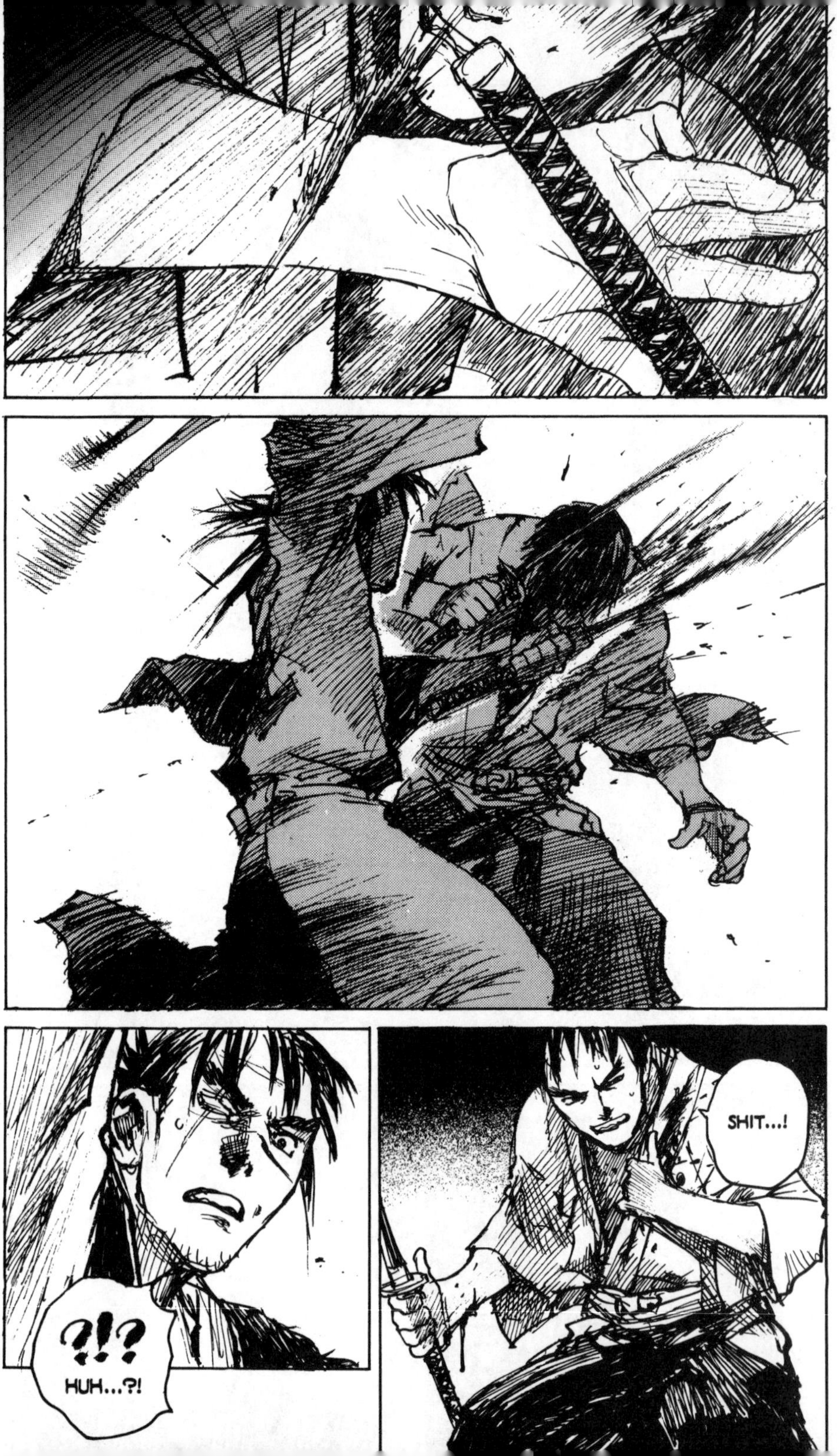
SHIT...!
?!?
HUH...?!

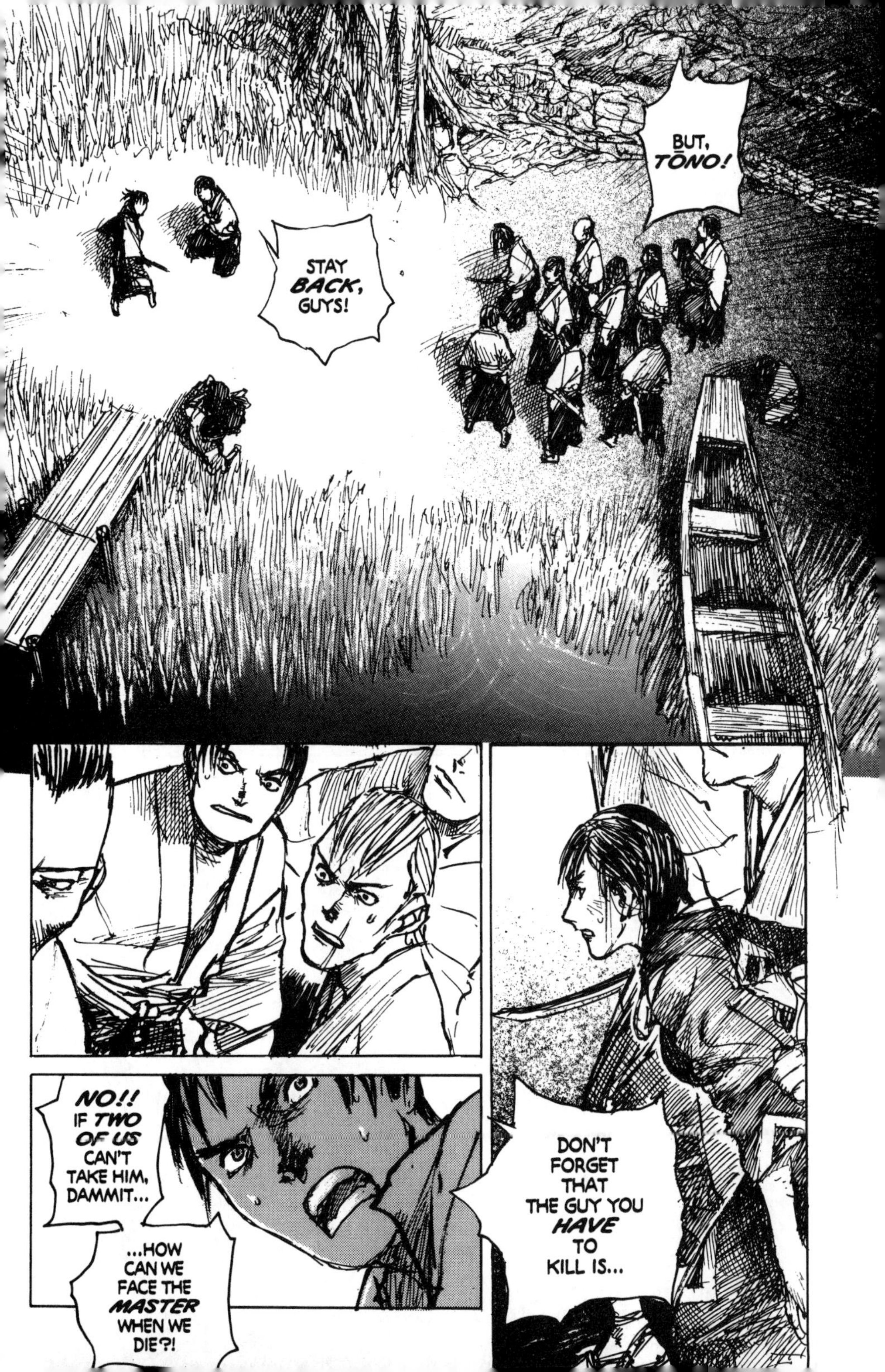
STAY BACK, GUYS!
BUT, TŌNO!
DON'T FORGET THAT THE GUY YOU HAVE TO KILL IS...
NO!! IF TWO OF US CAN'T TAKE HIM, DAMMIT...
...HOW CAN WE FACE THE MASTER WHEN WE DIE?!

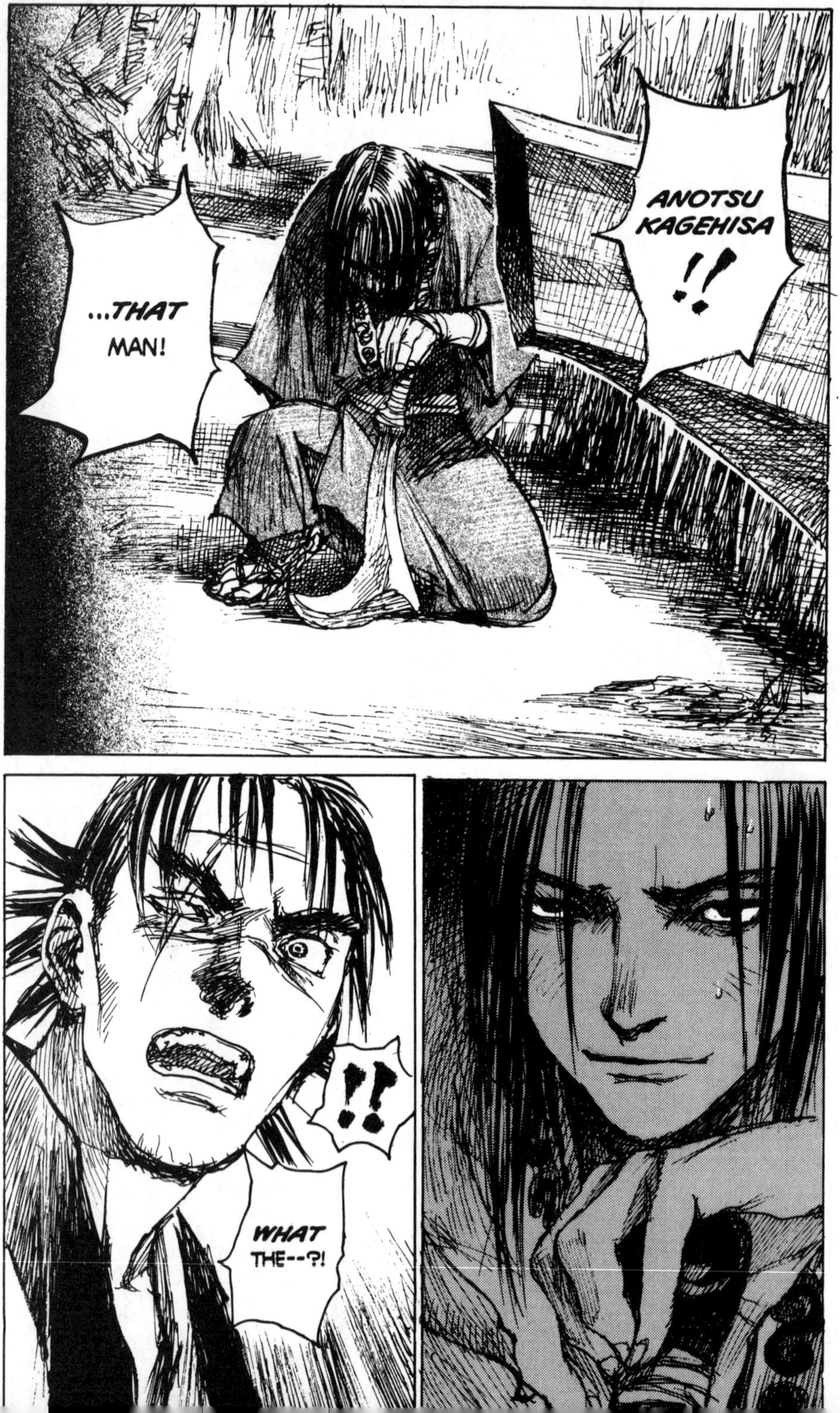
ANOTSU KAGEHISA !!
...THAT MAN!
!!
WHAT THE--?!

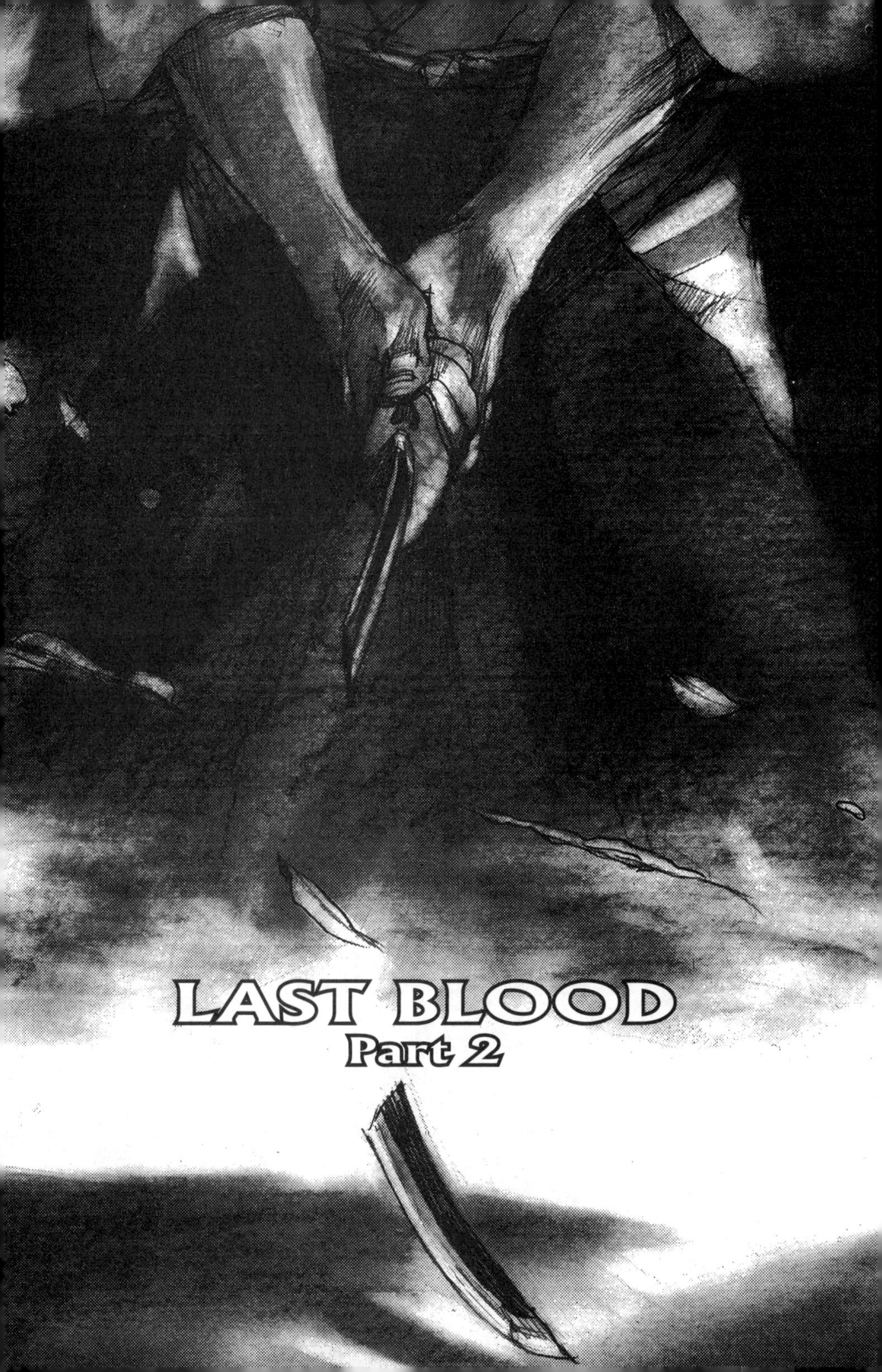
LAST BLOOD
Part 2

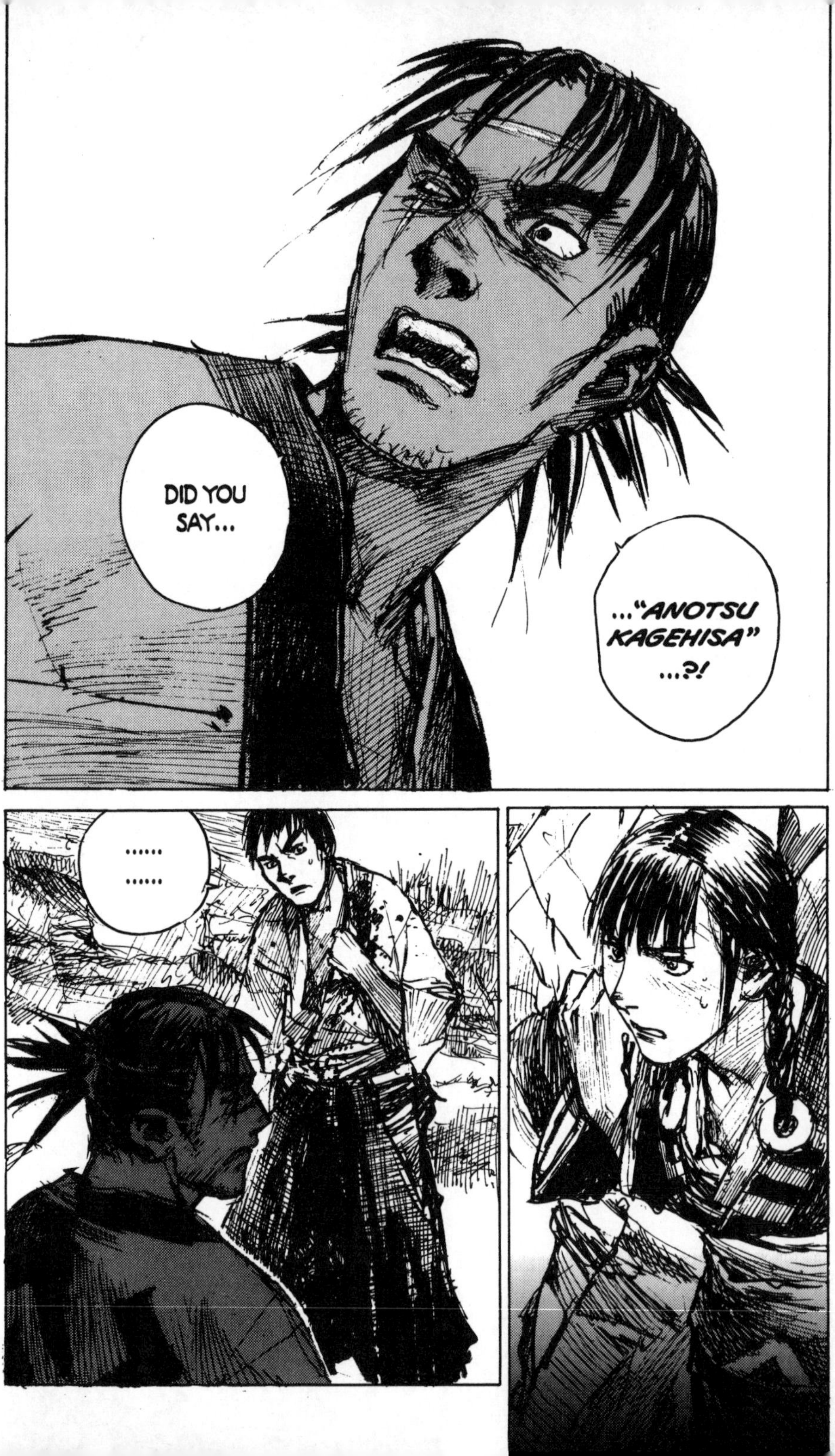
DID YOU SAY...
..."ANOTSU KAGEHISA" ...?!
....

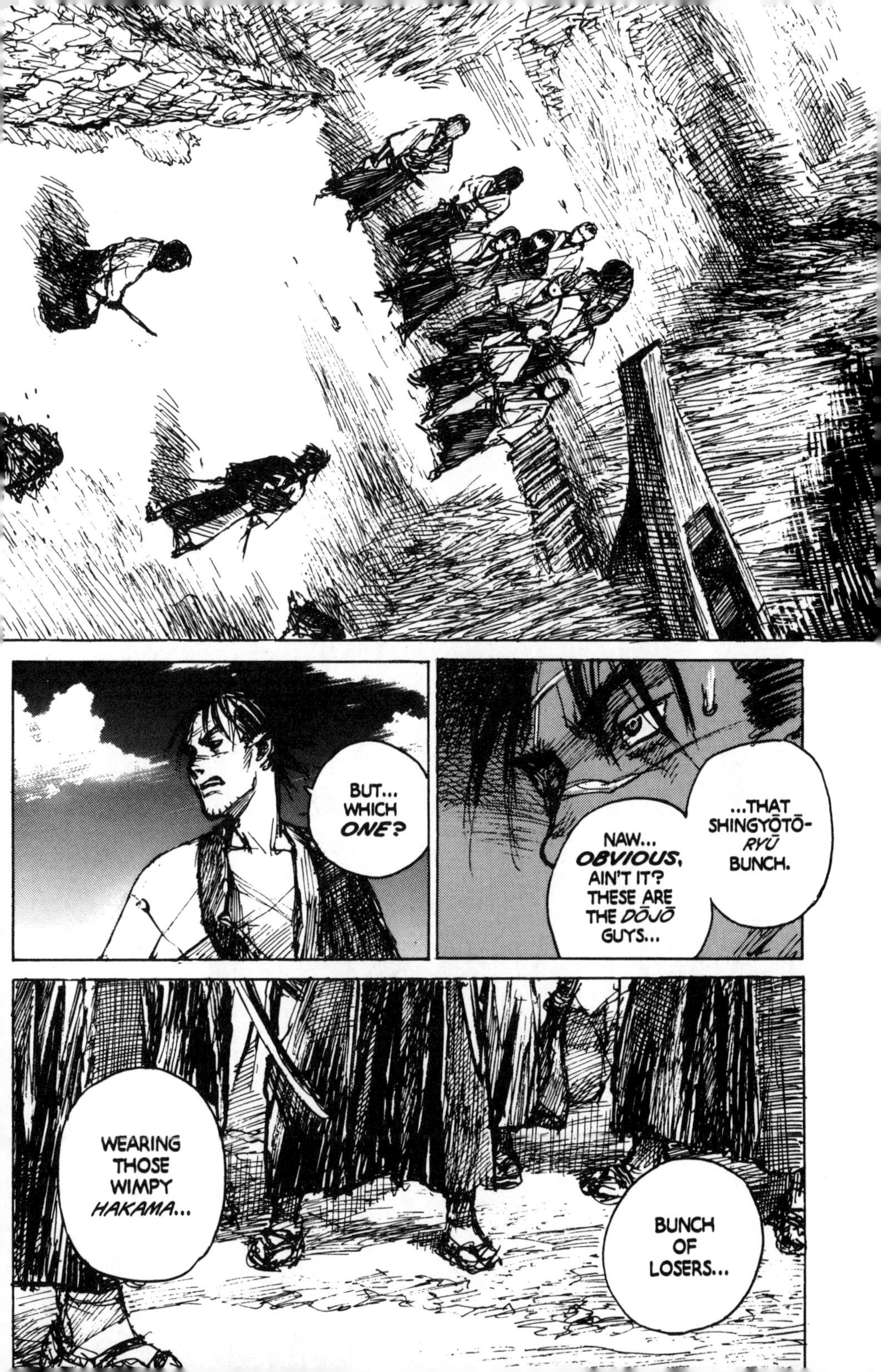
BUT... WHICH *ONE?*
NAW... ***OBVIOUS,*** AIN'T IT? THESE ARE THE *DŌJŌ* GUYS...
...THAT SHINGYŌTŌ-*RYŪ* BUNCH.
WEARING THOSE WIMPY *HAKAMA*...
BUNCH OF LOSERS...

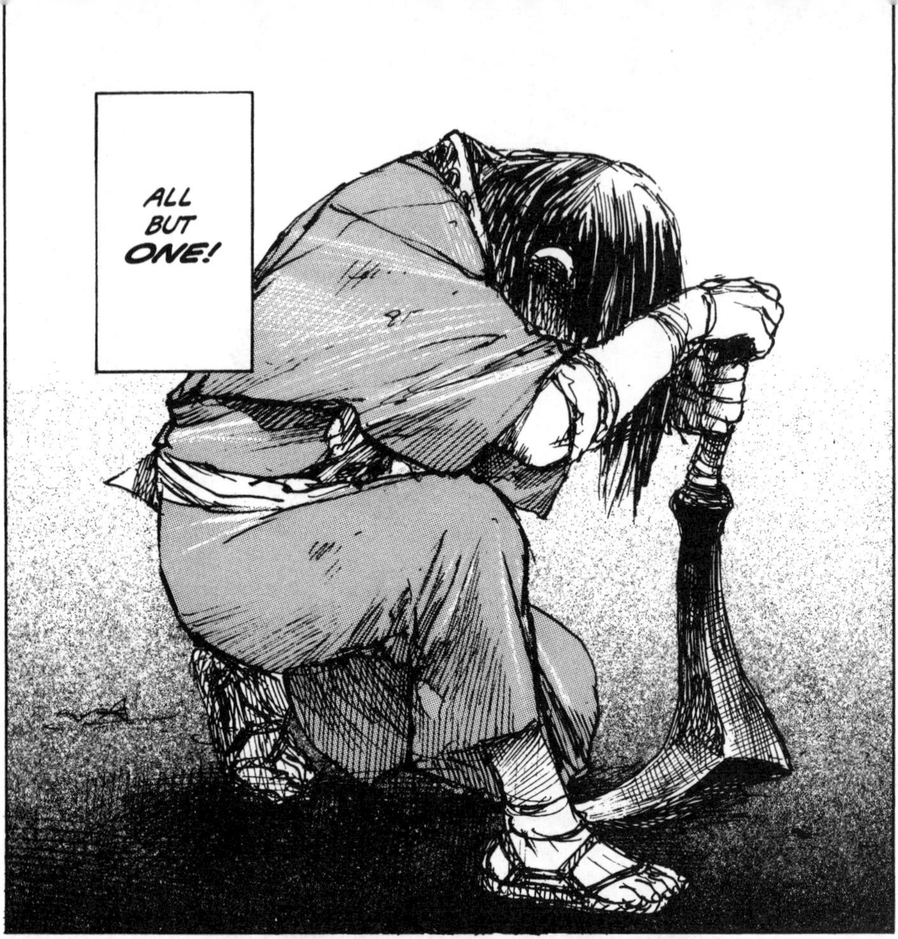
ALL BUT ONE!
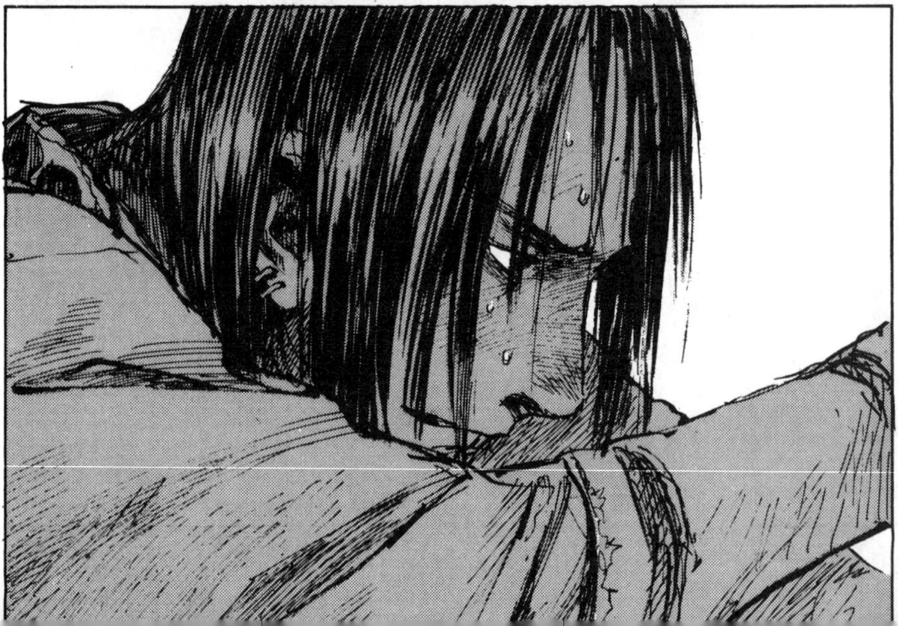

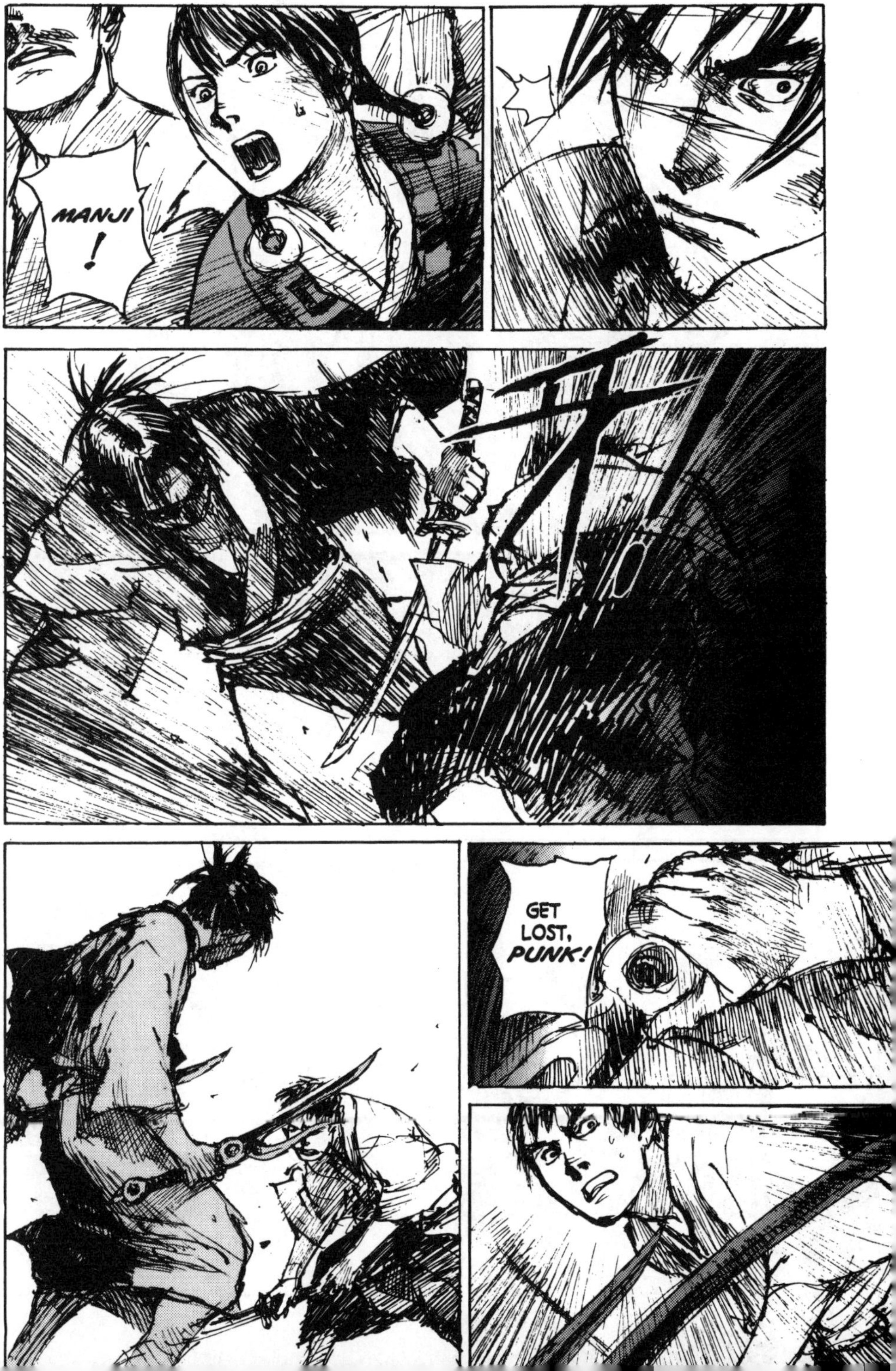
MANJI
!
GET
LOST,
PUNK!

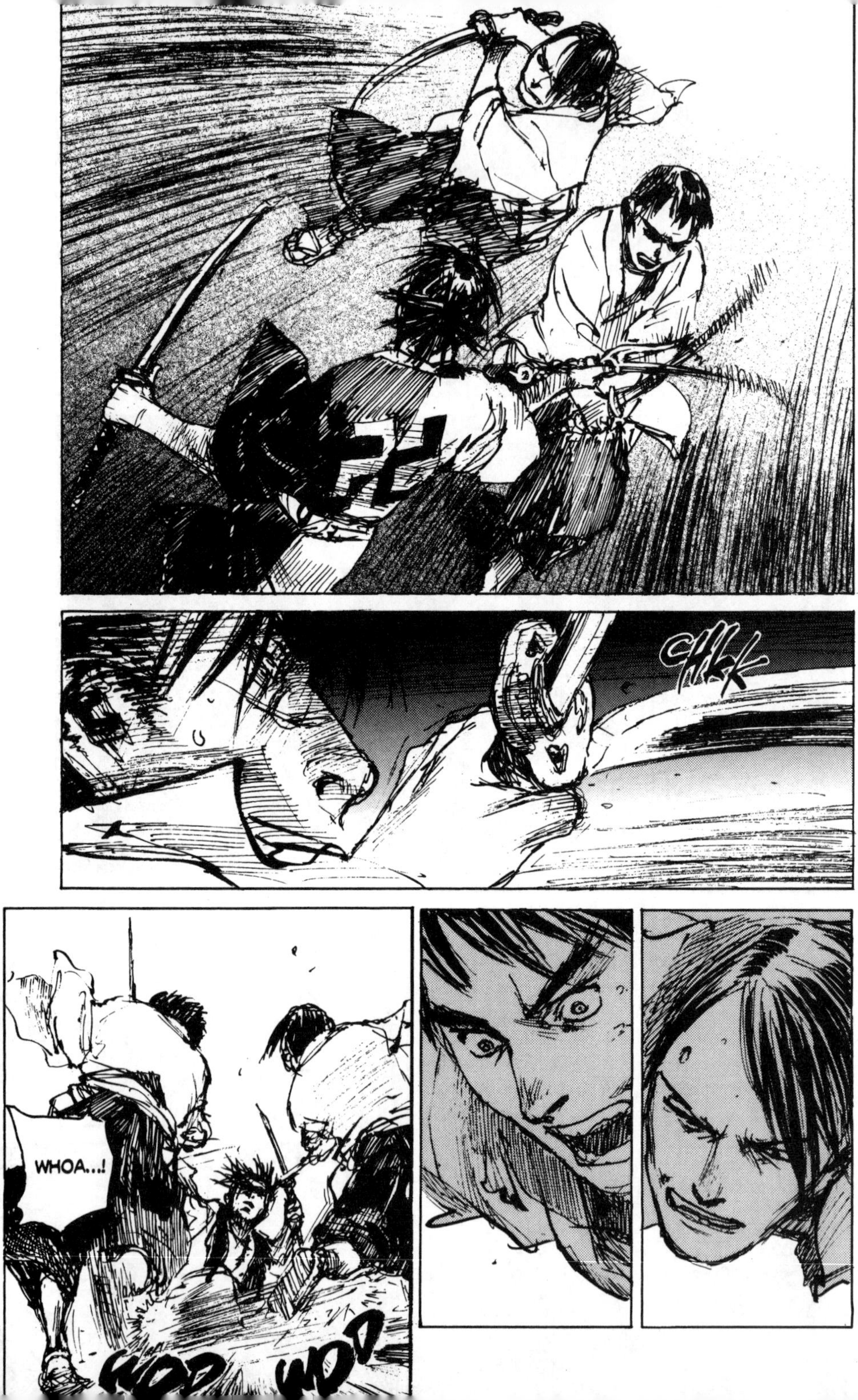
CHKK
WHOA...!
WOD WOD

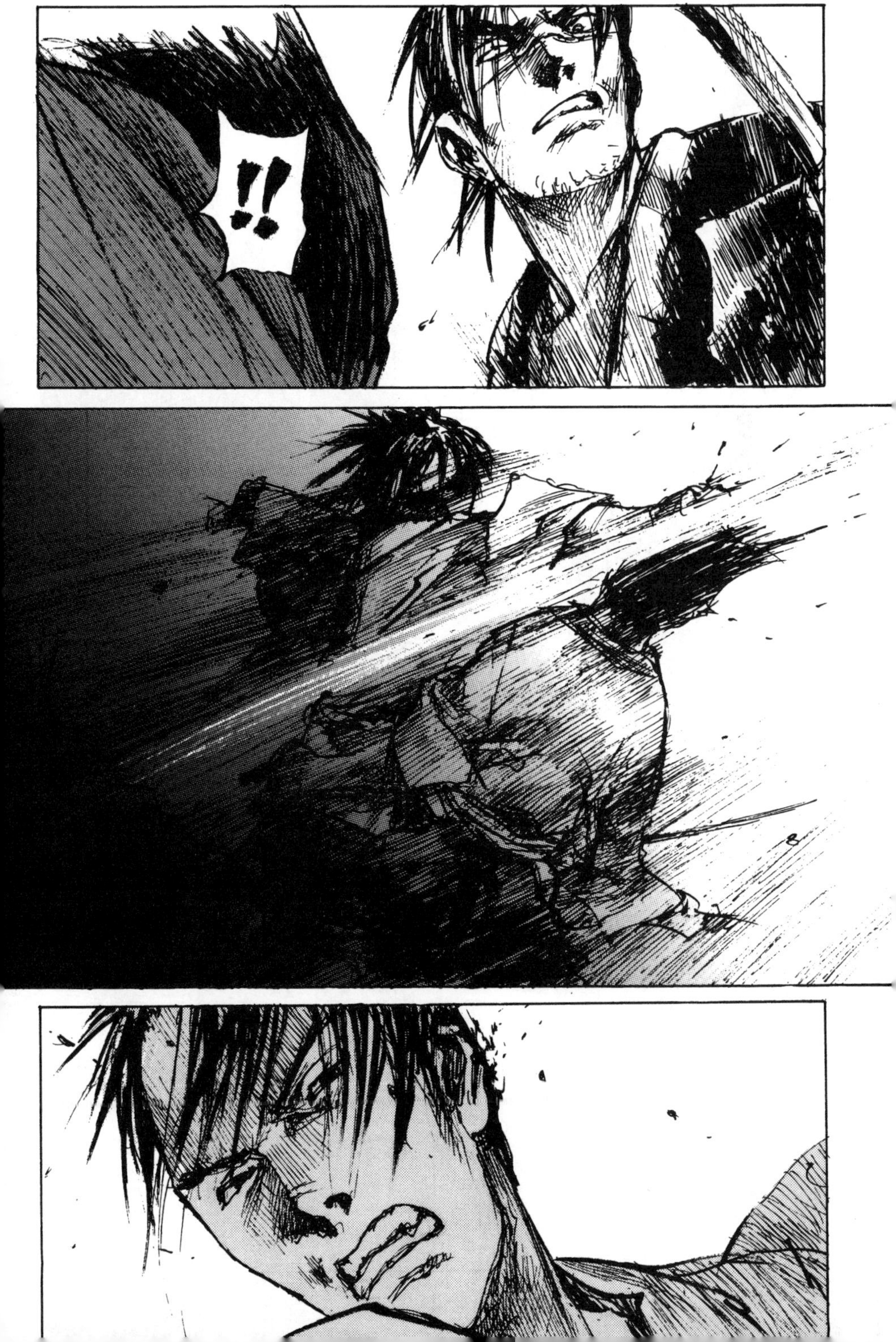
!!

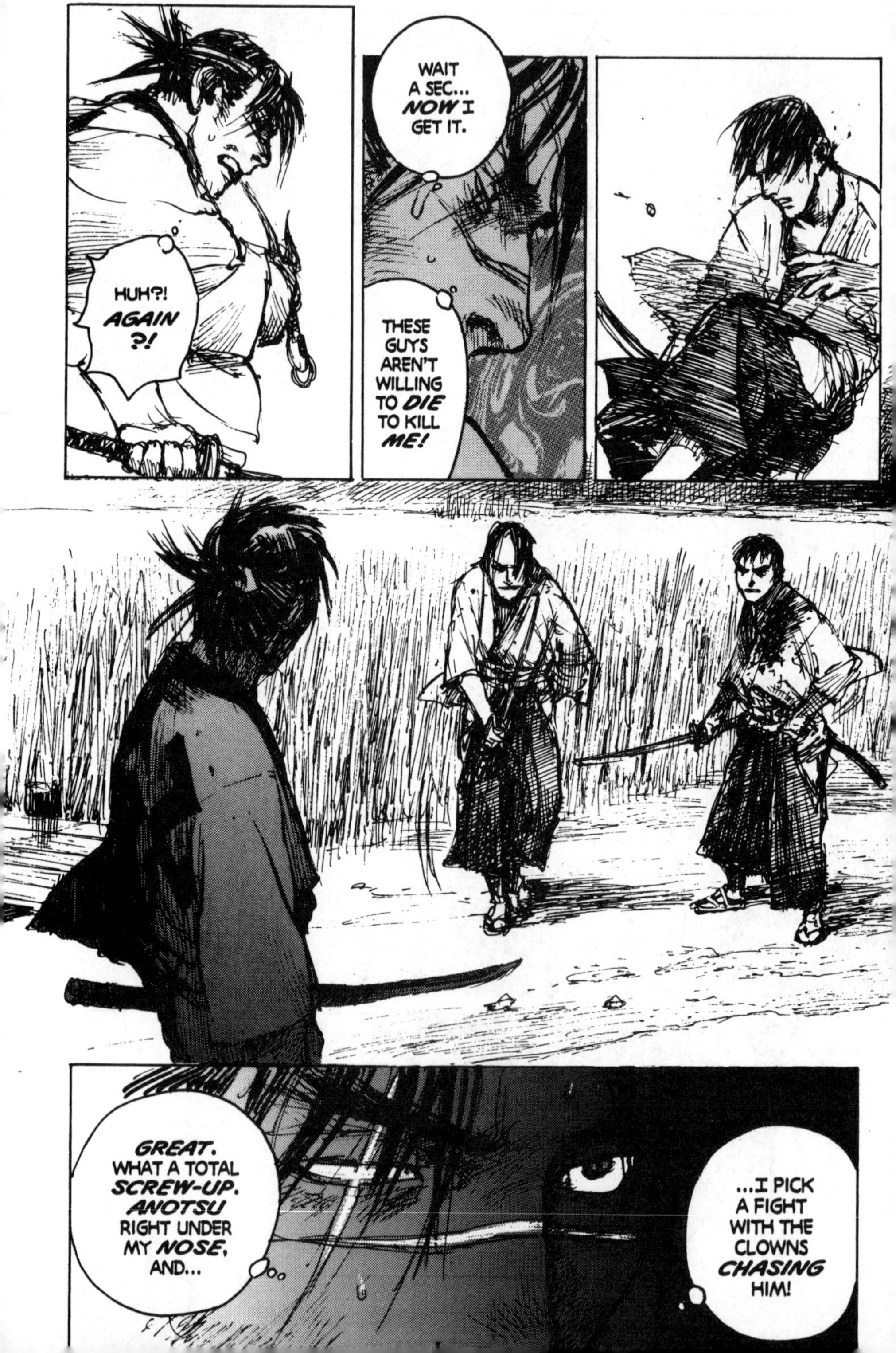
HUH?! AGAIN?!
WAIT A SEC... NOW I GET IT.
THESE GUYS AREN'T WILLING TO DIE TO KILL ME!
GREAT. WHAT A TOTAL SCREW-UP. ANOTSU RIGHT UNDER MY NOSE, AND...
...I PICK A FIGHT WITH THE CLOWNS CHASING HIM!

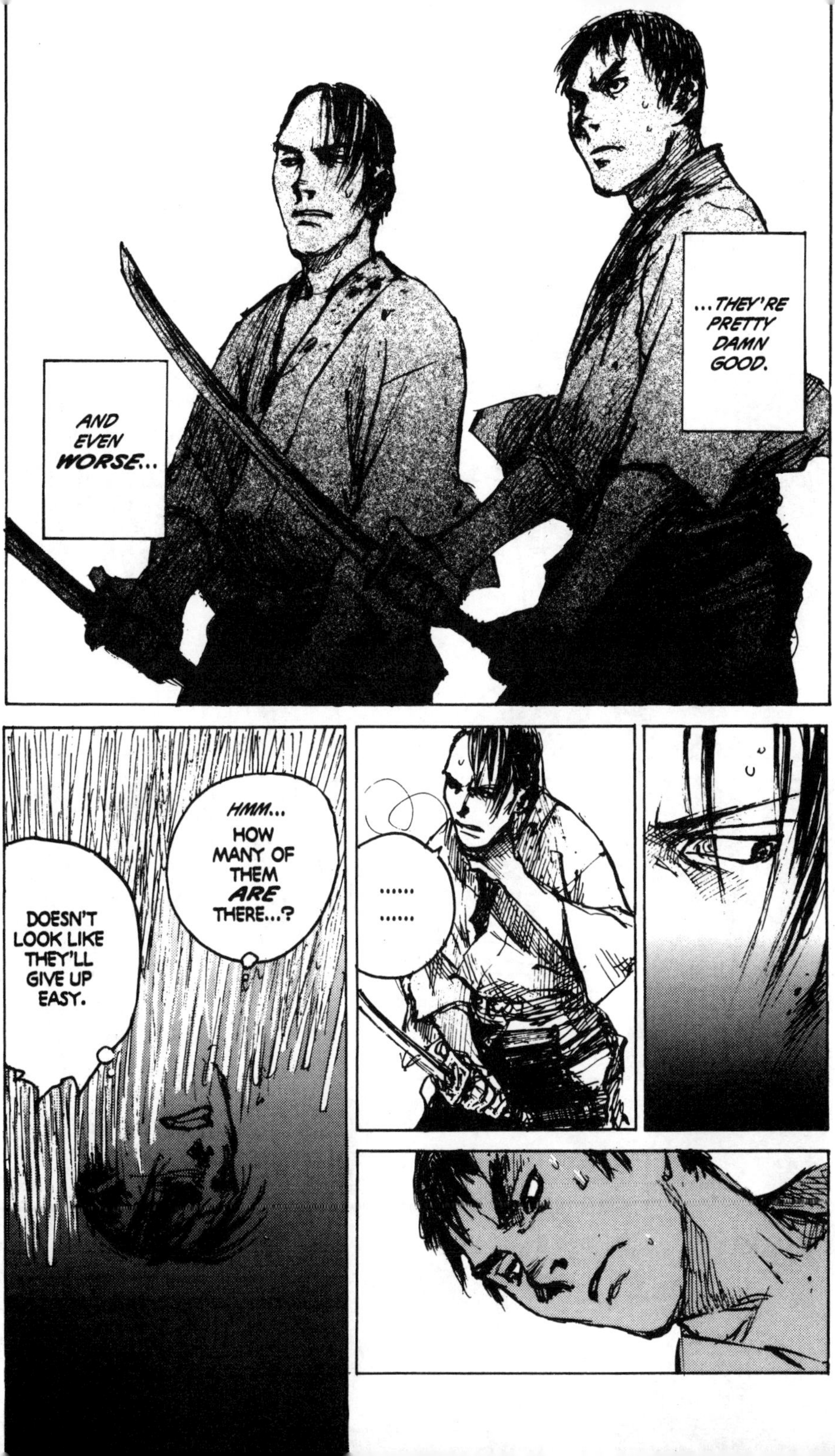
AND EVEN WORSE...
...THEY'RE PRETTY DAMN GOOD.
HMM... HOW MANY OF THEM ARE THERE...?
DOESN'T LOOK LIKE THEY'LL GIVE UP EASY.
....

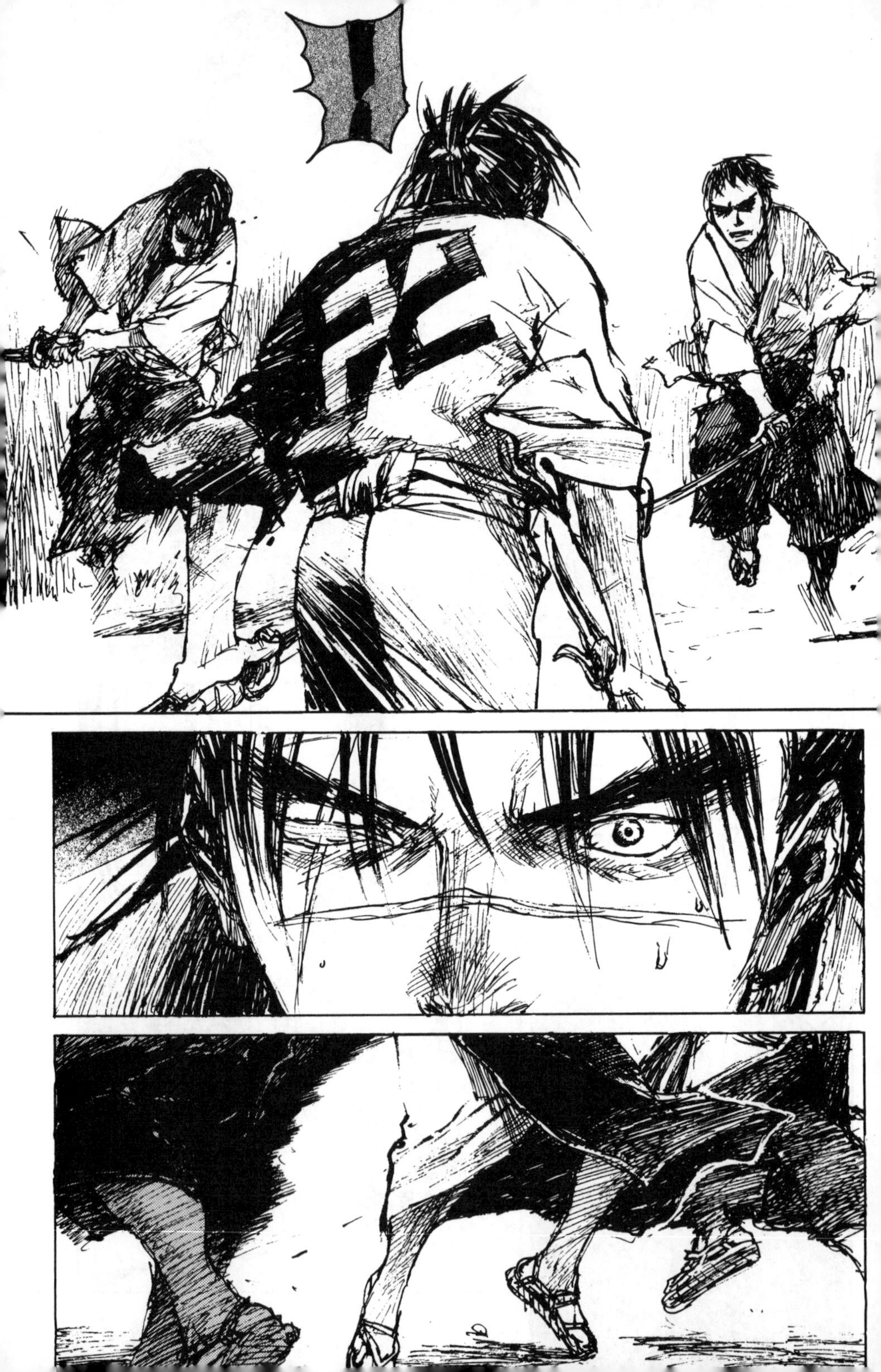
!

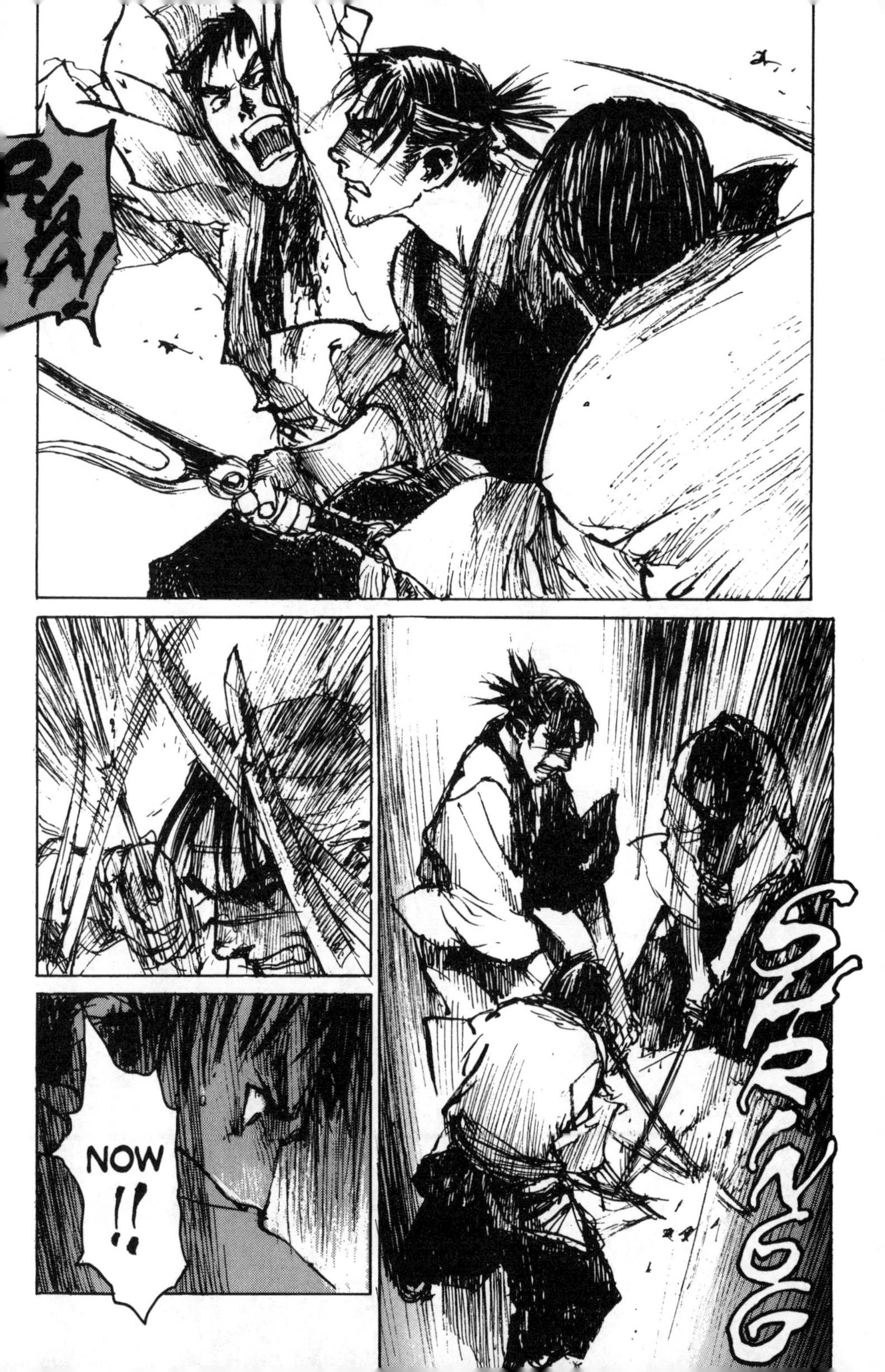
RYAA!
NOW !!

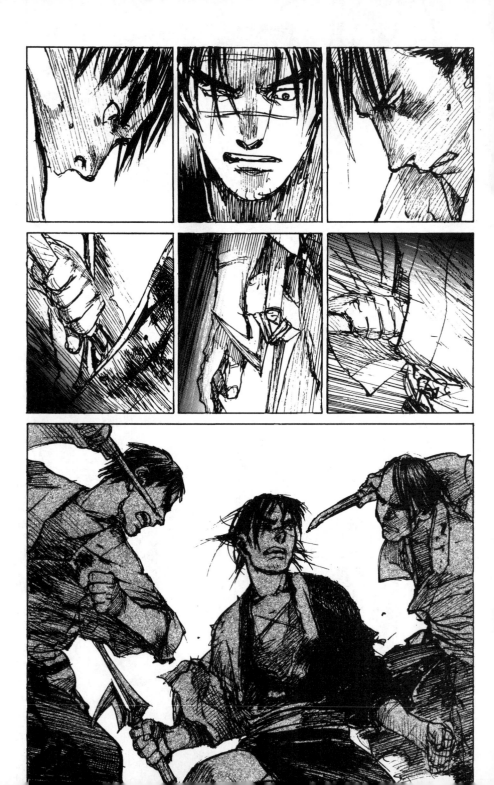

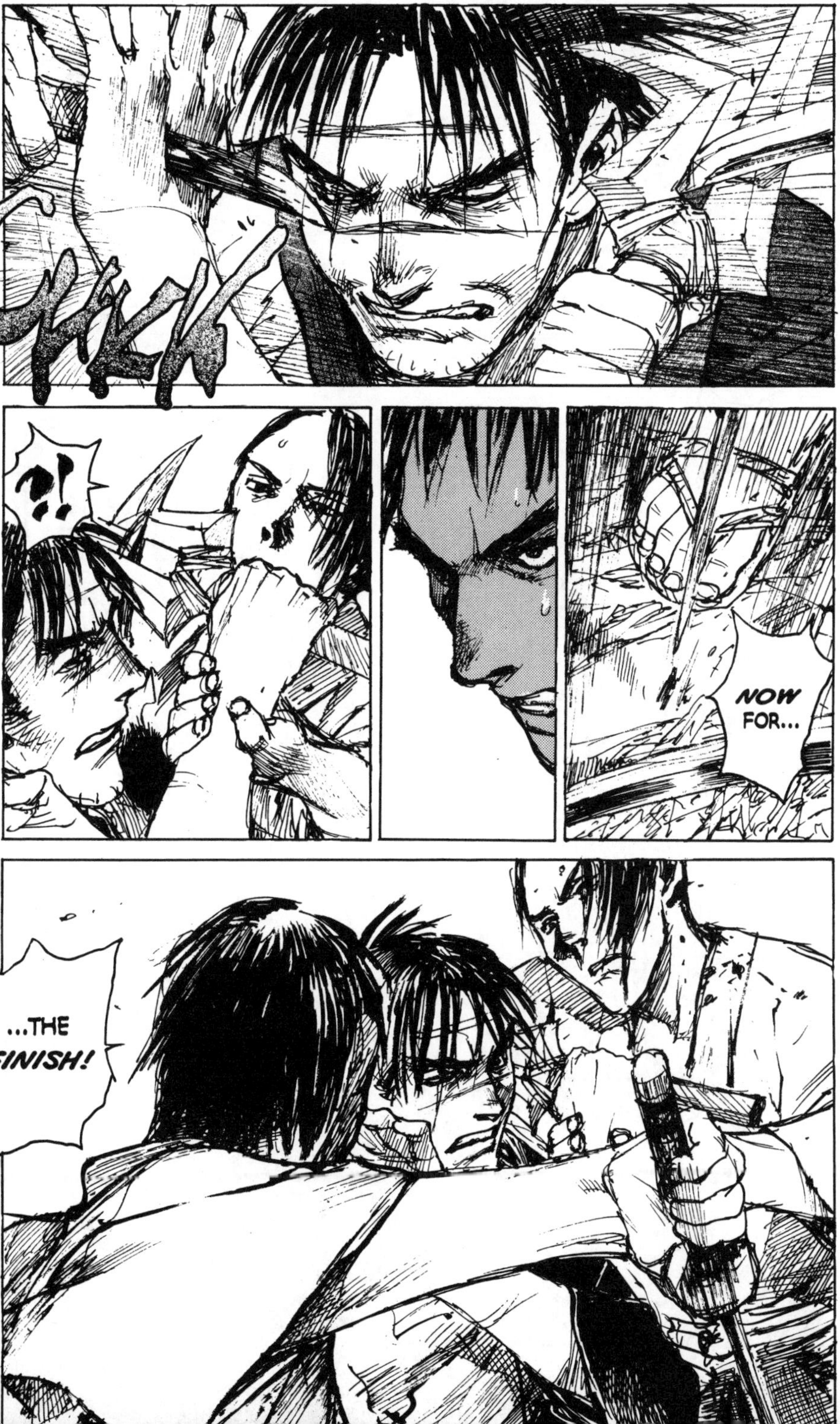
CHKK
NOW FOR...
?!
...THE FINISH!

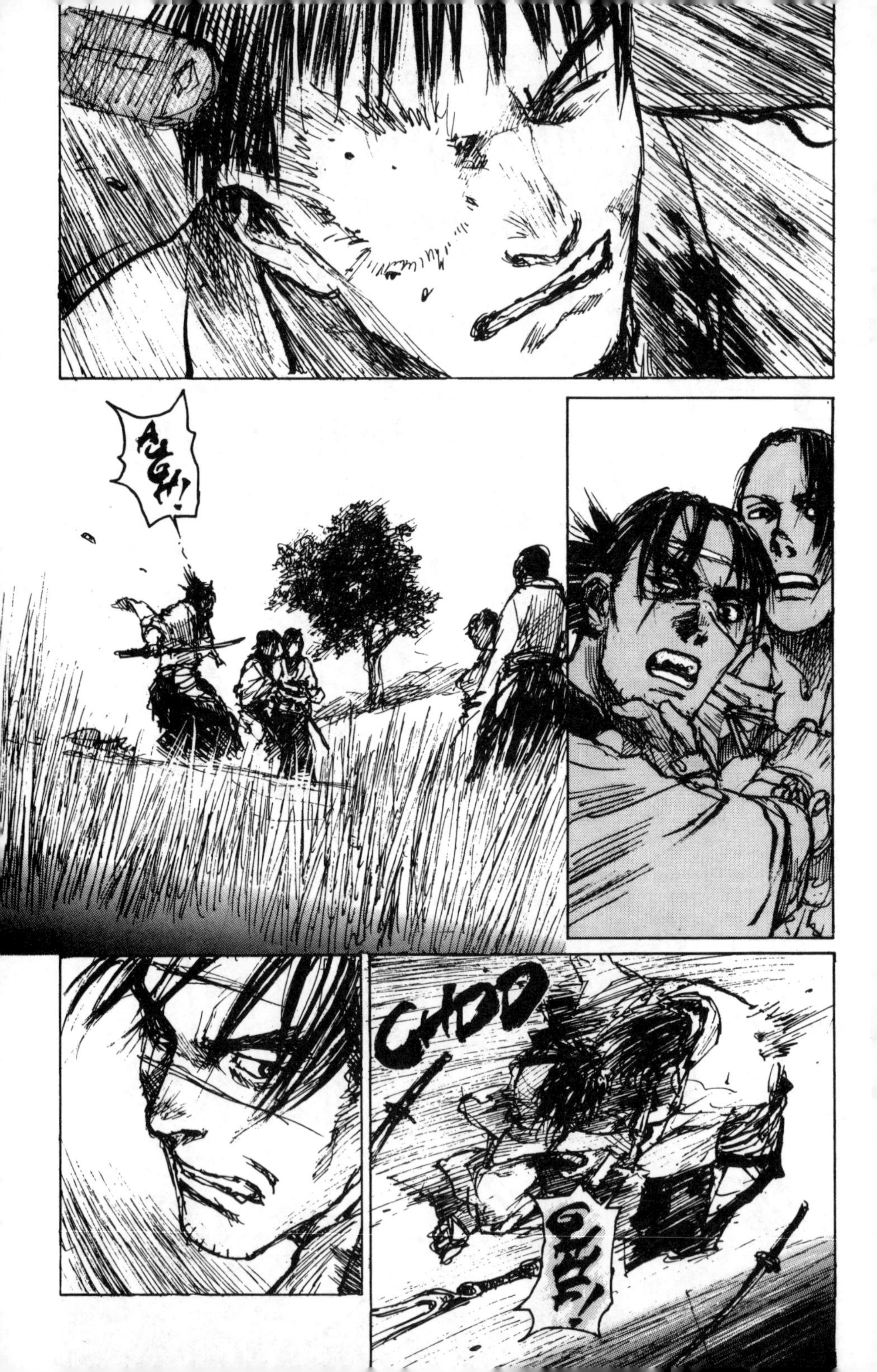
AUGH!
CHOO
GAH!

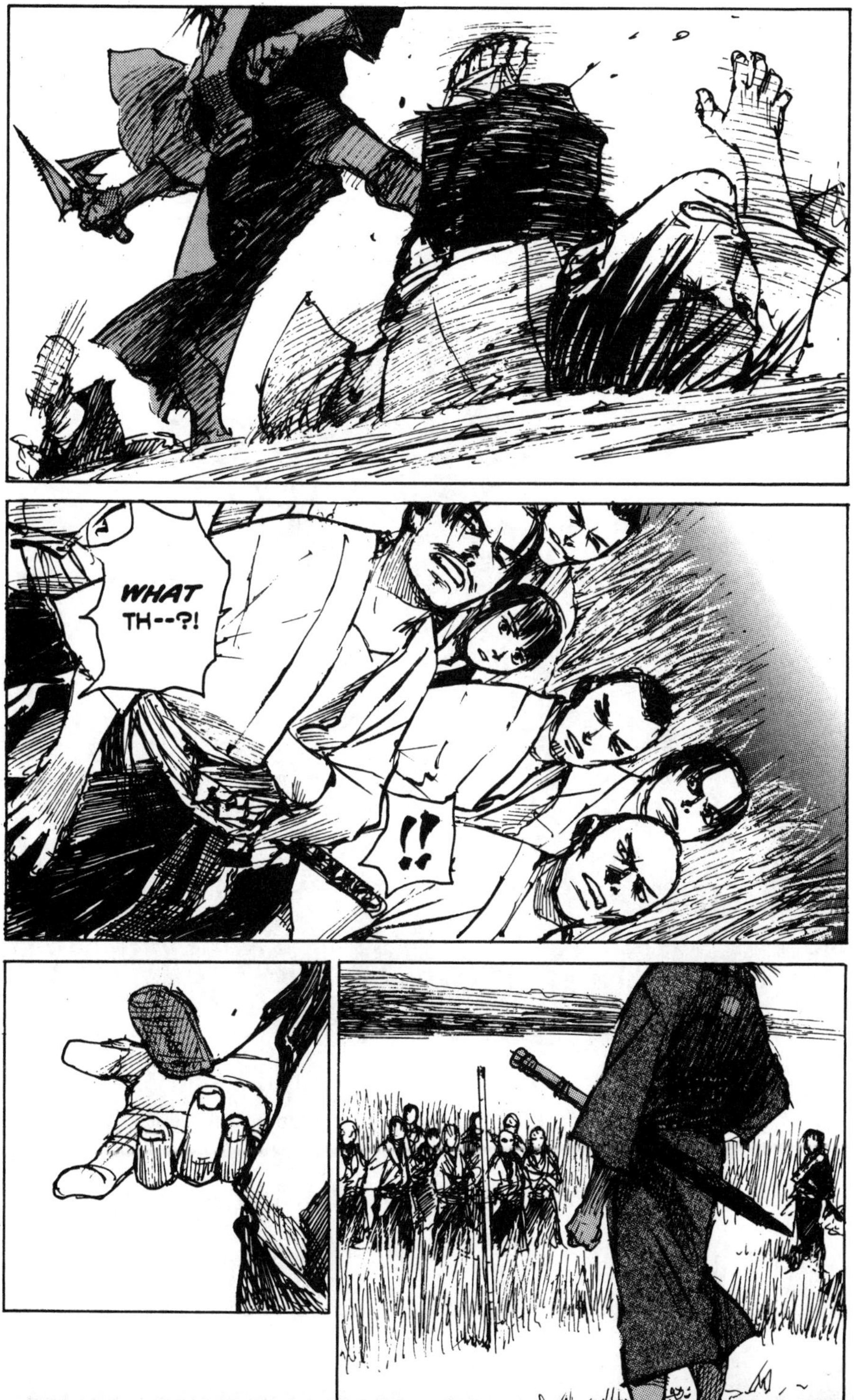
WHAT TH--?!
!!

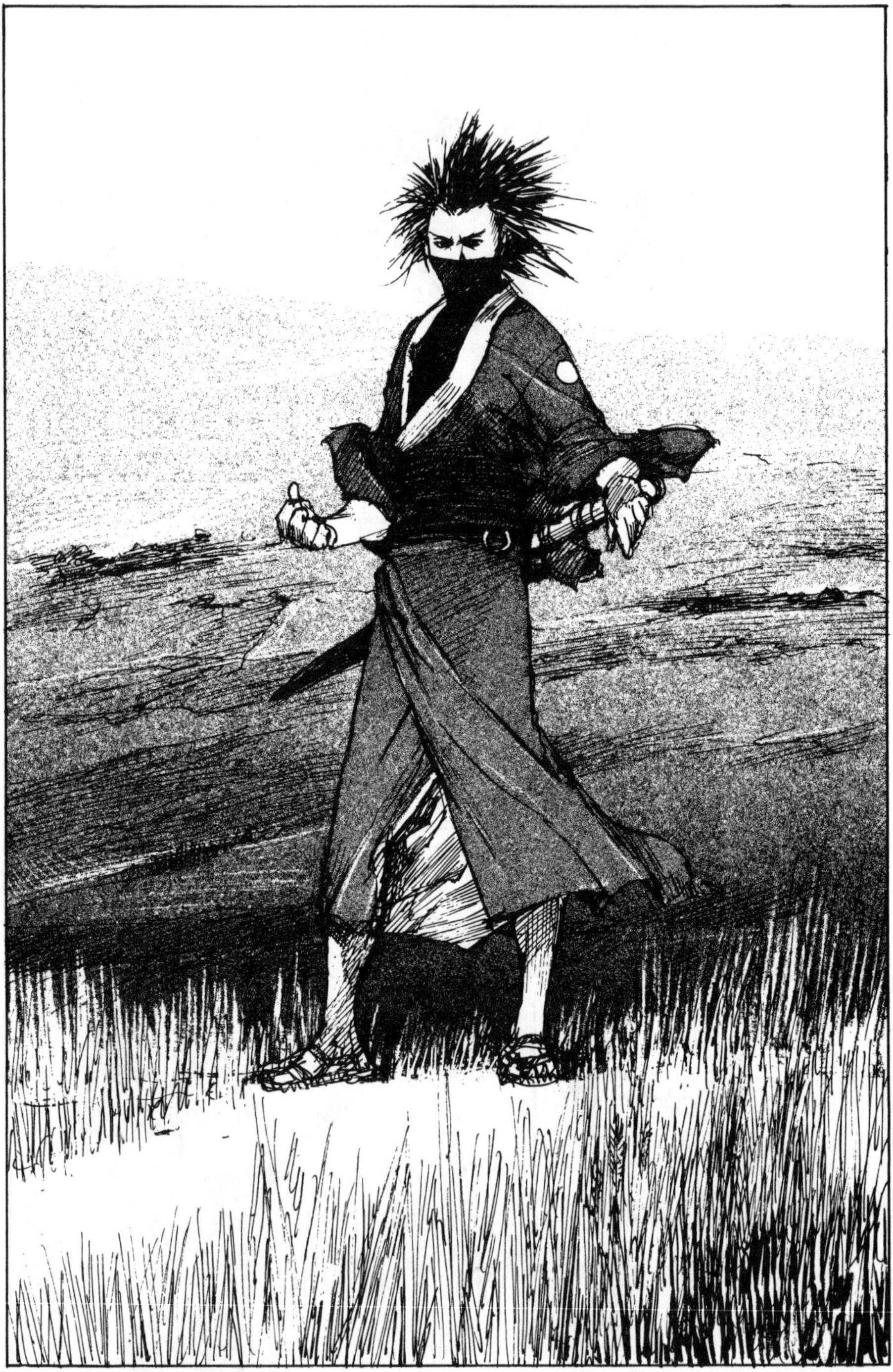

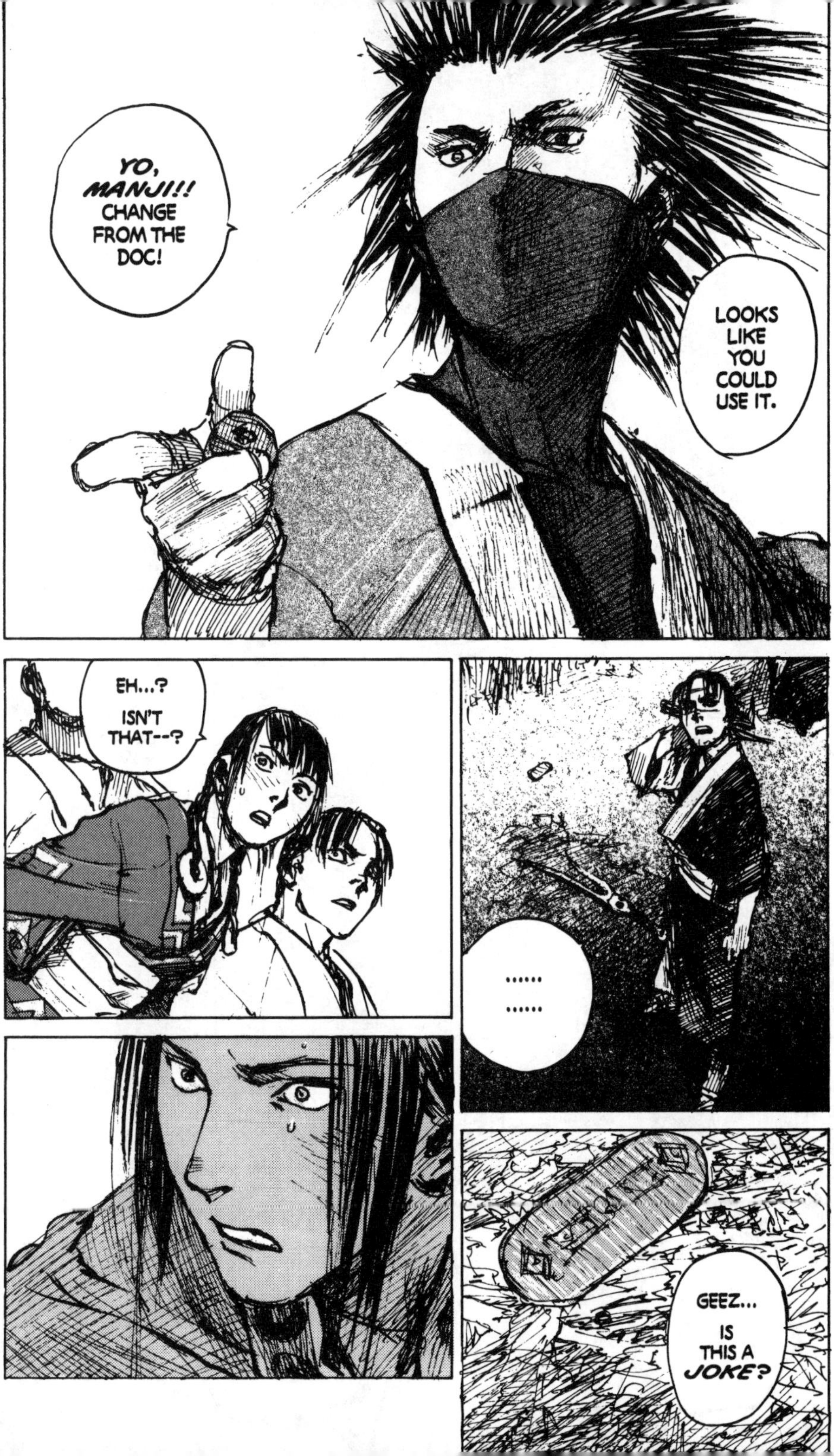
YO, MANJI!! CHANGE FROM THE DOC!
LOOKS LIKE YOU COULD USE IT.
....
GEEZ... IS THIS A JOKE?
EH...? ISN'T THAT--?

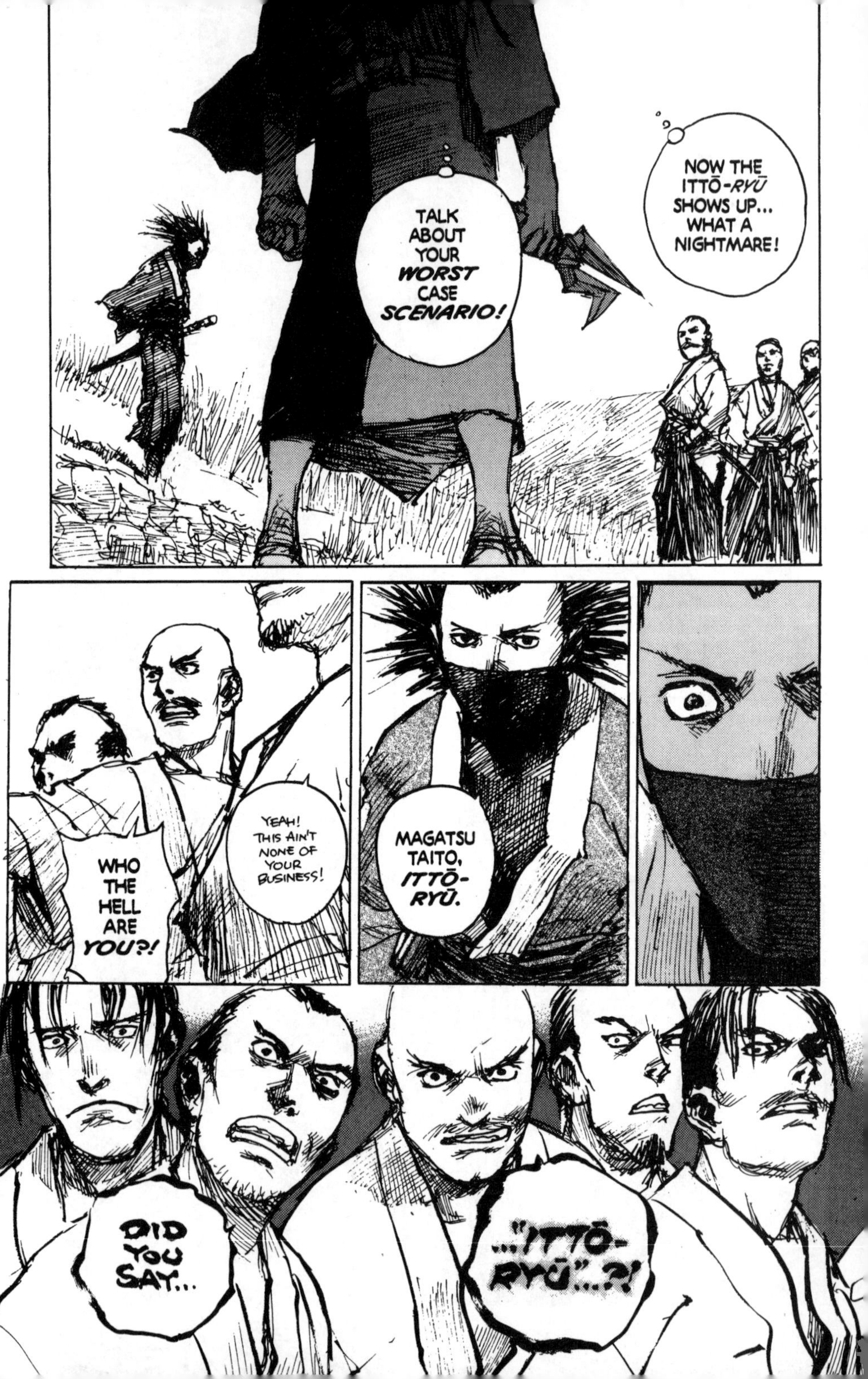
TALK ABOUT YOUR *WORST* CASE *SCENARIO!*
NOW THE ITTŌ-*RYŪ* SHOWS UP... WHAT A NIGHTMARE!
WHO THE HELL ARE *YOU?!*
YEAH! THIS AIN'T NONE OF YOUR BUSINESS!
MAGATSU TAITO, *ITTŌ-RYŪ.*
DID YOU SAY...
..."ITTŌ-RYŪ"...?!

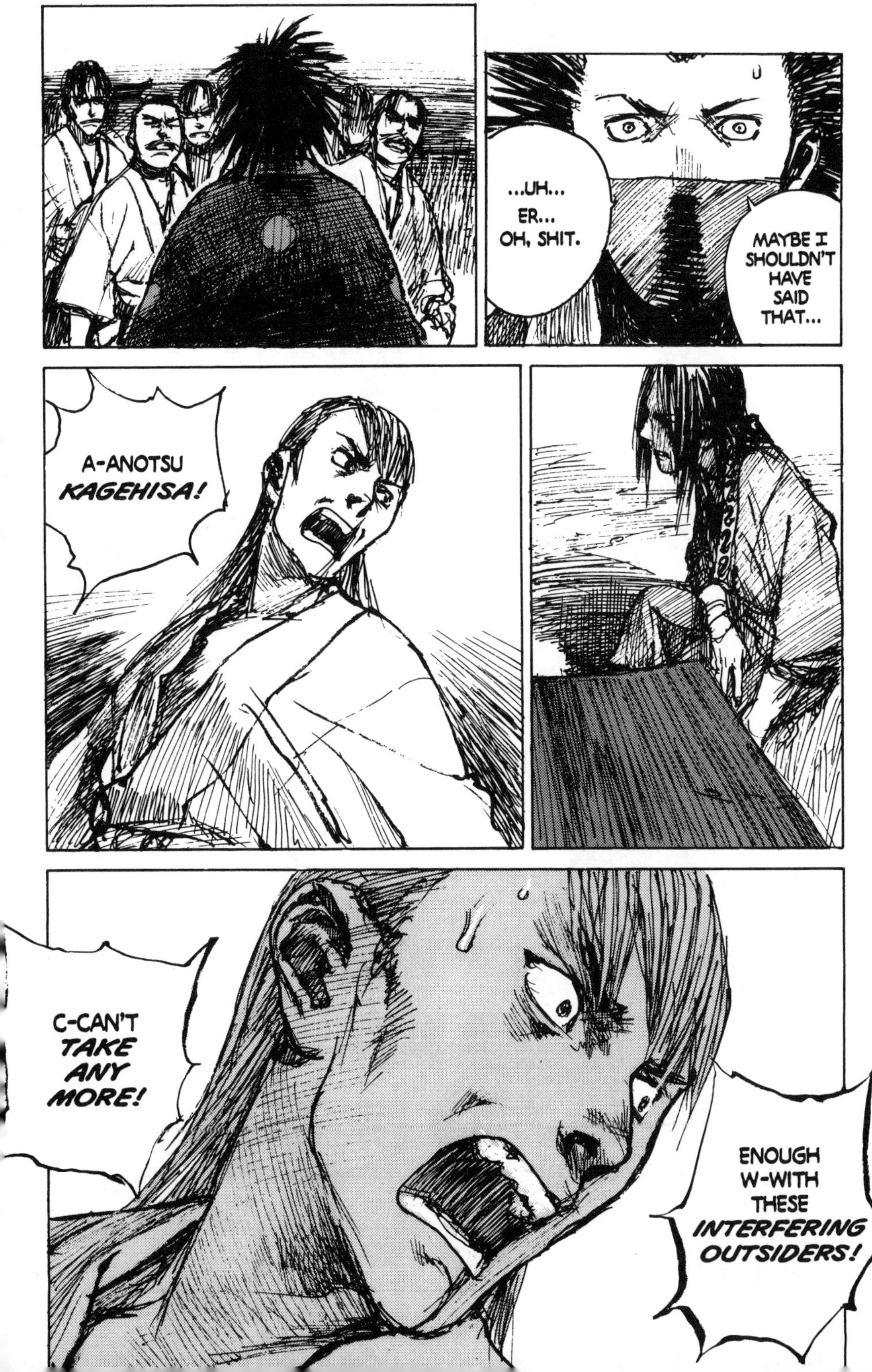
...UH... ER... OH, SHIT.
MAYBE I SHOULDN'T HAVE SAID THAT...
A-ANOTSU *KAGEHISA!*
C-CAN'T *TAKE ANY MORE!*
ENOUGH W-WITH THESE *INTERFERING OUTSIDERS!*

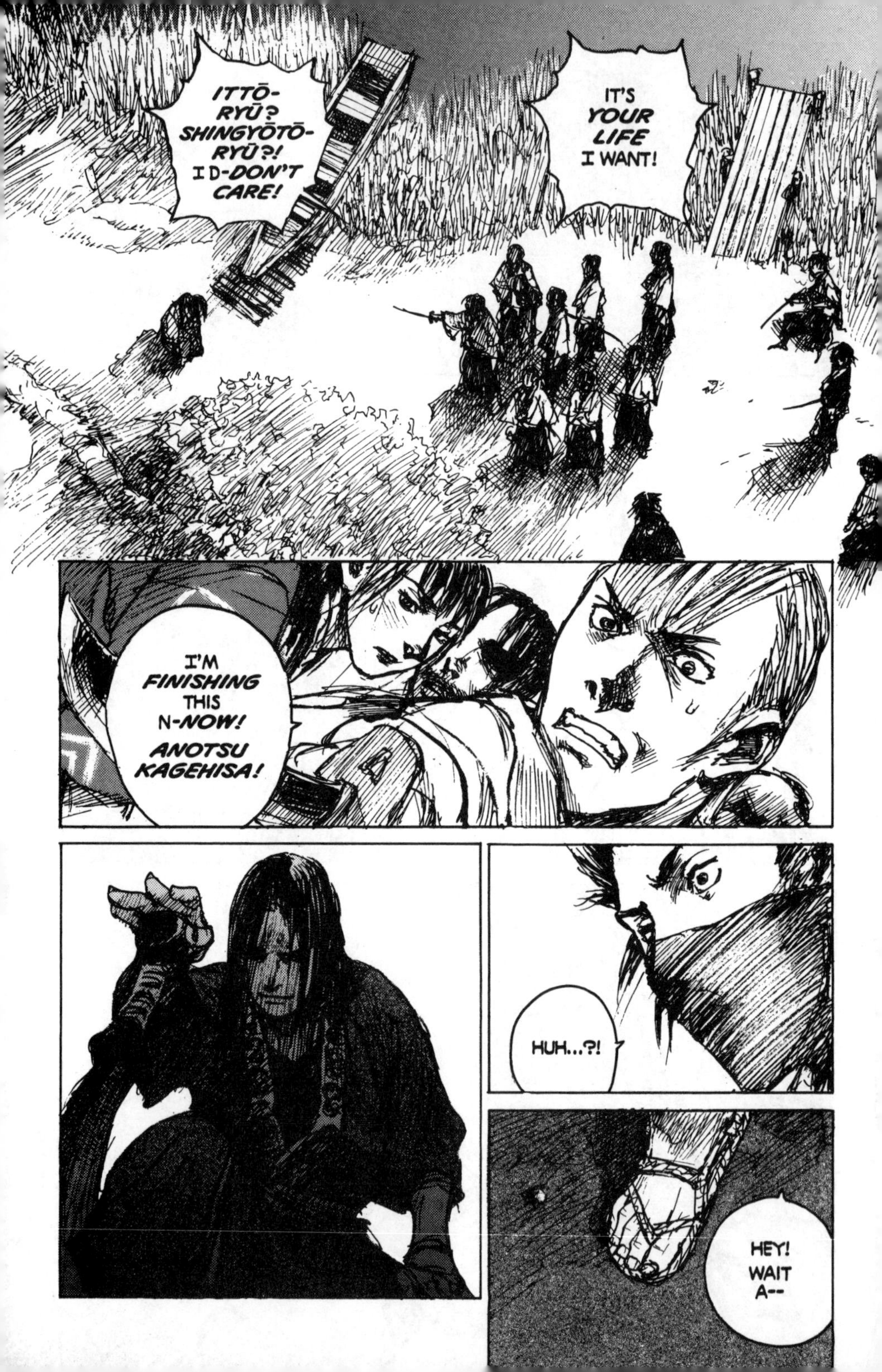
ITTŌ-RYŪ? SHINGYŌTŌ-RYŪ?! I D-DON'T CARE!
IT'S YOUR LIFE I WANT!
I'M FINISHING THIS N-NOW! ANOTSU KAGEHISA!
HUH...?!
HEY! WAIT A--

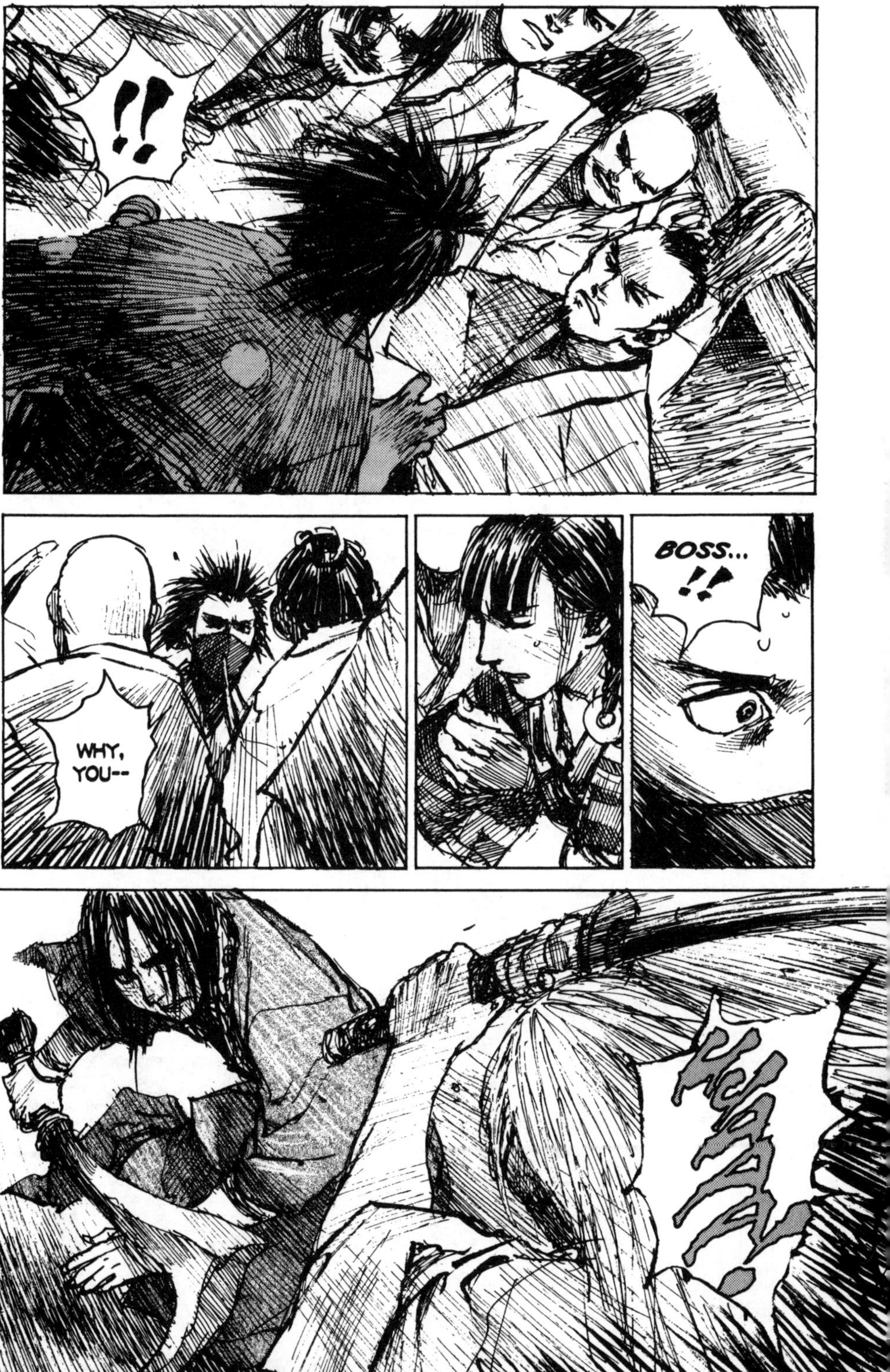
!!
BOSS... !!
WHY, YOU--

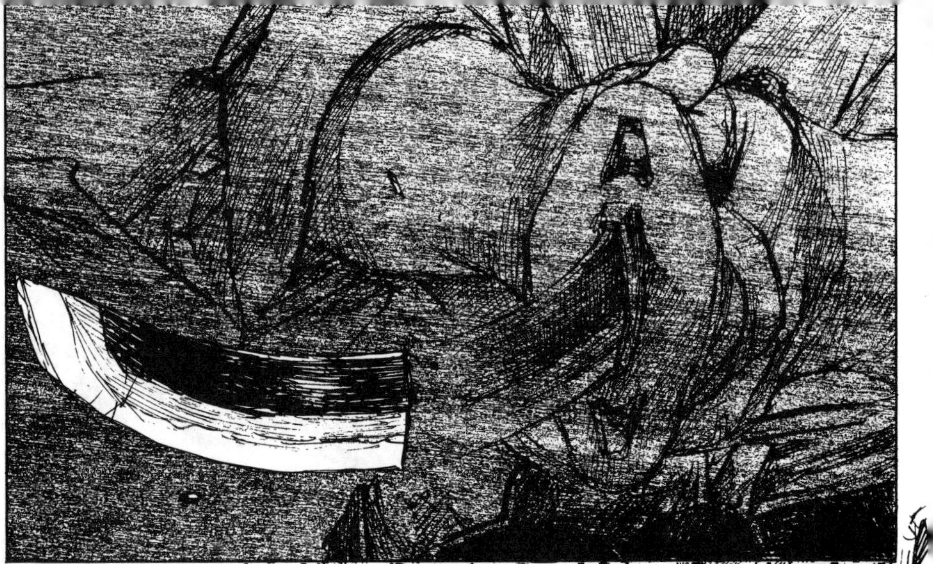
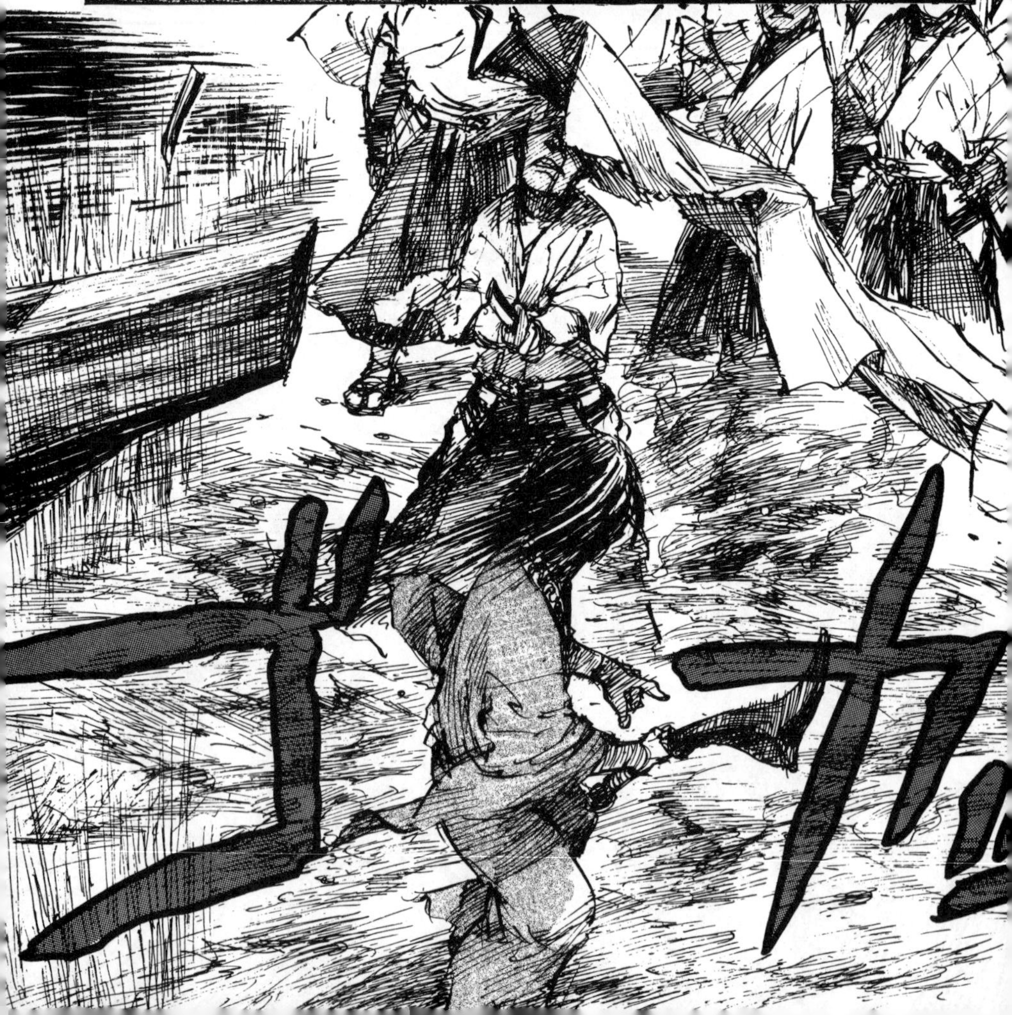
ゴカ!!

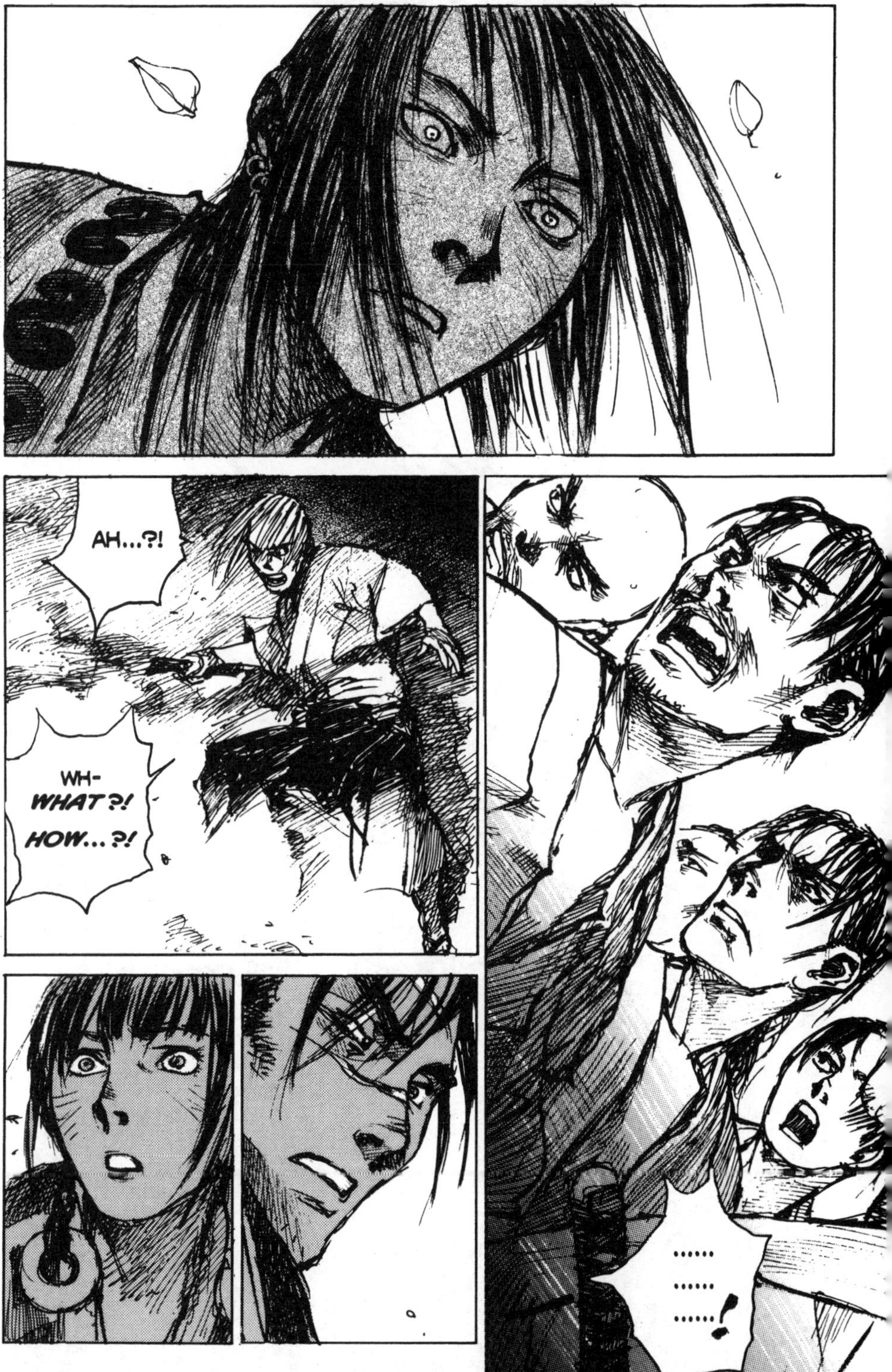
......
......
......!
AH...?!
WH- WHAT?! HOW...?!

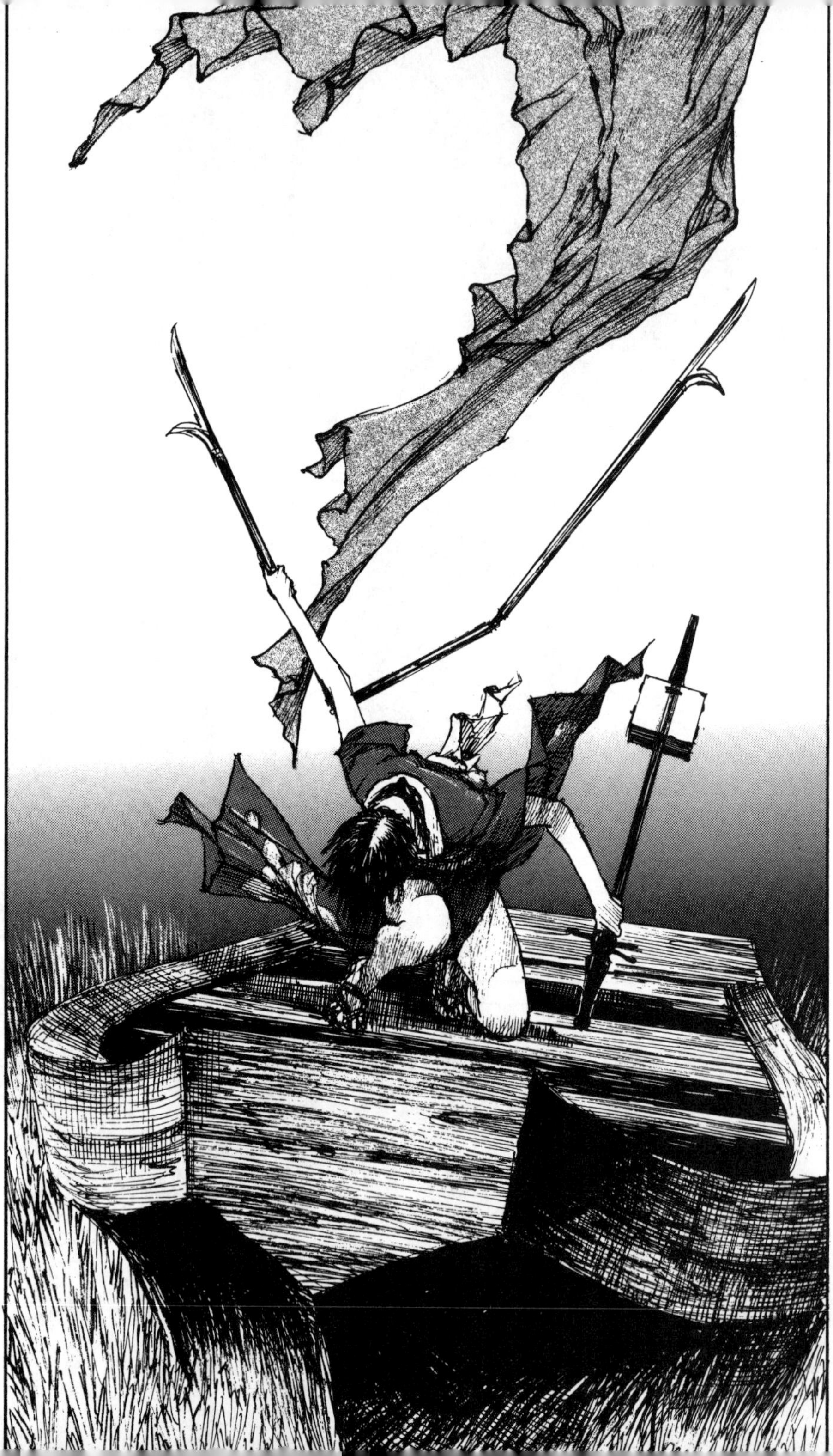

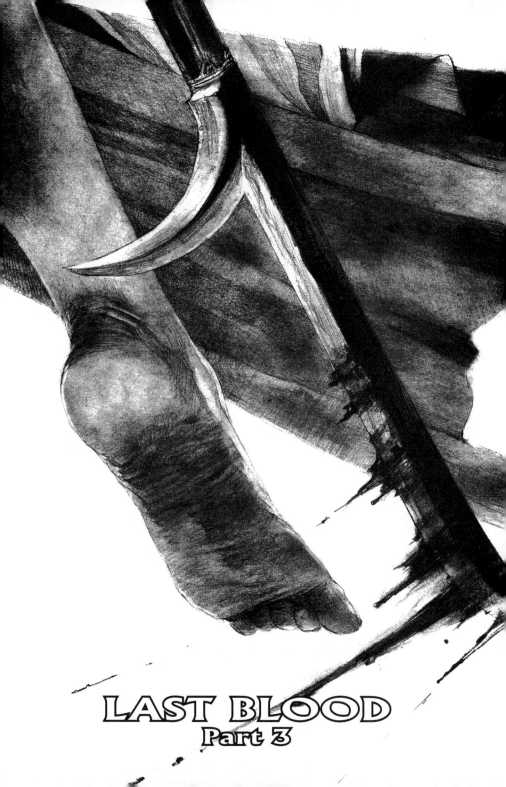

LAST BLOOD
Part 3

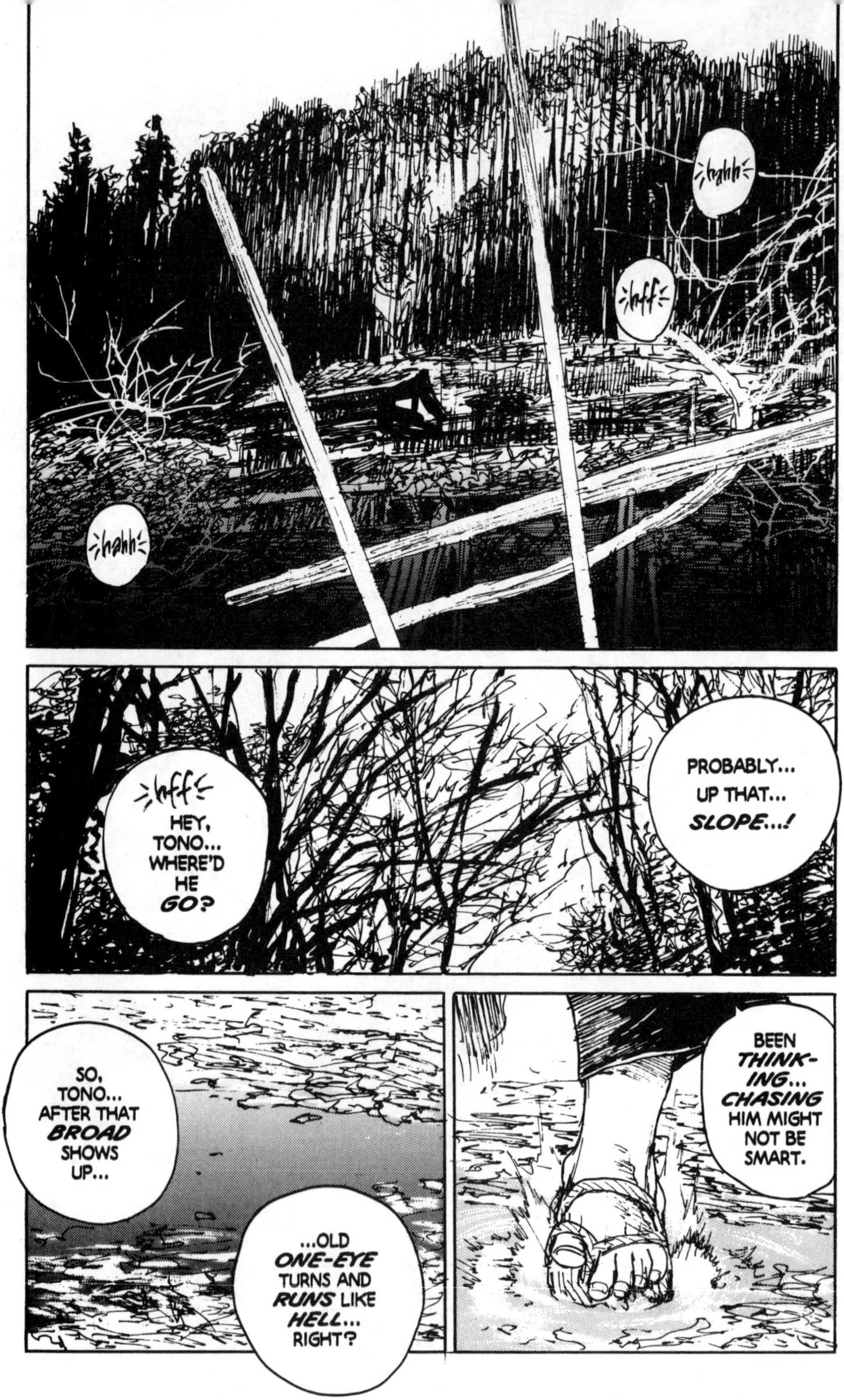
hahh
hff
hahh
hff HEY, TONO... WHERE'D HE GO?
PROBABLY... UP THAT... SLOPE...!
SO, TONO... AFTER THAT BROAD SHOWS UP...
...OLD ONE-EYE TURNS AND RUNS LIKE HELL... RIGHT?
BEEN THINKING... CHASING HIM MIGHT NOT BE SMART.

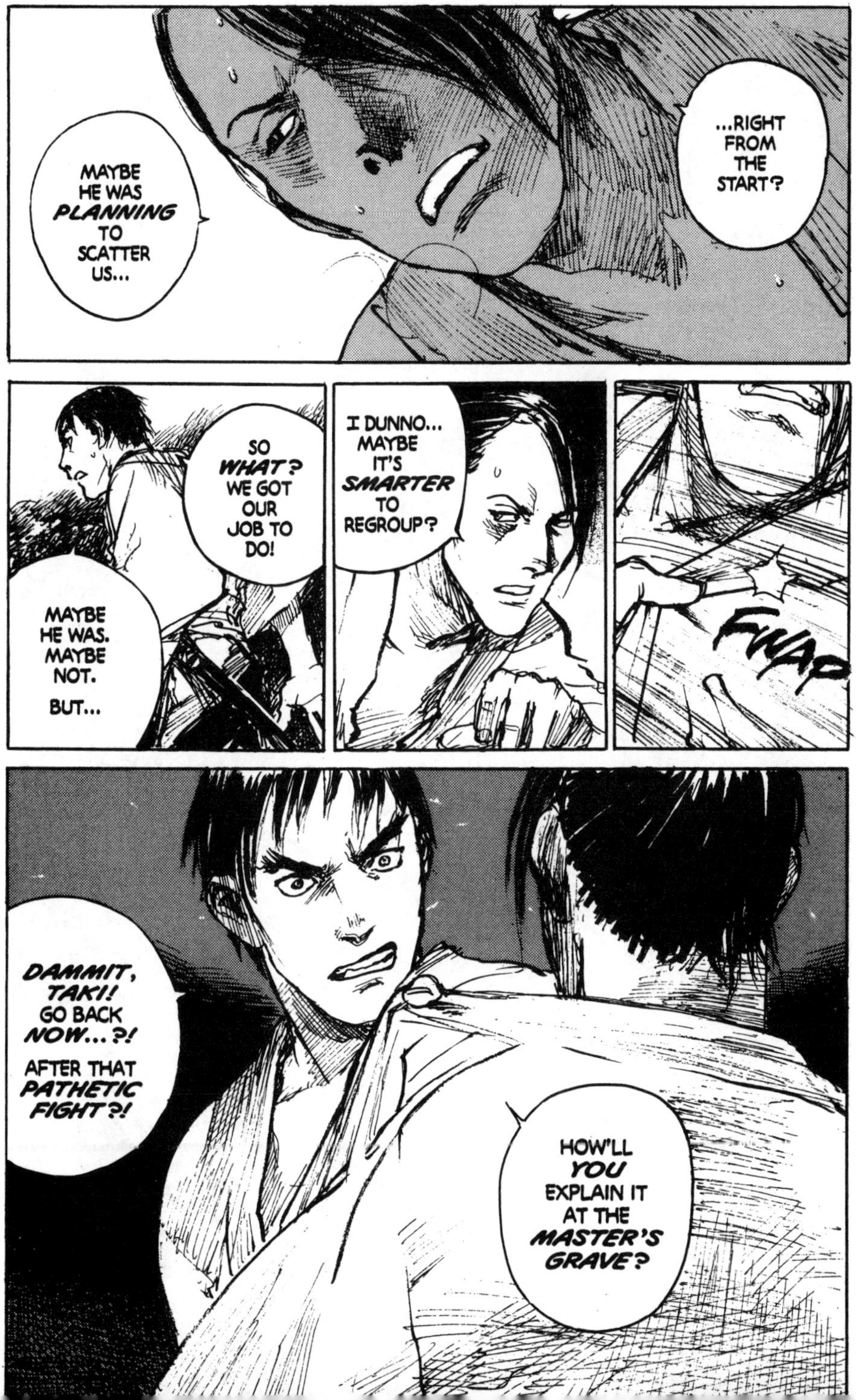
MAYBE HE WAS *PLANNING* TO SCATTER US...
...RIGHT FROM THE START?
MAYBE HE WAS. MAYBE NOT.
BUT...
SO *WHAT?* WE GOT OUR JOB TO DO!
I DUNNO... MAYBE IT'S *SMARTER* TO REGROUP?
FWAP
DAMMIT, TAKI! GO BACK *NOW...?!*
AFTER THAT *PATHETIC FIGHT?!*
HOW'LL *YOU* EXPLAIN IT AT THE *MASTER'S GRAVE?*

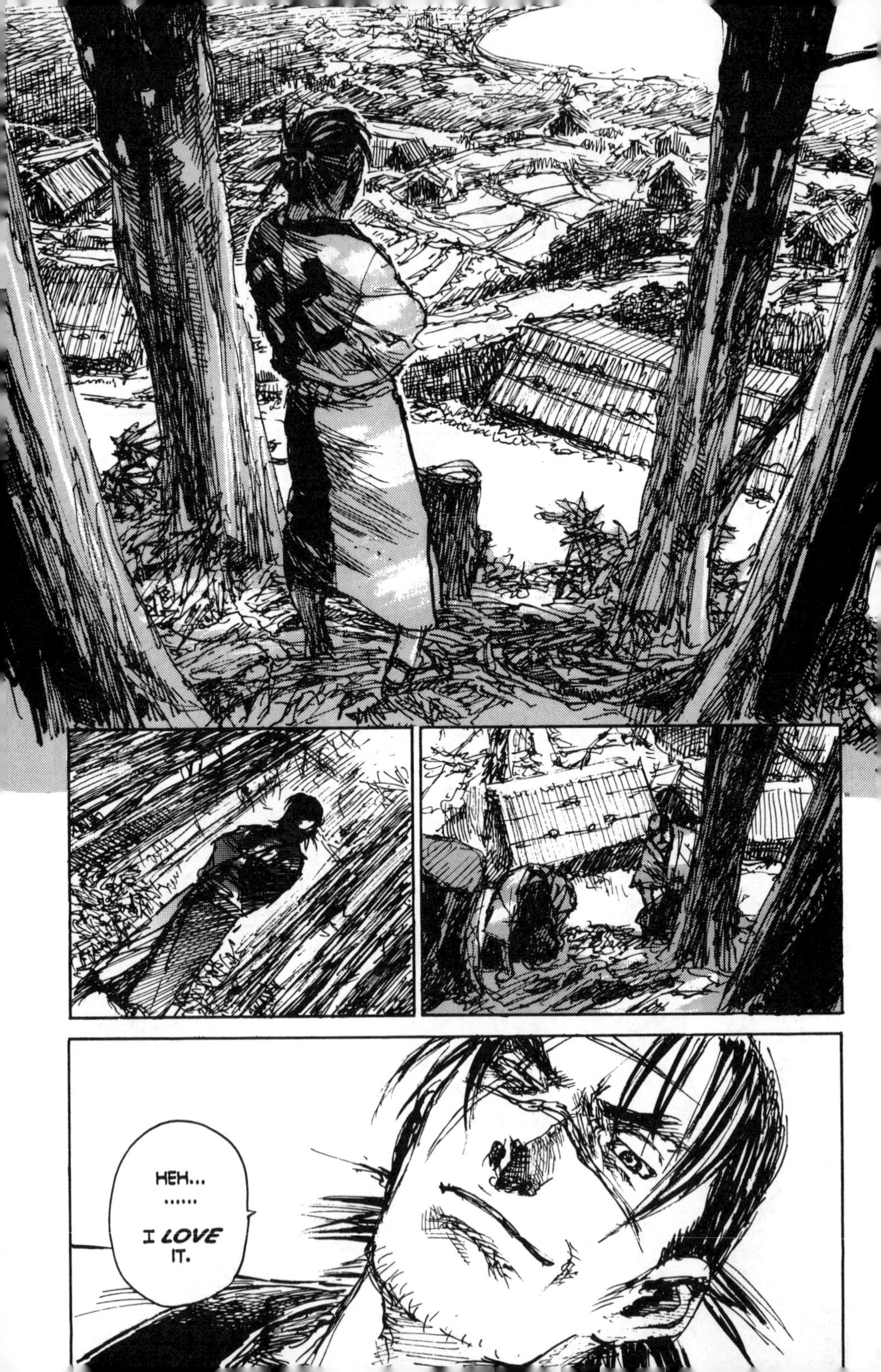
HEH... ...... I *LOVE* IT.

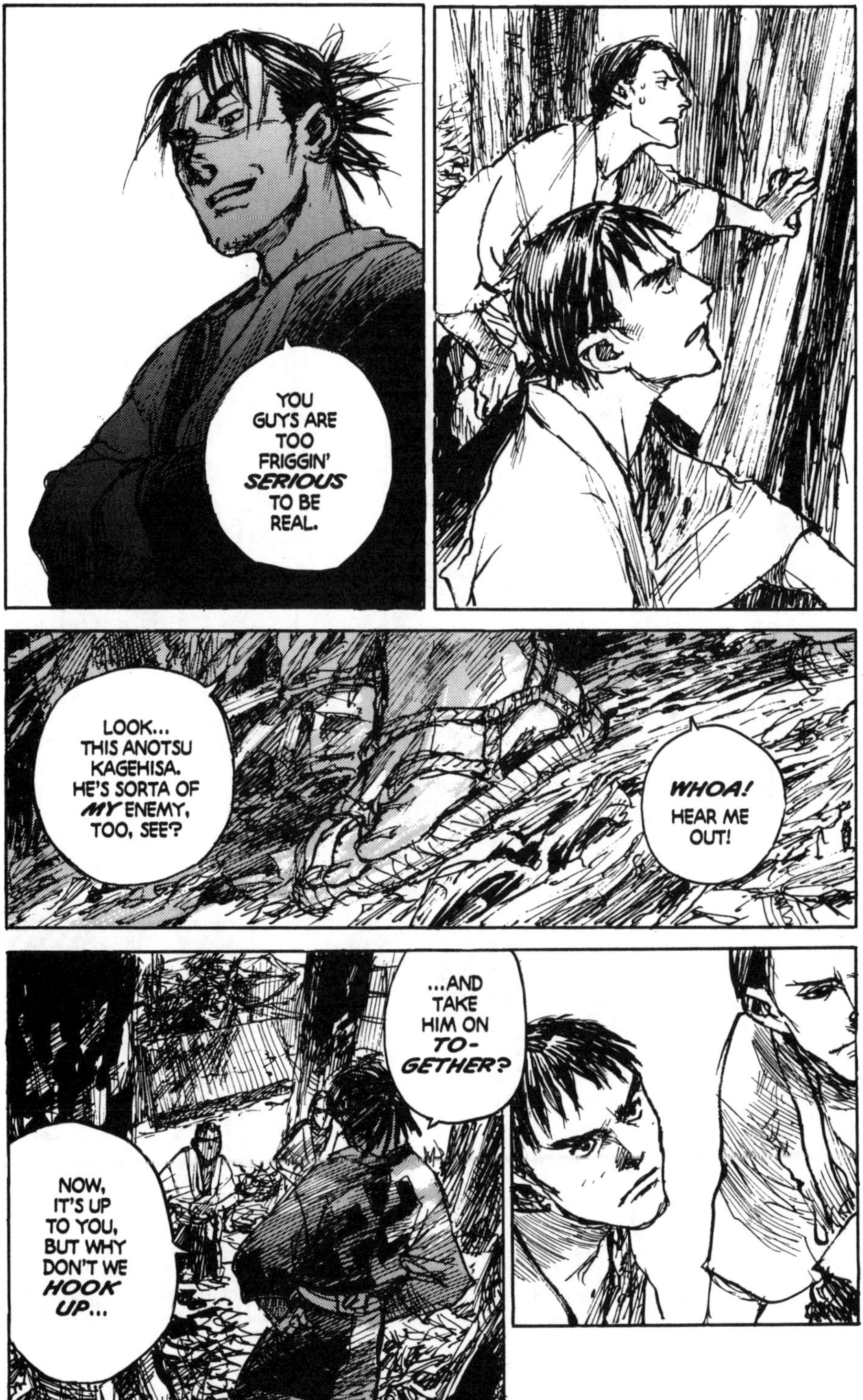
YOU GUYS ARE TOO FRIGGIN' *SERIOUS* TO BE REAL.
WHOA! HEAR ME OUT!
LOOK... THIS ANOTSU KAGEHISA. HE'S SORTA OF *MY* ENEMY, TOO, SEE?
NOW, IT'S UP TO YOU, BUT WHY DON'T WE *HOOK UP*...
...AND TAKE HIM ON *TO-GETHER?*

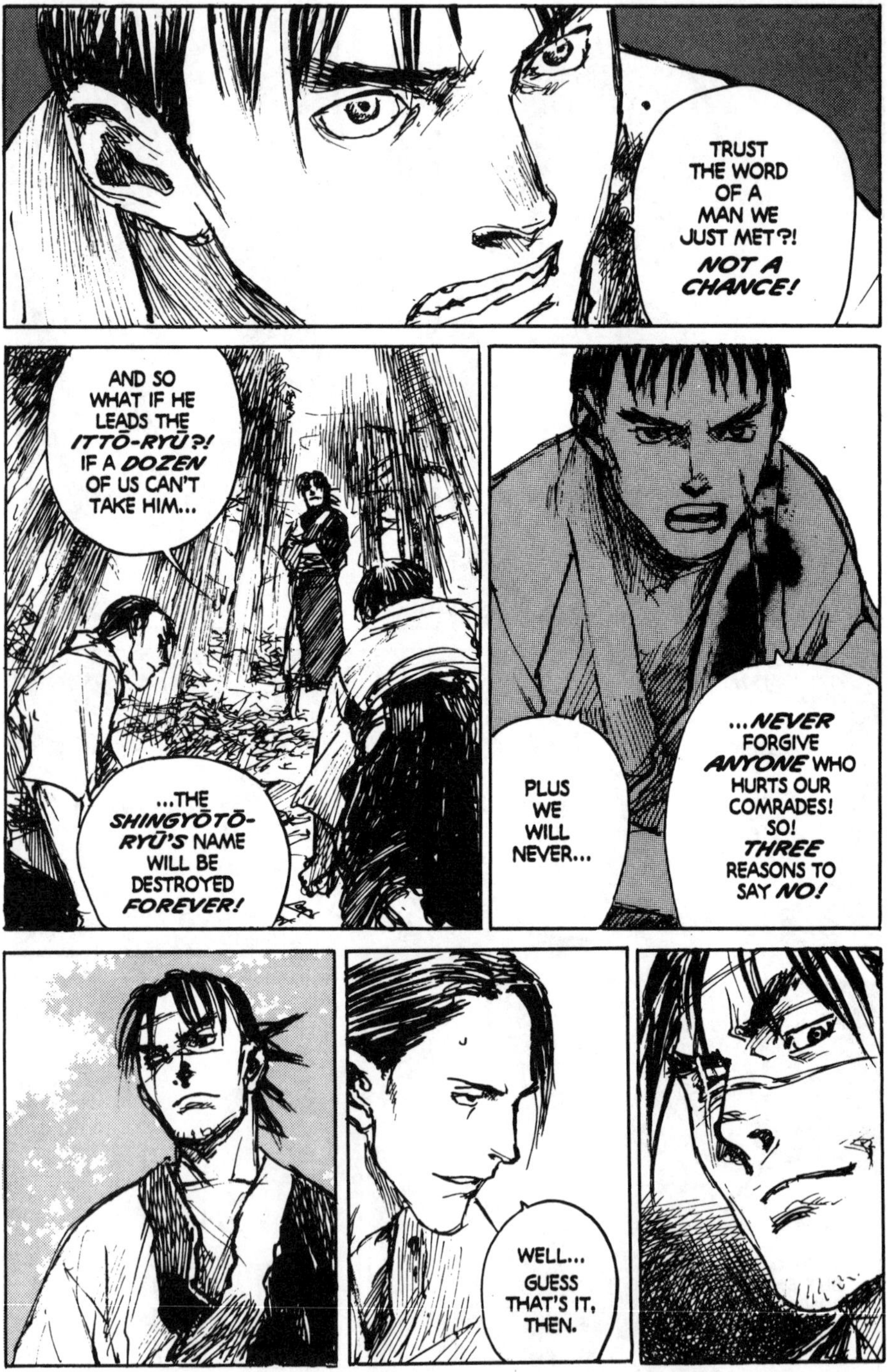
TRUST THE WORD OF A MAN WE JUST MET?! *NOT A CHANCE!*
AND SO WHAT IF HE LEADS THE *ITTŌ-RYŪ*?! IF A *DOZEN* OF US CAN'T TAKE HIM...
...THE *SHINGYŌTŌ-RYŪ'S* NAME WILL BE DESTROYED *FOREVER!*
PLUS WE WILL NEVER...
...*NEVER* FORGIVE *ANYONE* WHO HURTS OUR COMRADES! SO! *THREE* REASONS TO SAY *NO!*
WELL... GUESS THAT'S IT, THEN.

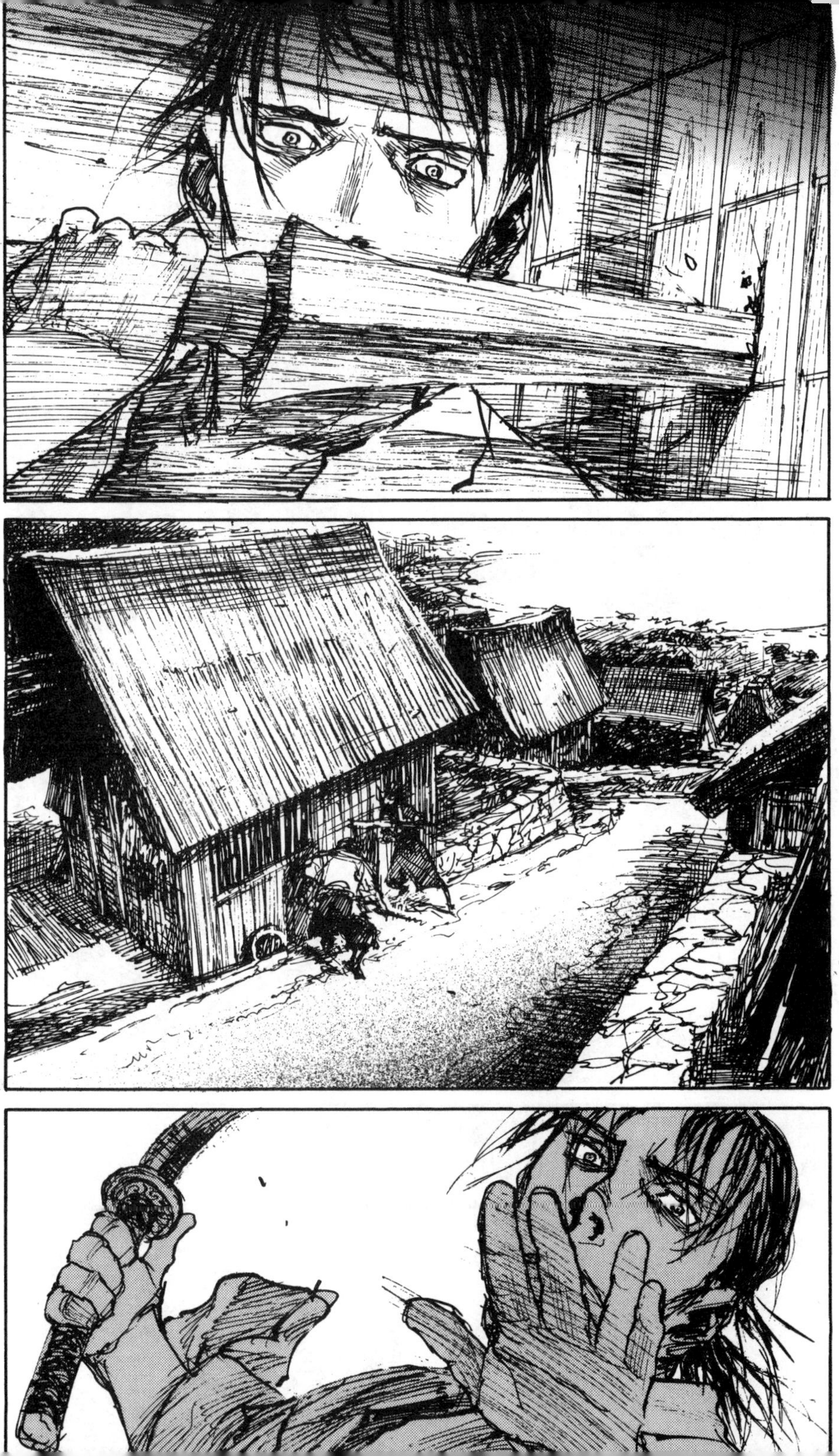

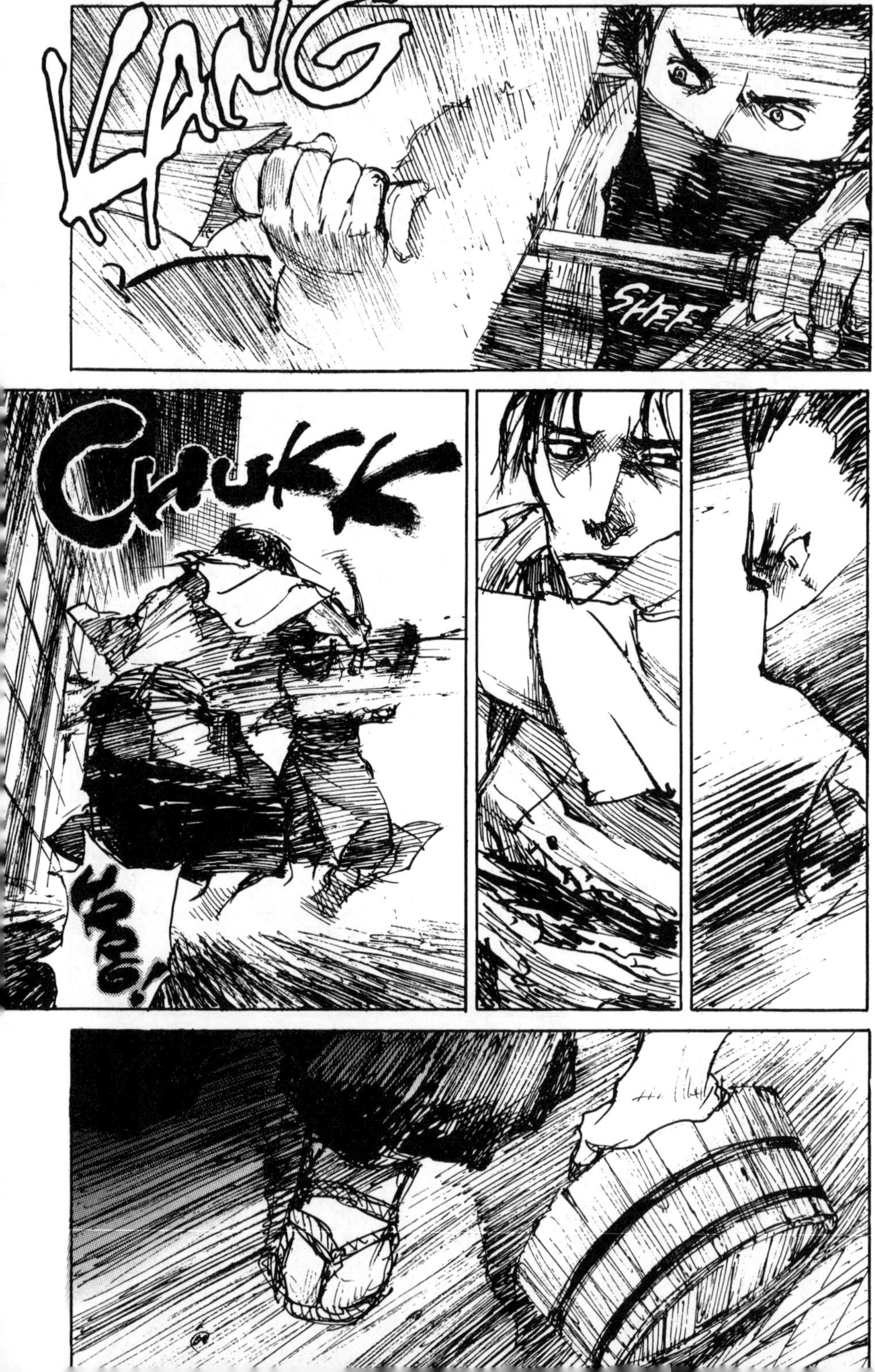
KANG
SHFF
CHUKK

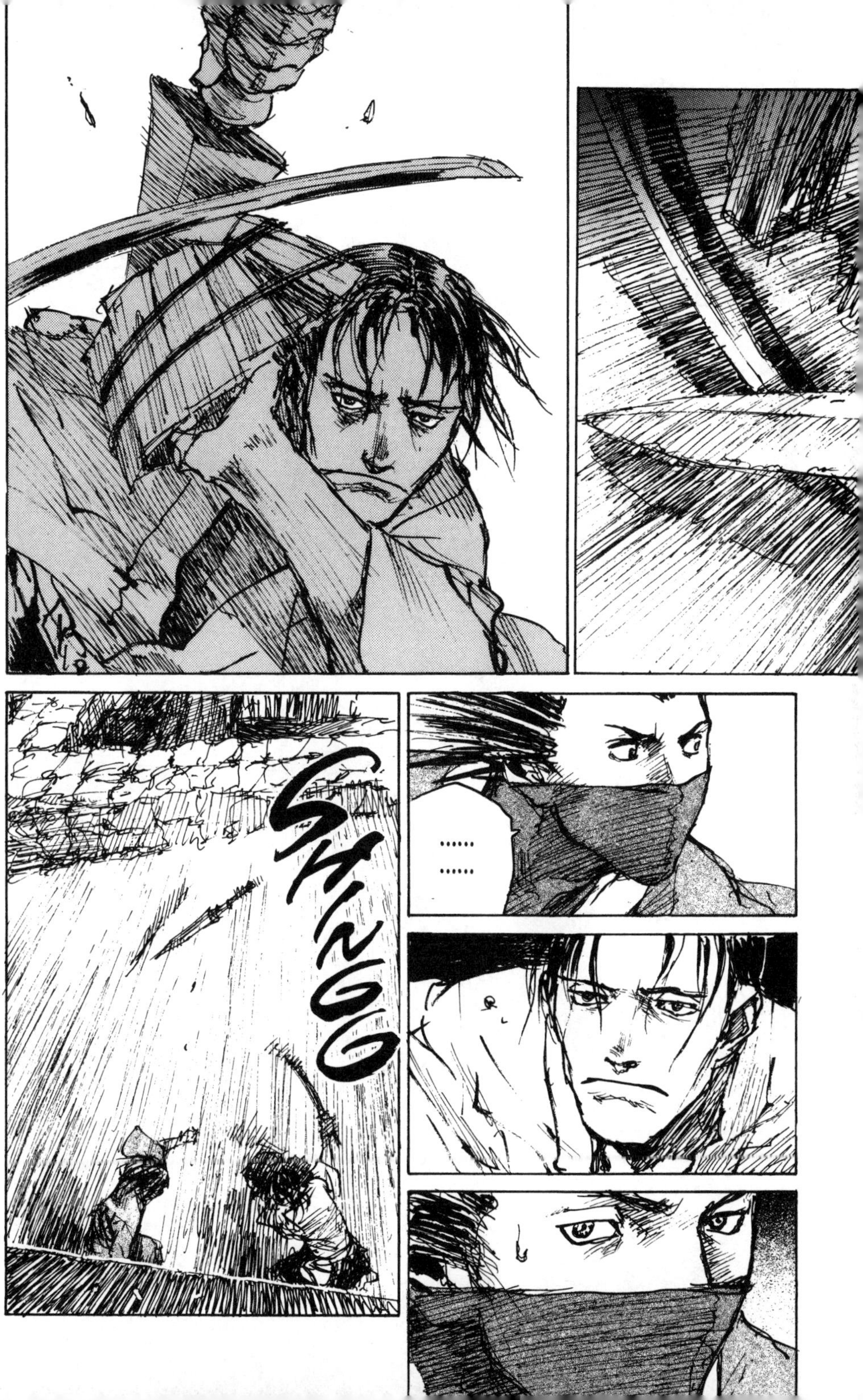
SHINGG
......
......

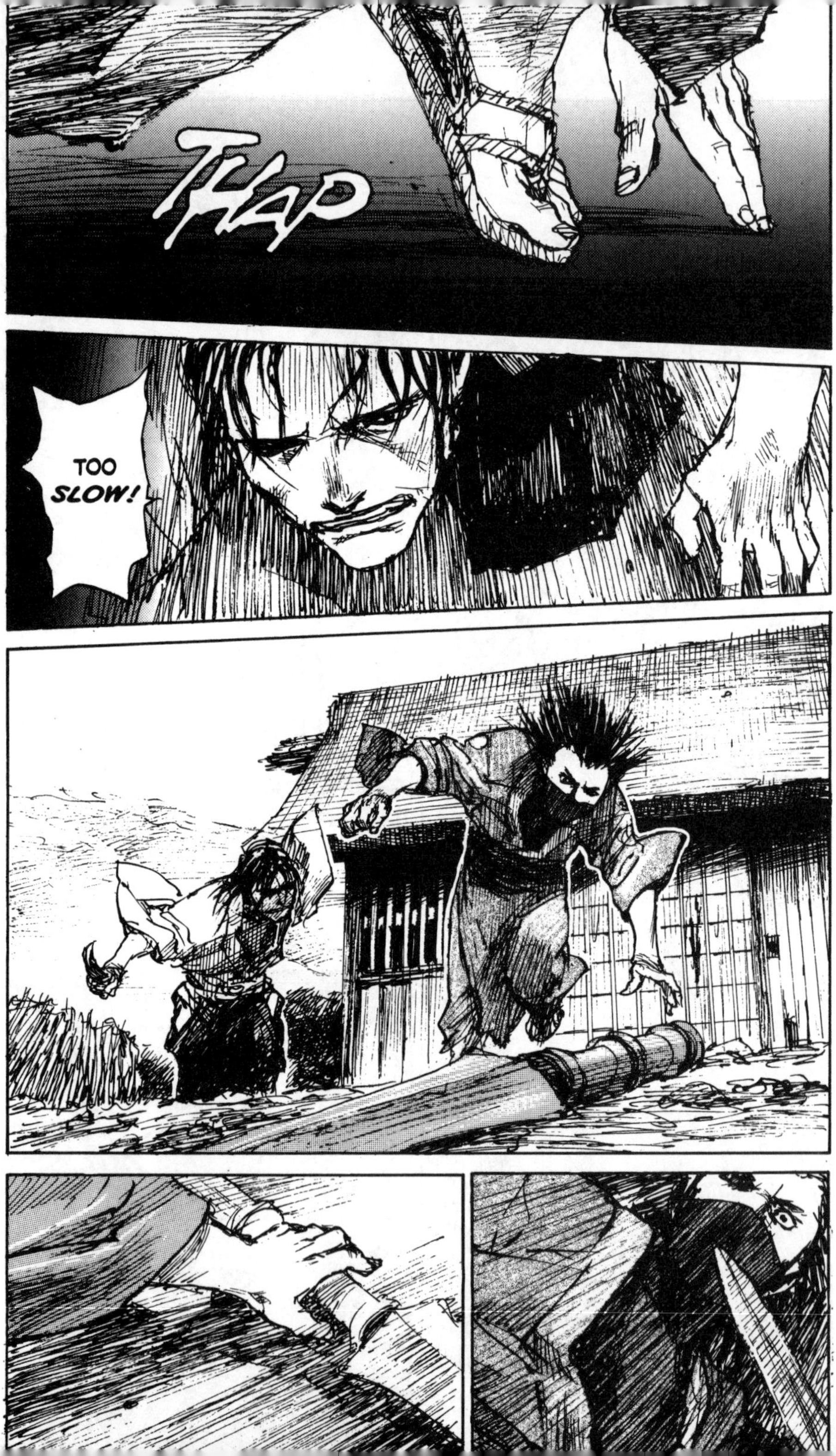
THAP
TOO SLOW!

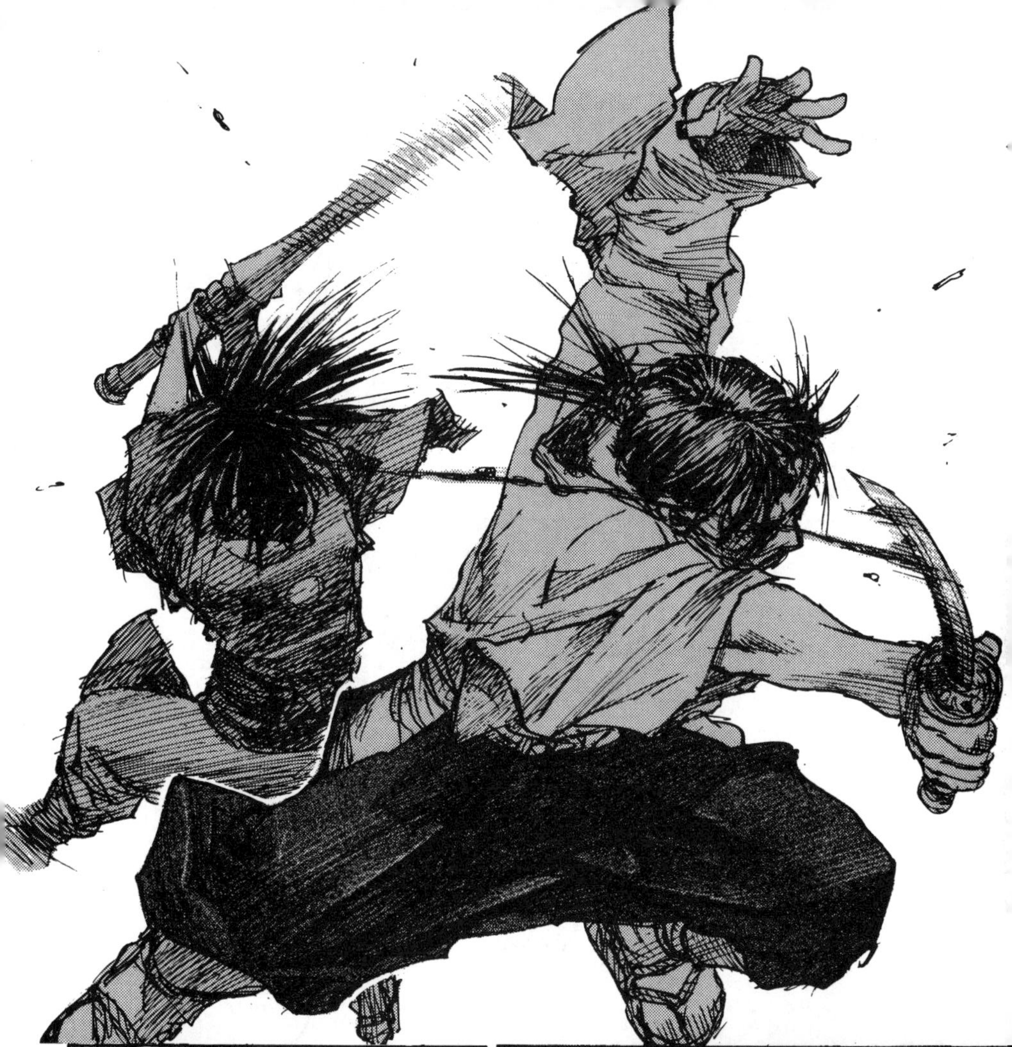
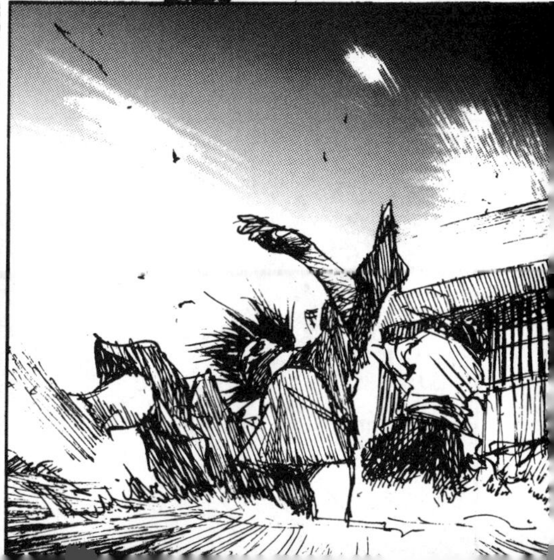
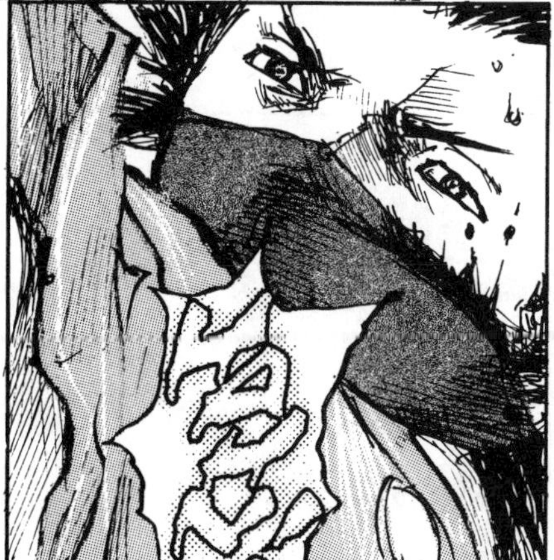

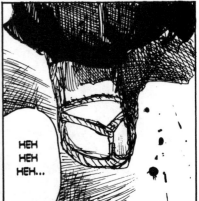

HEH
HEH
HEH...

SO...
THE
ITTŌ-RYŪ!
NO WORSE...
AND NO
BETTER
THAN THEY
SAY.

...AT
LEAST,
FOR A GUY
IN *MY*
CONDITION!

YEAH?
WELL, *YOU*
GUYS ARE
A BIT
TOUGH TO
SWALLOW...

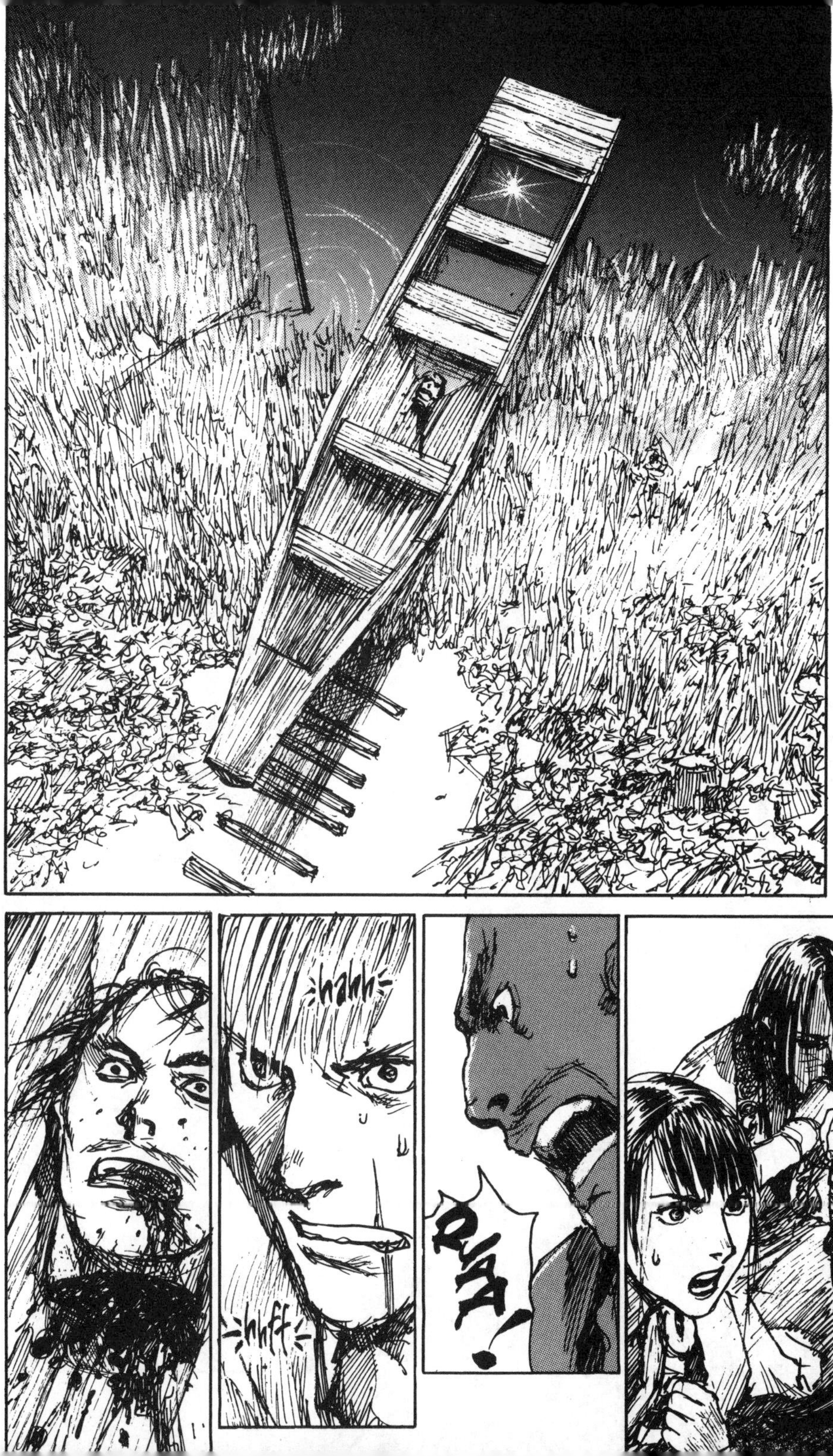
QUA!
hahh
hhff

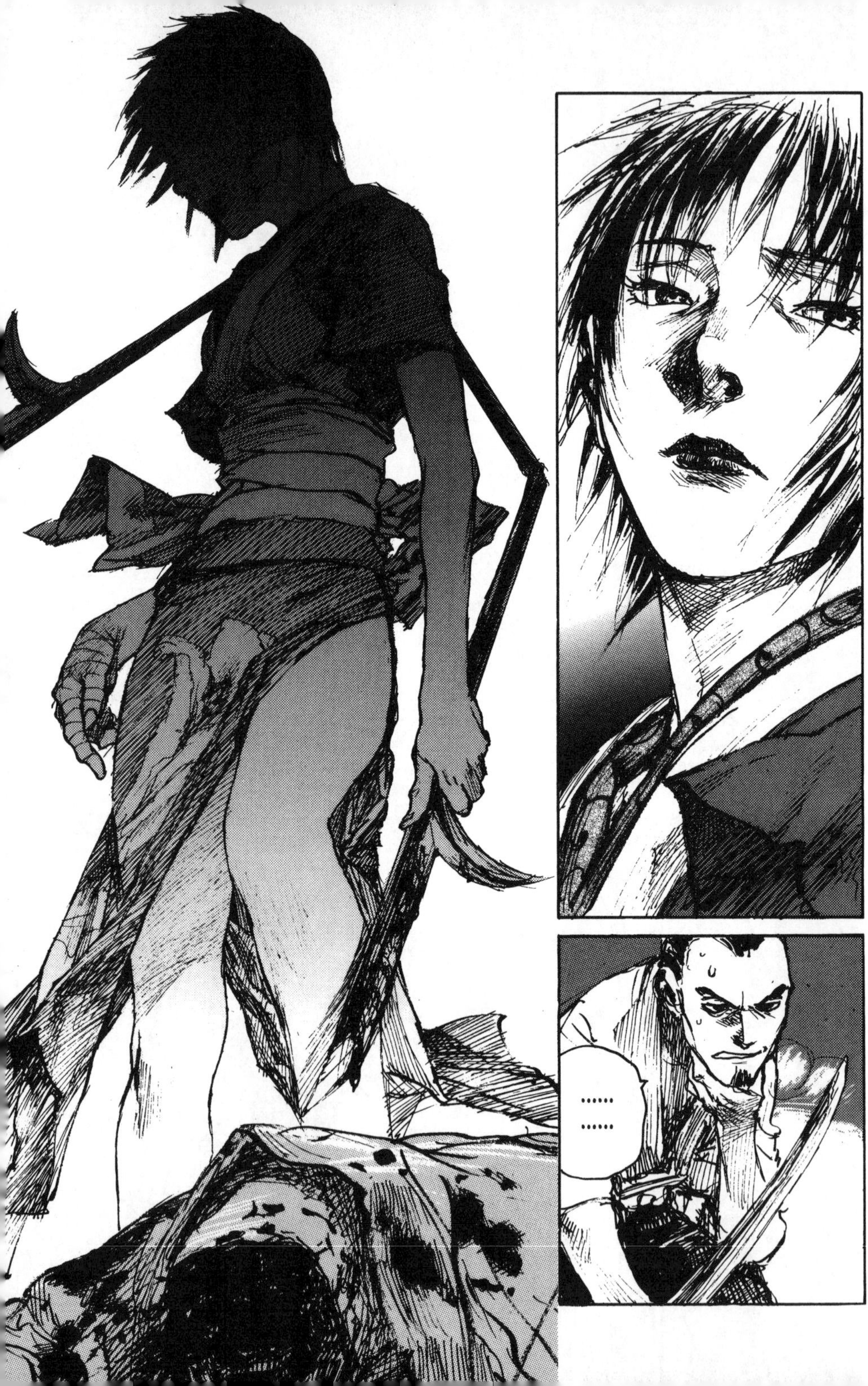
......
......

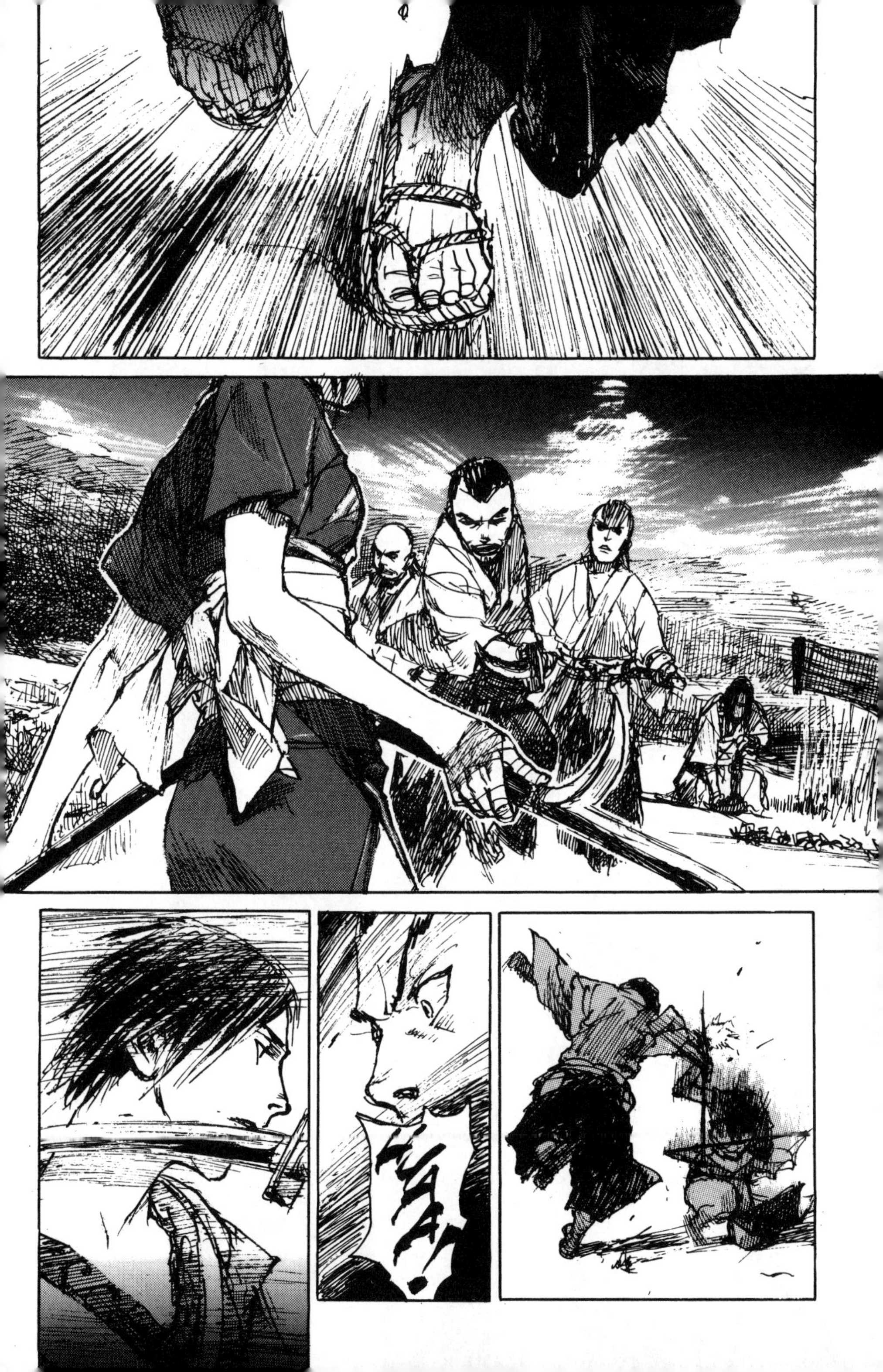
HAA!

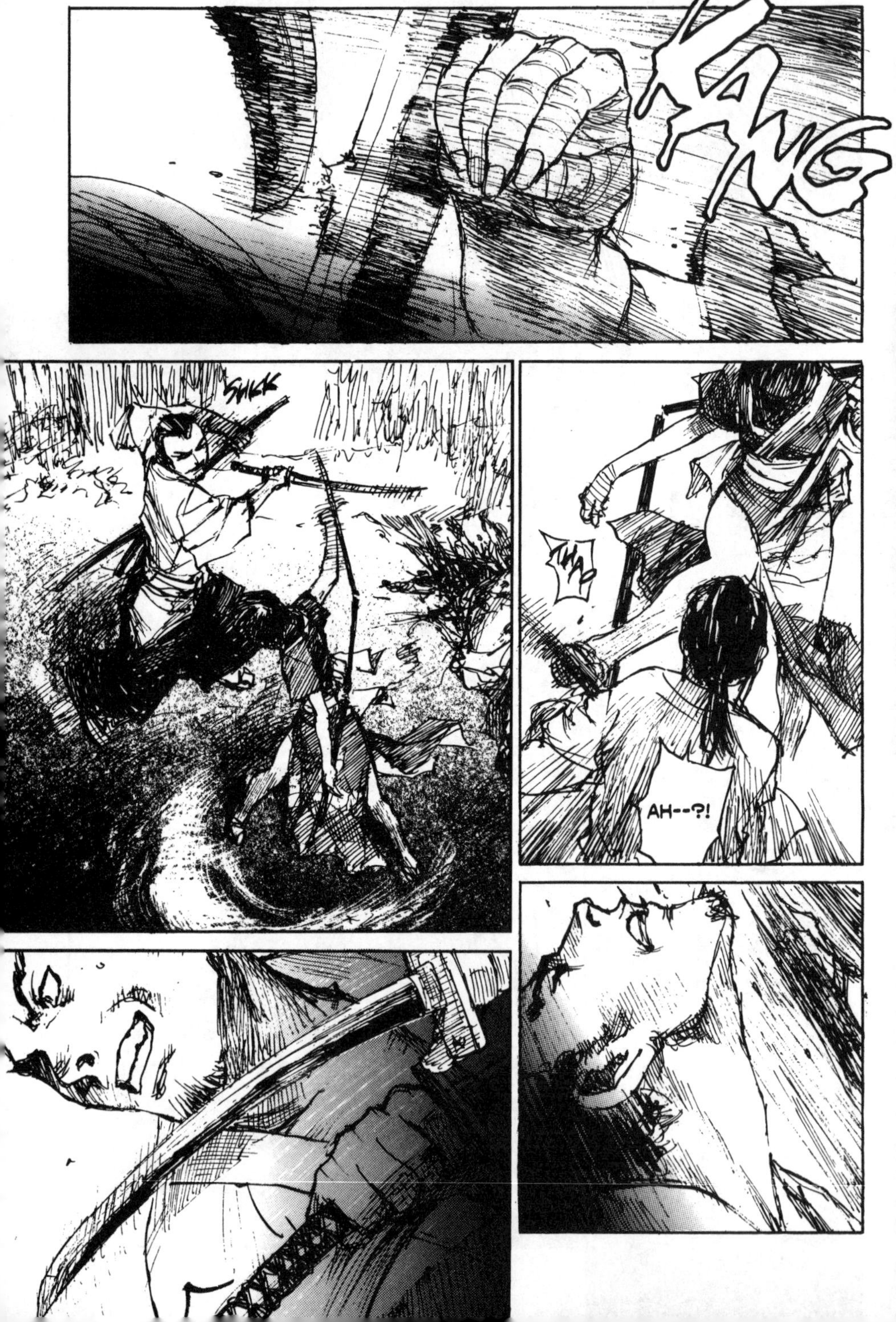
KANG
THAP
AH--?!
SHICK

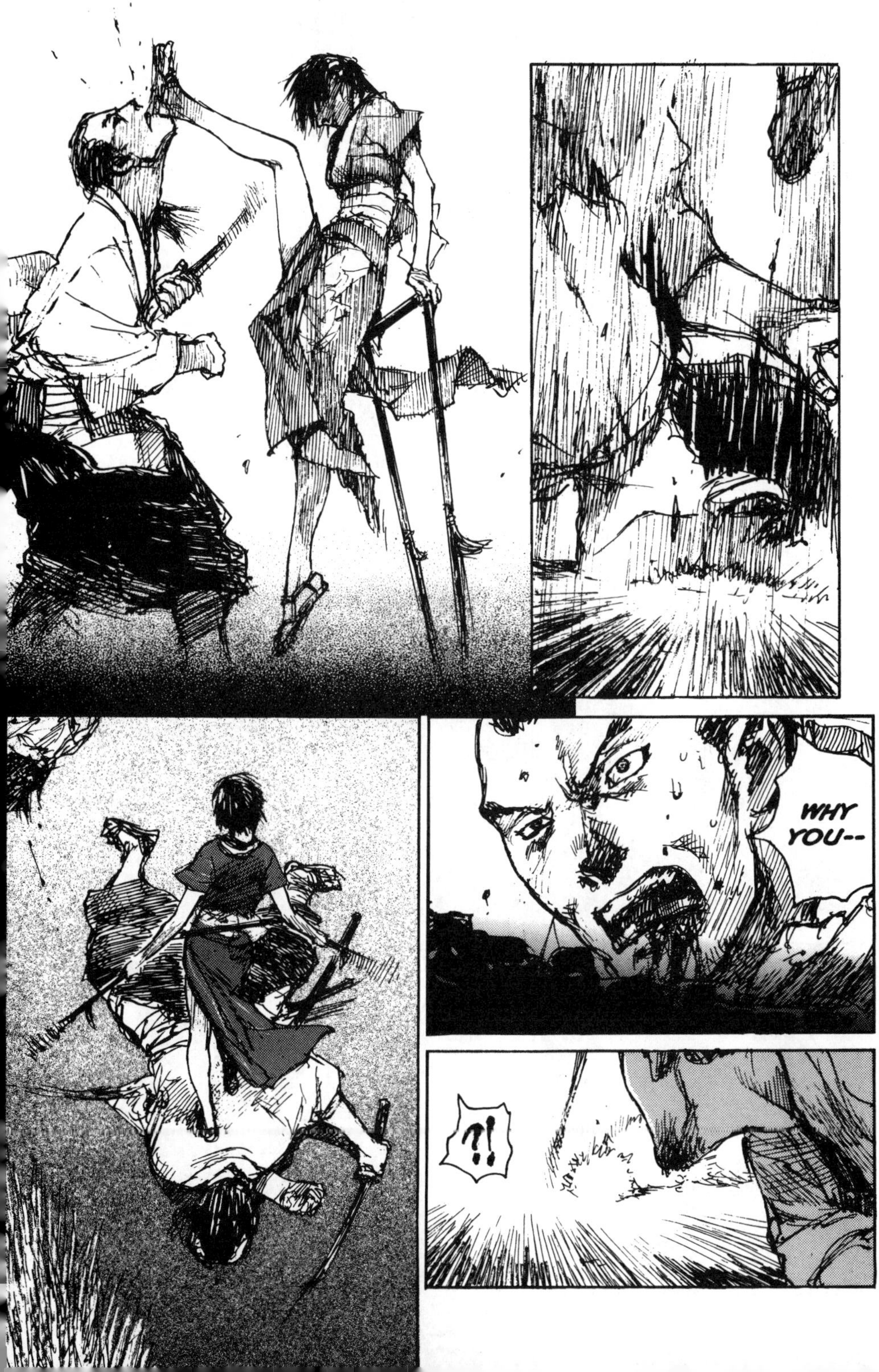
WHY YOU--
?!

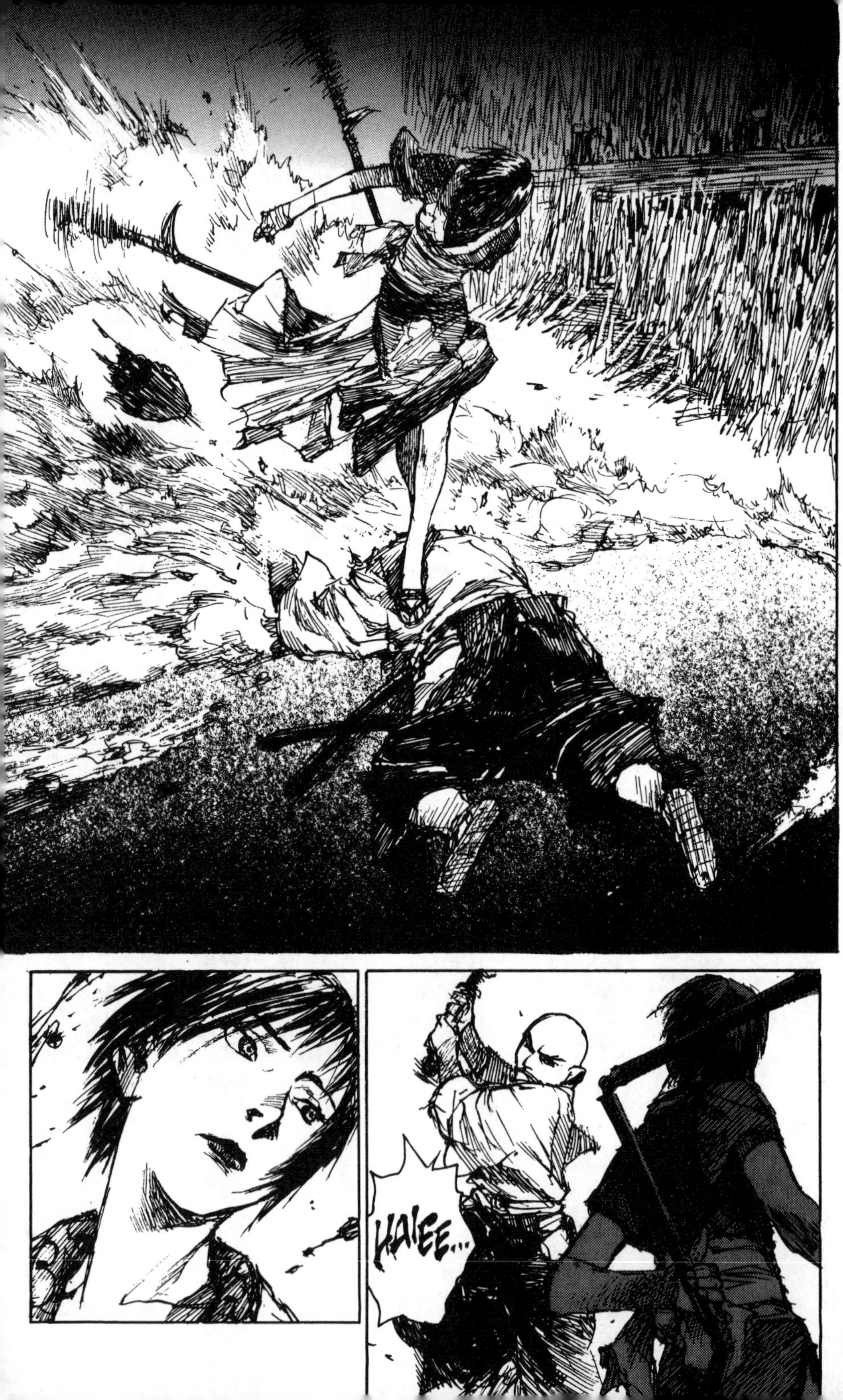
HAIEE...

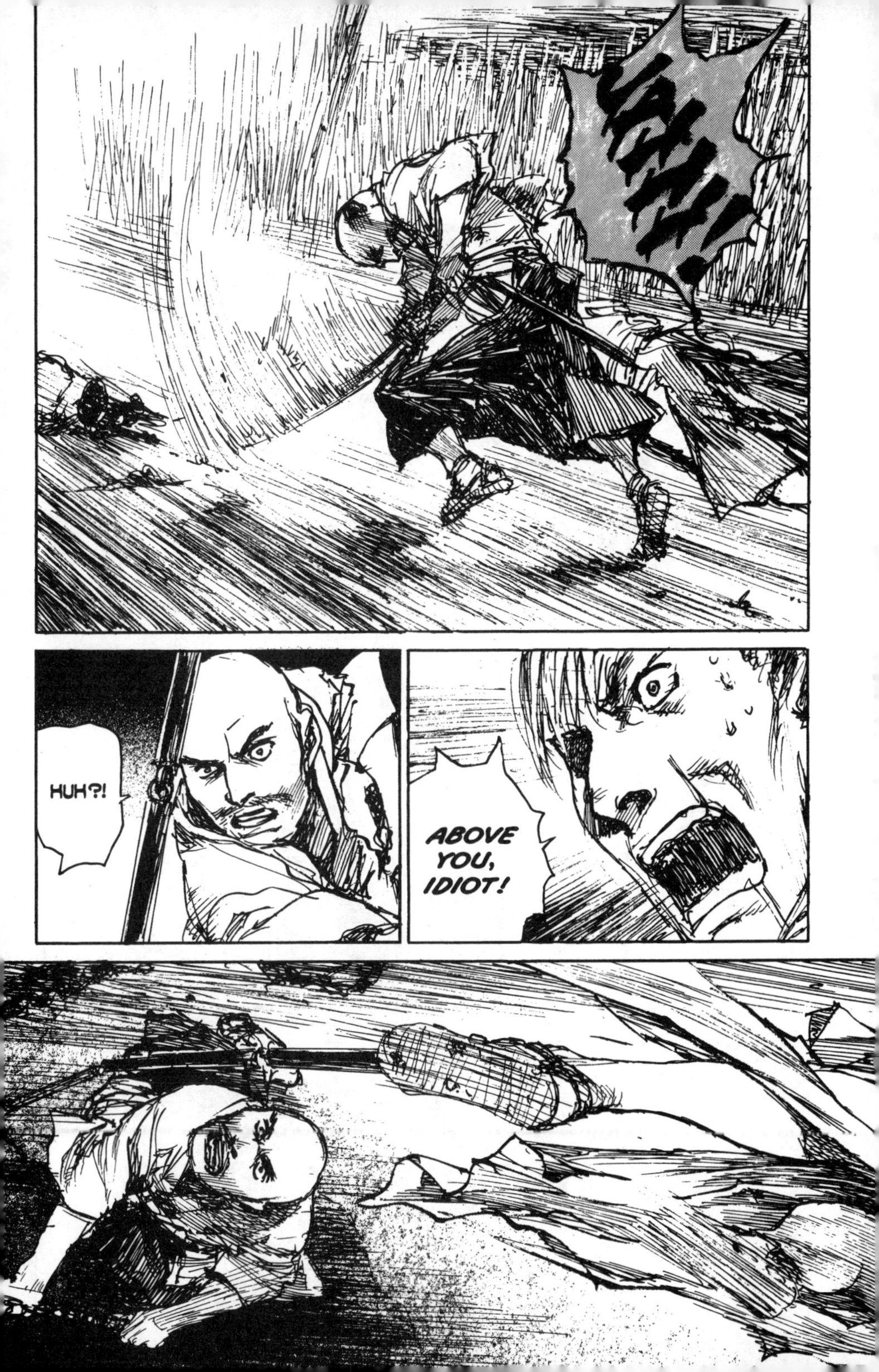
ABOVE YOU, IDIOT!
HUH?!

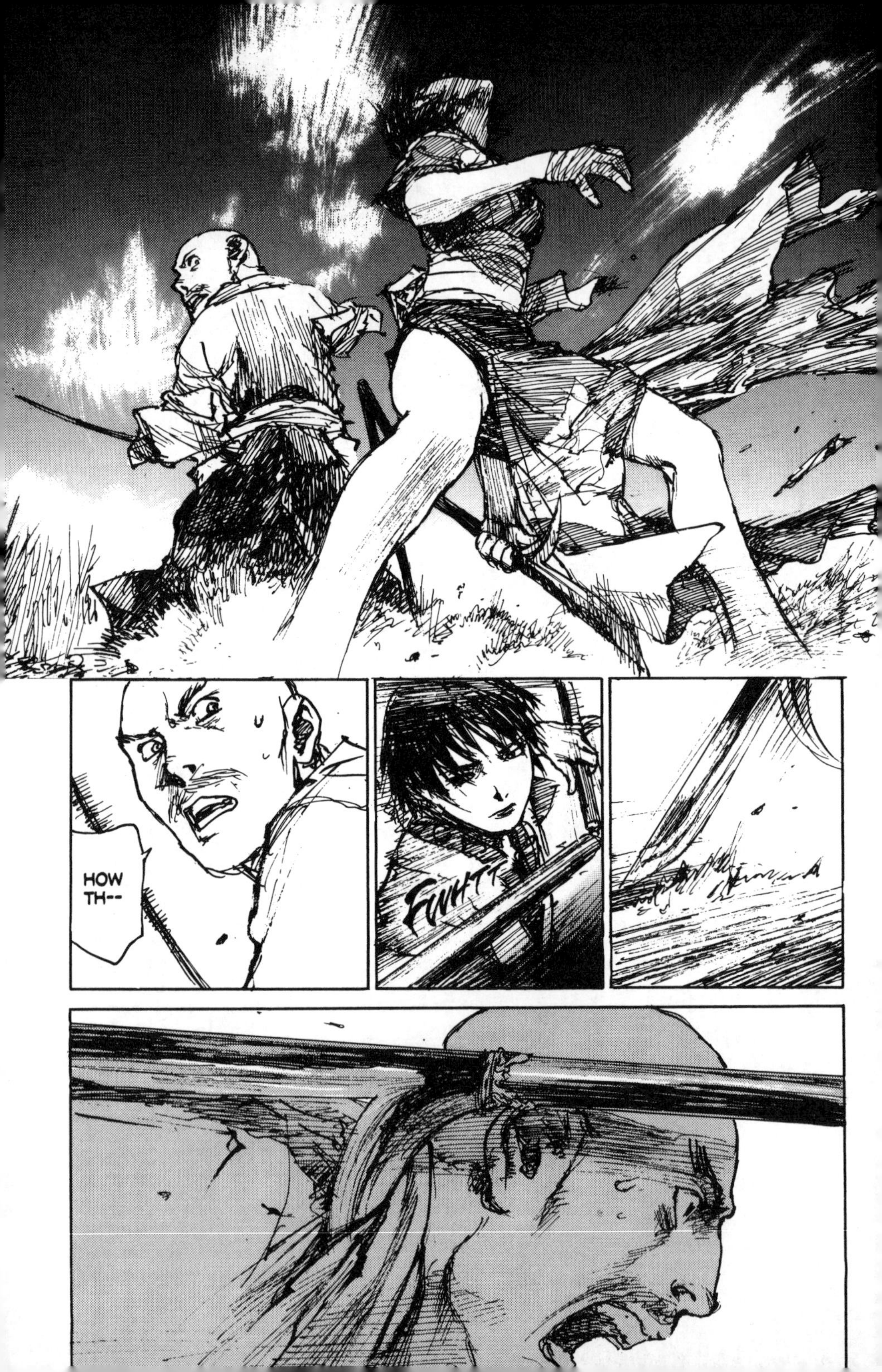
FWHT
HOW TH--

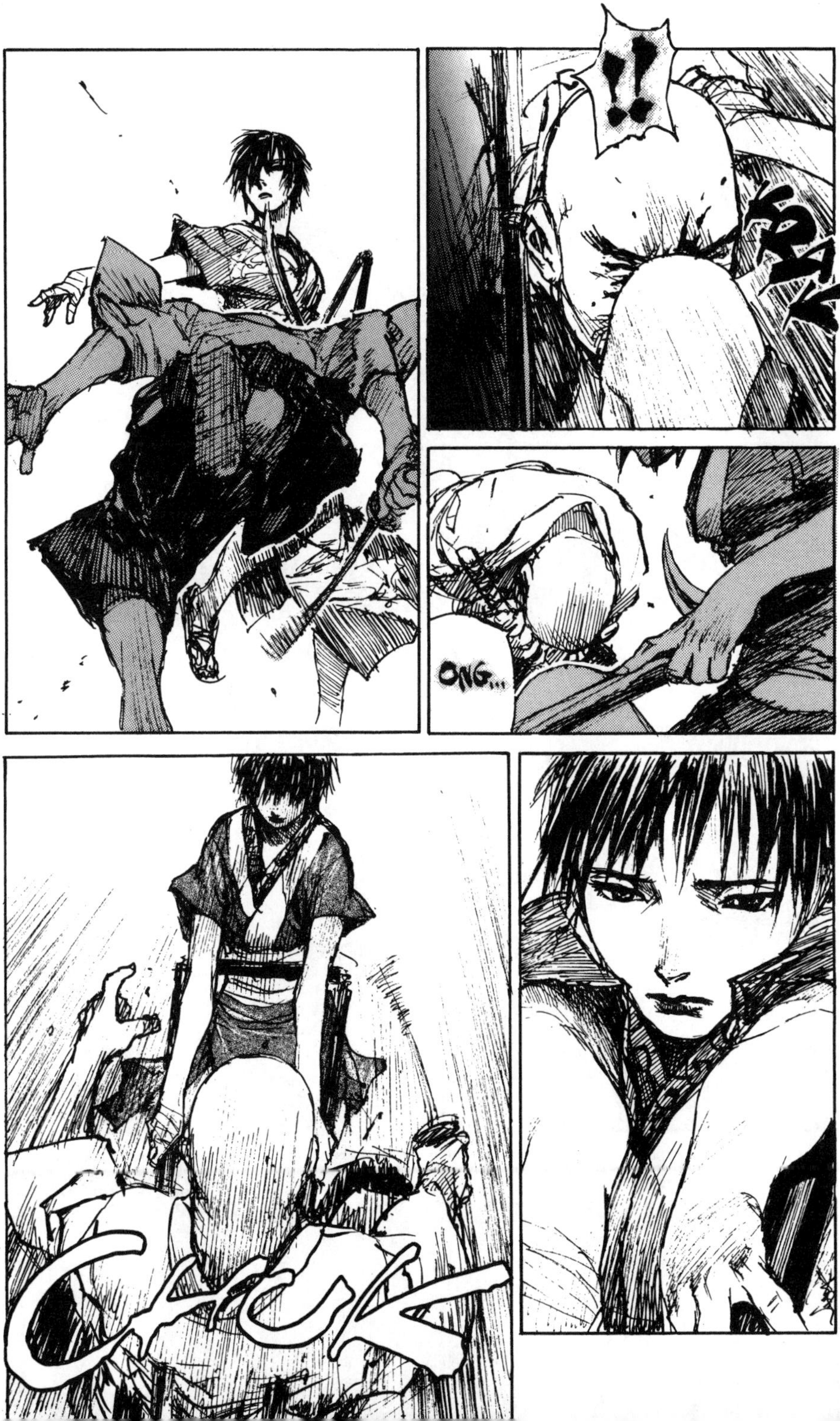
!!
ONG...
CRACK

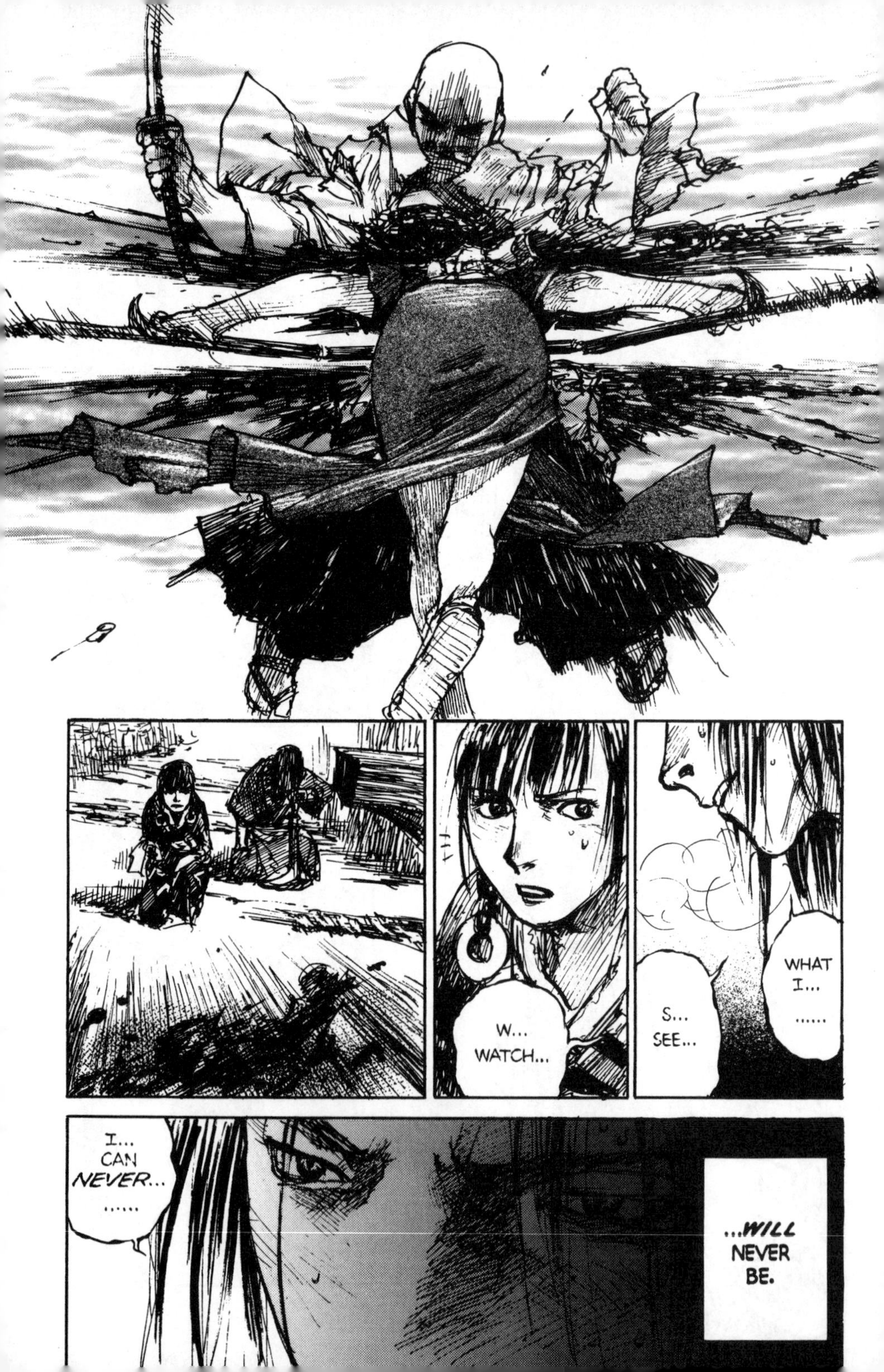
WHAT I... ......
S... SEE...
W... WATCH...
...*WILL* NEVER BE.
I... CAN *NEVER*... ......

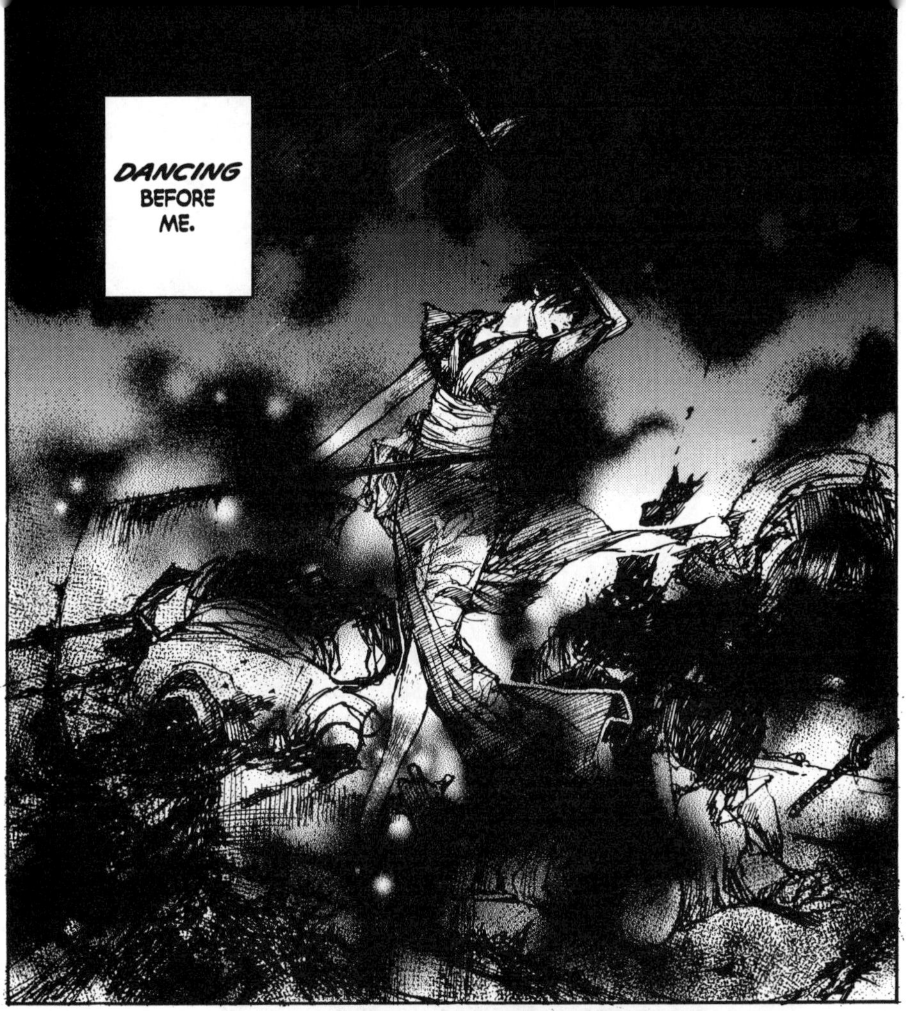
DANCING
BEFORE
ME.
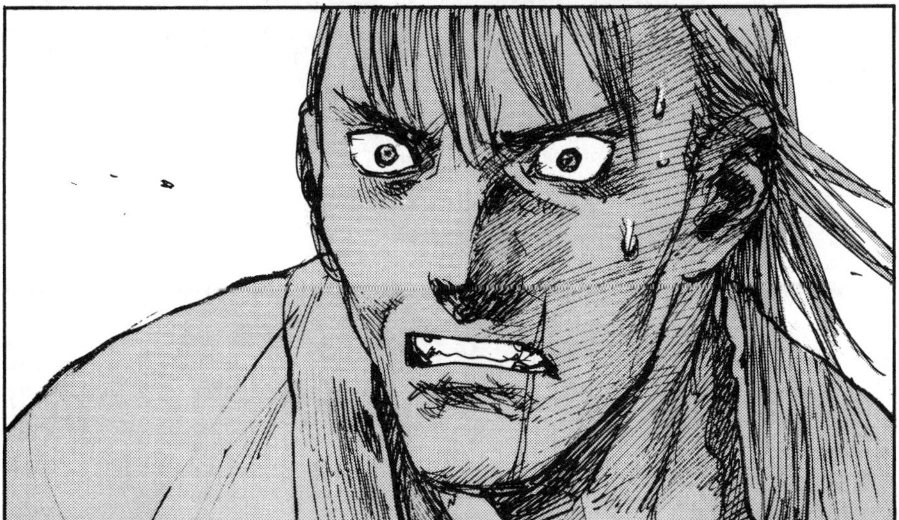

WHEN I WAS A CHILD, *AFRAID* OF A SINGLE WILD DOG...

...AND THAT GIRL APPEARED, NO MORE THAN TEN, *SLICING* IT IN HALF... THE *SAME* FEELING.

ONLY *NOW*, REMEMBERING MY *EMOTION*... IT WASN'T *FEAR* OF HER. NO...

I *ALREADY* KNEW... *INSTINCTIVELY*... THAT SHE'D WALK AHEAD OF ME THE REST OF MY LIFE.

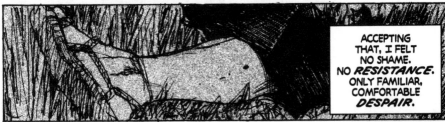

ACCEPTING THAT, I FELT NO SHAME. NO *RESISTANCE*. ONLY FAMILIAR, COMFORTABLE *DESPAIR*.

I *REMEMBER* IT NOW... WHAT I FELT THEN...

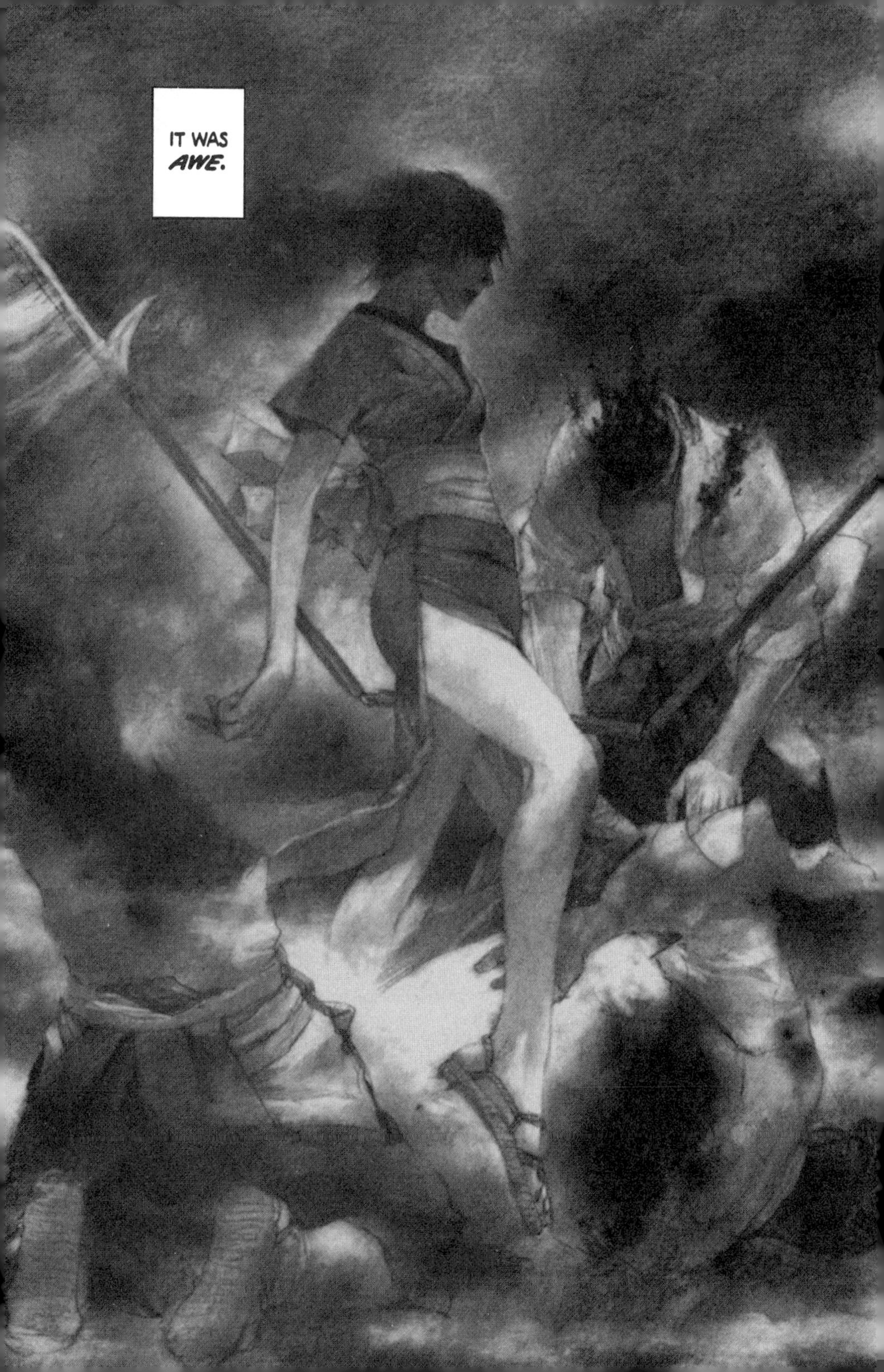
IT WAS
AWE.

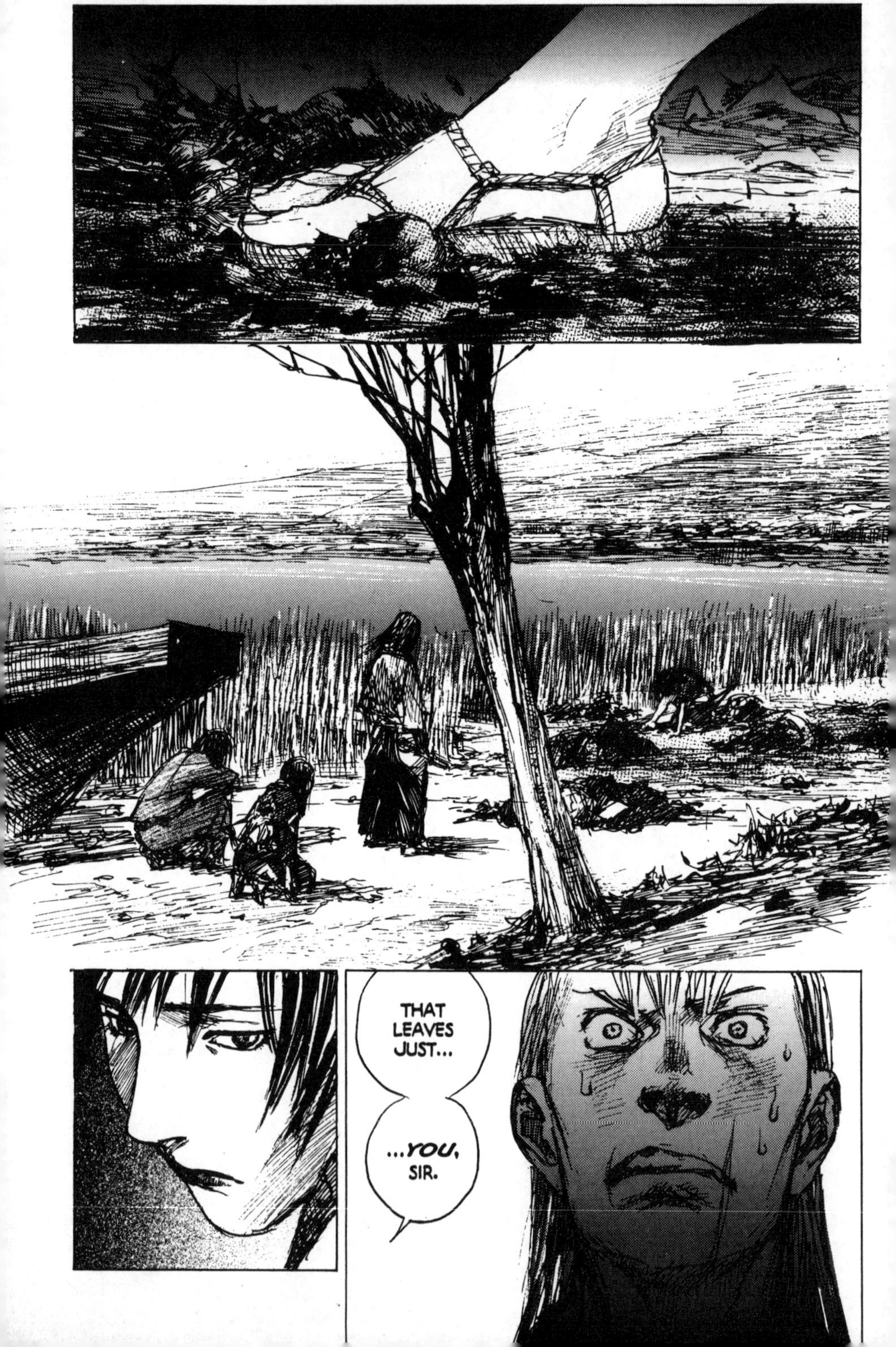
THAT LEAVES JUST...
...YOU, SIR.

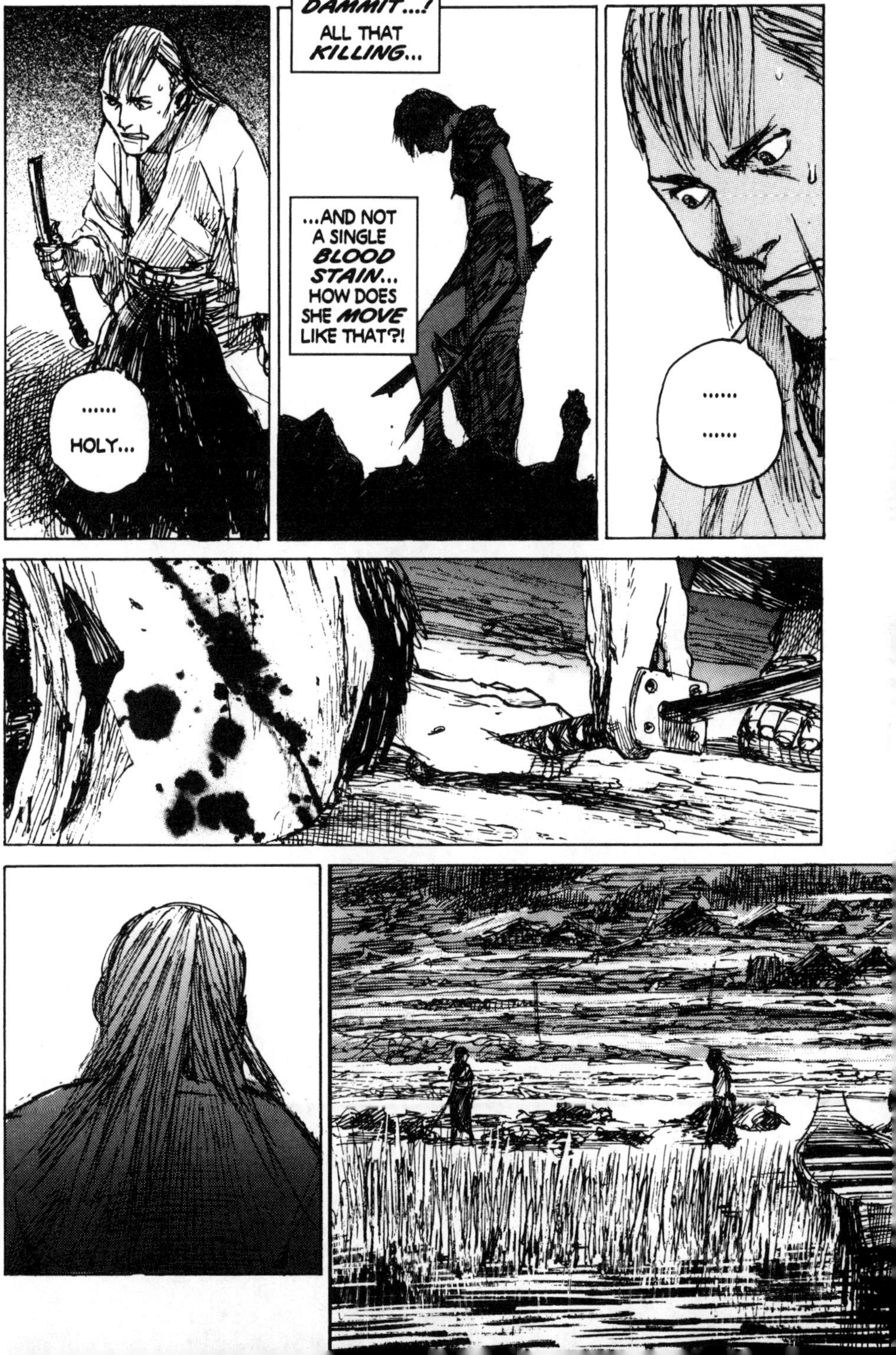
....
DAMMIT...! ALL THAT KILLING...
...AND NOT A SINGLE BLOOD STAIN... HOW DOES SHE MOVE LIKE THAT?!
...... HOLY...

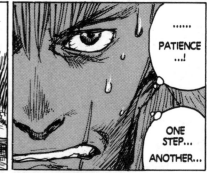

......
PATIENCE
...!

ONE
STEP...
ANOTHER...

STEP
BY STEP,
CLOSE
ON
HER.

UNTIL
THE
INSTANT
BEFORE
SHE
STRIKES!

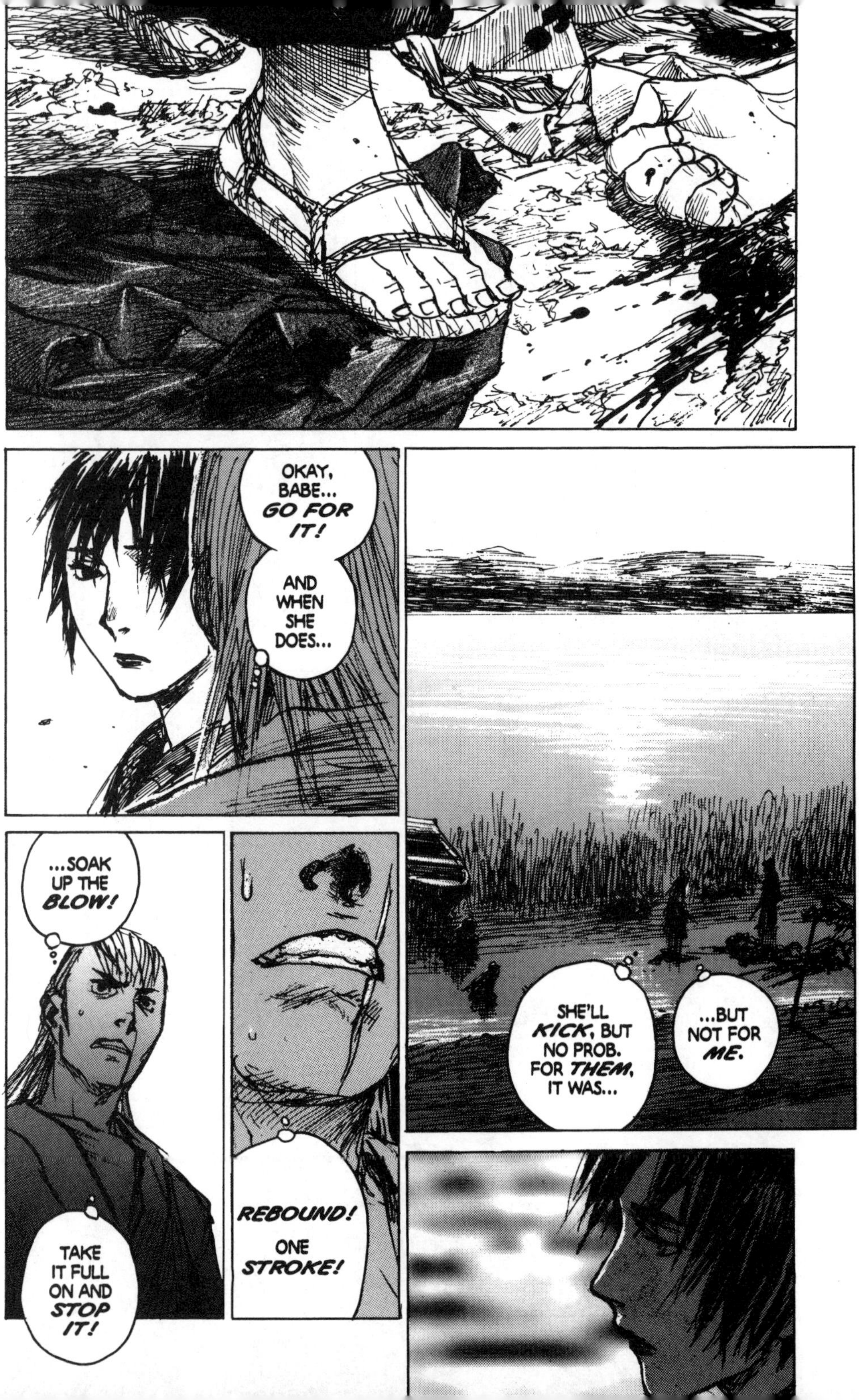
OKAY, BABE... GO FOR IT!
AND WHEN SHE DOES...
...SOAK UP THE BLOW!
TAKE IT FULL ON AND STOP IT!
REBOUND!
ONE STROKE!
SHE'LL KICK, BUT NO PROB. FOR THEM, IT WAS...
...BUT NOT FOR ME.

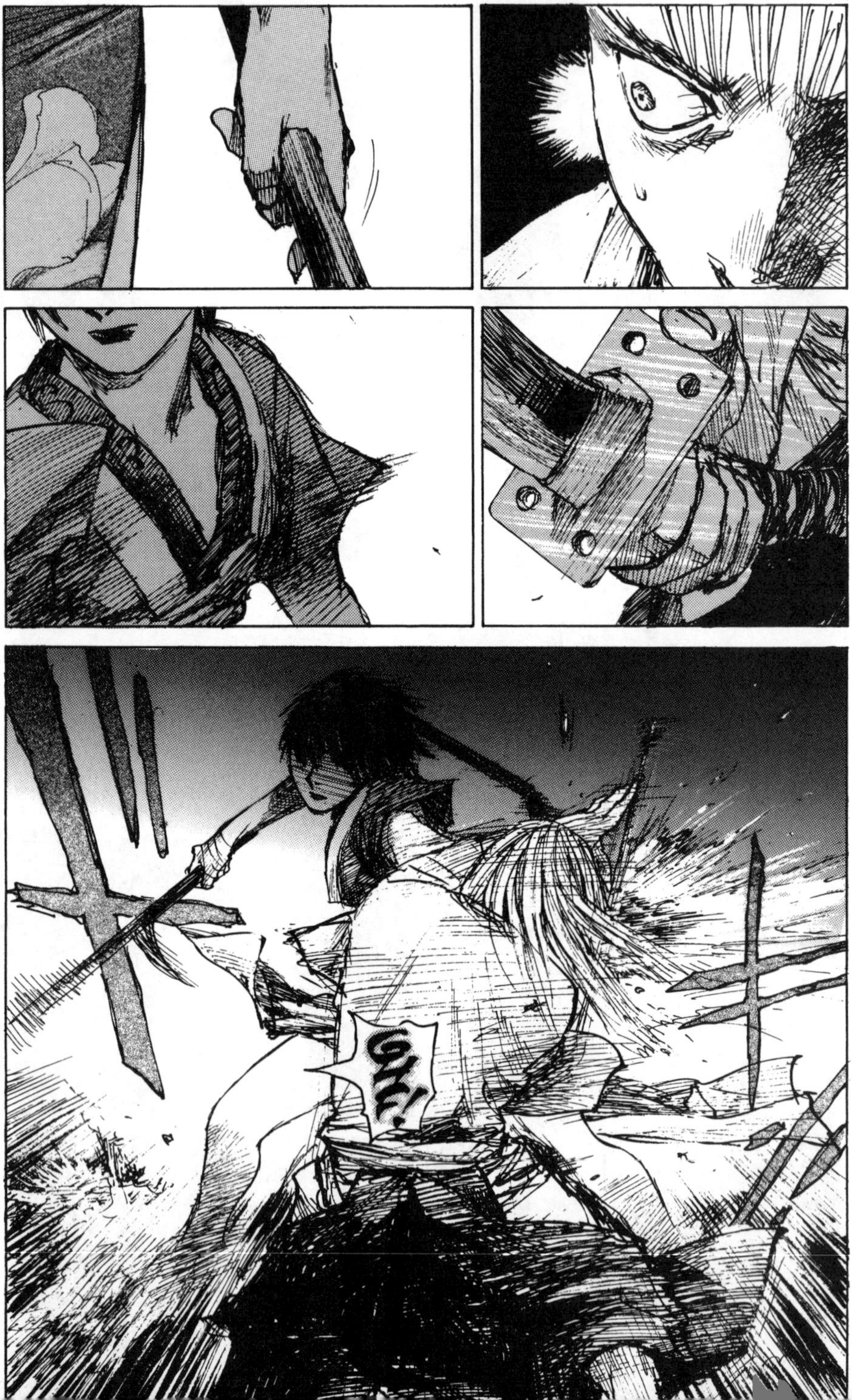
GAH!

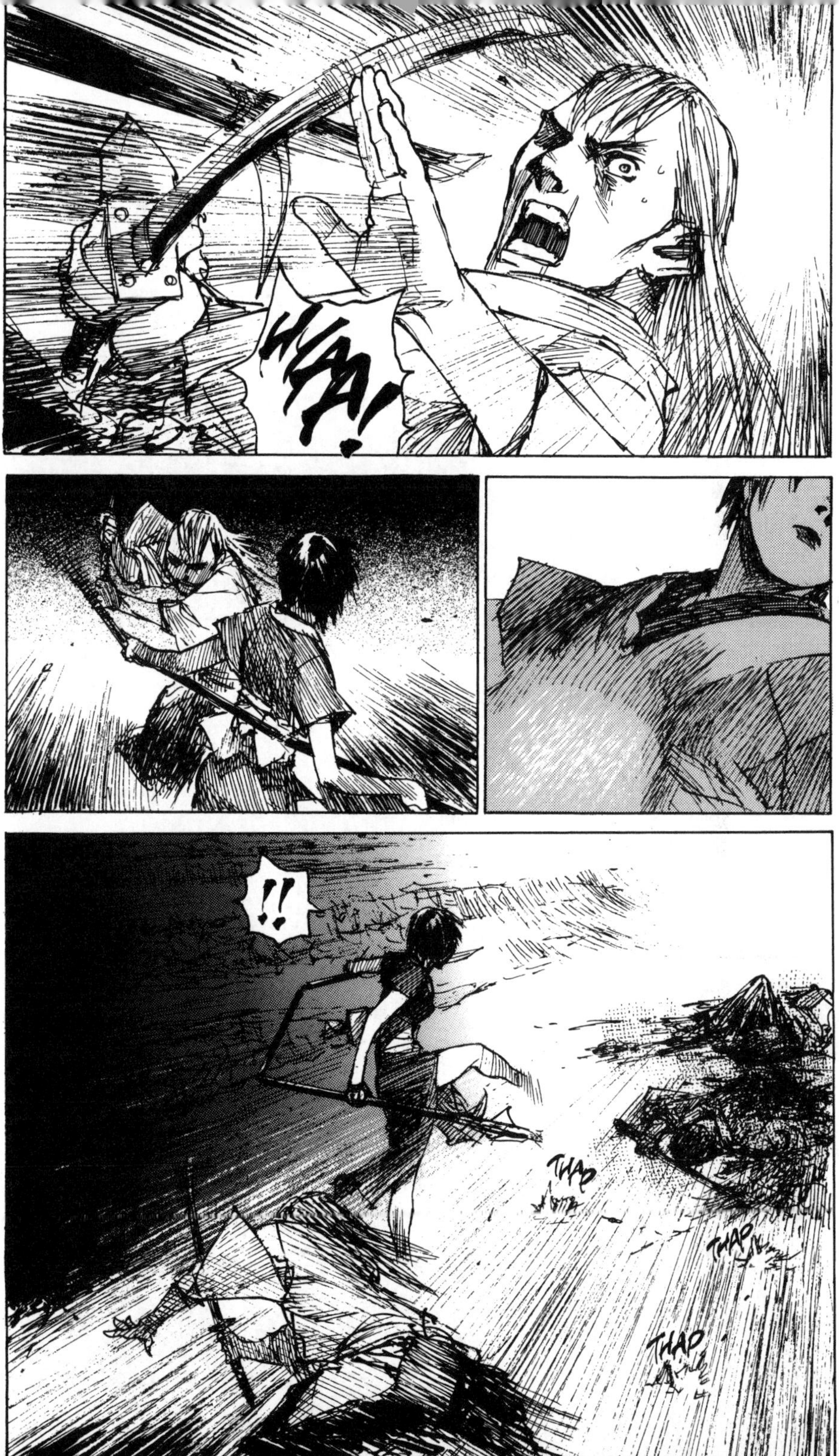
WAA!
!!
THAP
THAP
THAP

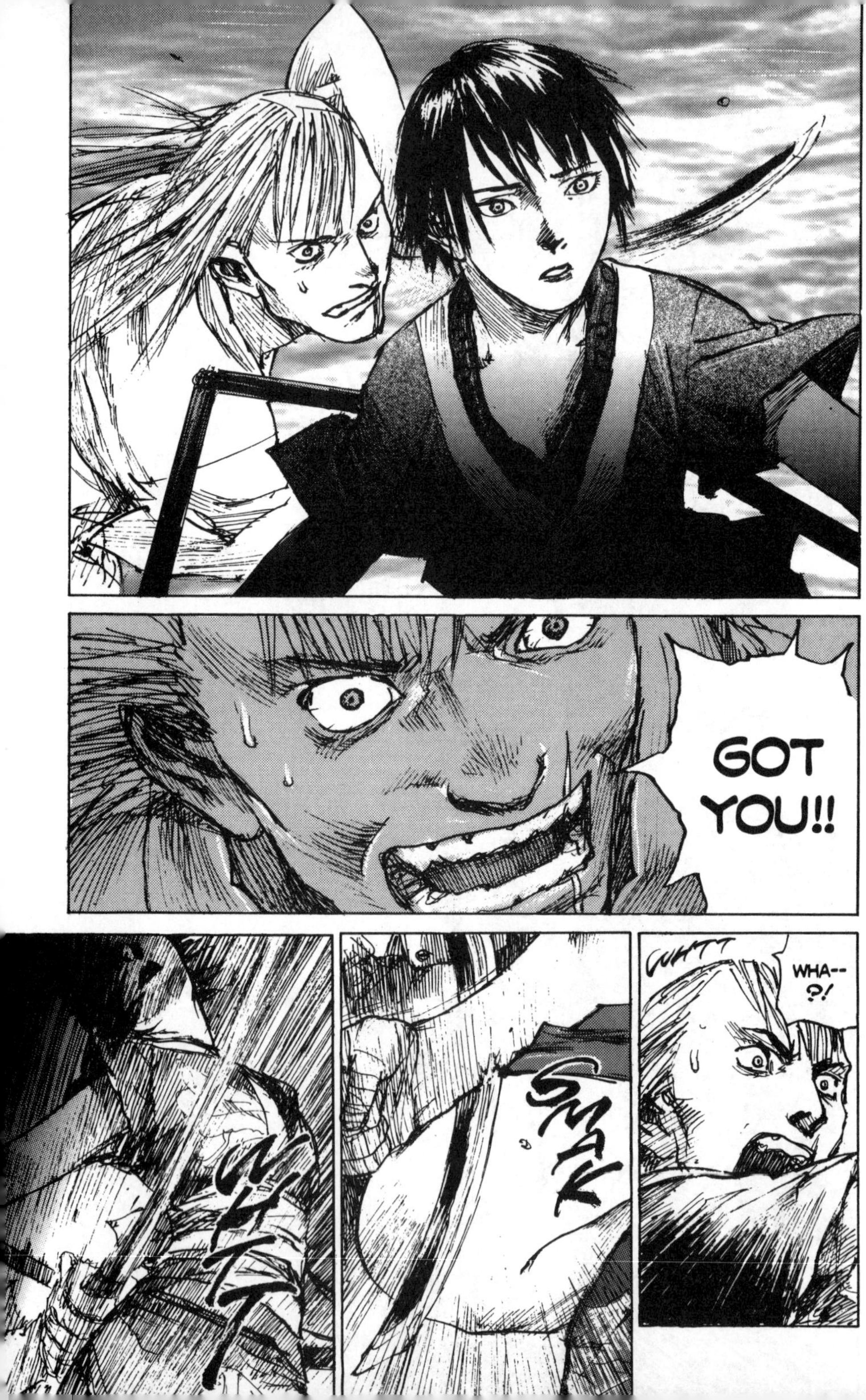
GOT YOU!!
WHA-- ?!
SMAK

CHUK

NNG...

AH...?!

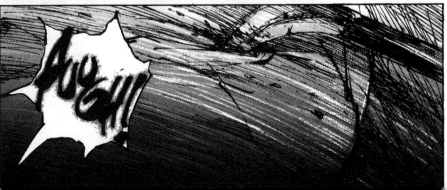

AUGH!!

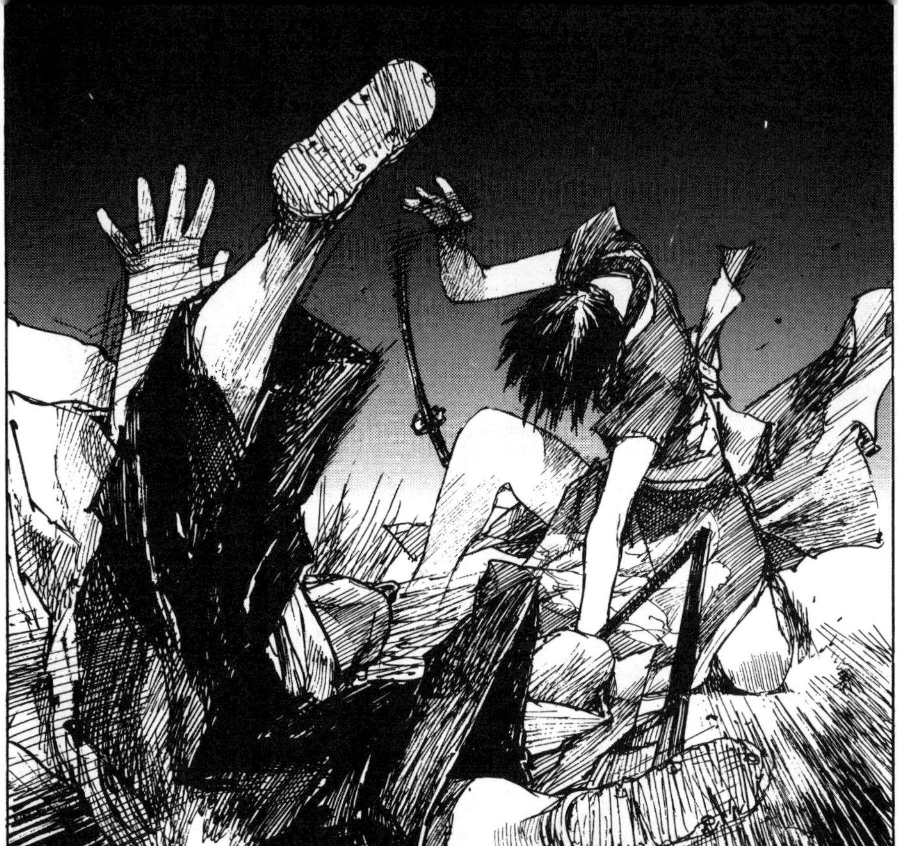
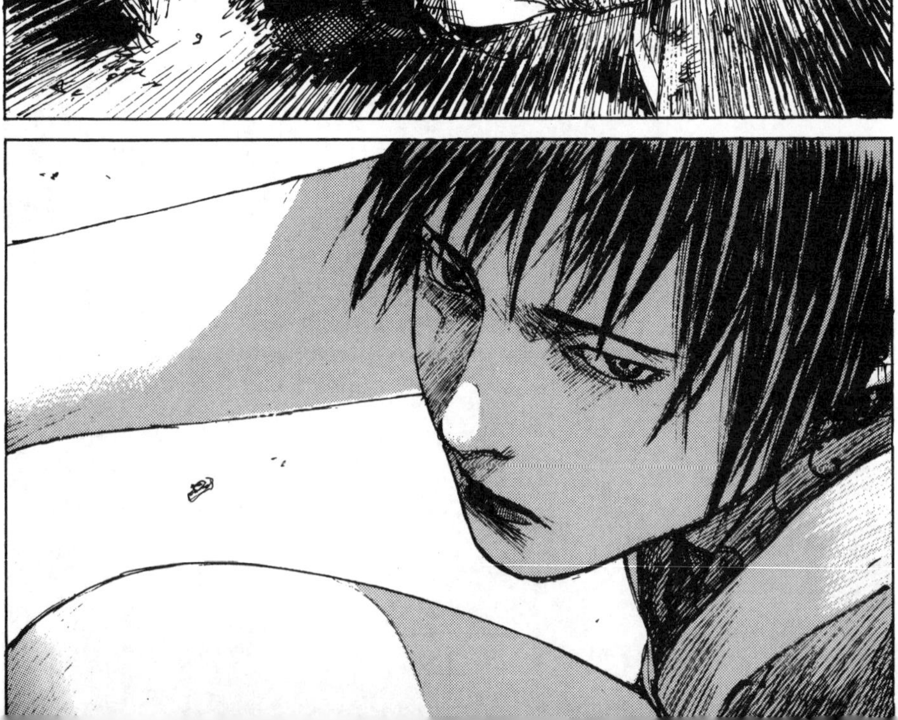

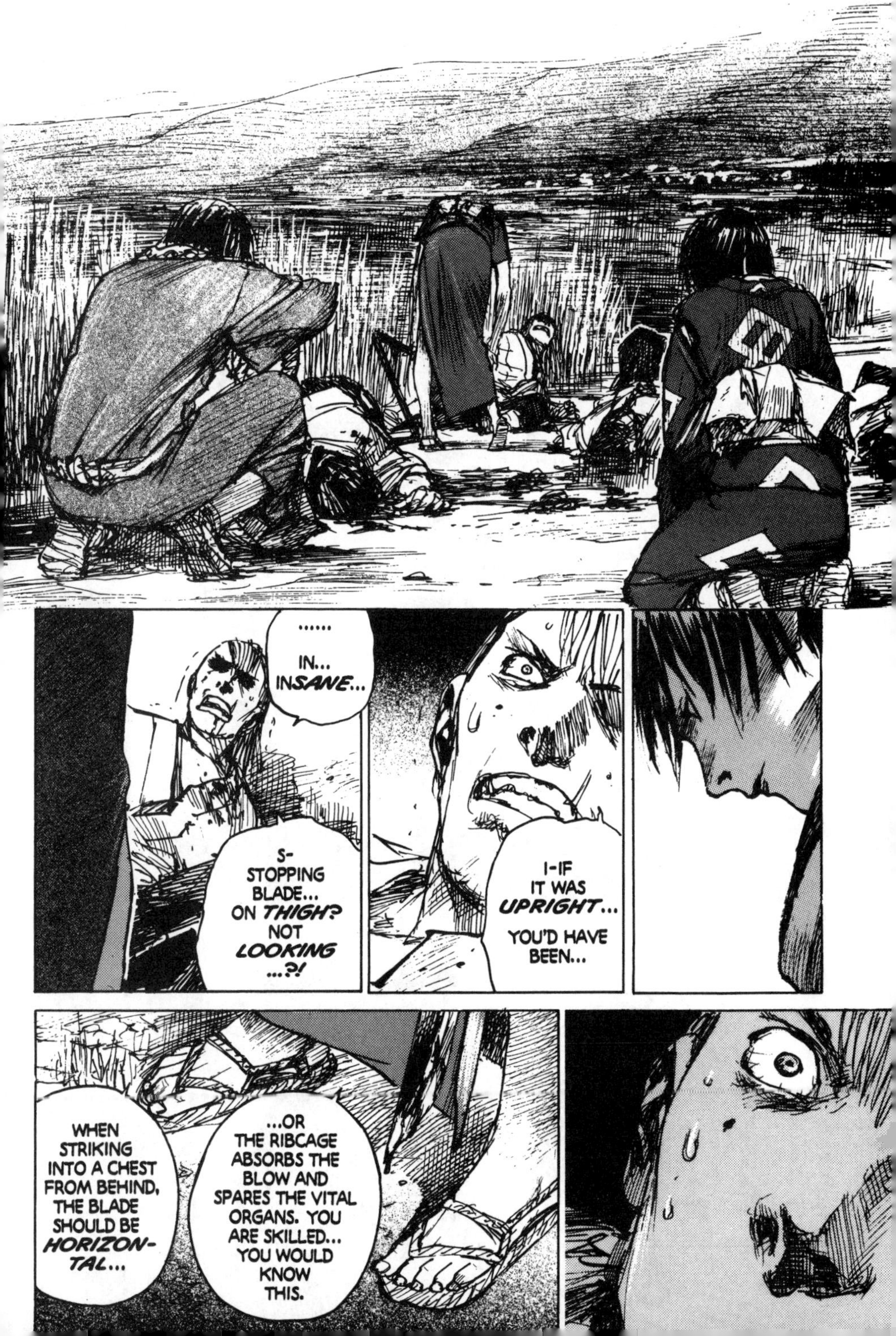
......
IN... INSANE...
S-STOPPING BLADE... ON THIGH? NOT LOOKING ...?!
I-IF IT WAS UPRIGHT... YOU'D HAVE BEEN...
WHEN STRIKING INTO A CHEST FROM BEHIND, THE BLADE SHOULD BE HORIZON-TAL...
...OR THE RIBCAGE ABSORBS THE BLOW AND SPARES THE VITAL ORGANS. YOU ARE SKILLED... YOU WOULD KNOW THIS.

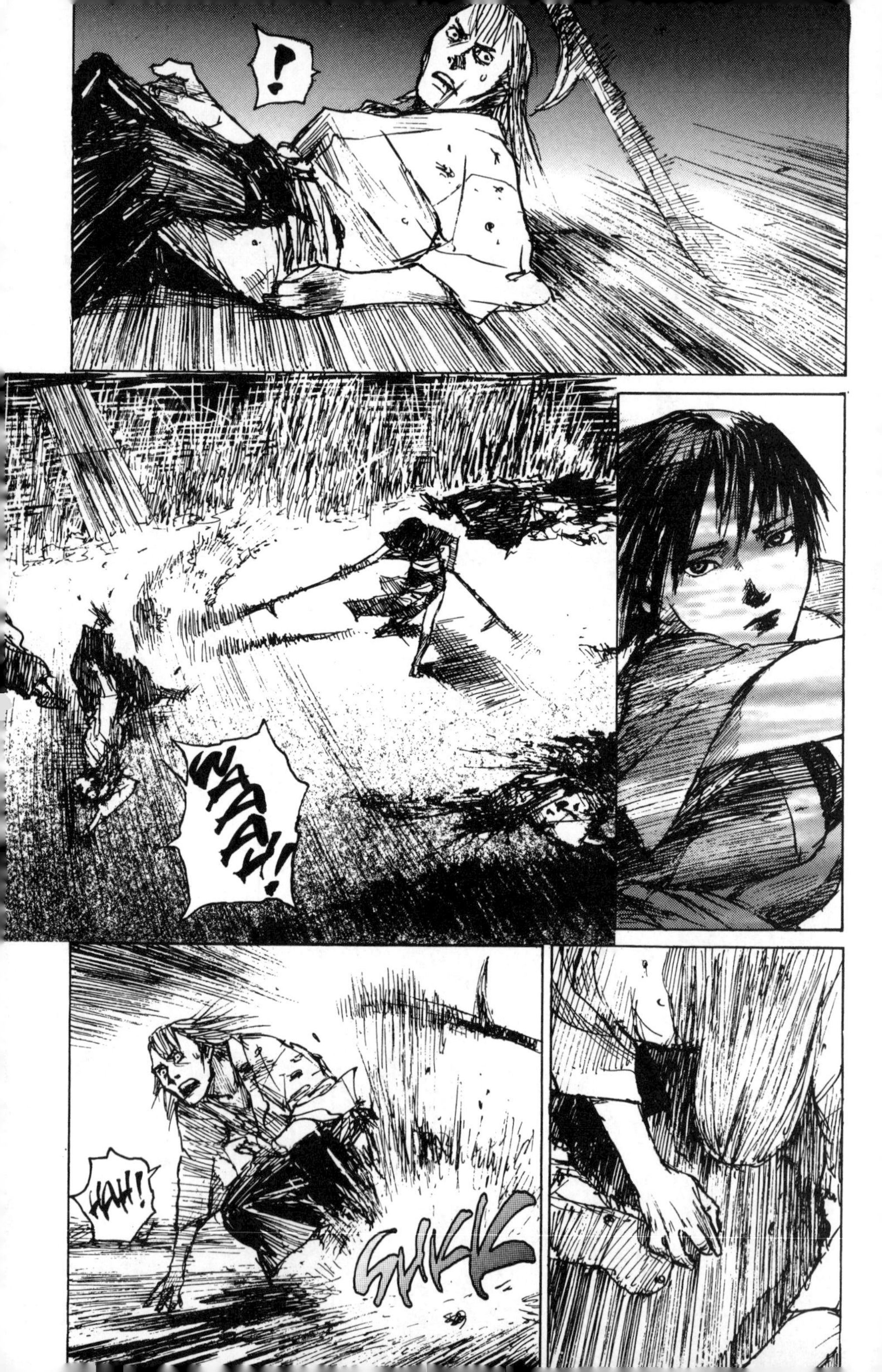
!
SWAY!
HAH!
SHKK

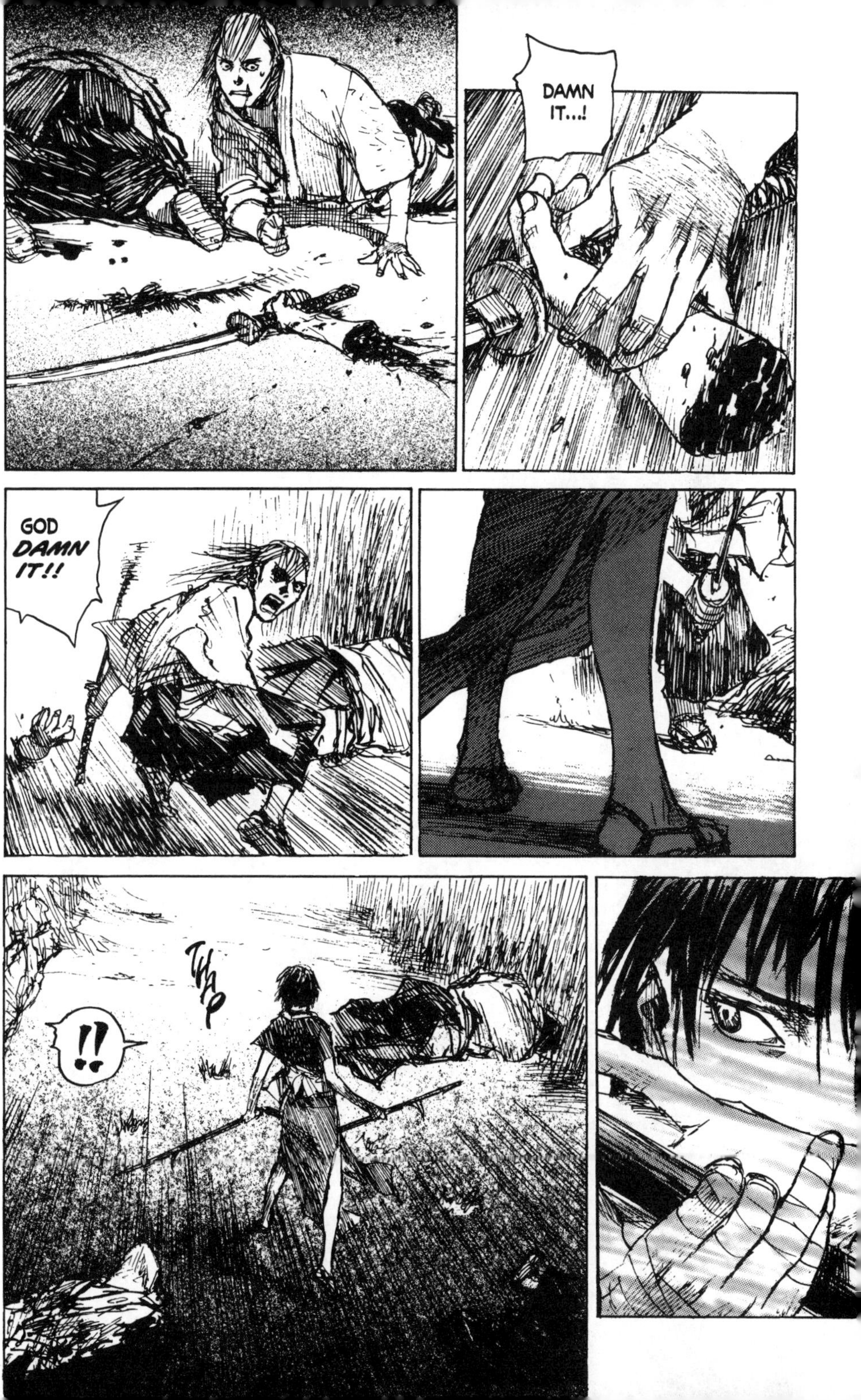
DAMN IT...!
GOD DAMN IT!!
THAP
!!

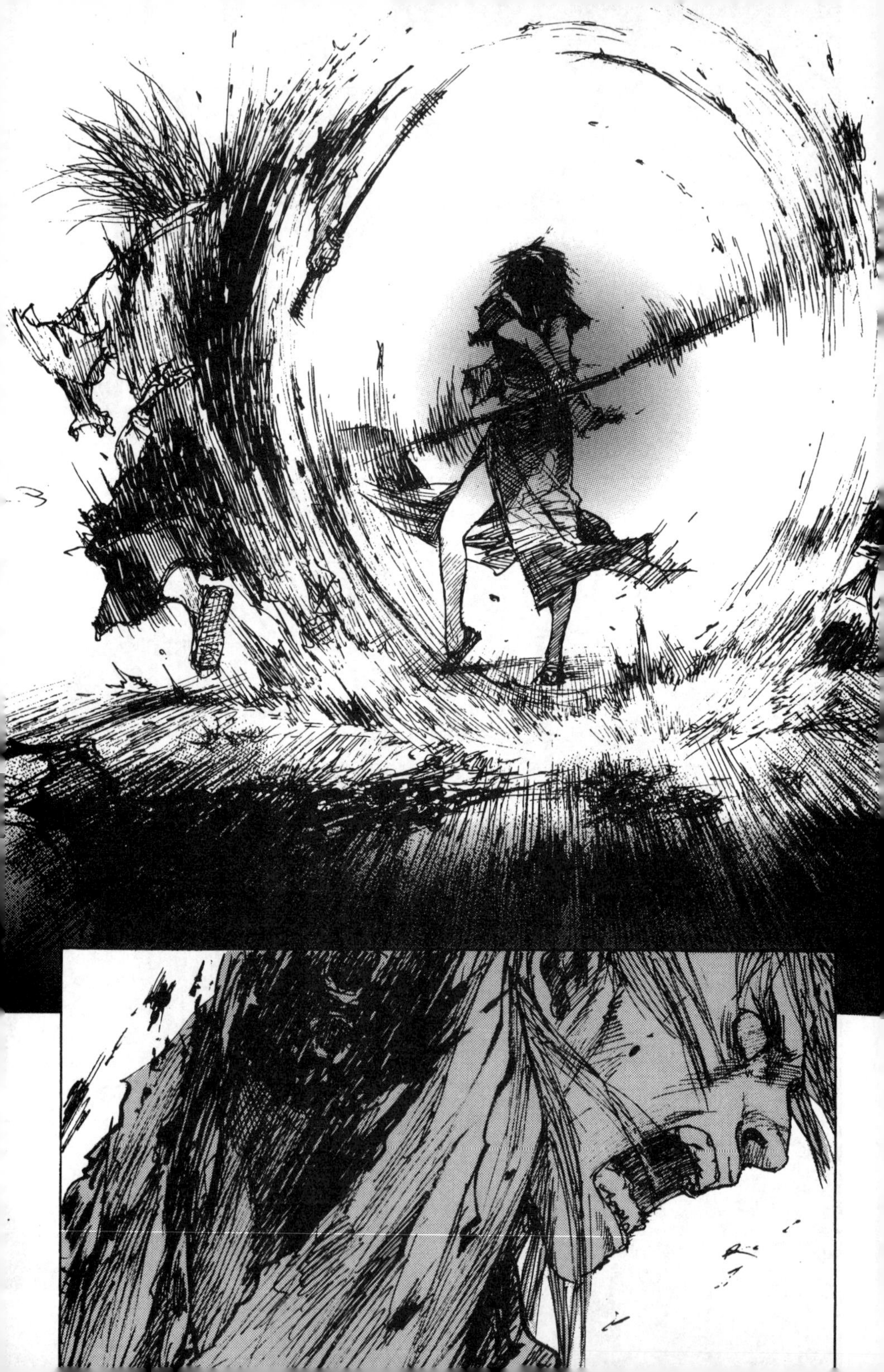

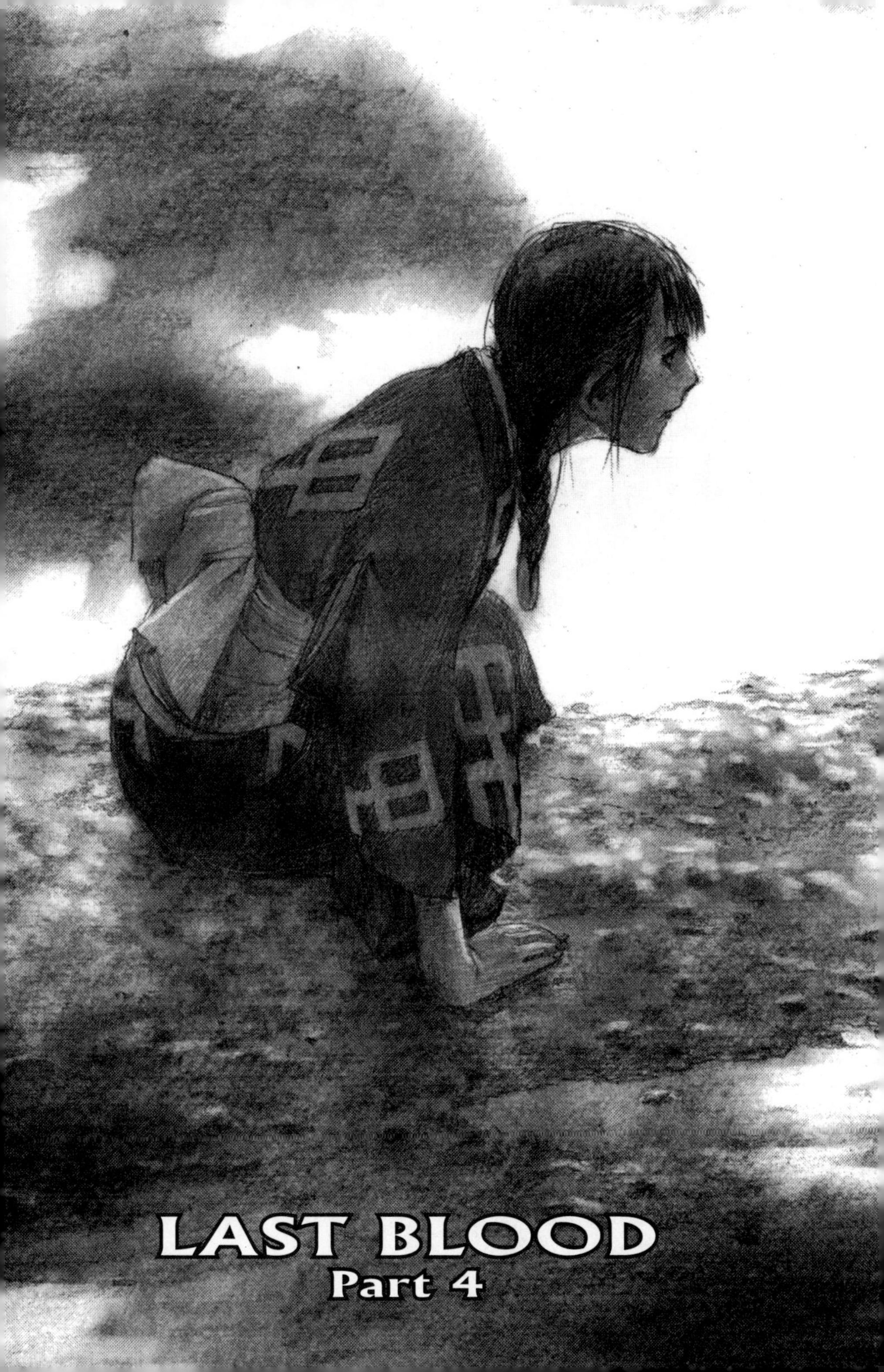

LAST BLOOD
Part 4

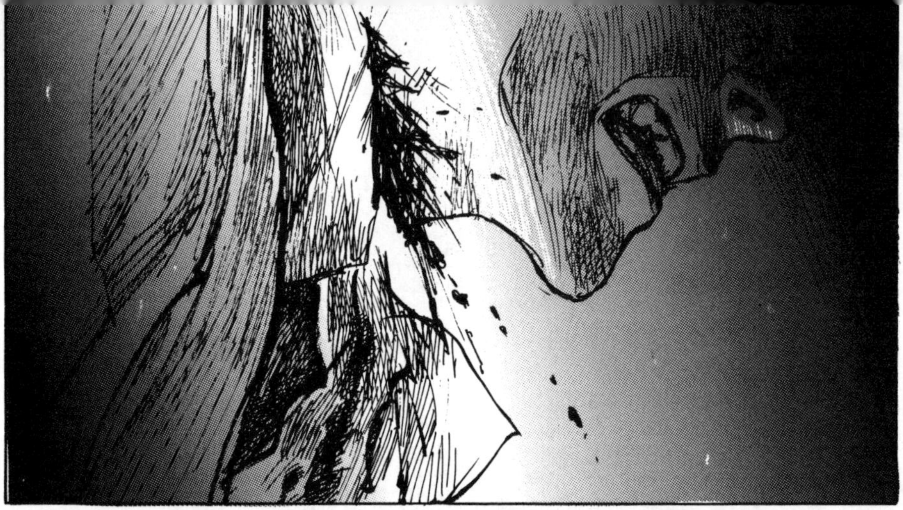
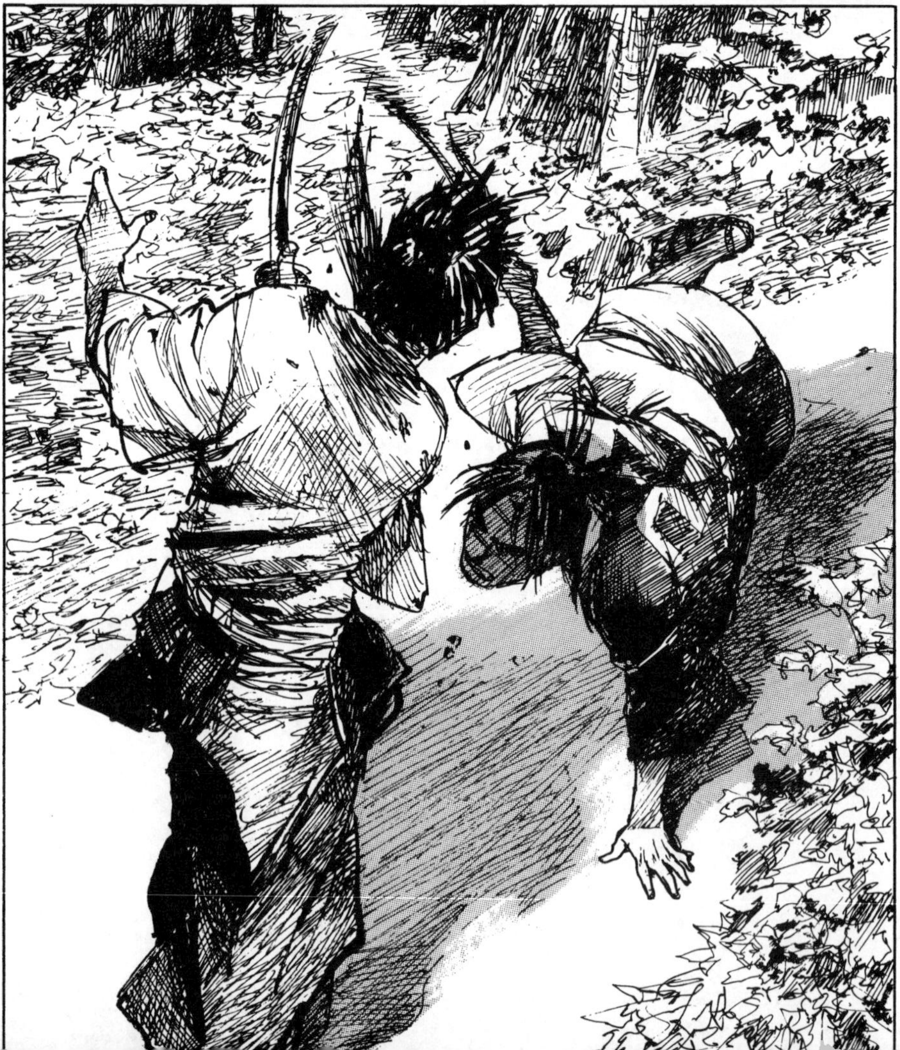

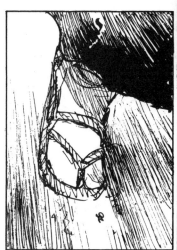

SORRY, GUYS.

I'M A MOUNTAIN BOY, SEE?

IT'S EASY, TRICKING *DŌJŌ* KIDS LIKE YOU ONTO THIS FOOTING.

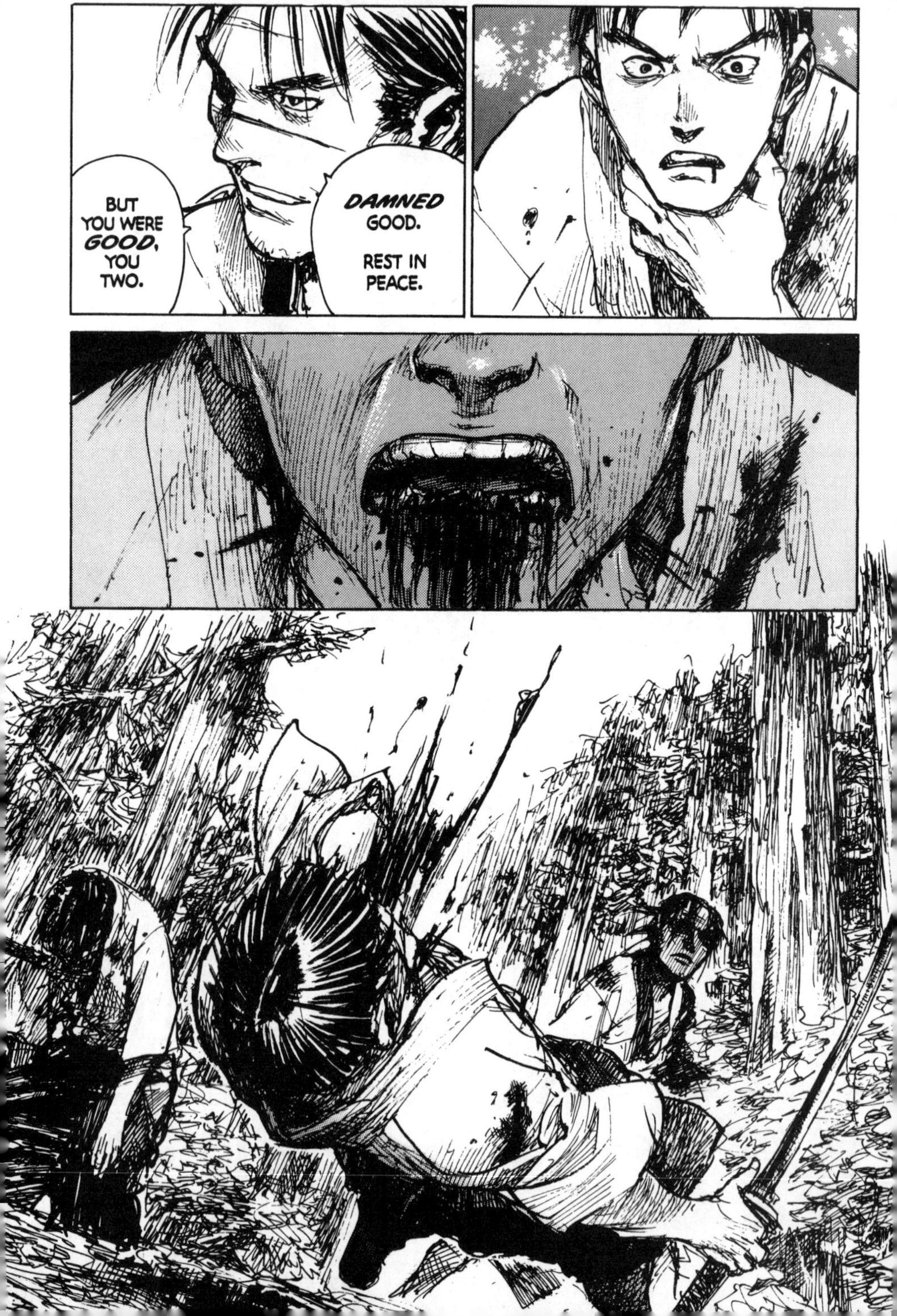
BUT YOU WERE ***GOOD***, YOU TWO.
DAMNED GOOD.
REST IN PEACE.

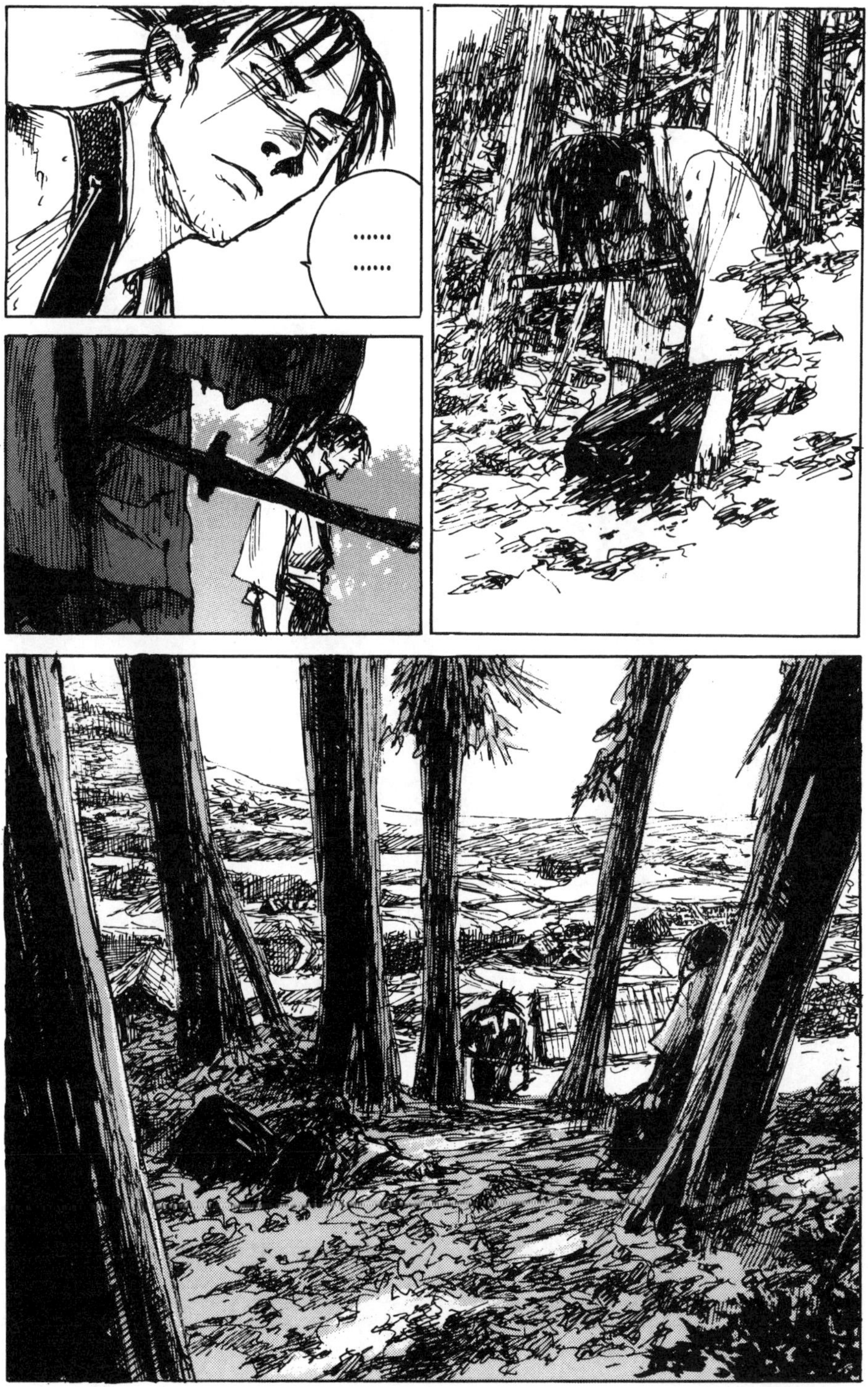
……
……

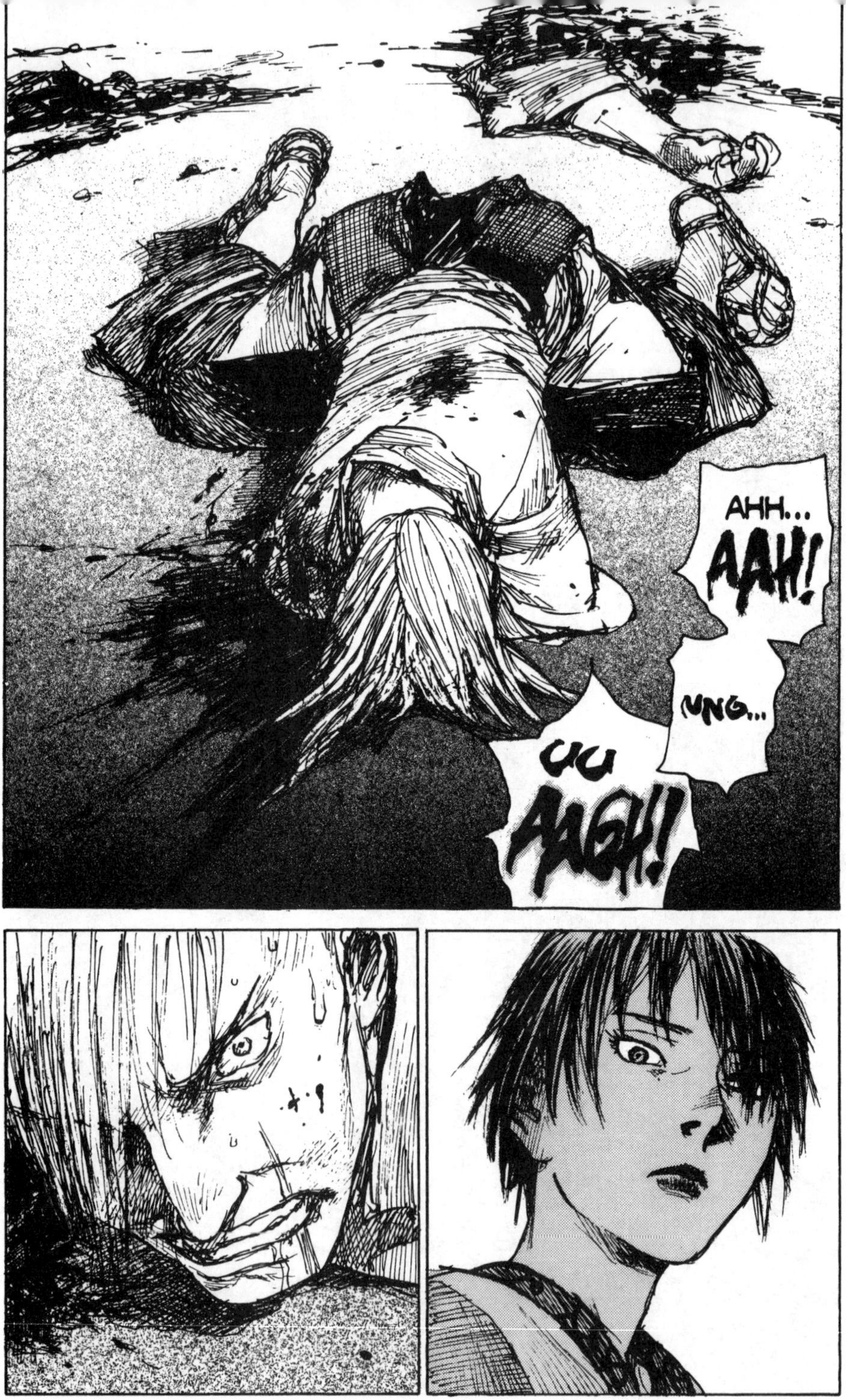
AHH... AAH!
UNG...
UU AAGH!

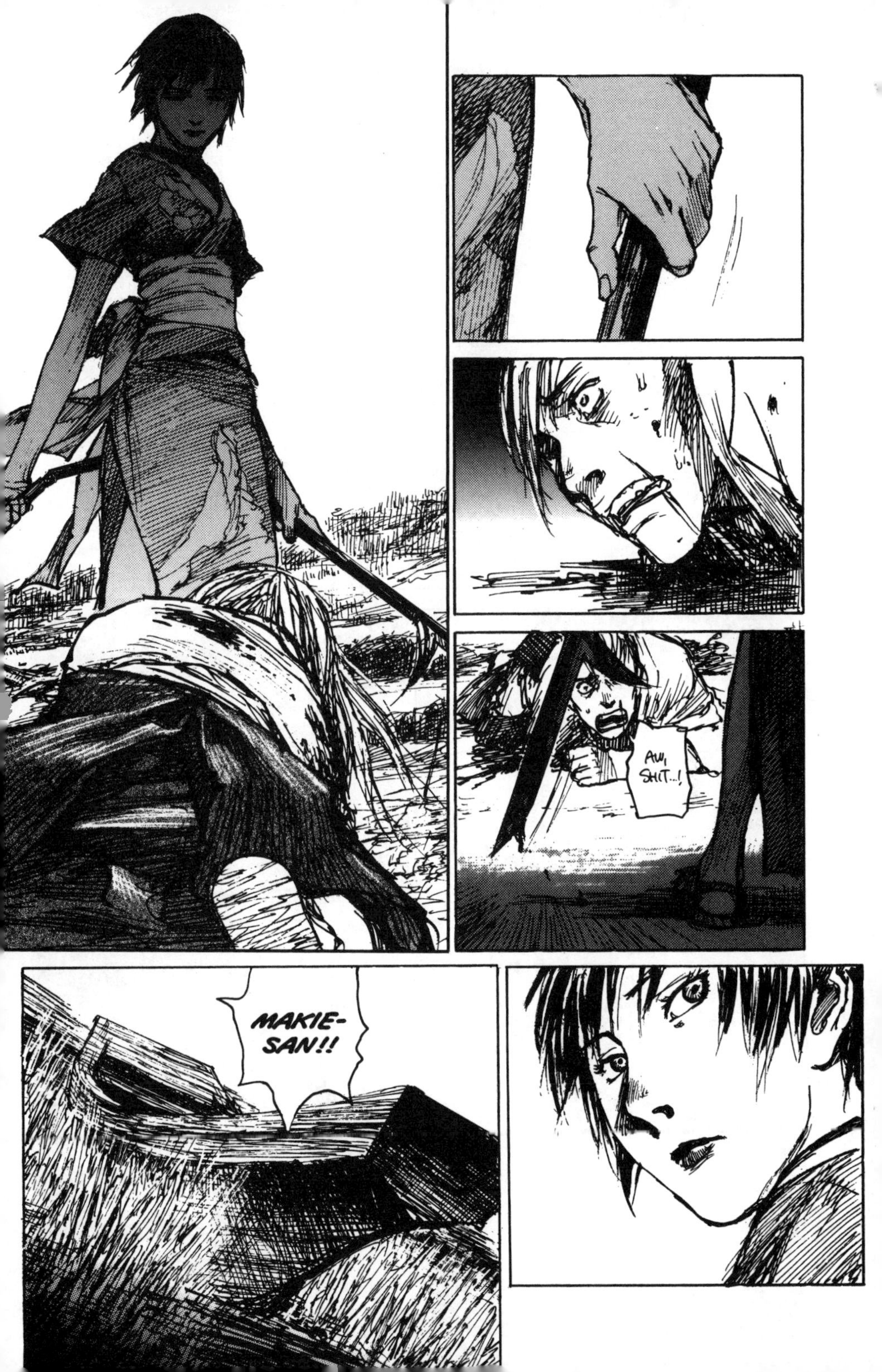
AW, SHIT...!
MAKIE-SAN!!

HE'S ALREADY... ......

I MEAN... YOU'VE *WON*, RIGHT?

NO...

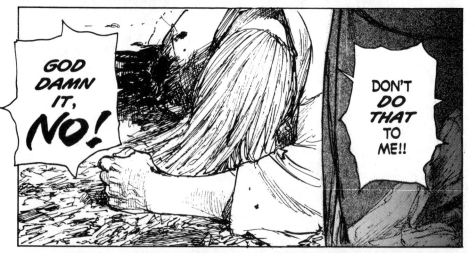

GOD DAMN IT, NO!

DON'T *DO THAT* TO ME!!

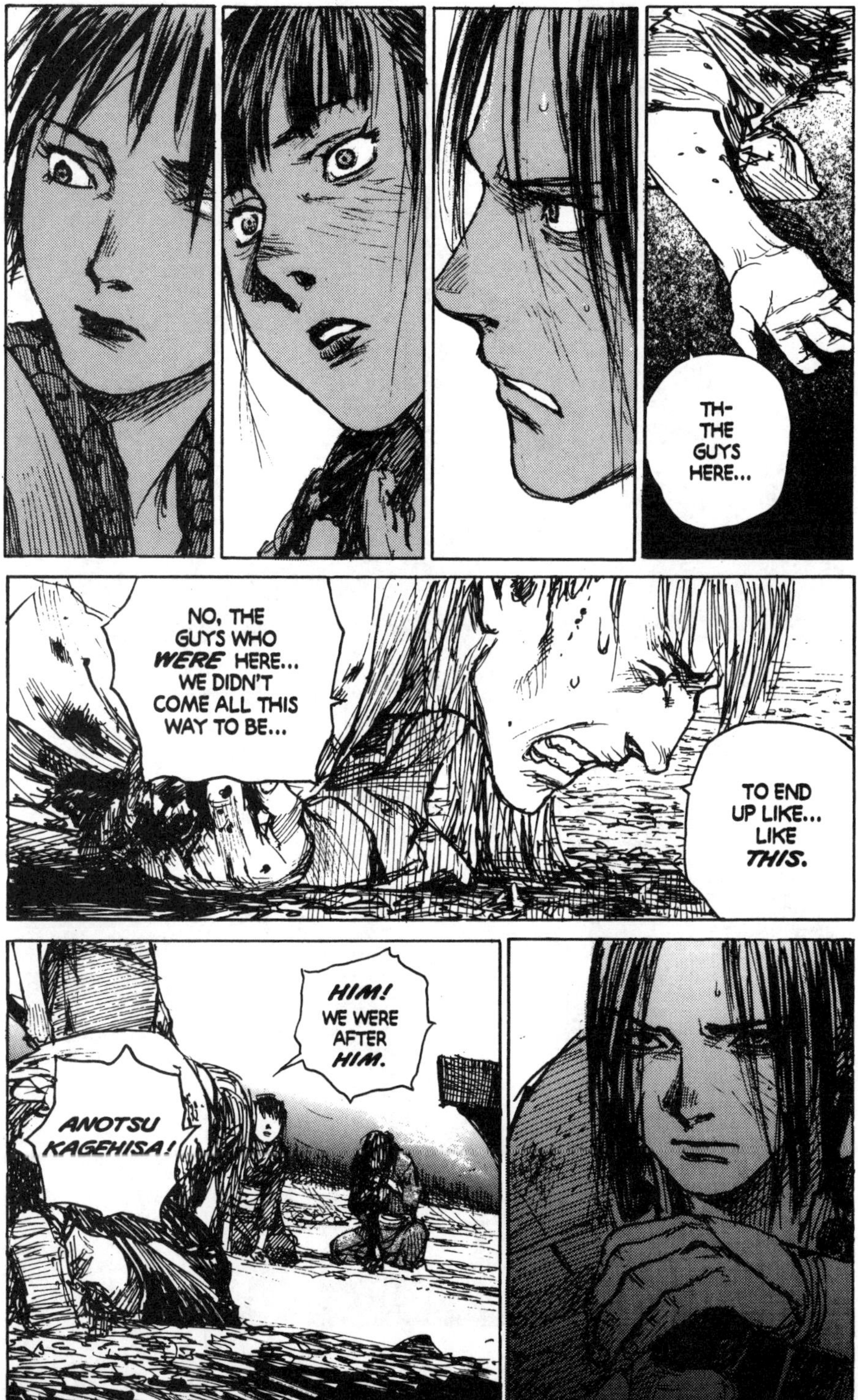
TH- THE GUYS HERE...
NO, THE GUYS WHO *WERE* HERE... WE DIDN'T COME ALL THIS WAY TO BE...
TO END UP LIKE... LIKE *THIS*.
HIM! WE WERE AFTER *HIM*.
ANOTSU KAGEHISA!

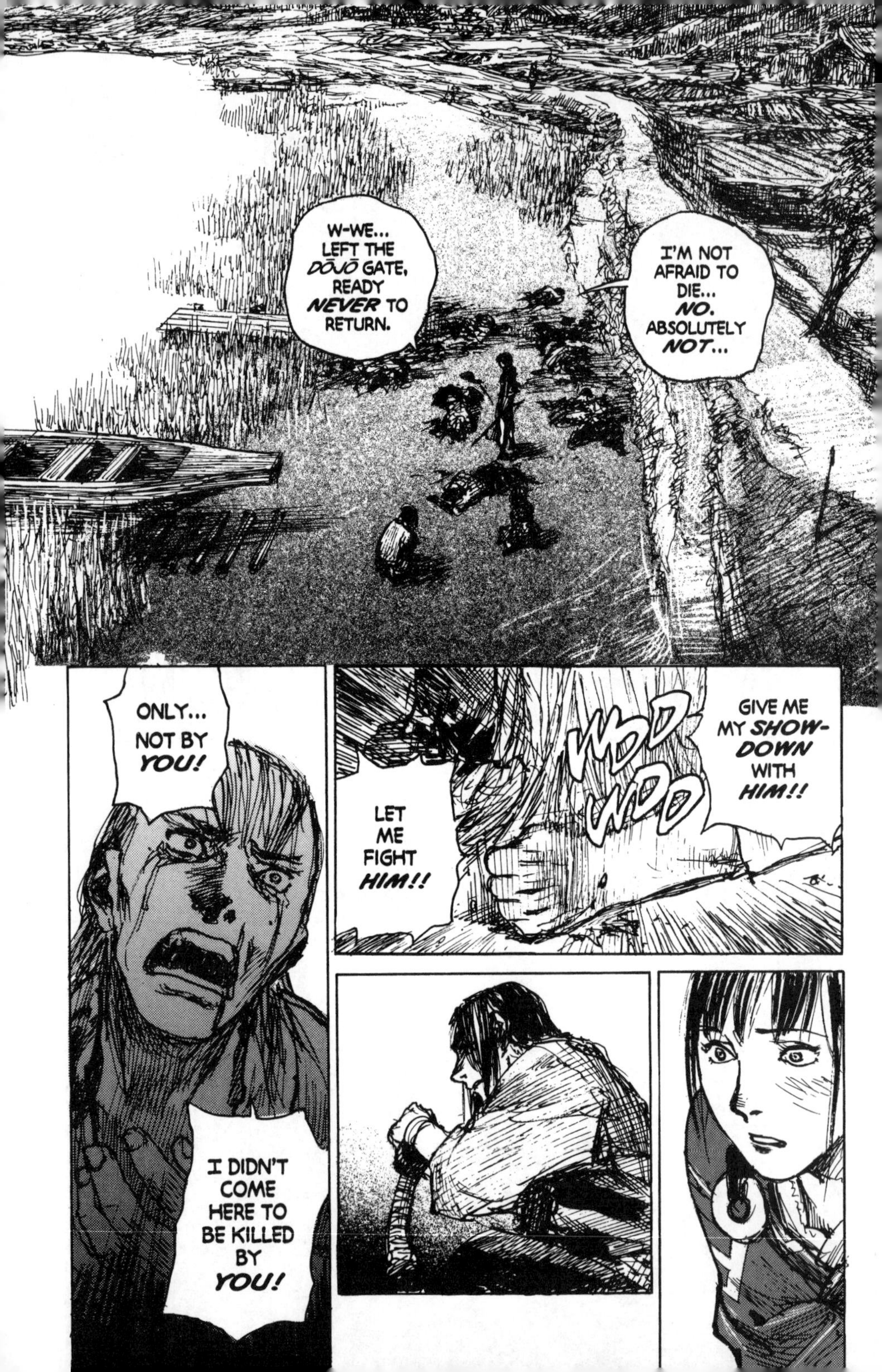
I'M NOT AFRAID TO DIE... NO. ABSOLUTELY NOT...
W-WE... LEFT THE DŌJŌ GATE, READY NEVER TO RETURN.
GIVE ME MY SHOW-DOWN WITH HIM!!
WDD WDD
LET ME FIGHT HIM!!
ONLY... NOT BY YOU!
I DIDN'T COME HERE TO BE KILLED BY YOU!

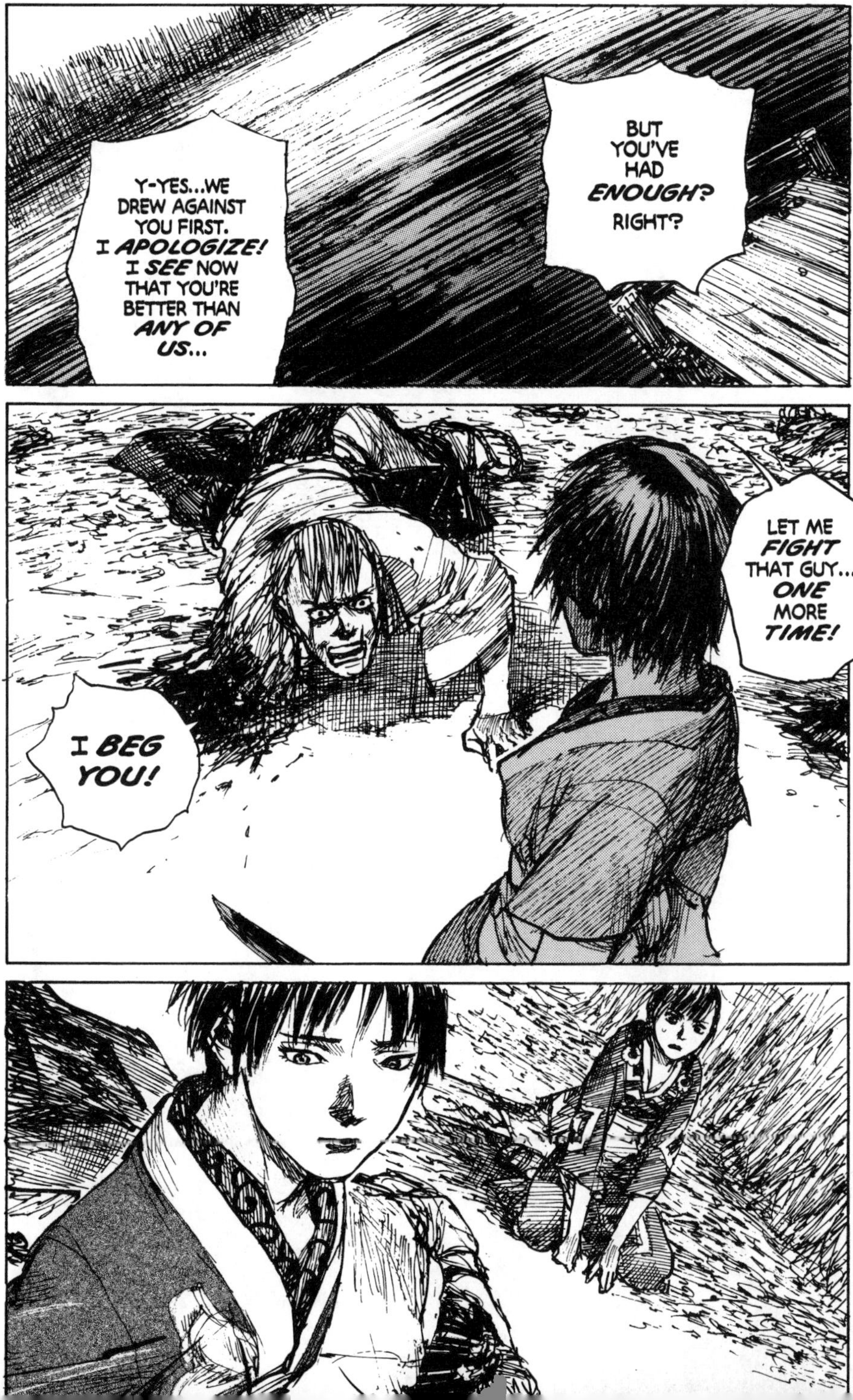
BUT YOU'VE HAD ENOUGH? RIGHT?
Y-YES...WE DREW AGAINST YOU FIRST. I APOLOGIZE! I SEE NOW THAT YOU'RE BETTER THAN ANY OF US...
LET ME FIGHT THAT GUY... ONE MORE TIME!
I BEG YOU!

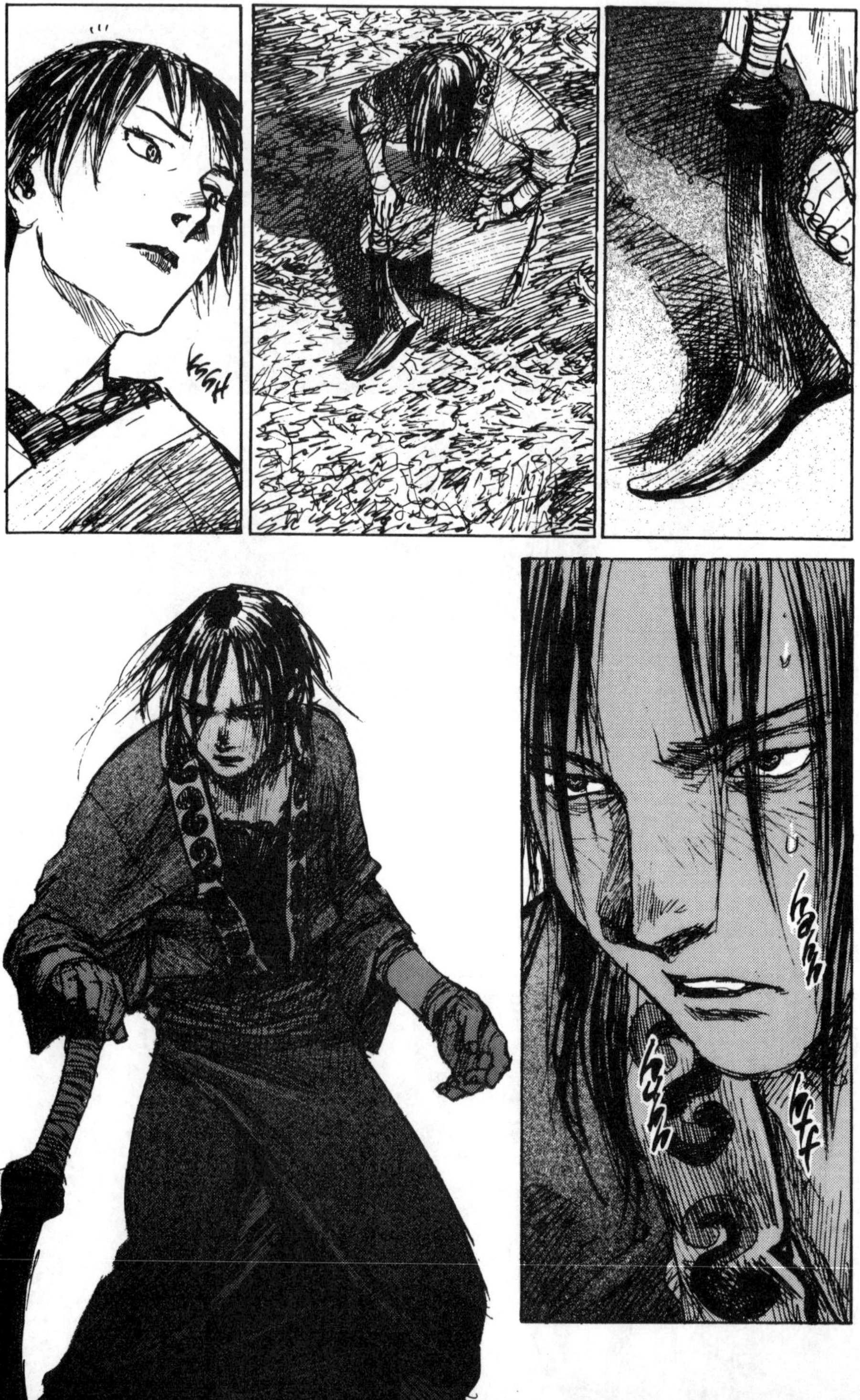
haaa
hff

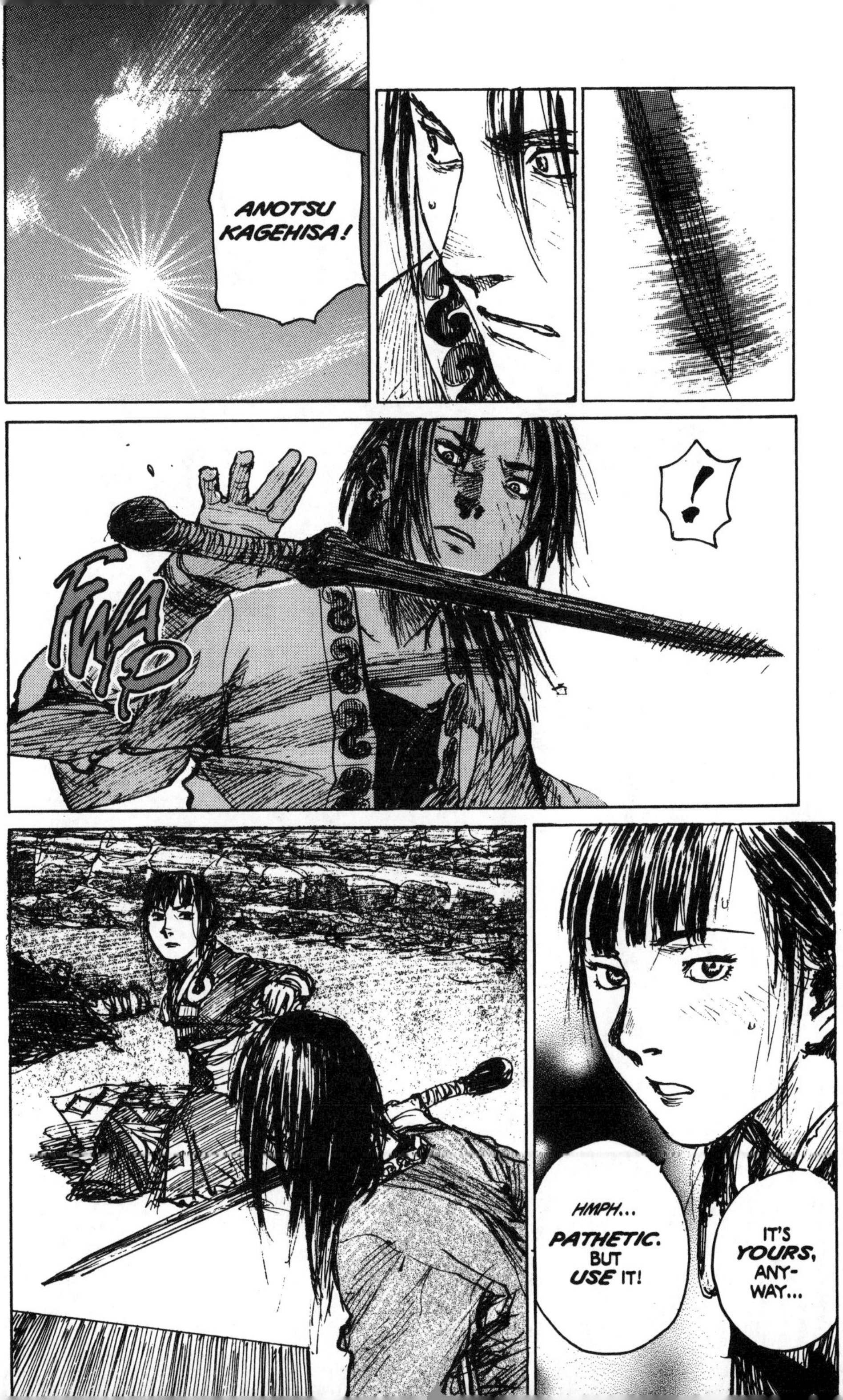
ANOTSU KAGEHISA!
!
FWAP
HMPH... PATHETIC. BUT USE IT!
IT'S YOURS, ANYWAY...

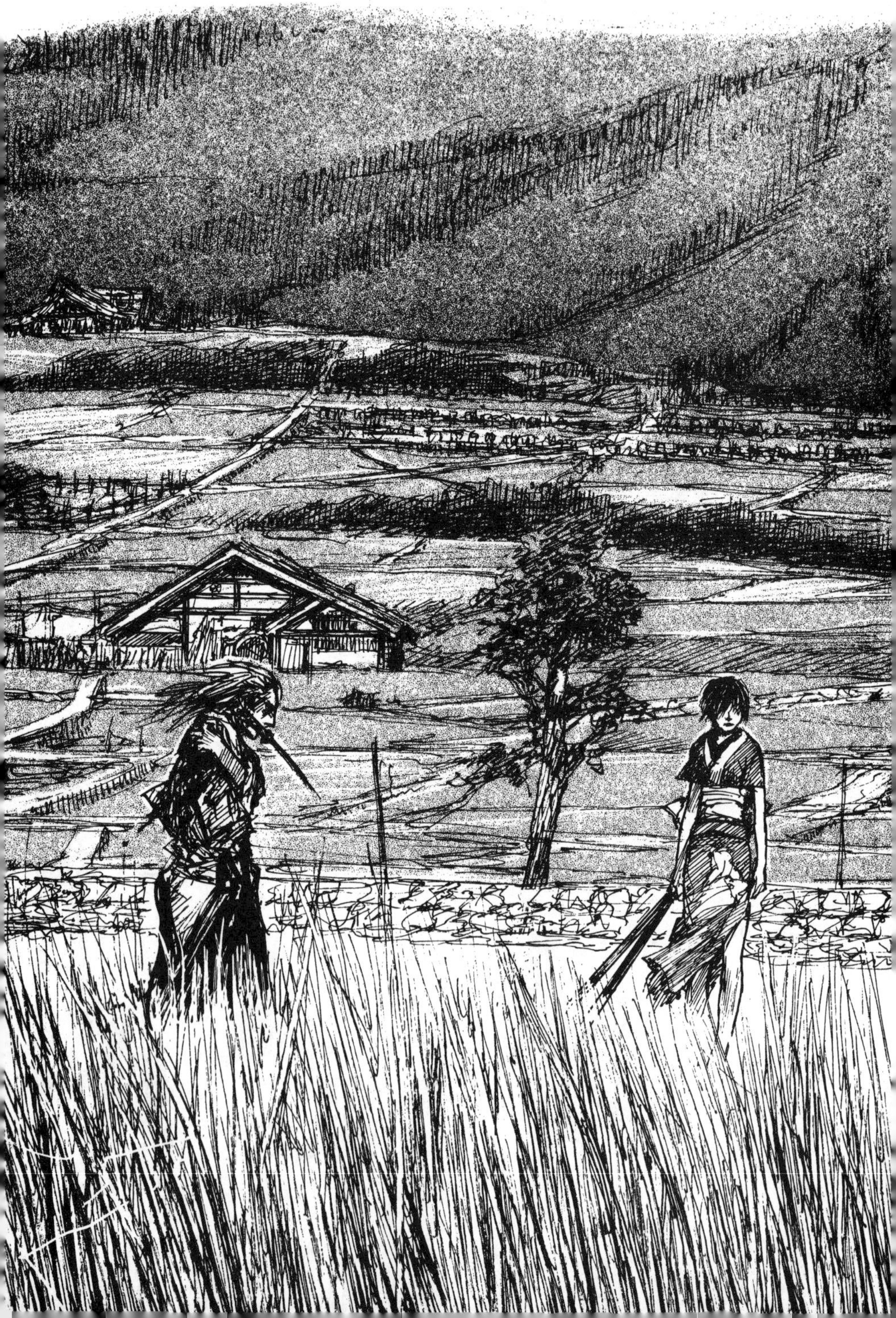

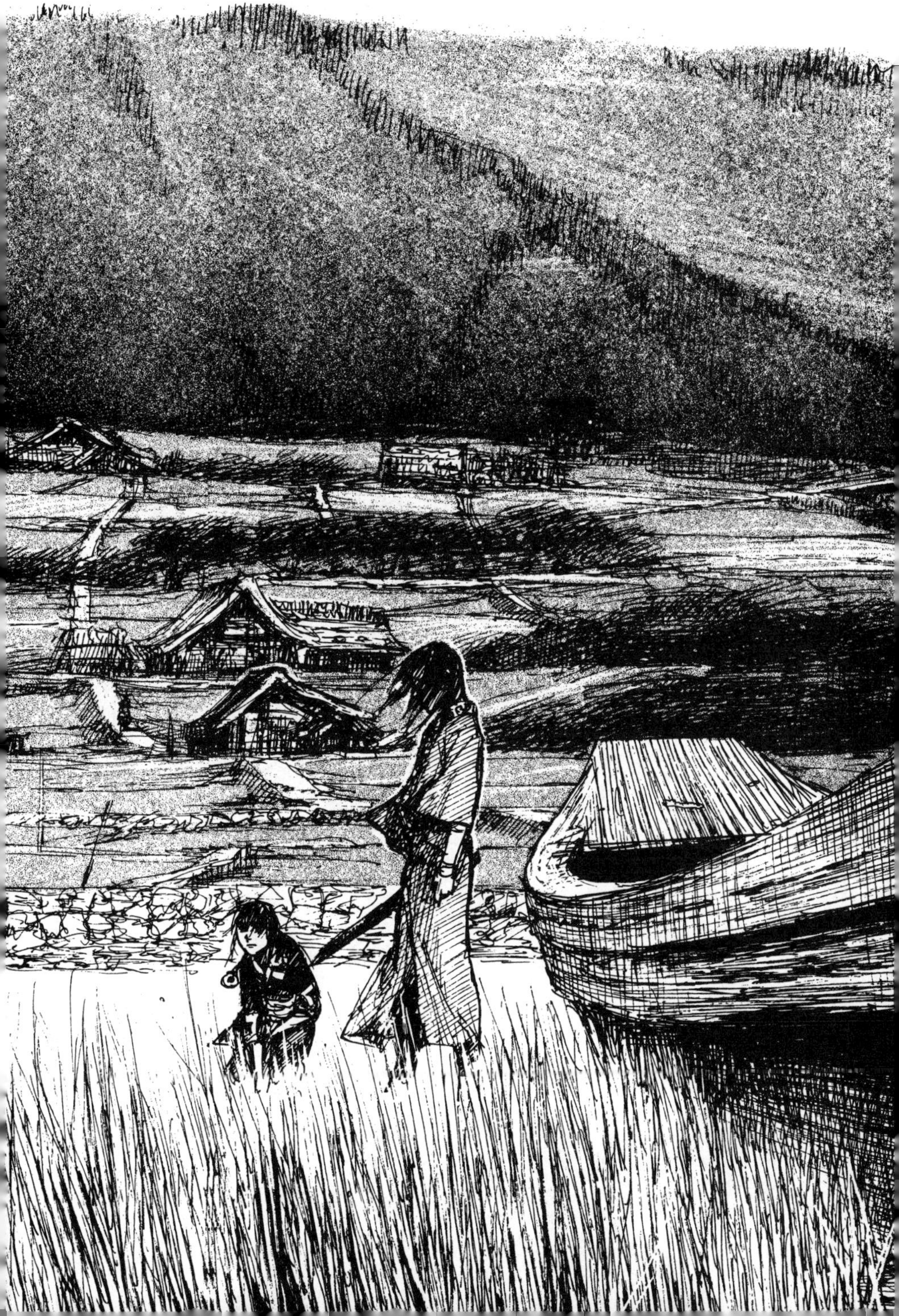

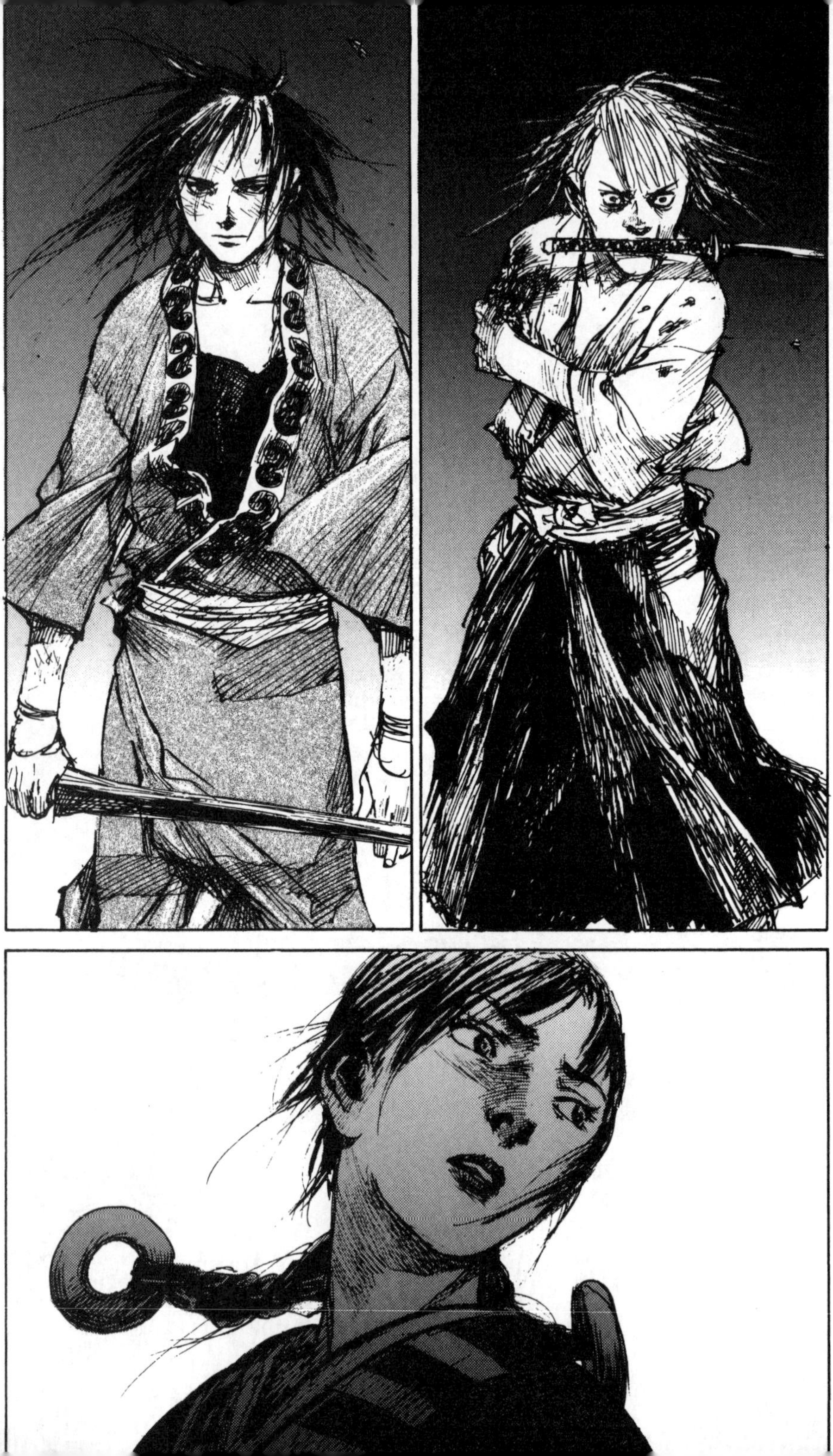

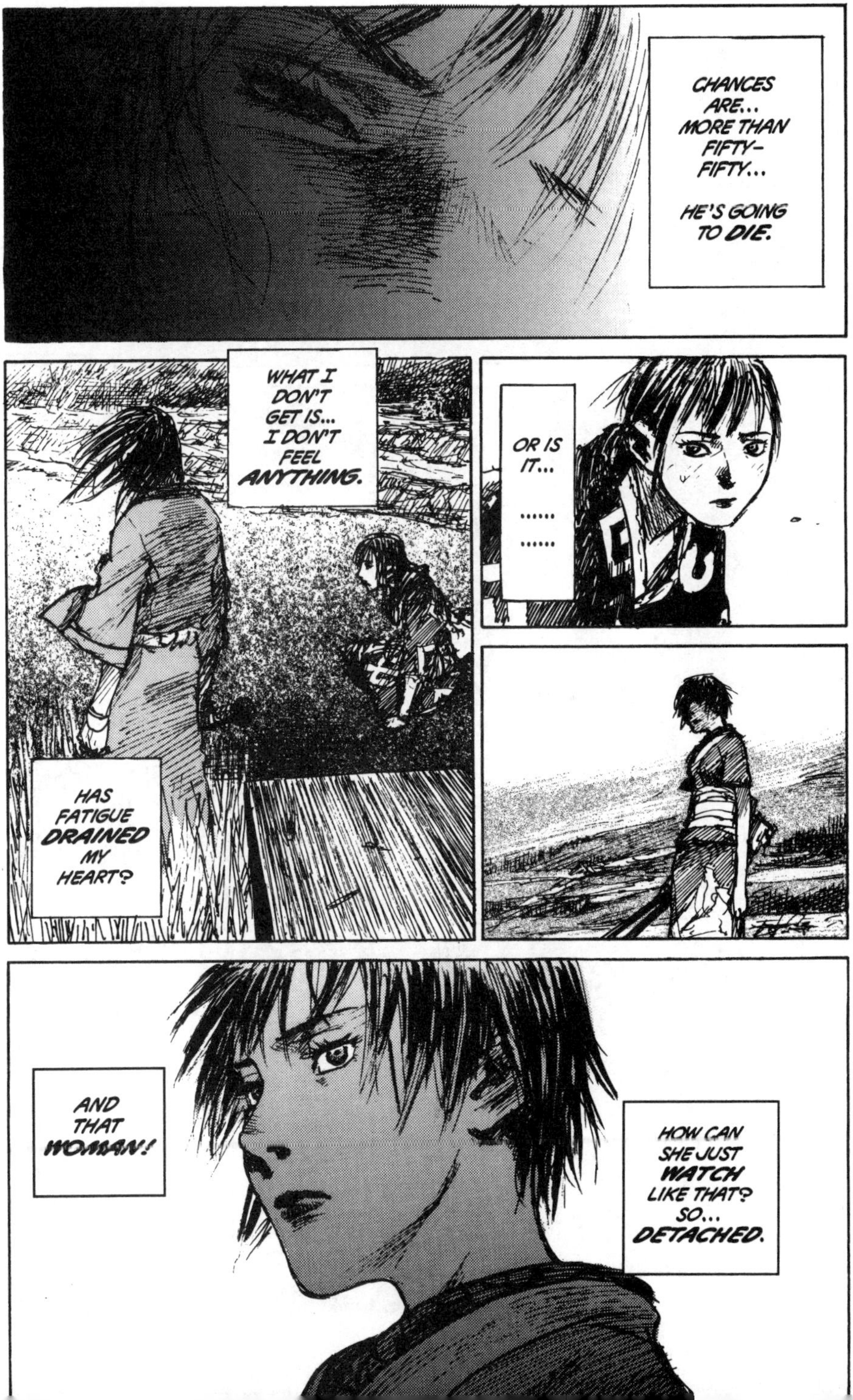
CHANCES ARE... MORE THAN FIFTY-FIFTY... HE'S GOING TO DIE.
WHAT I DON'T GET IS... I DON'T FEEL ANYTHING.
HAS FATIGUE DRAINED MY HEART?
OR IS IT... ....
AND THAT WOMAN!
HOW CAN SHE JUST WATCH LIKE THAT? SO... DETACHED.

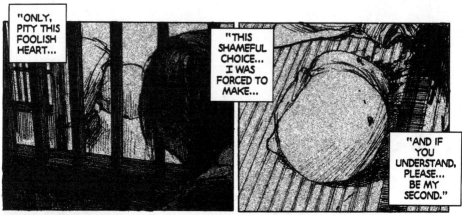

"ONLY, PITY THIS FOOLISH HEART...

"THIS SHAMEFUL CHOICE... I WAS FORCED TO MAKE...

"AND IF YOU UNDERSTAND, PLEASE... BE MY SECOND."

≶hahh≶

≶hff≶

≶huhh≶

≶hahh≶

"YEAH, WE CAN'T DO ANYTHING WITHOUT A SWORD.

"THAT'S WHY THEY CALL US *KENSHI*."

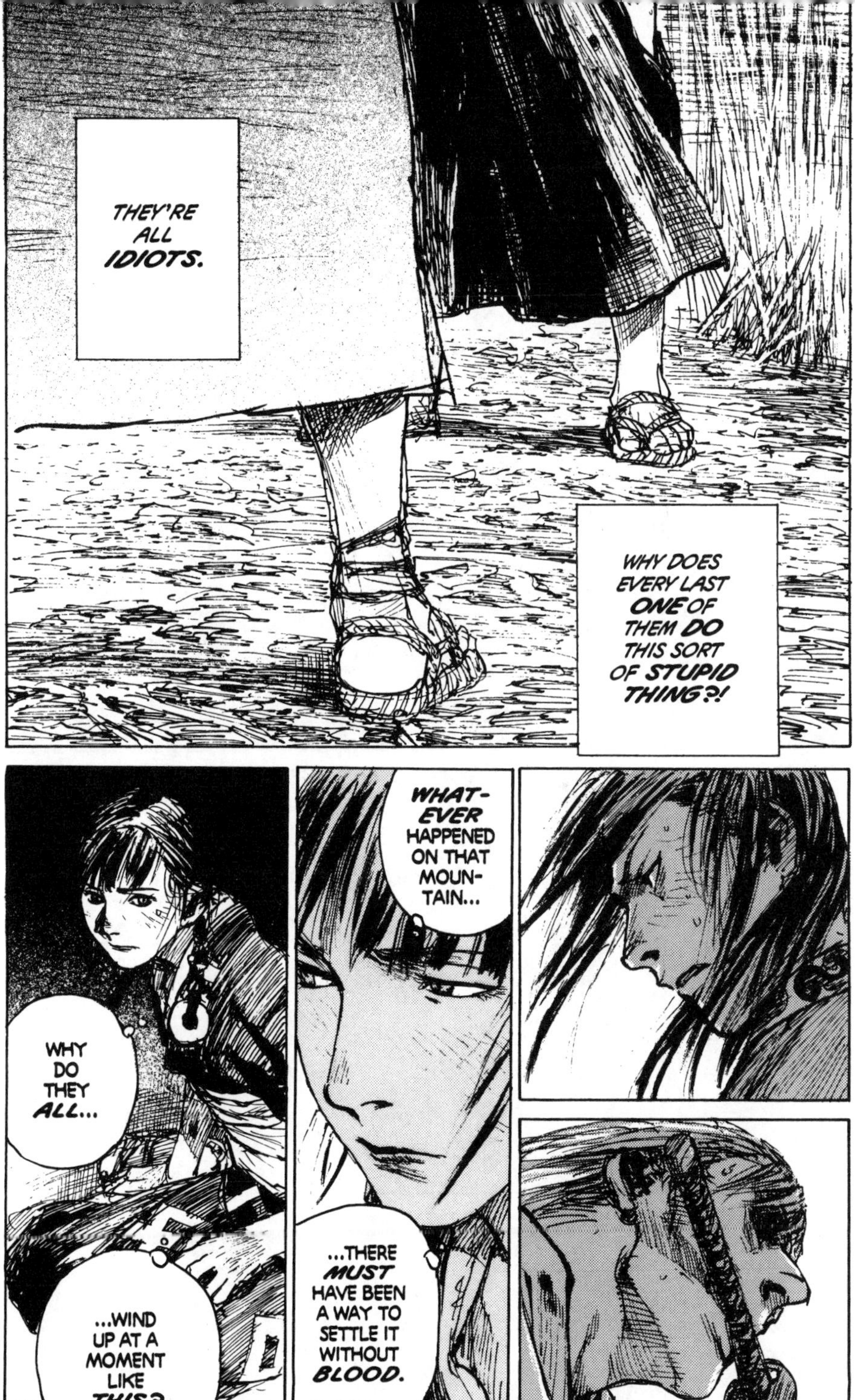
THEY'RE ALL IDIOTS.
WHY DOES EVERY LAST ONE OF THEM DO THIS SORT OF STUPID THING?!
WHY DO THEY ALL...
...WIND UP AT A MOMENT LIKE THIS?
WHAT-EVER HAPPENED ON THAT MOUN-TAIN...
...THERE MUST HAVE BEEN A WAY TO SETTLE IT WITHOUT BLOOD.

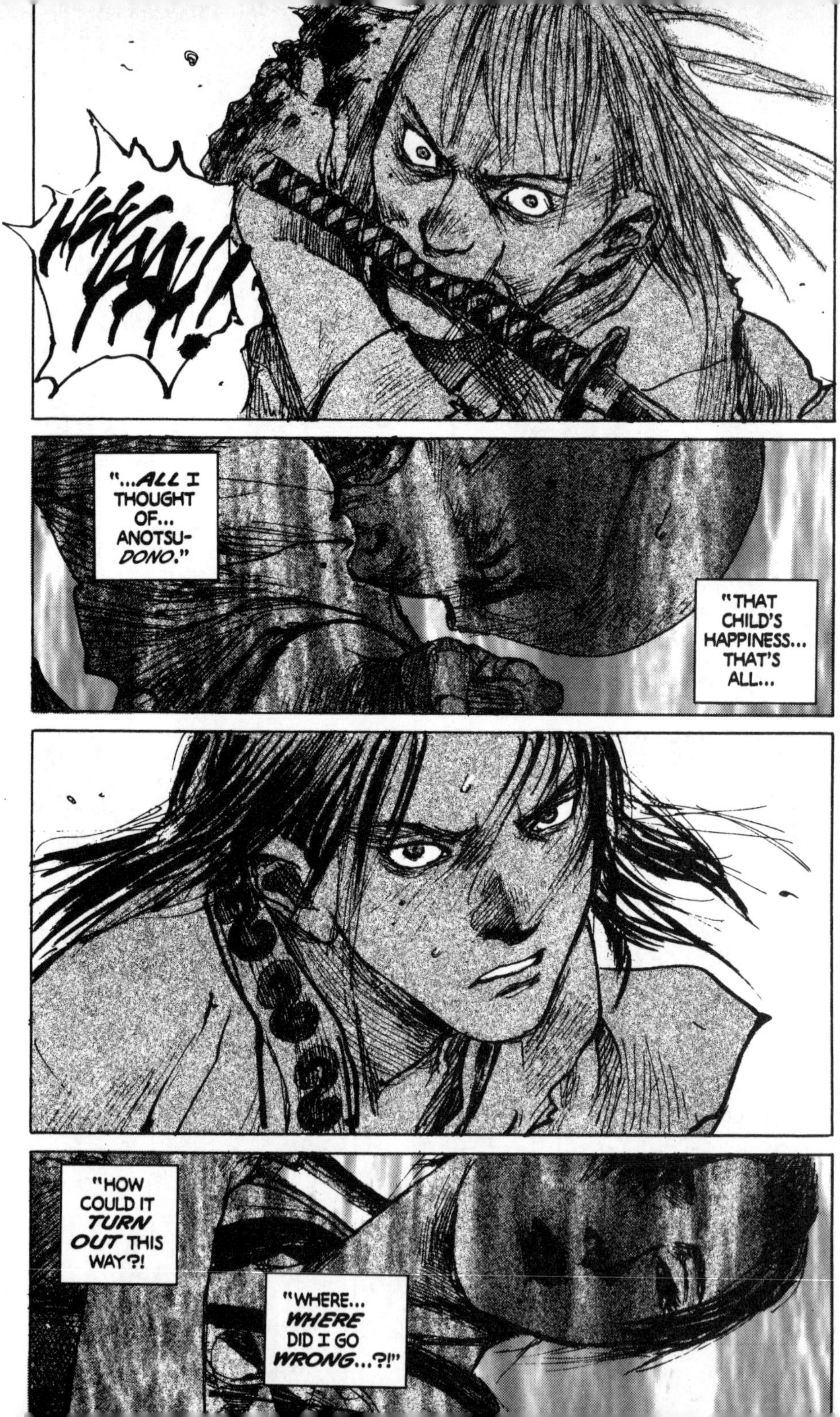
"THAT CHILD'S HAPPINESS... THAT'S ALL...
"...*ALL* I THOUGHT OF... ANOTSU-*DONO*."
"HOW COULD IT *TURN OUT* THIS WAY?!
"WHERE... *WHERE* DID I GO *WRONG*...?!"

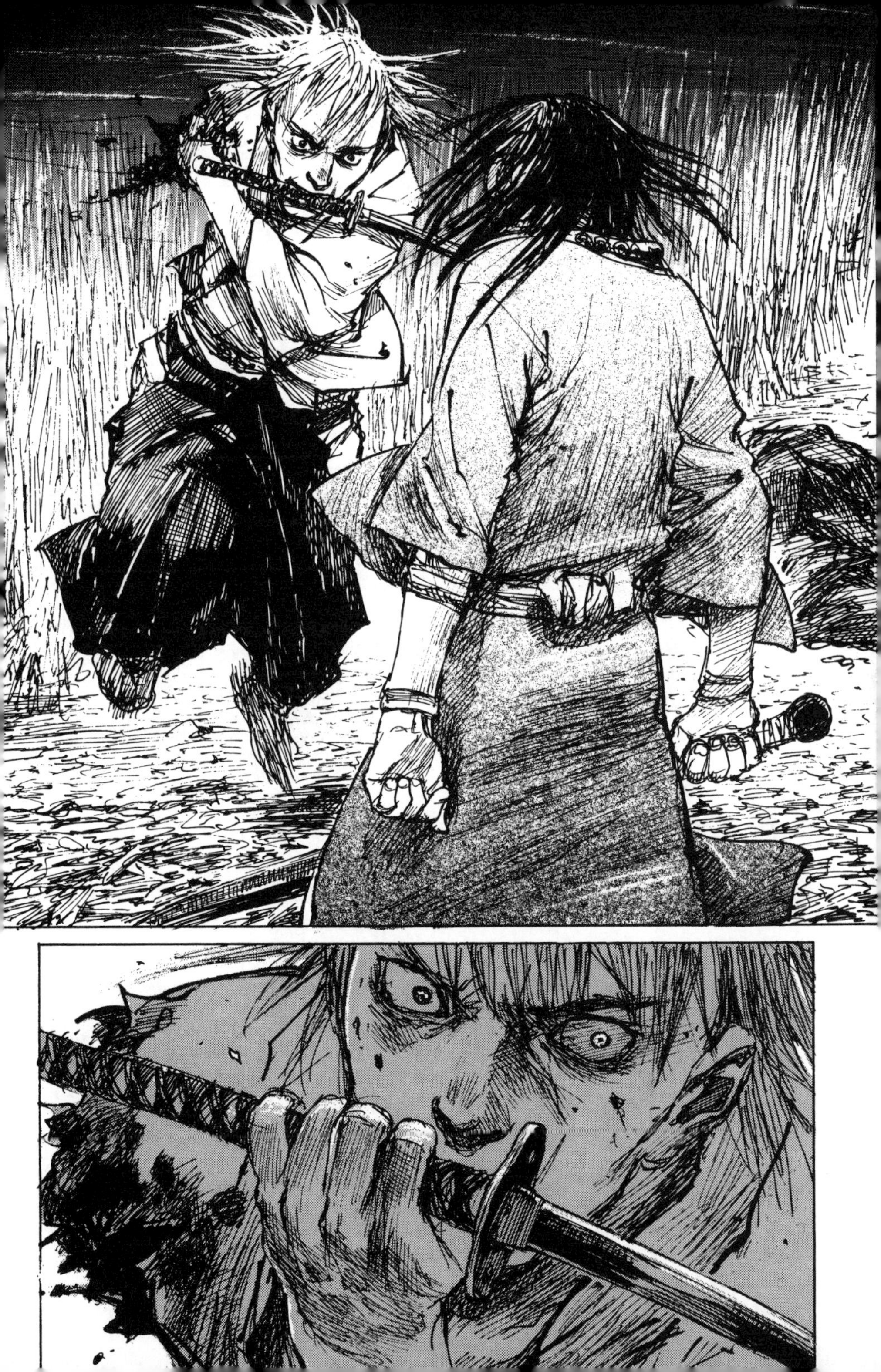

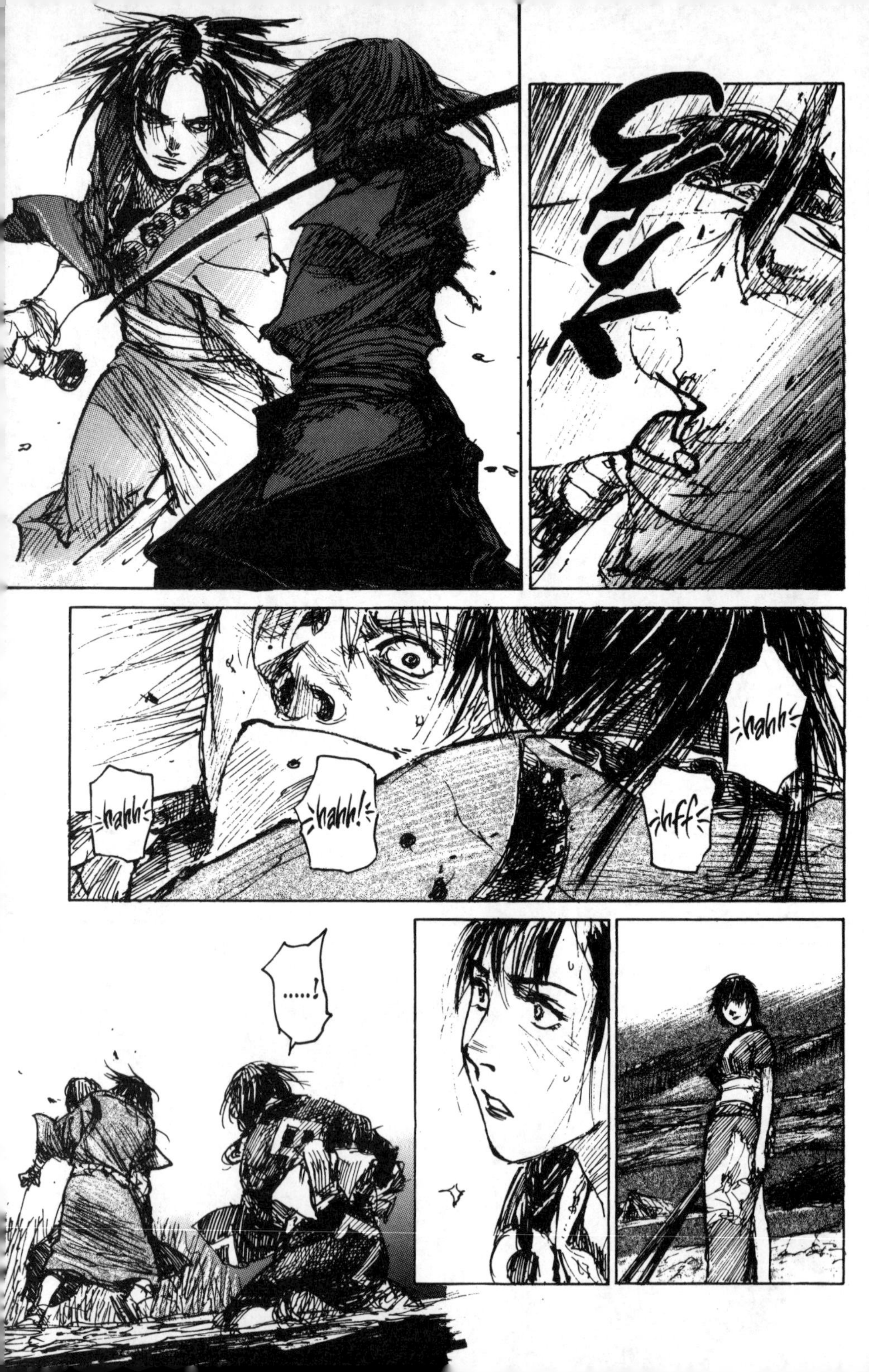
hahh
hff
hahh!
hahh
......!

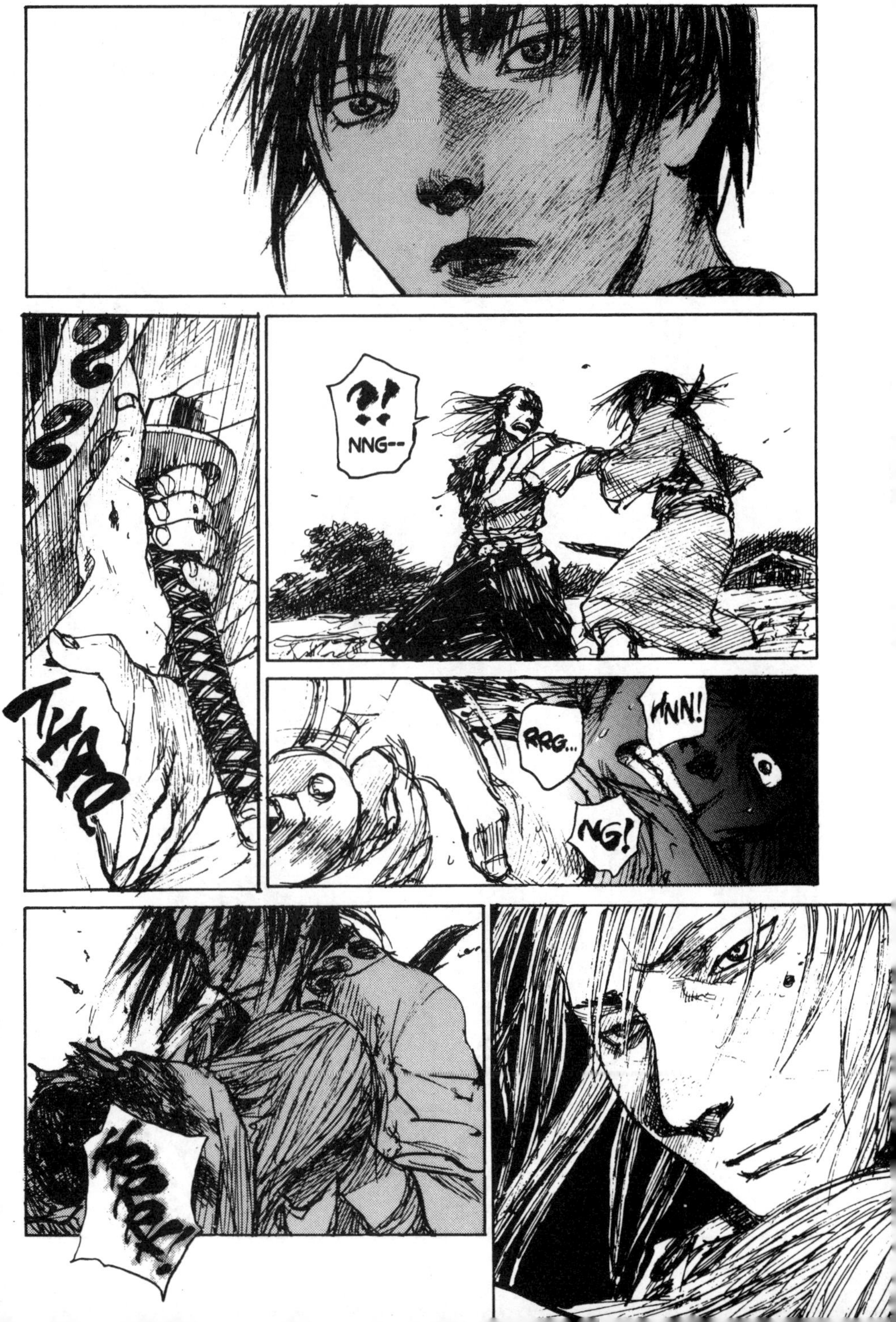
?! NNG--
HNN!
RRG...
NG!

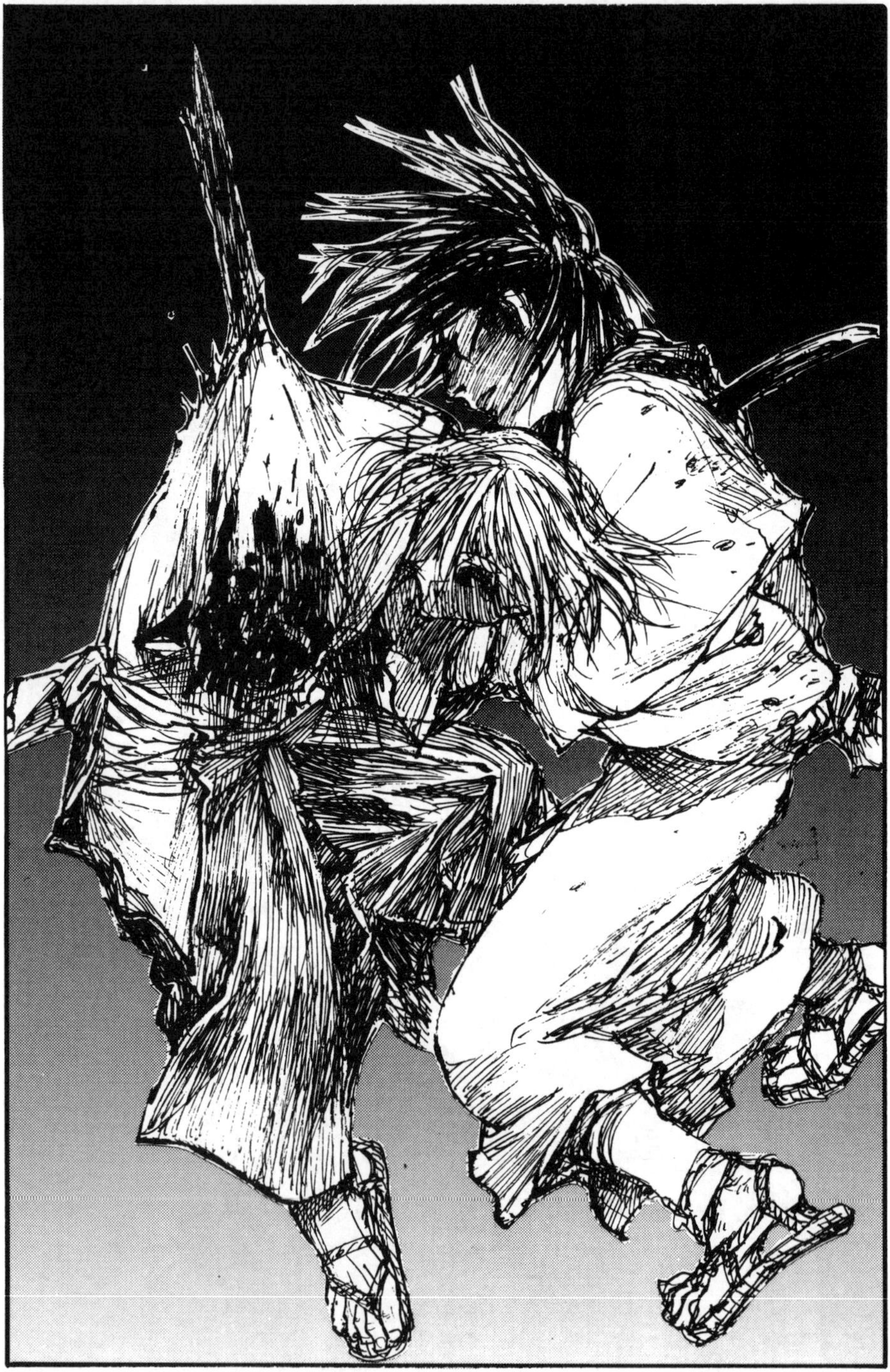

LAST BLOOD
Part 5

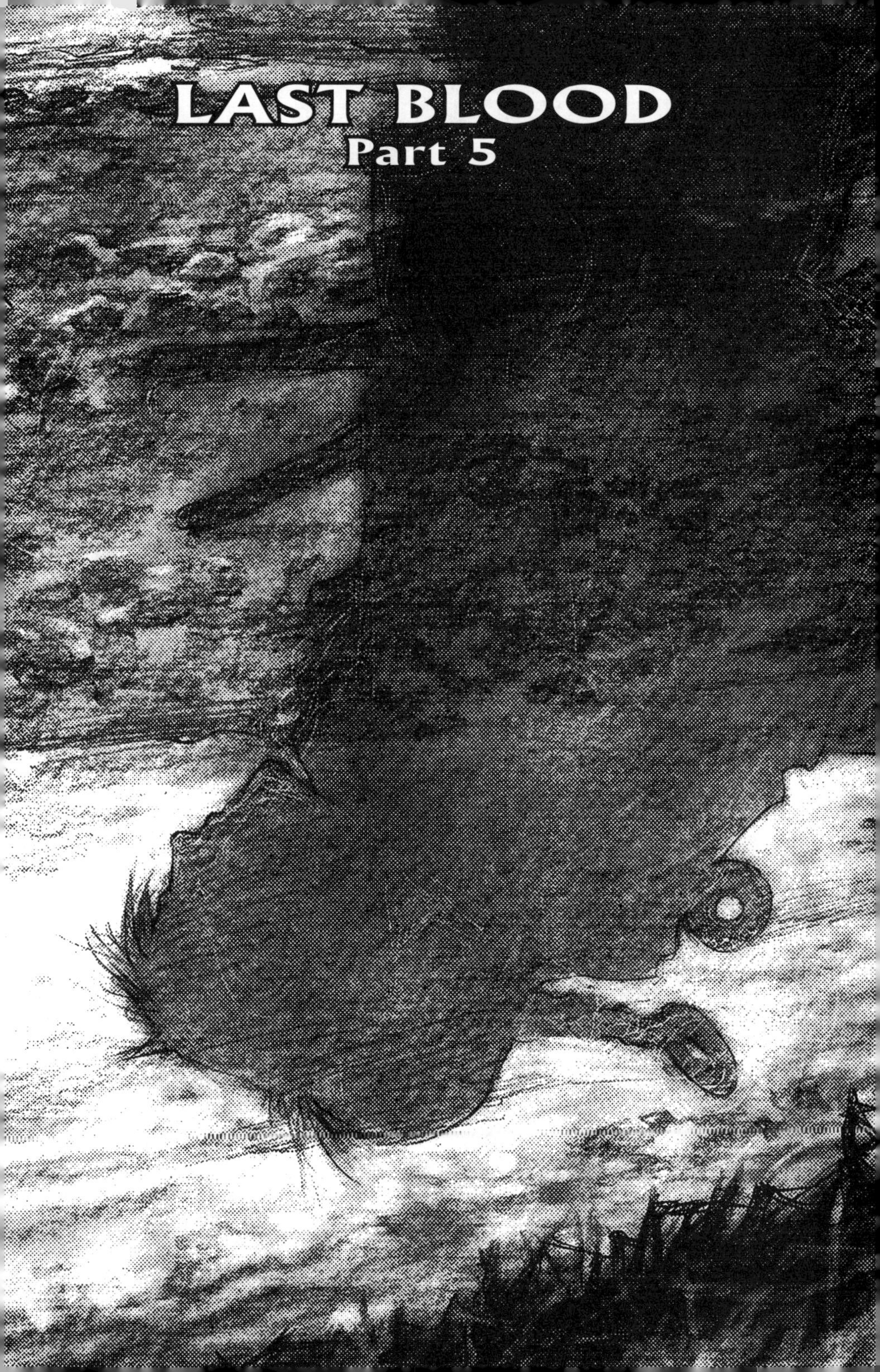

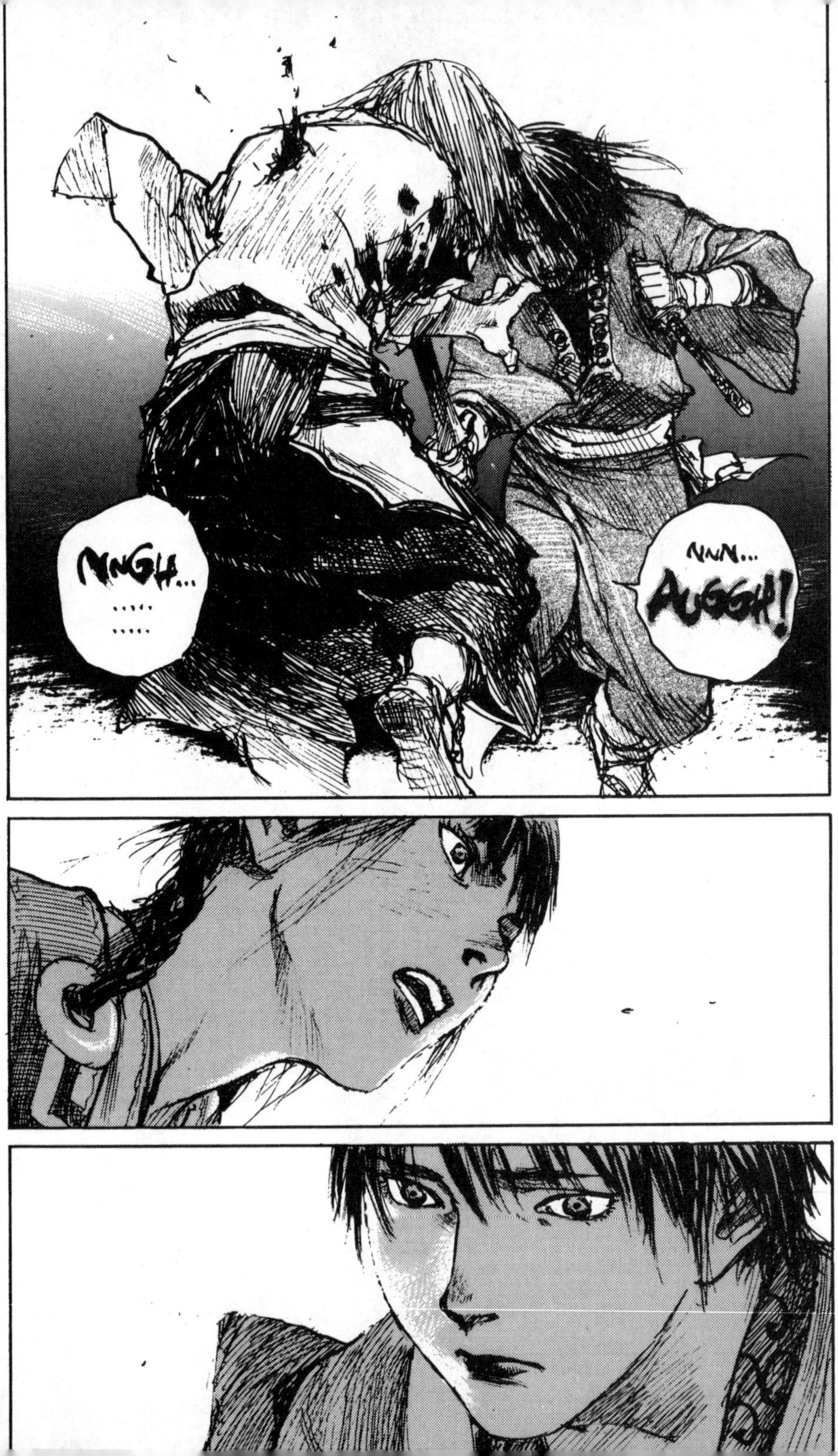
NNN... AUGGH!
MNGH... ....

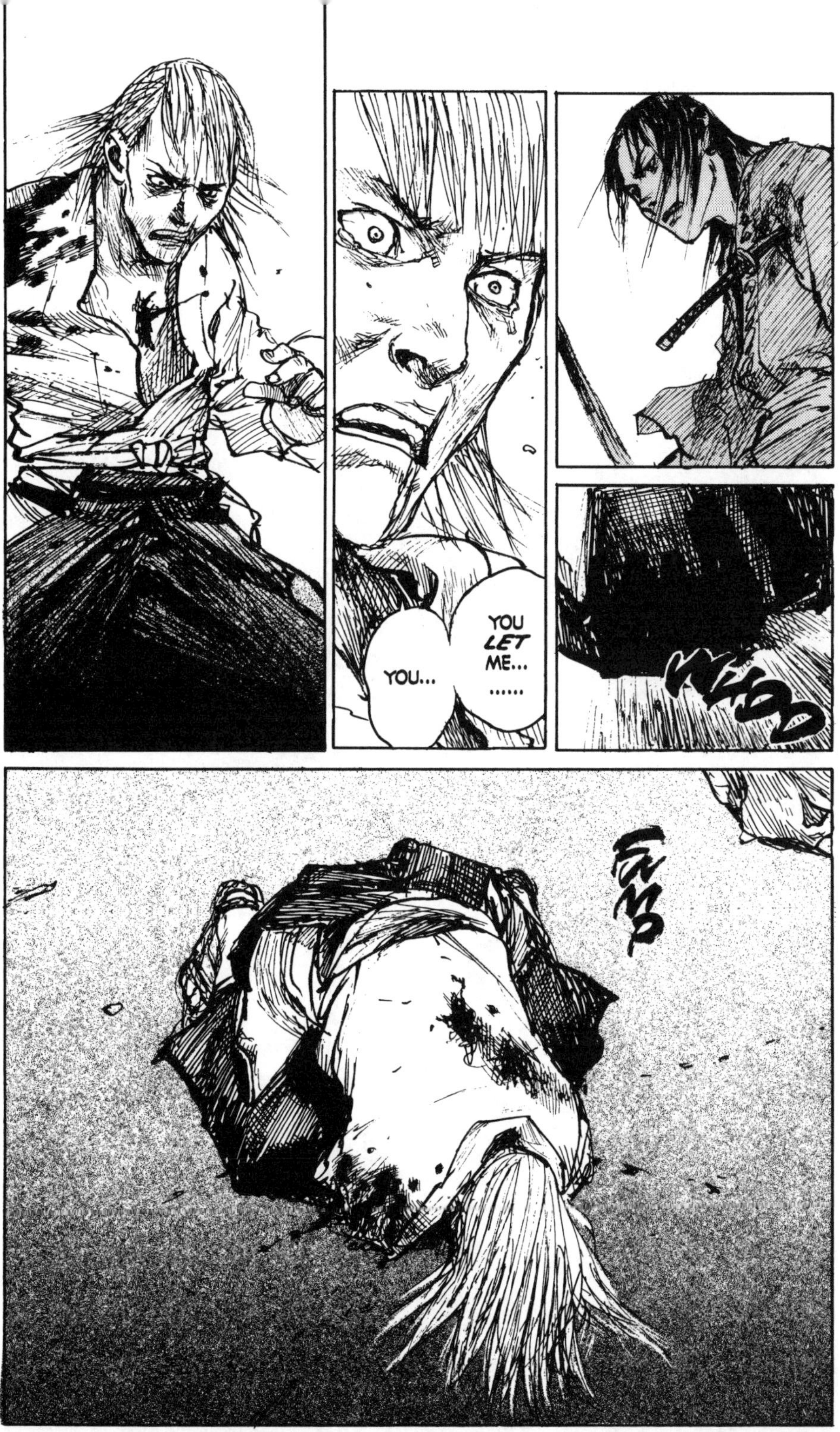
YOU LET ME... ......
YOU...
FUMP

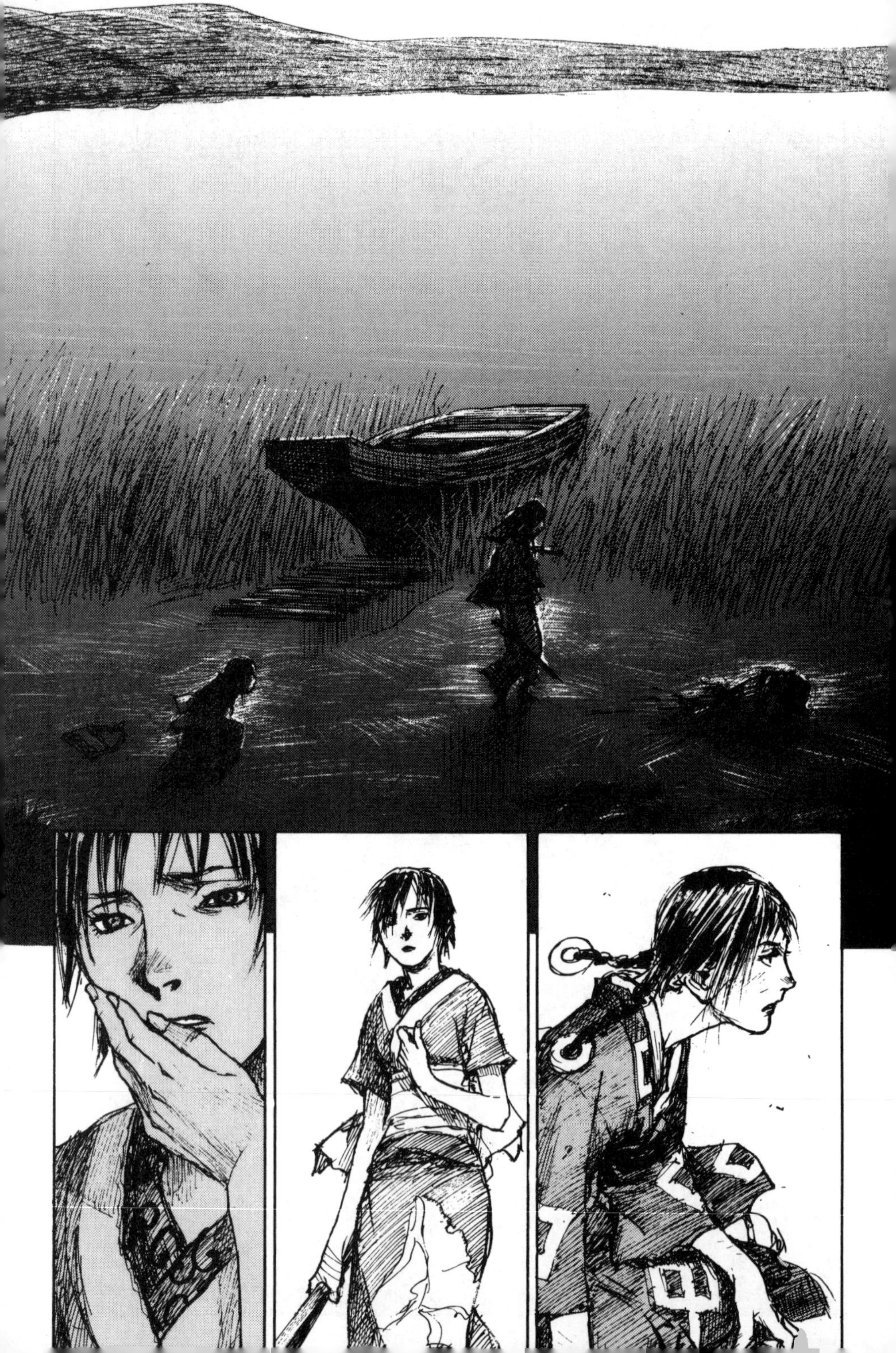

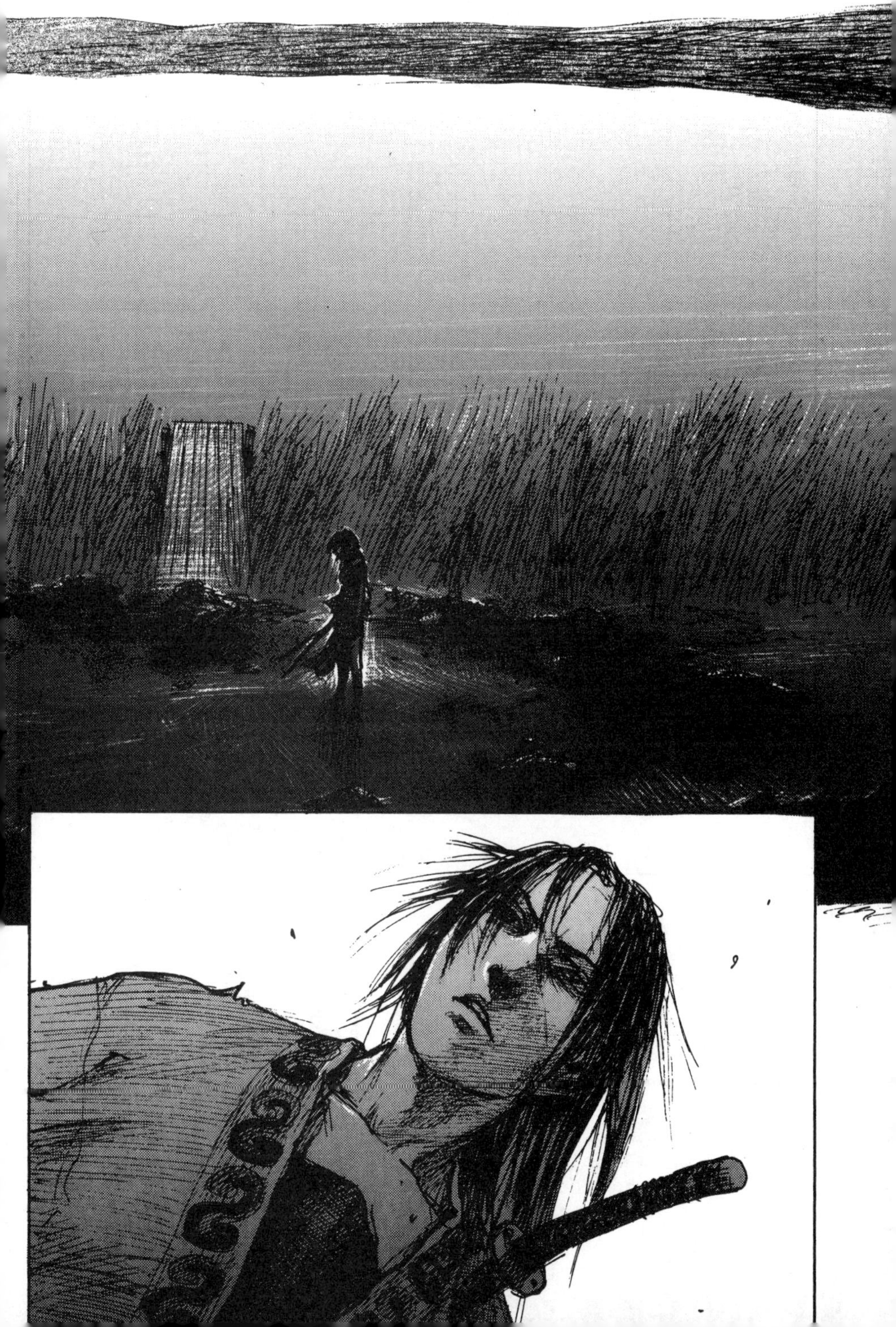

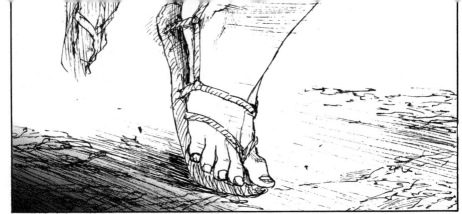

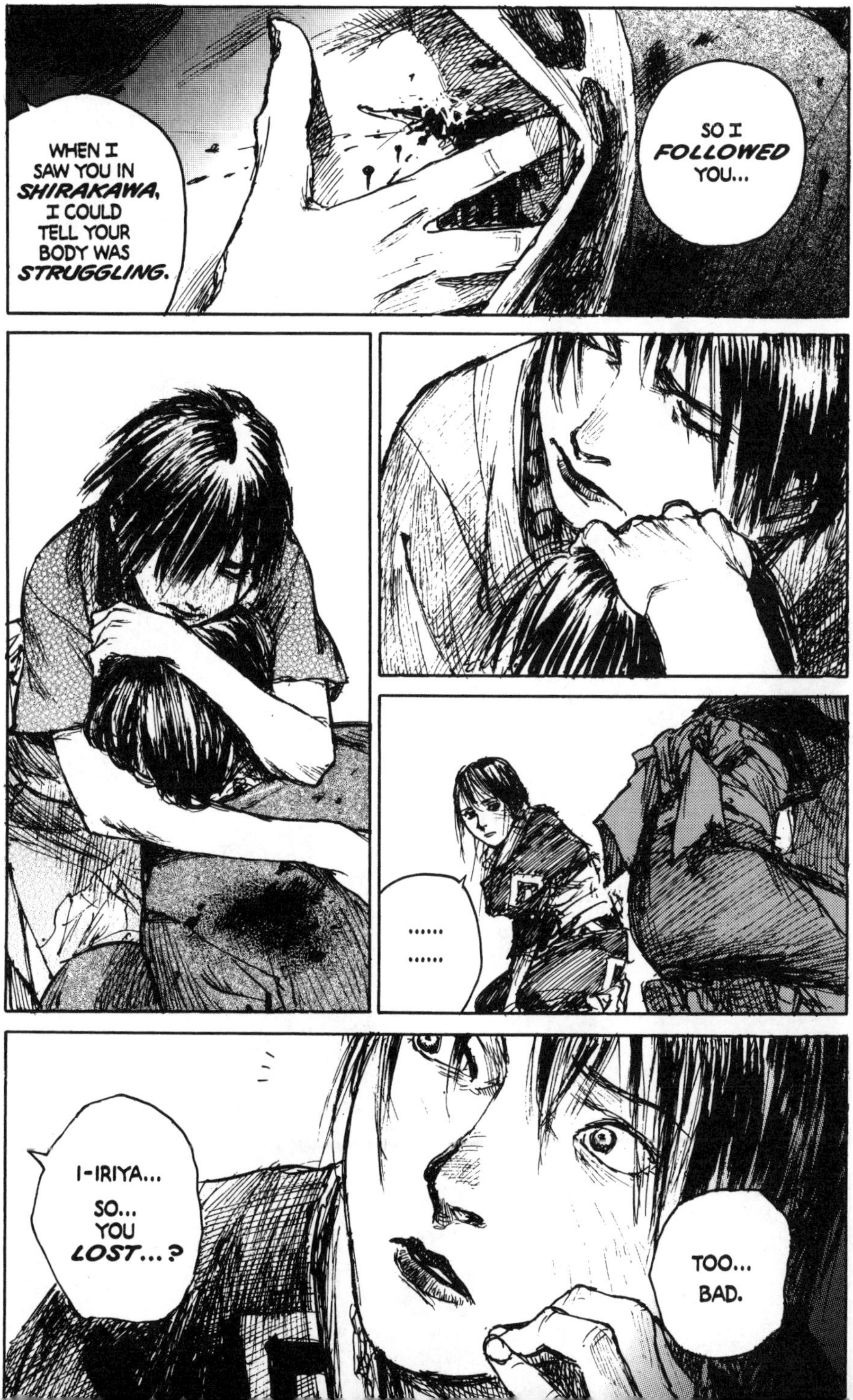
WHEN I SAW YOU IN SHIRAKAWA, I COULD TELL YOUR BODY WAS STRUGGLING.
SO I FOLLOWED YOU...
......
......
I-IRIYA...
SO... YOU LOST...?
TOO... BAD.

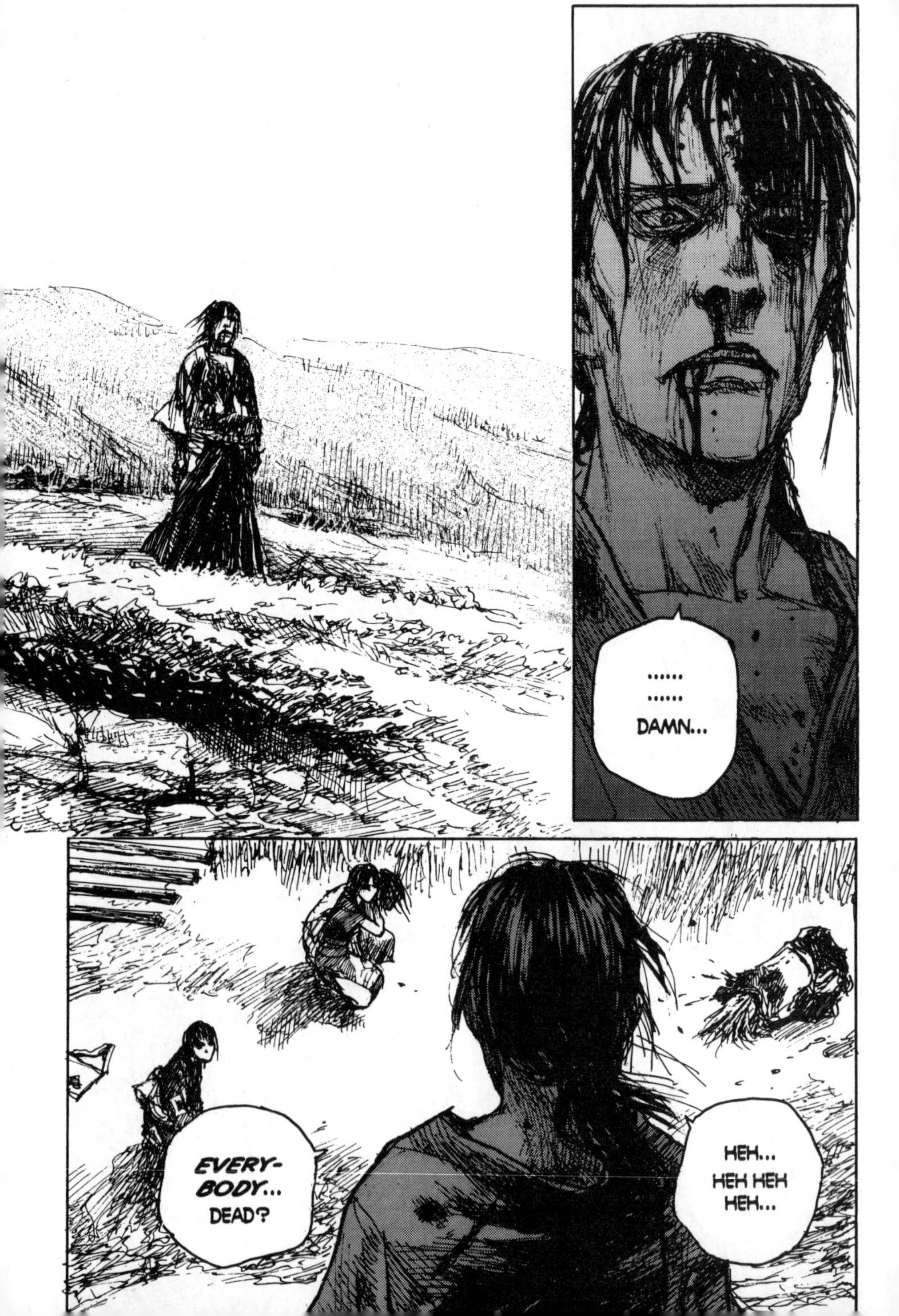
......
......
DAMN...
HEH...
HEH HEH
HEH...
EVERY-
BODY...
DEAD?

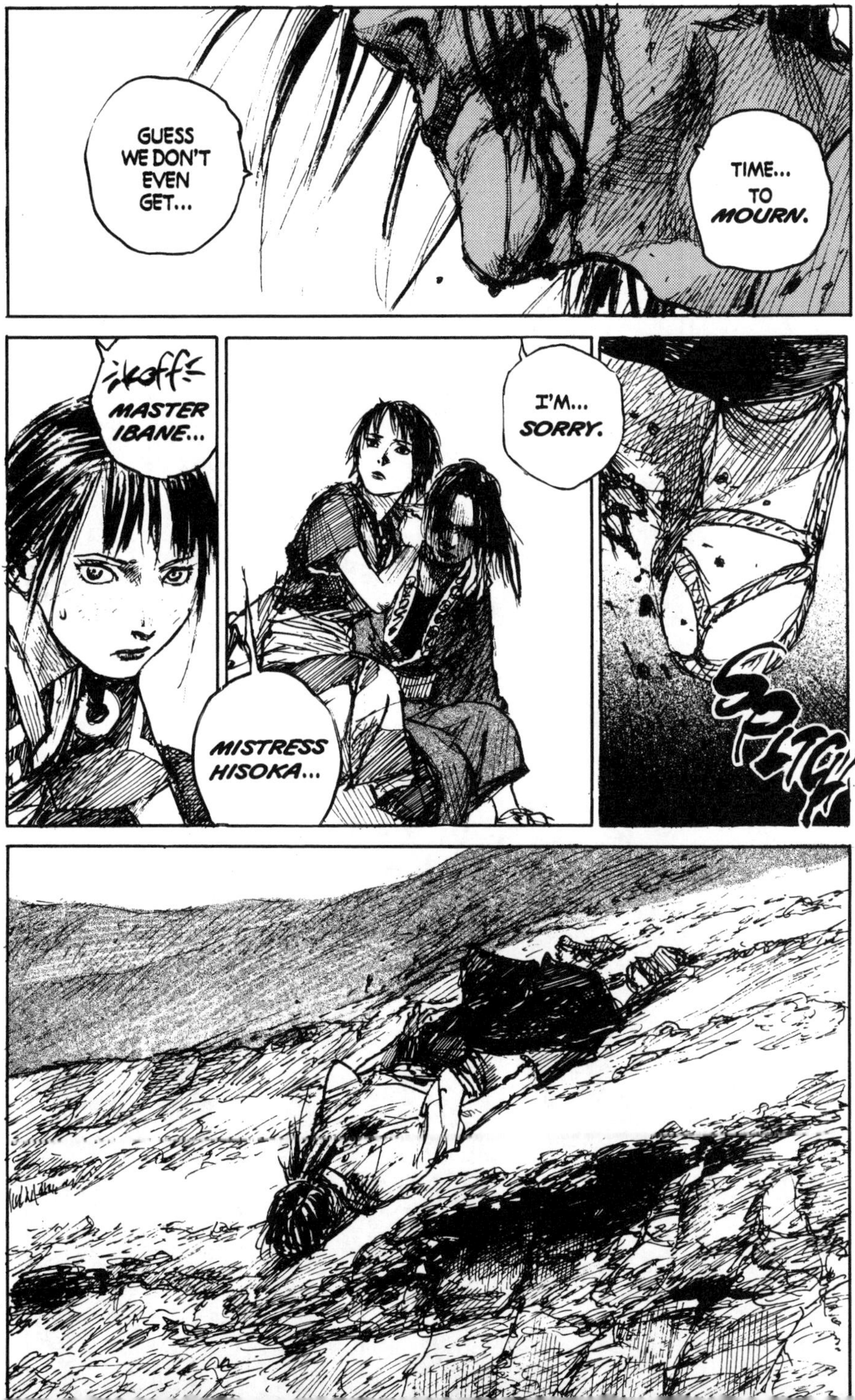
GUESS WE DON'T EVEN GET...
TIME... TO MOURN.
koff
MASTER IBANE...
I'M... SORRY.
MISTRESS HISOKA...
SPLTCH

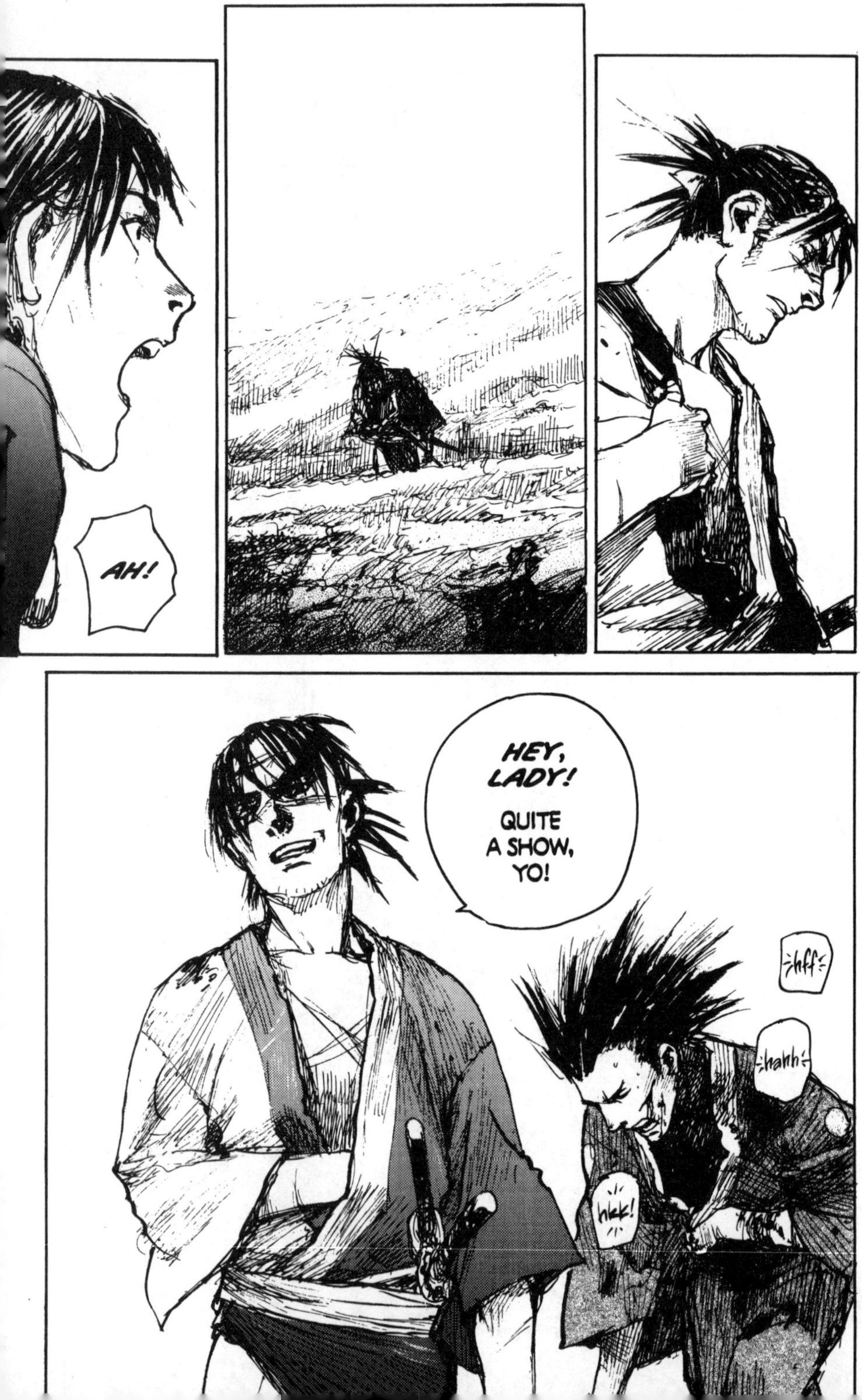
AH!
HEY, LADY! QUITE A SHOW, YO!
hff
hahh
hkk!

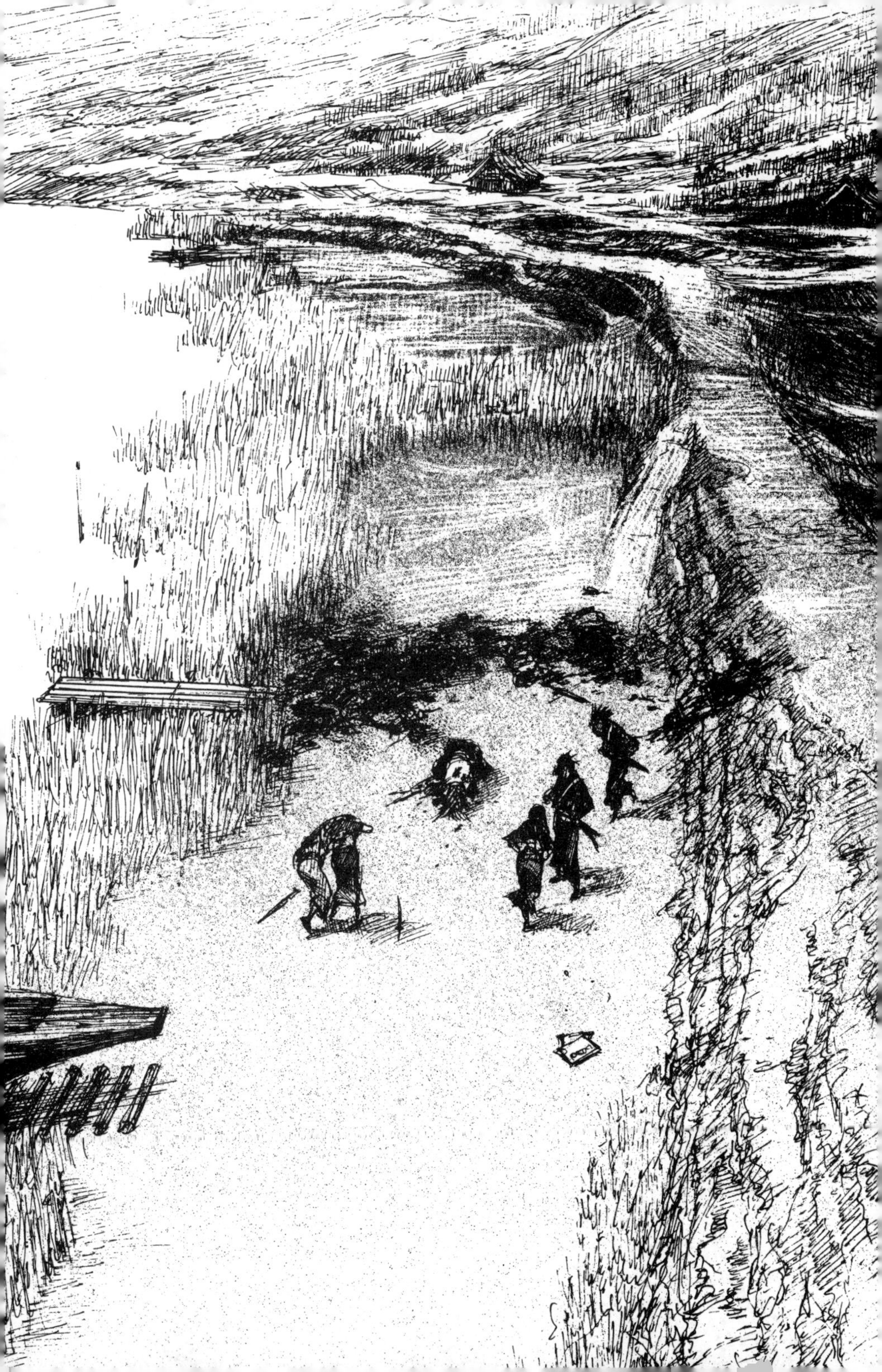

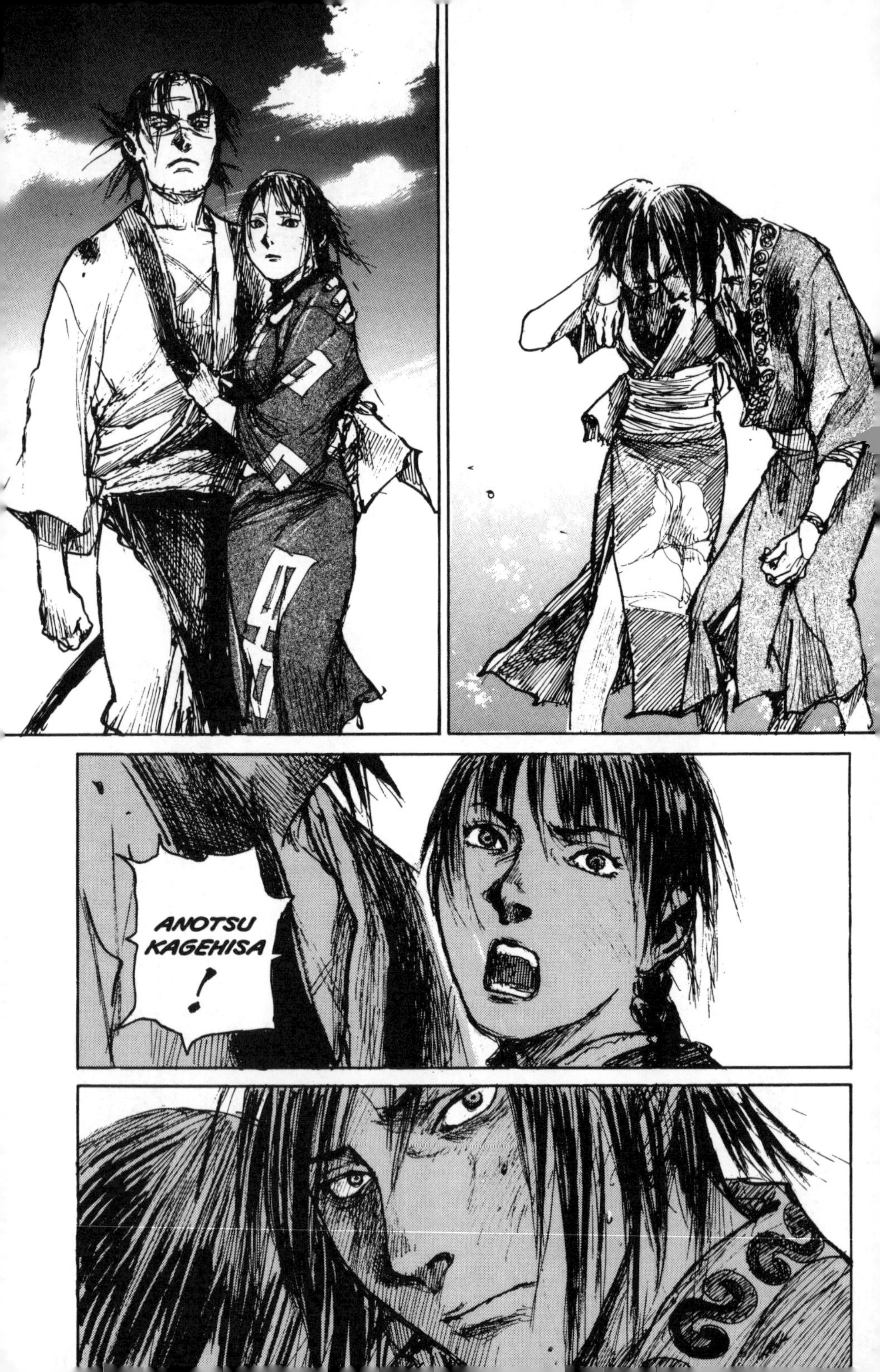
ANOTSU KAGEHISA!

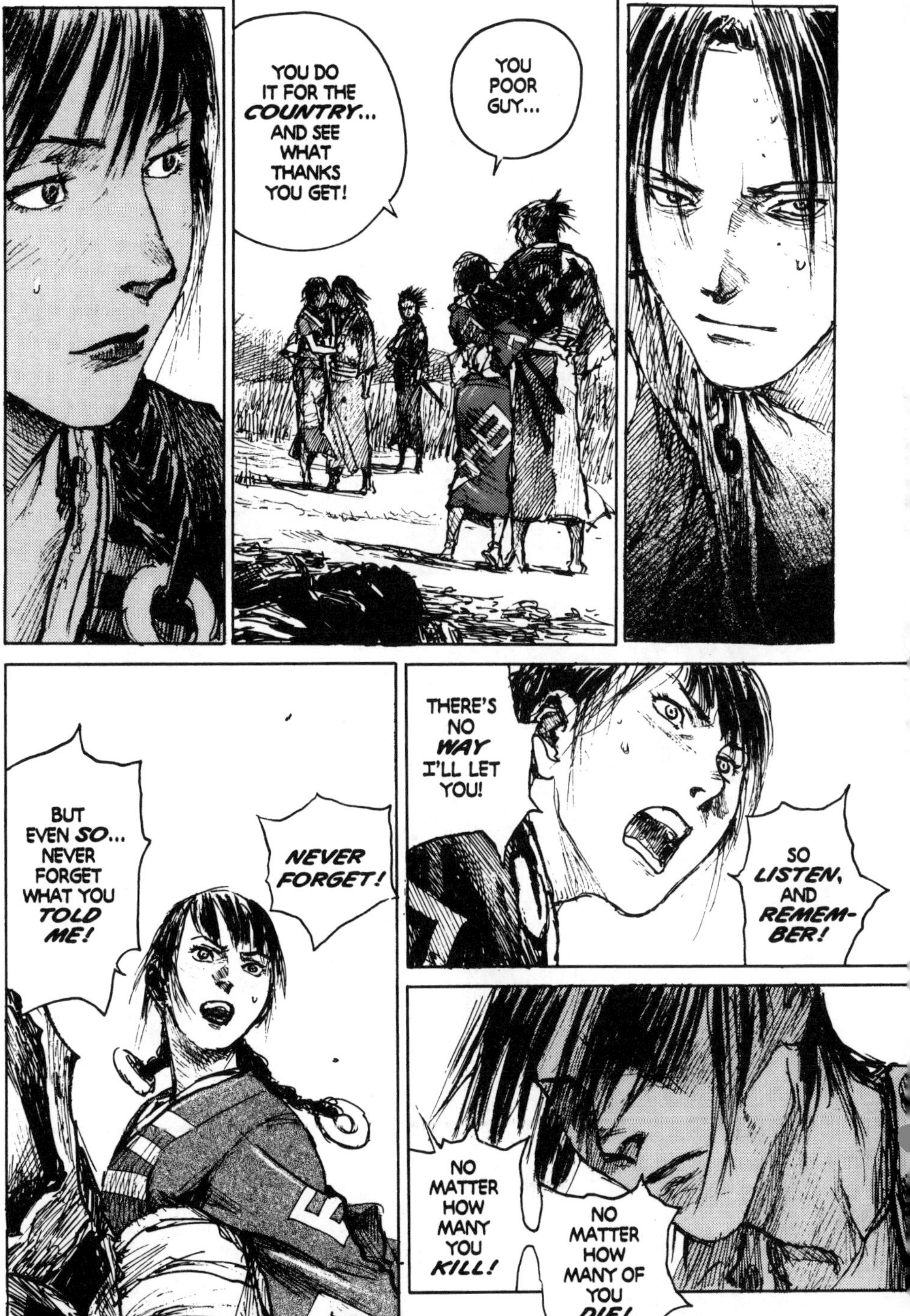
YOU DO IT FOR THE COUNTRY... AND SEE WHAT THANKS YOU GET!
YOU POOR GUY...
BUT EVEN SO... NEVER FORGET WHAT YOU TOLD ME!
NEVER FORGET!
THERE'S NO WAY I'LL LET YOU!
SO LISTEN, AND REMEMBER!
NO MATTER HOW MANY YOU KILL!
NO MATTER HOW MANY OF YOU DIE!

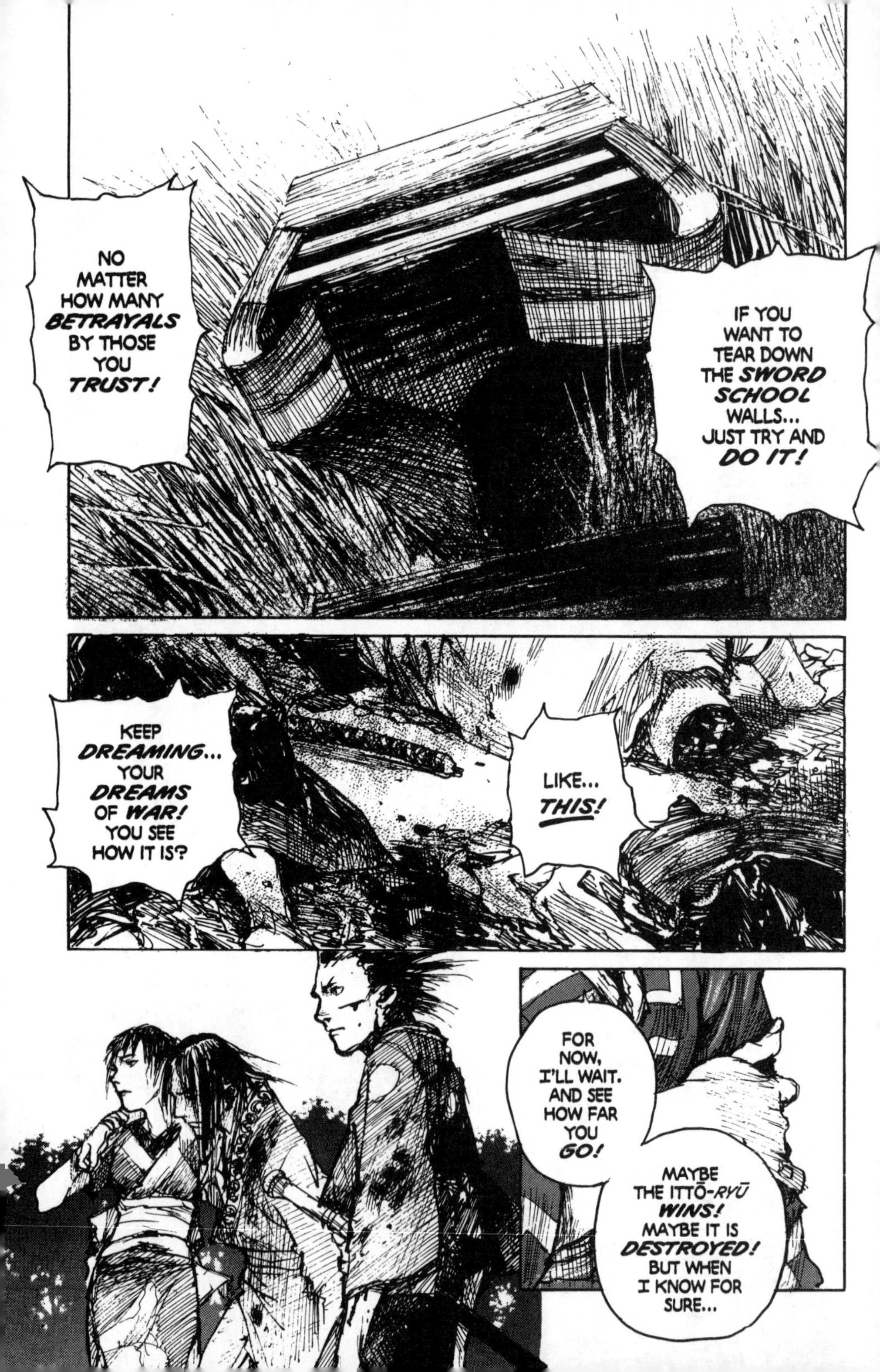
IF YOU WANT TO TEAR DOWN THE SWORD SCHOOL WALLS... JUST TRY AND DO IT!
NO MATTER HOW MANY BETRAYALS BY THOSE YOU TRUST!
LIKE... THIS!
KEEP DREAMING... YOUR DREAMS OF WAR! YOU SEE HOW IT IS?
FOR NOW, I'LL WAIT. AND SEE HOW FAR YOU GO!
MAYBE THE ITTŌ-RYŪ WINS! MAYBE IT IS DESTROYED! BUT WHEN I KNOW FOR SURE...

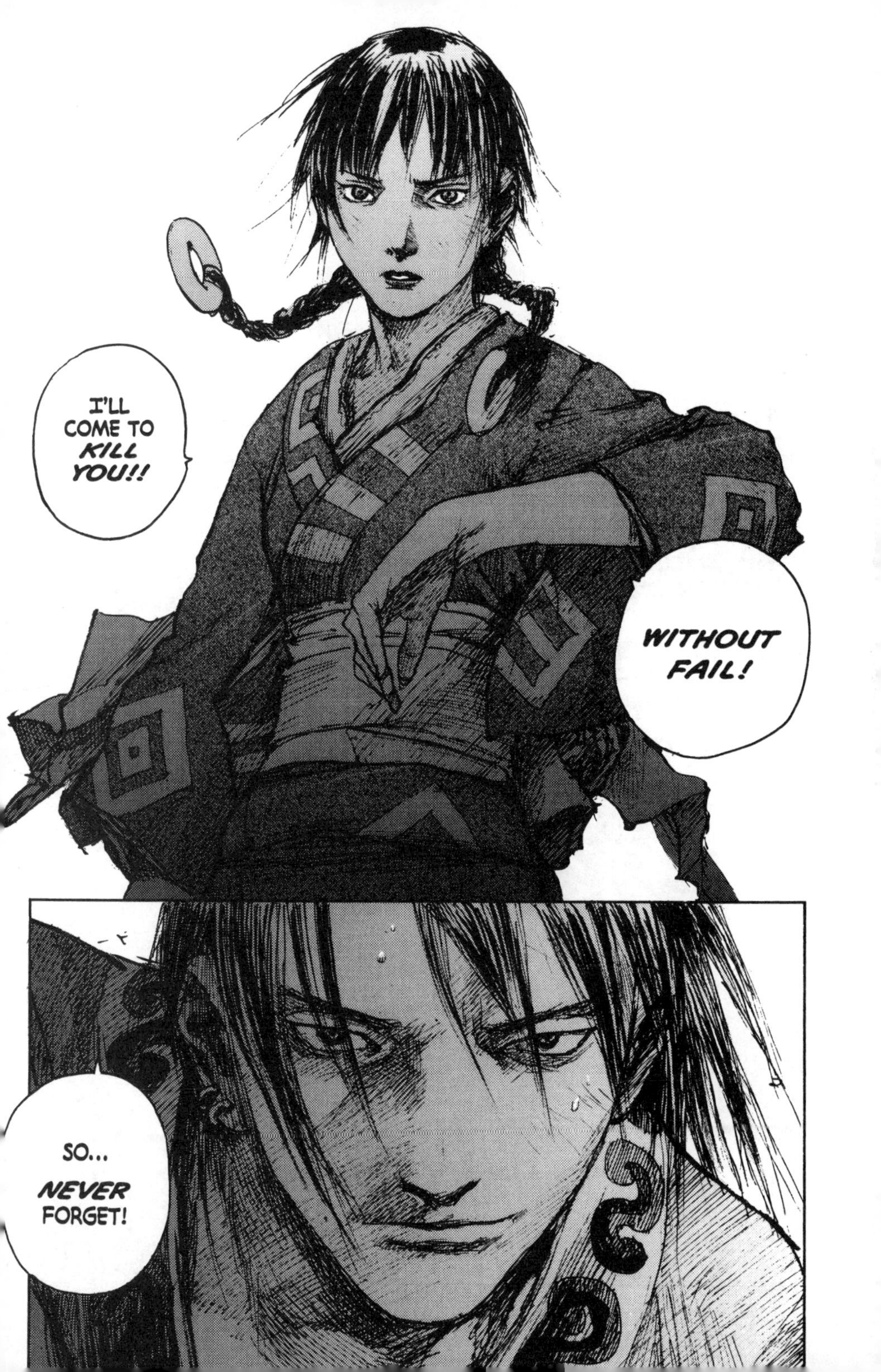
I'LL COME TO KILL YOU!!
WITHOUT FAIL!
SO... NEVER FORGET!

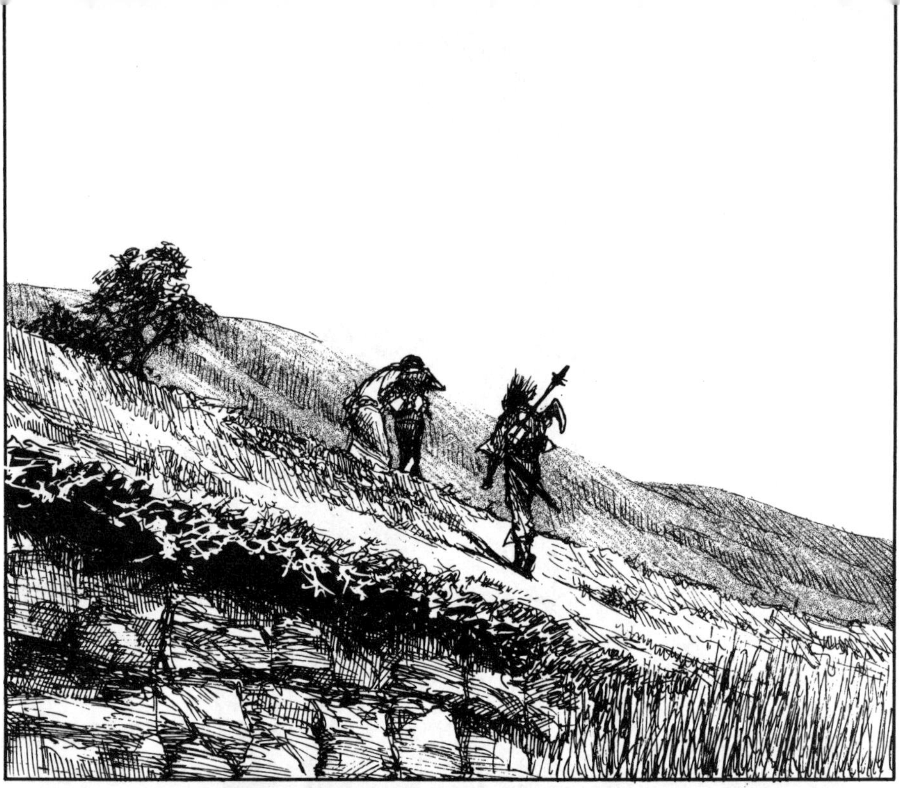
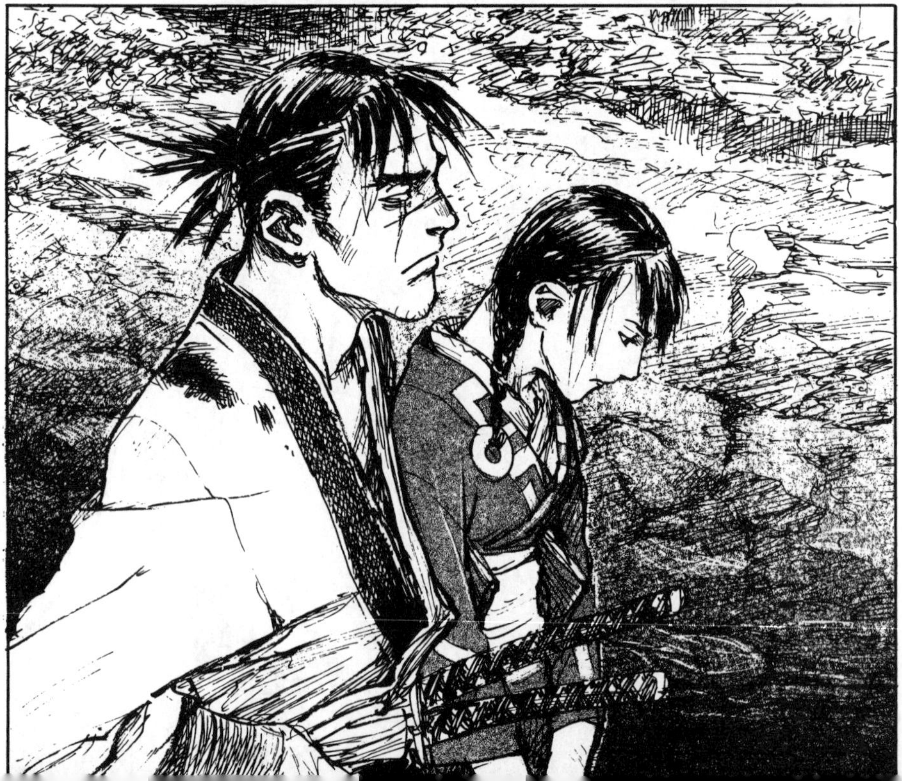

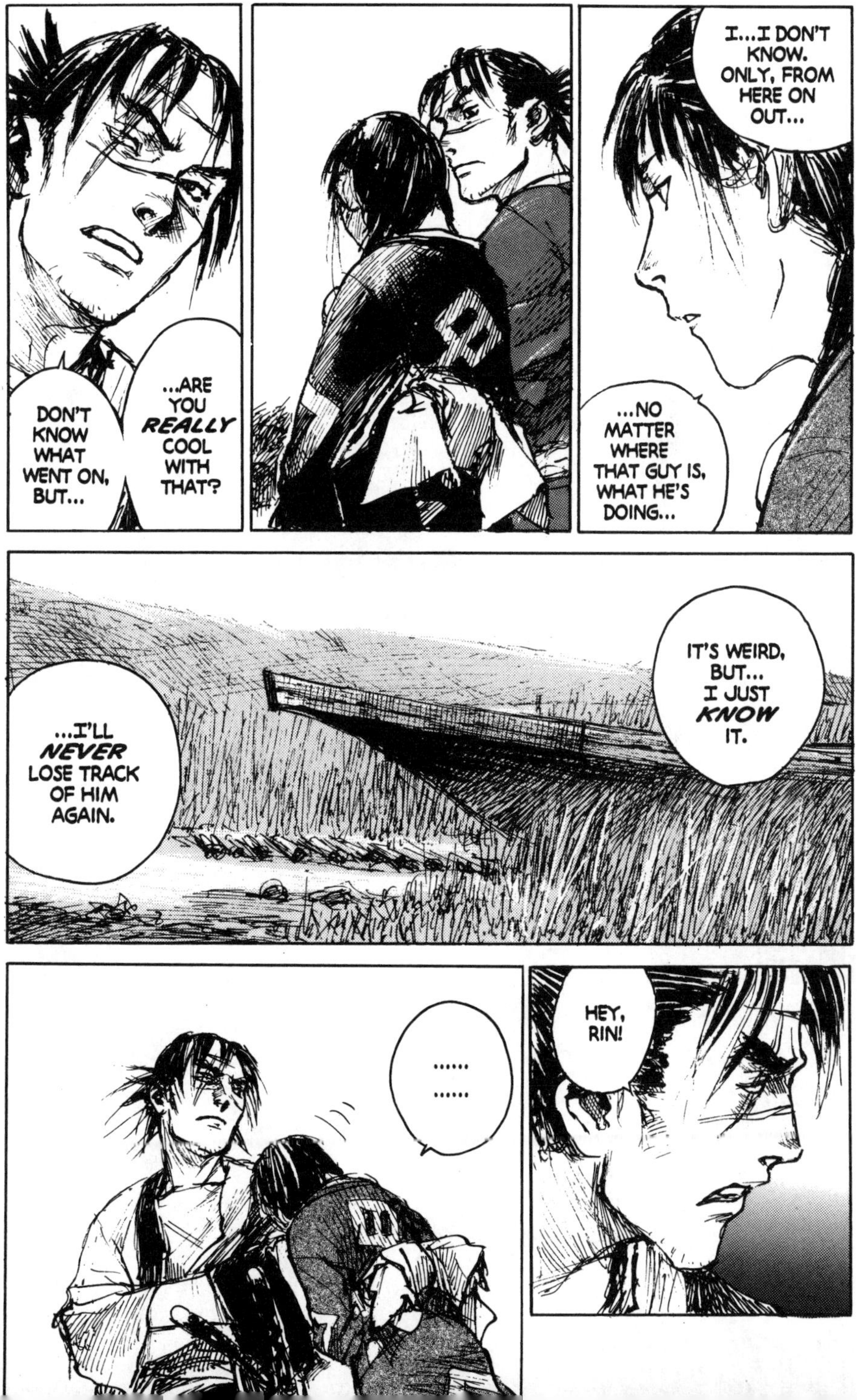
DON'T KNOW WHAT WENT ON, BUT...
...ARE YOU *REALLY* COOL WITH THAT?
I...I DON'T KNOW. ONLY, FROM HERE ON OUT...
...NO MATTER WHERE THAT GUY IS, WHAT HE'S DOING...
...I'LL *NEVER* LOSE TRACK OF HIM AGAIN.
IT'S WEIRD, BUT... I JUST *KNOW* IT.
....
HEY, RIN!

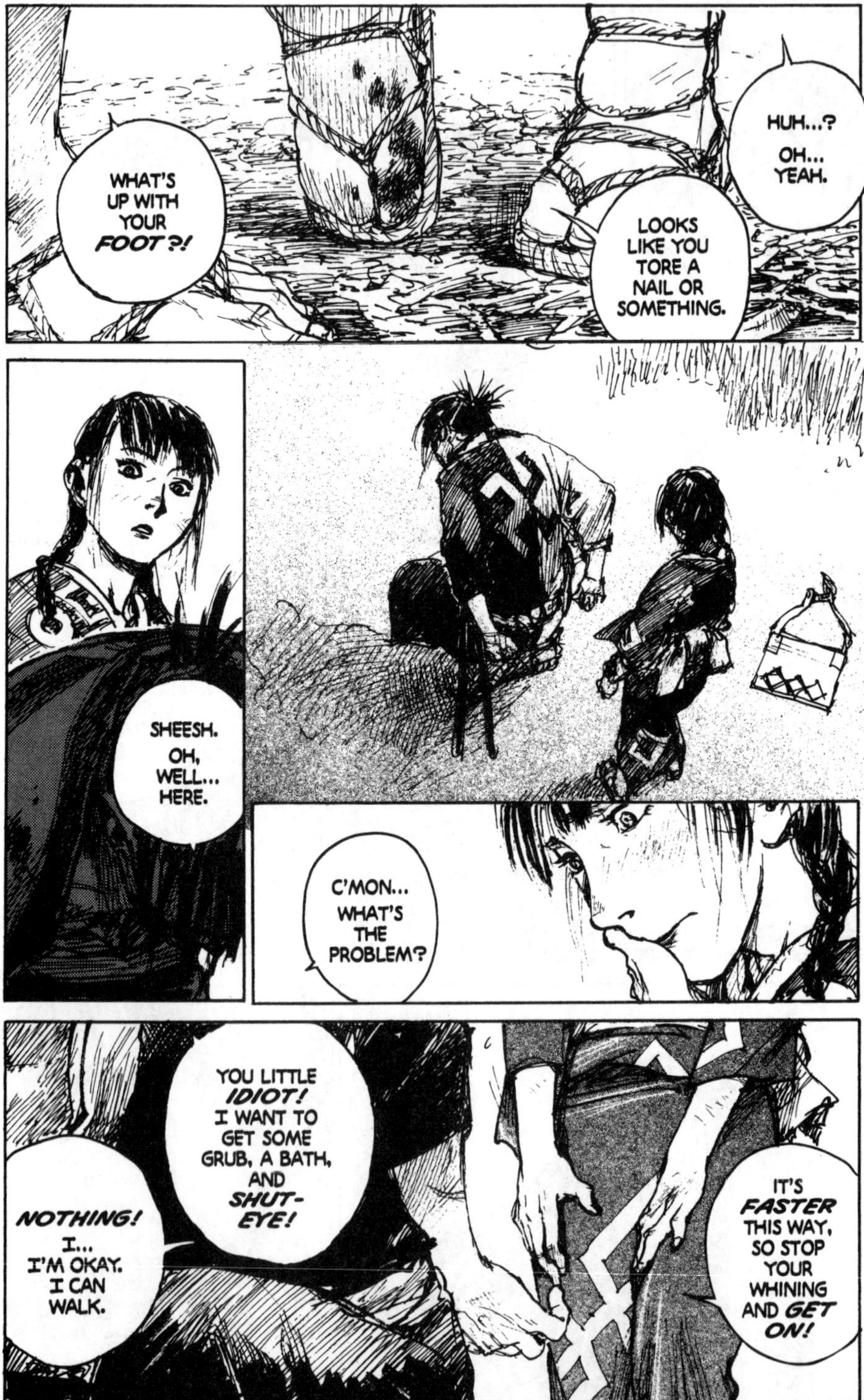
WHAT'S UP WITH YOUR *FOOT*?!
HUH...? OH... YEAH.
LOOKS LIKE YOU TORE A NAIL OR SOMETHING.
SHEESH. OH, WELL... HERE.
C'MON... WHAT'S THE PROBLEM?
NOTHING! I... I'M OKAY. I CAN WALK.
YOU LITTLE *IDIOT!* I WANT TO GET SOME GRUB, A BATH, AND *SHUT-EYE!*
IT'S *FASTER* THIS WAY, SO STOP YOUR WHINING AND *GET ON!*

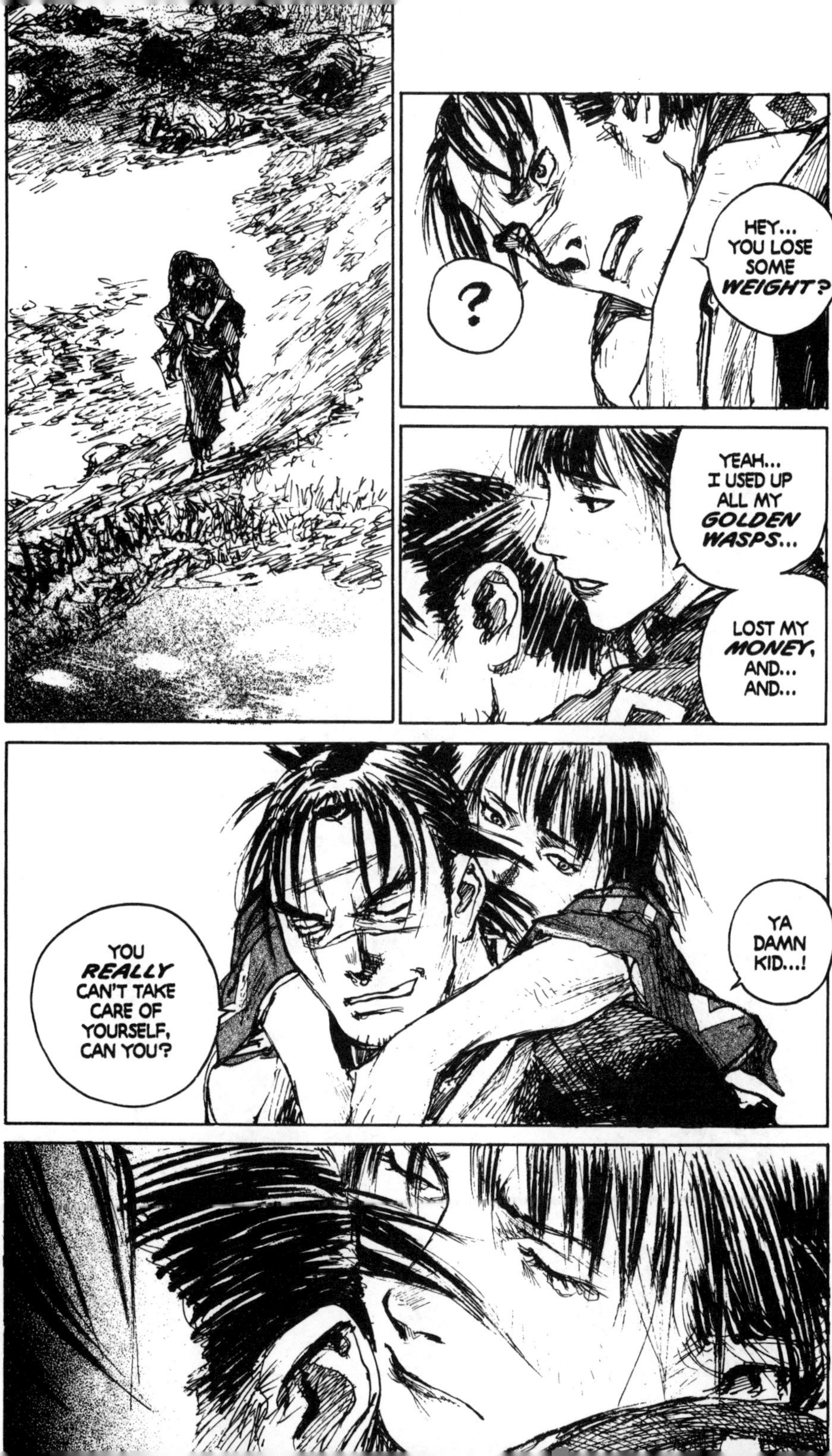
HEY... YOU LOSE SOME WEIGHT?
?
YEAH... I USED UP ALL MY GOLDEN WASPS...
LOST MY MONEY, AND... AND...
YA DAMN KID...!
YOU REALLY CAN'T TAKE CARE OF YOURSELF, CAN YOU?

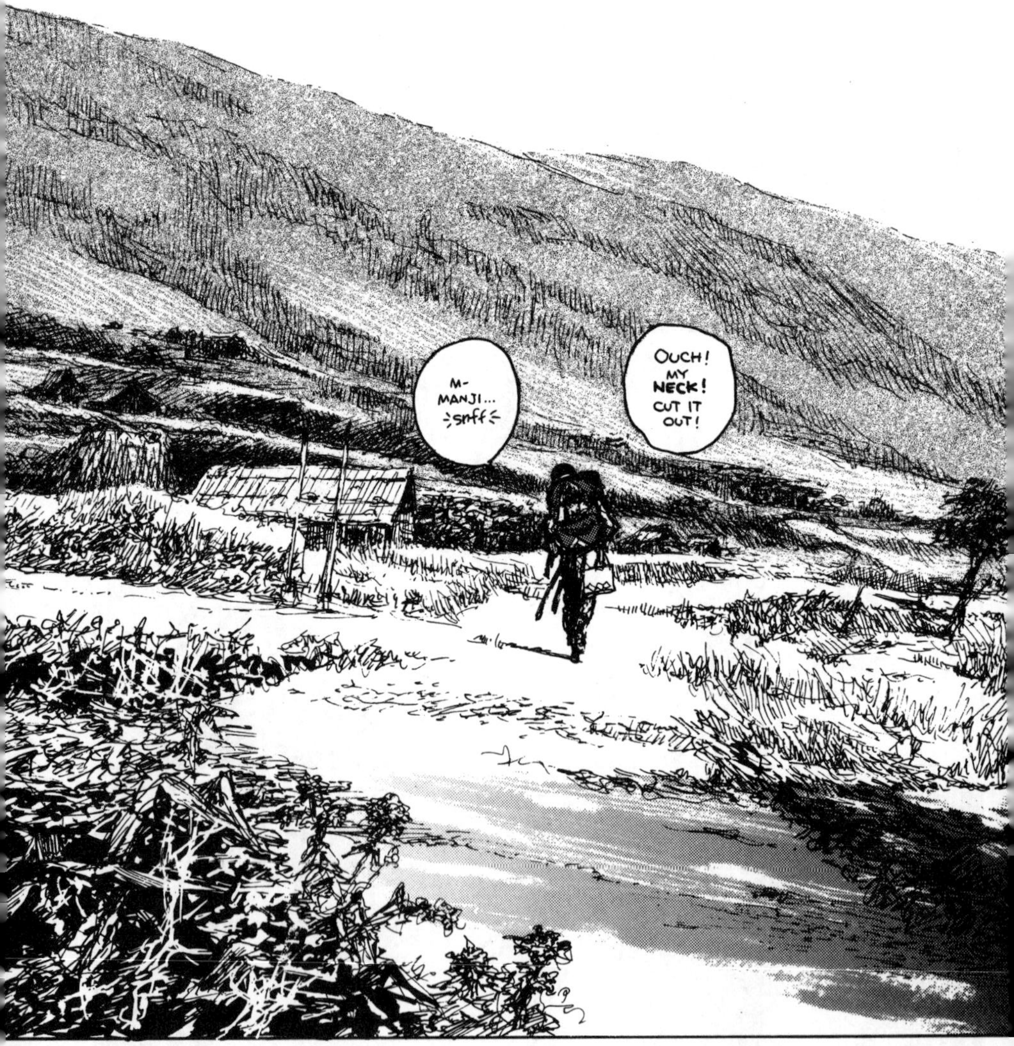
OUCH! MY NECK! CUT IT OUT!
M-MANJI... snff

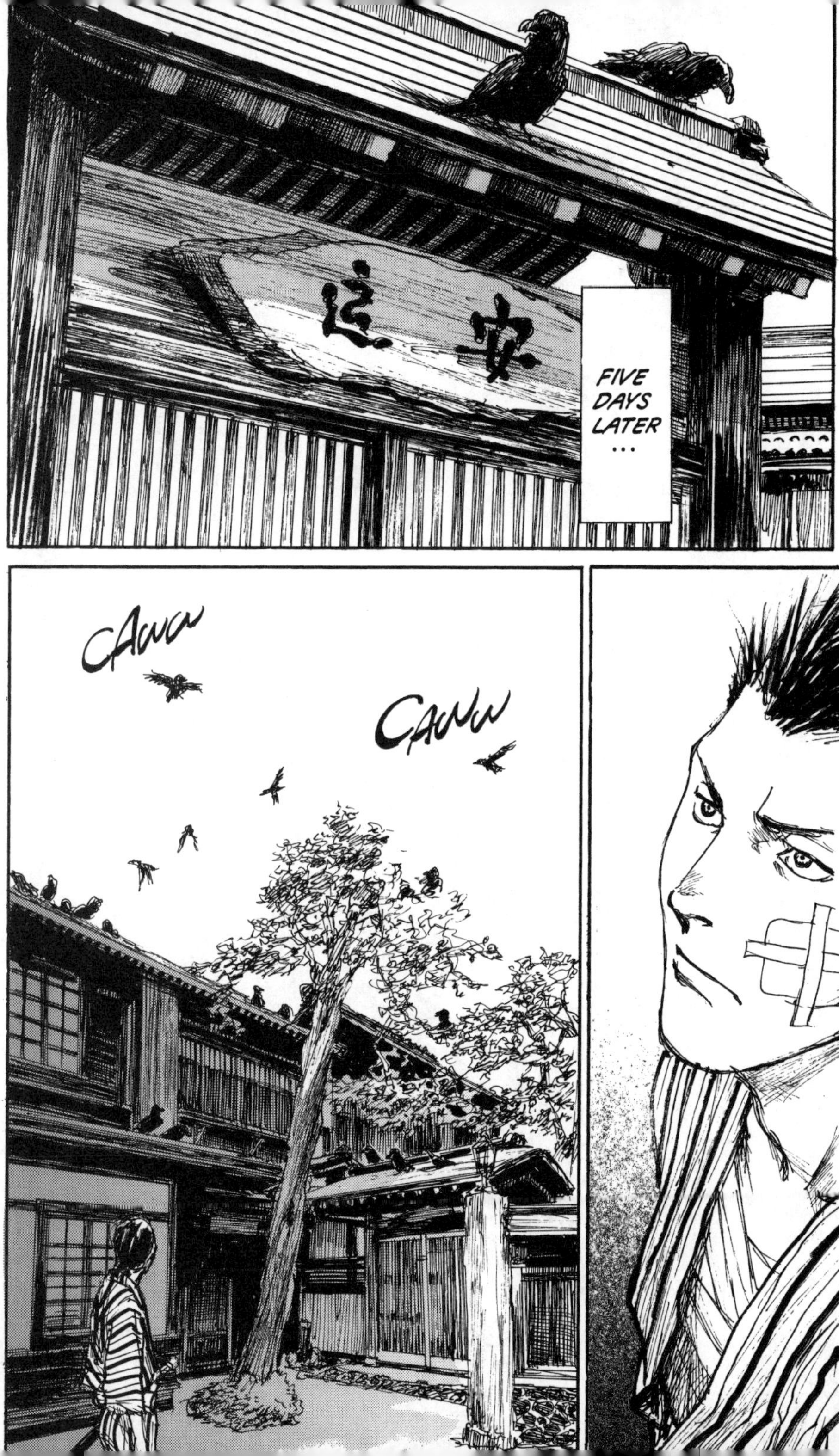
FIVE DAYS LATER ...
CAWW
CAWW

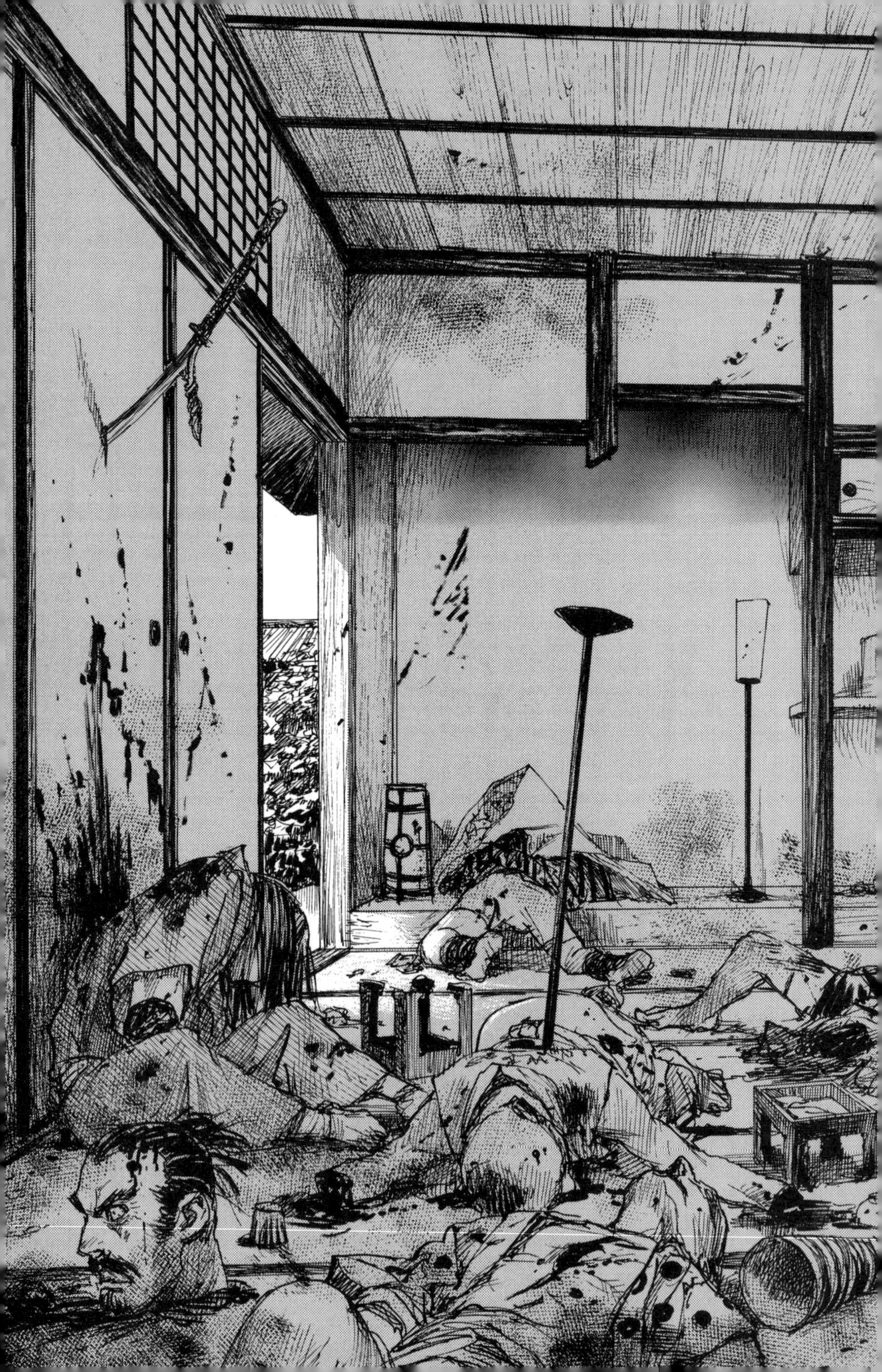

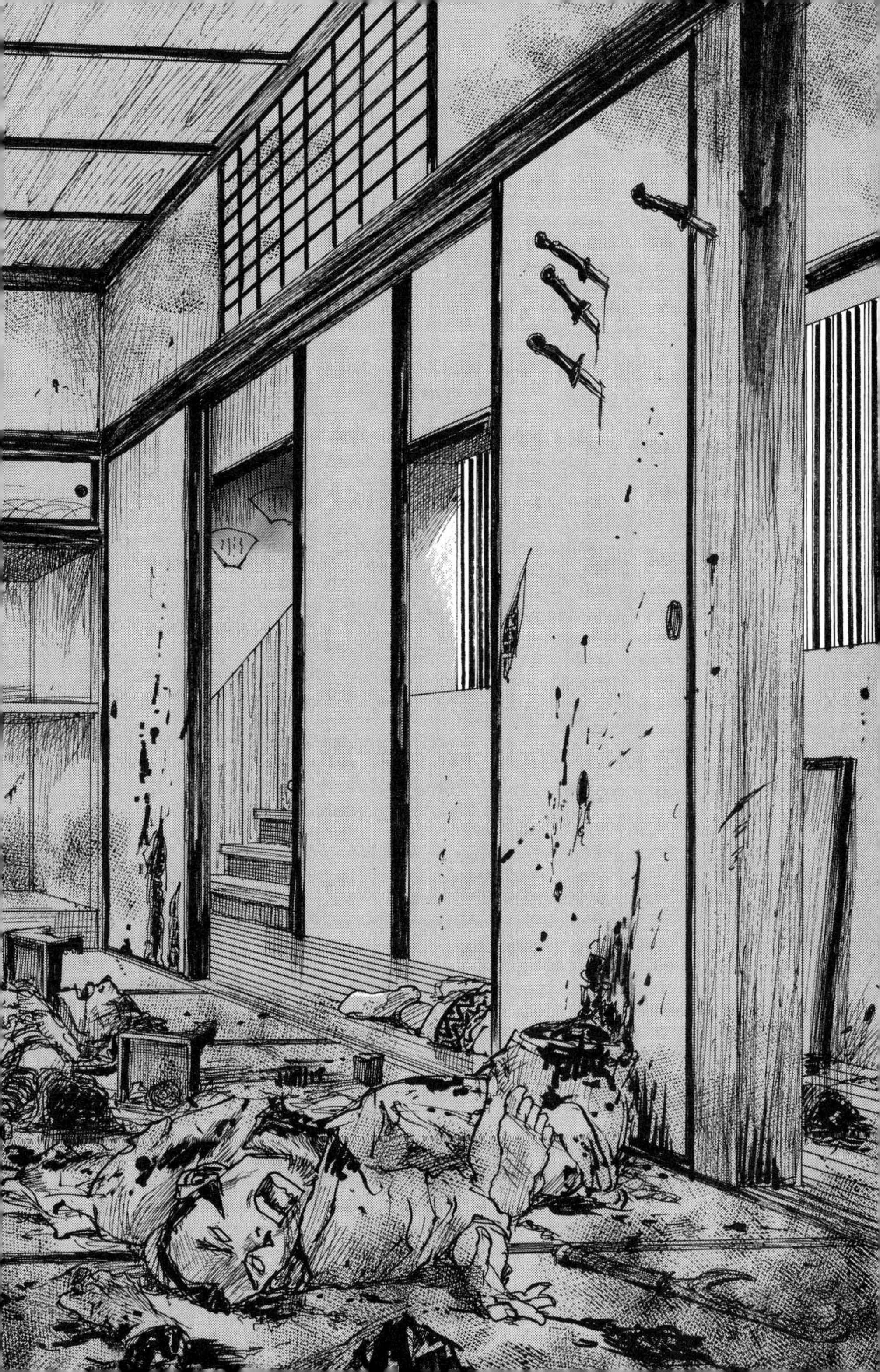

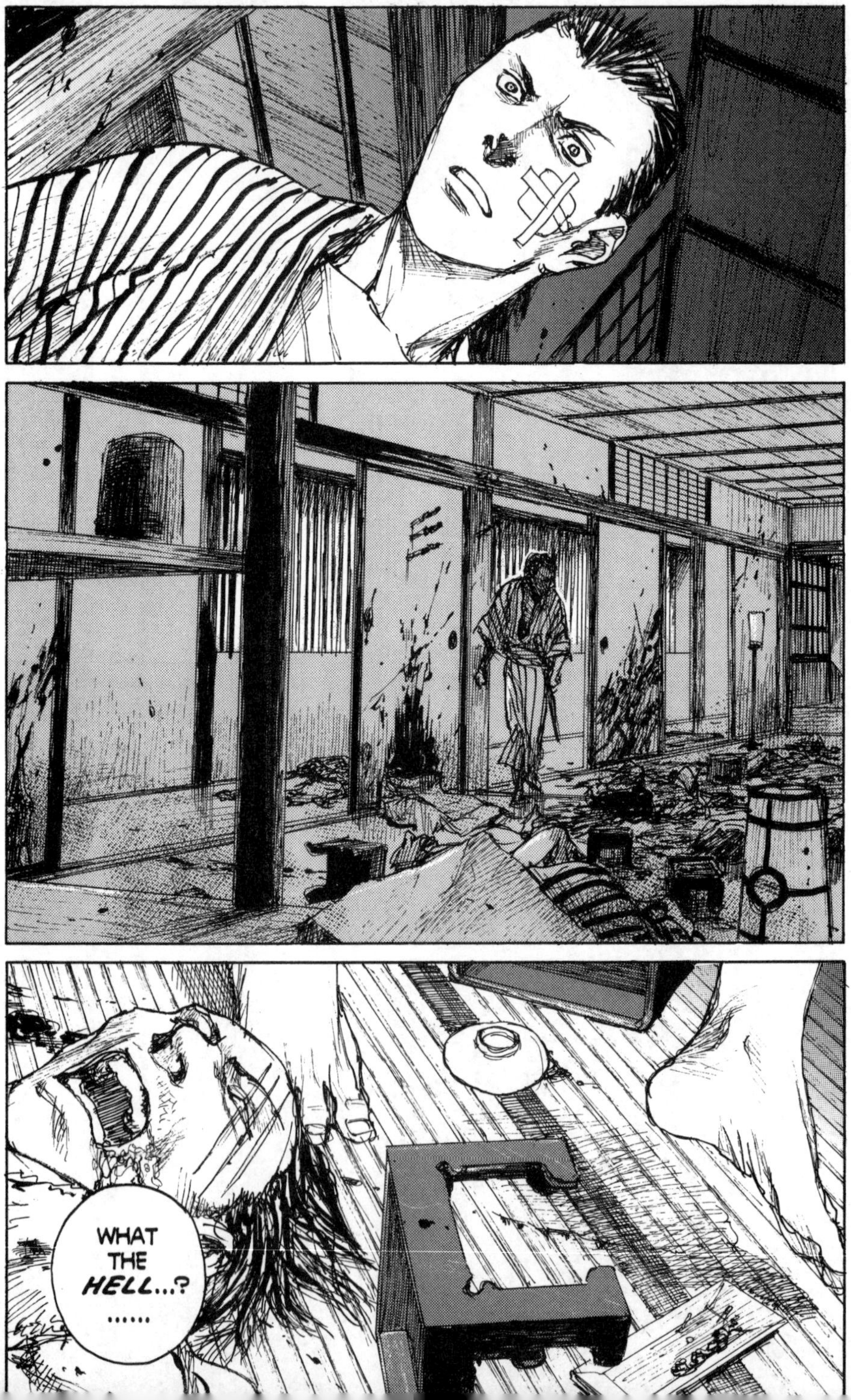
WHAT THE HELL...? ......

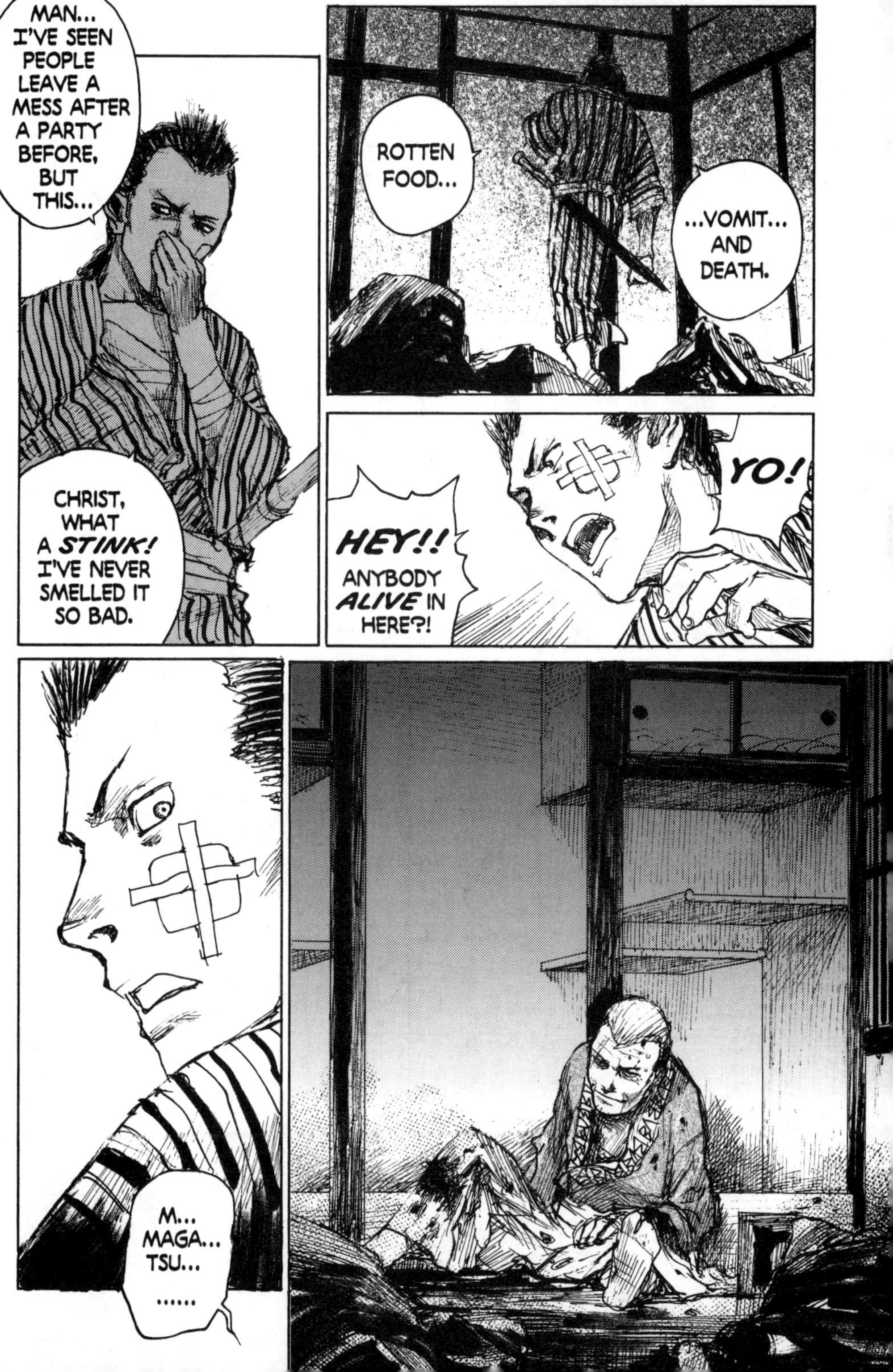
ROTTEN FOOD...
...VOMIT... AND DEATH.
YO!
HEY!! ANYBODY ALIVE IN HERE?!
MAN... I'VE SEEN PEOPLE LEAVE A MESS AFTER A PARTY BEFORE, BUT THIS...
CHRIST, WHAT A STINK! I'VE NEVER SMELLED IT SO BAD.
M... MAGA... TSU...
......

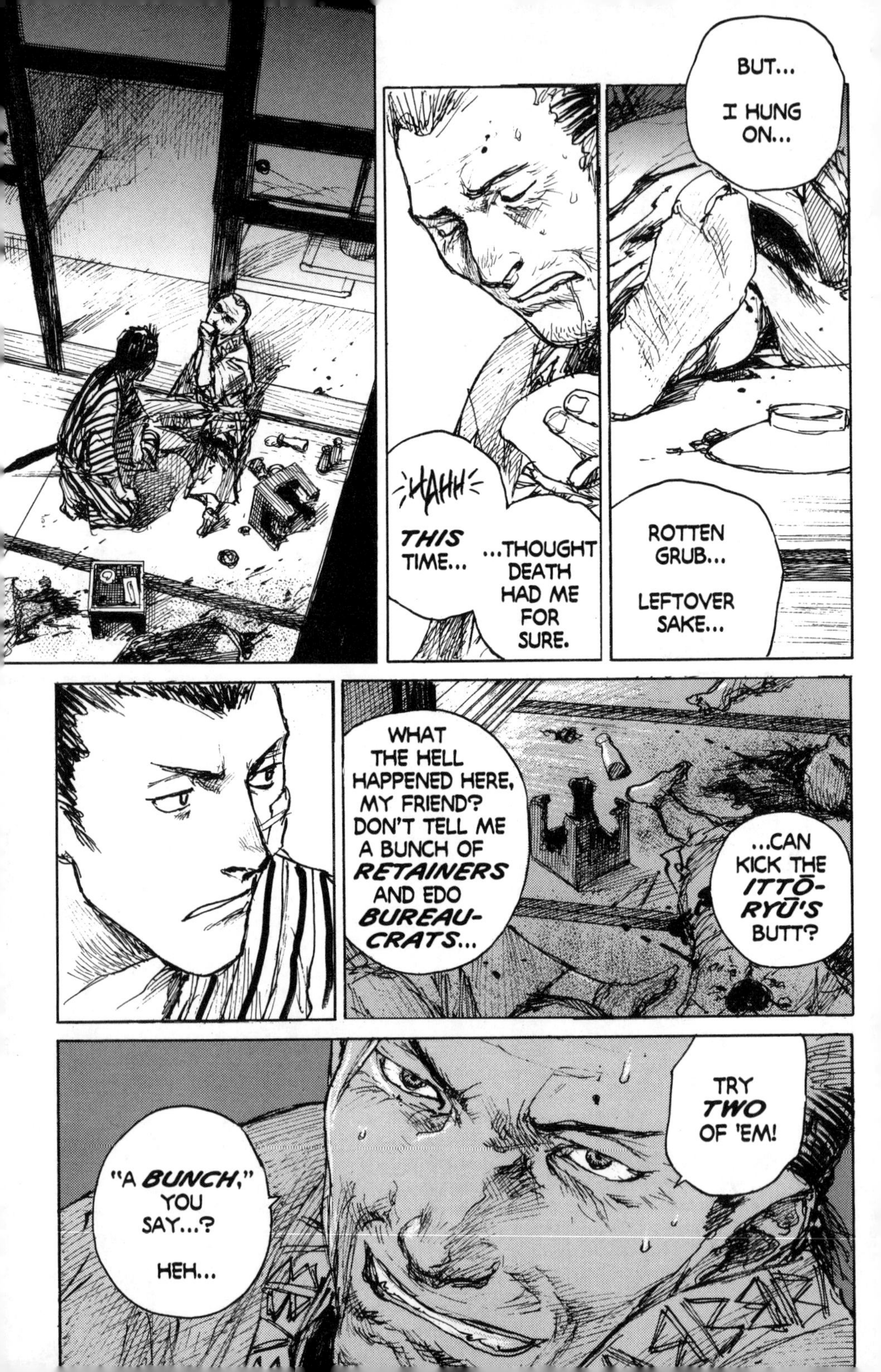
HAHH
THIS TIME...
...THOUGHT DEATH HAD ME FOR SURE.
BUT... I HUNG ON...
ROTTEN GRUB... LEFTOVER SAKE...
WHAT THE HELL HAPPENED HERE, MY FRIEND? DON'T TELL ME A BUNCH OF *RETAINERS* AND EDO *BUREAUCRATS*...
...CAN KICK THE *ITTŌ-RYŪ'S* BUTT?
"A *BUNCH*," YOU SAY...? HEH...
TRY *TWO* OF 'EM!

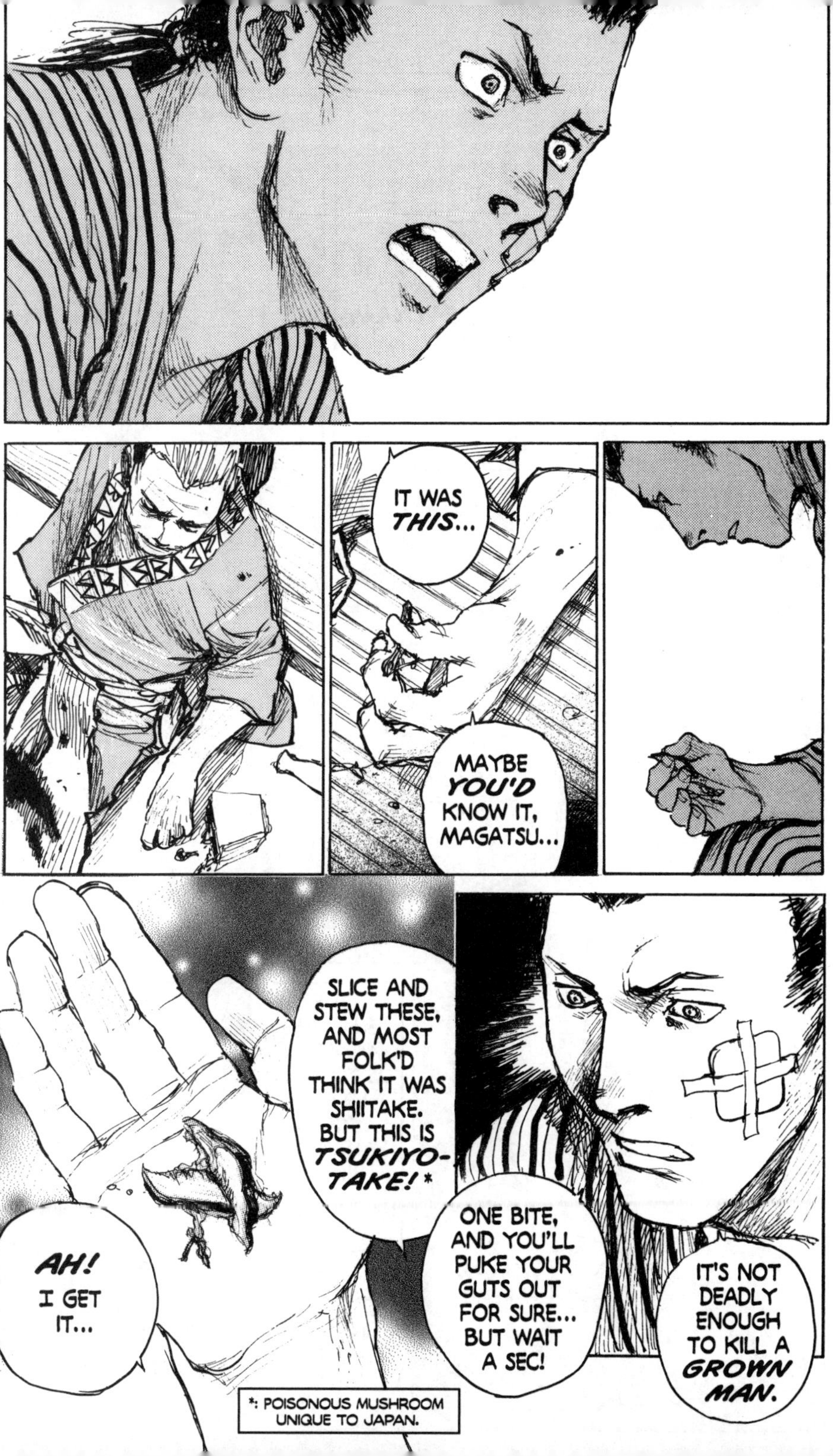

IT WAS *THIS*...
MAYBE *YOU'D* KNOW IT, MAGATSU...
SLICE AND STEW THESE, AND MOST FOLK'D THINK IT WAS SHIITAKE. BUT THIS IS *TSUKIYO-TAKE!* *
AH! I GET IT...
ONE BITE, AND YOU'LL PUKE YOUR GUTS OUT FOR SURE... BUT WAIT A SEC!
IT'S NOT DEADLY ENOUGH TO KILL A *GROWN MAN.*
*: POISONOUS MUSHROOM UNIQUE TO JAPAN.

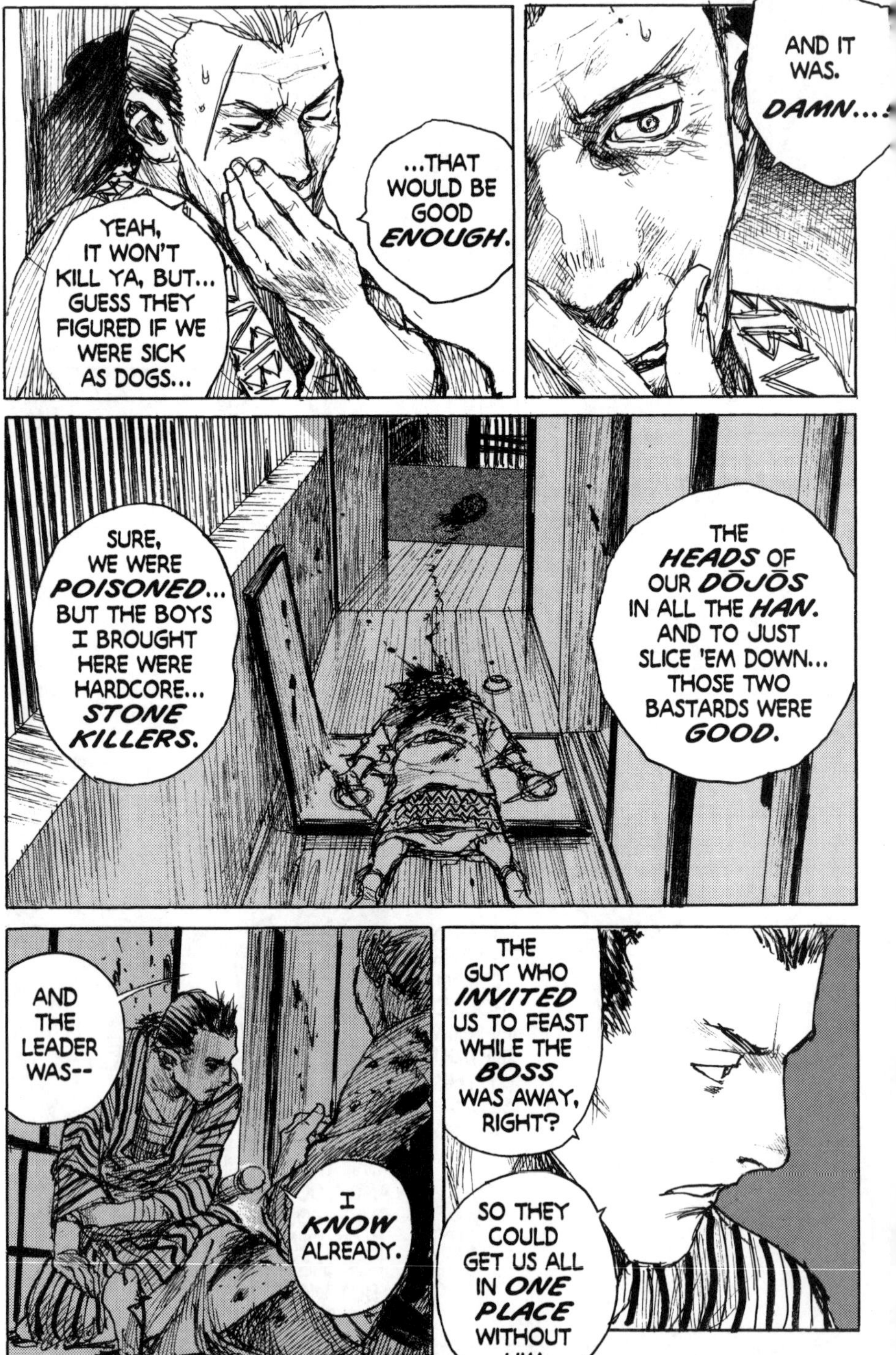
YEAH, IT WON'T KILL YA, BUT... GUESS THEY FIGURED IF WE WERE SICK AS DOGS...
...THAT WOULD BE GOOD ENOUGH.
AND IT WAS. DAMN...
SURE, WE WERE POISONED... BUT THE BOYS I BROUGHT HERE WERE HARDCORE... STONE KILLERS.
THE HEADS OF OUR DŌJŌS IN ALL THE HAN. AND TO JUST SLICE 'EM DOWN... THOSE TWO BASTARDS WERE GOOD.
AND THE LEADER WAS--
I KNOW ALREADY.
THE GUY WHO INVITED US TO FEAST WHILE THE BOSS WAS AWAY, RIGHT?
SO THEY COULD GET US ALL IN ONE PLACE WITHOUT HIM.

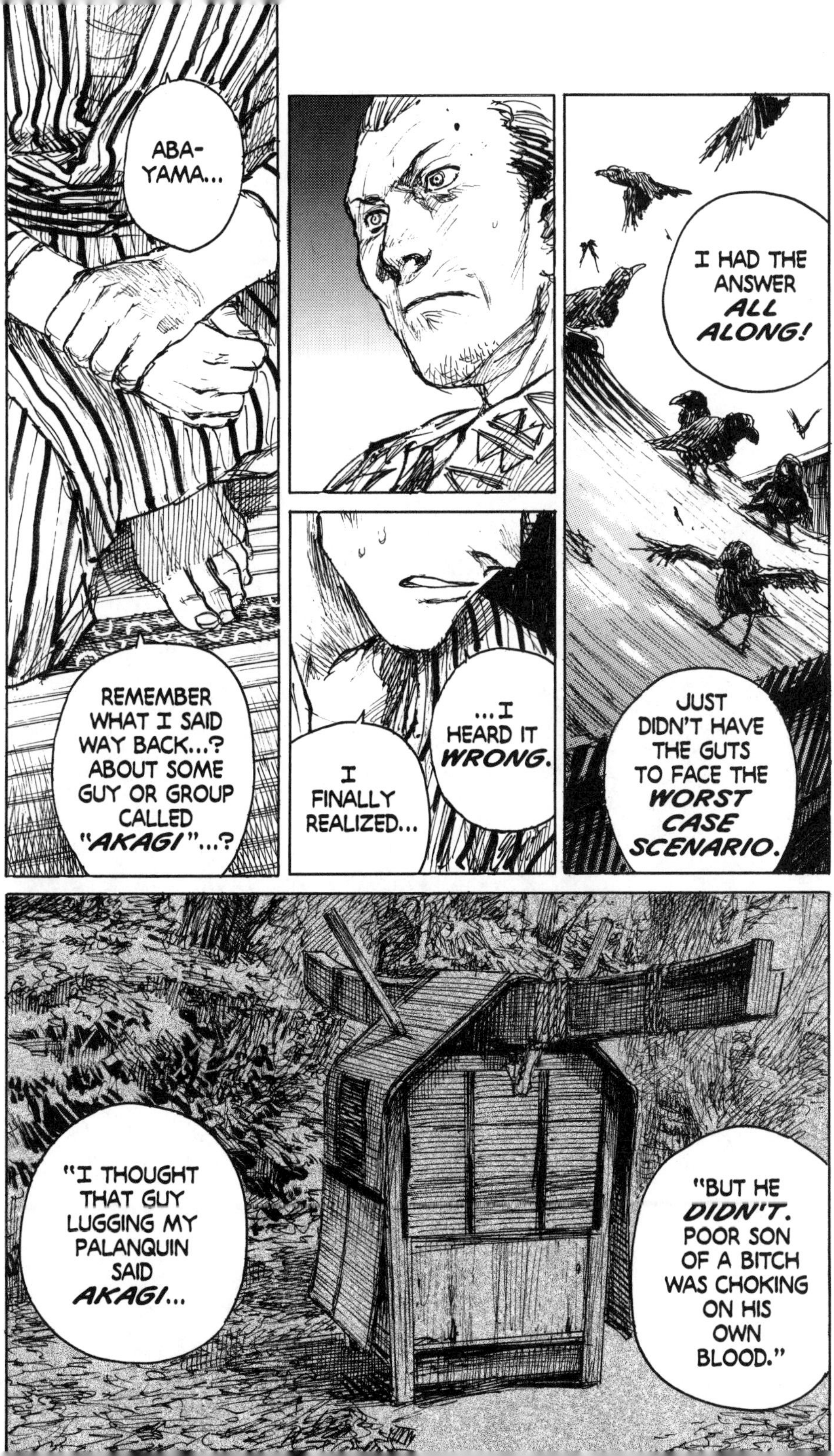
ABA-YAMA...
REMEMBER WHAT I SAID WAY BACK...? ABOUT SOME GUY OR GROUP CALLED "AKAGI"...?
I FINALLY REALIZED...
...I HEARD IT WRONG.
I HAD THE ANSWER ALL ALONG!
JUST DIDN'T HAVE THE GUTS TO FACE THE WORST CASE SCENARIO.
"I THOUGHT THAT GUY LUGGING MY PALANQUIN SAID AKAGI...
"BUT HE DIDN'T. POOR SON OF A BITCH WAS CHOKING ON HIS OWN BLOOD."

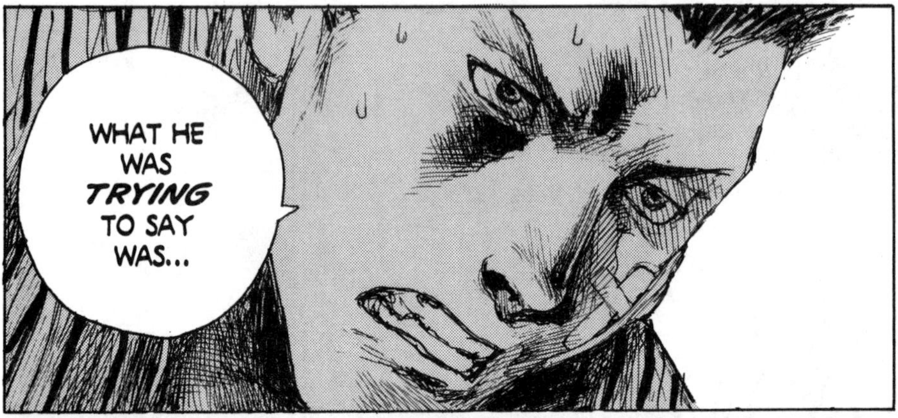
WHAT HE WAS *TRYING* TO SAY WAS...
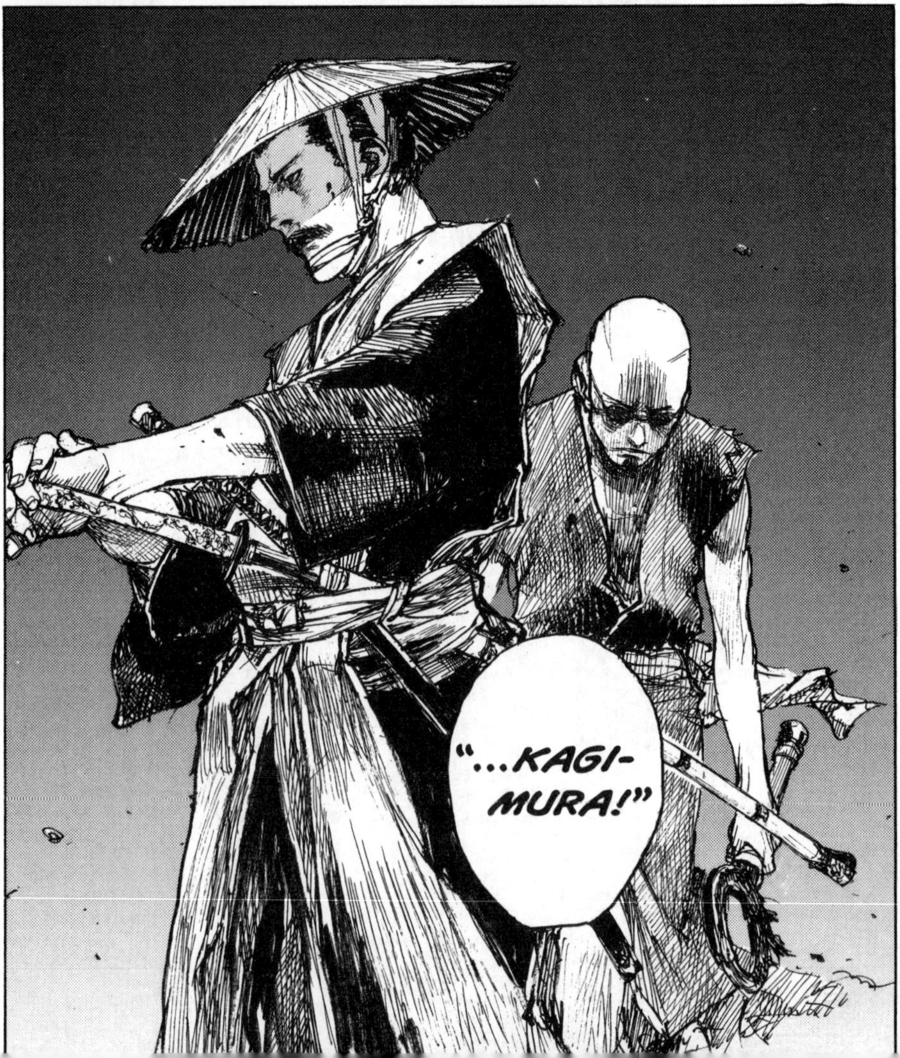
"...KAGI-MURA!"

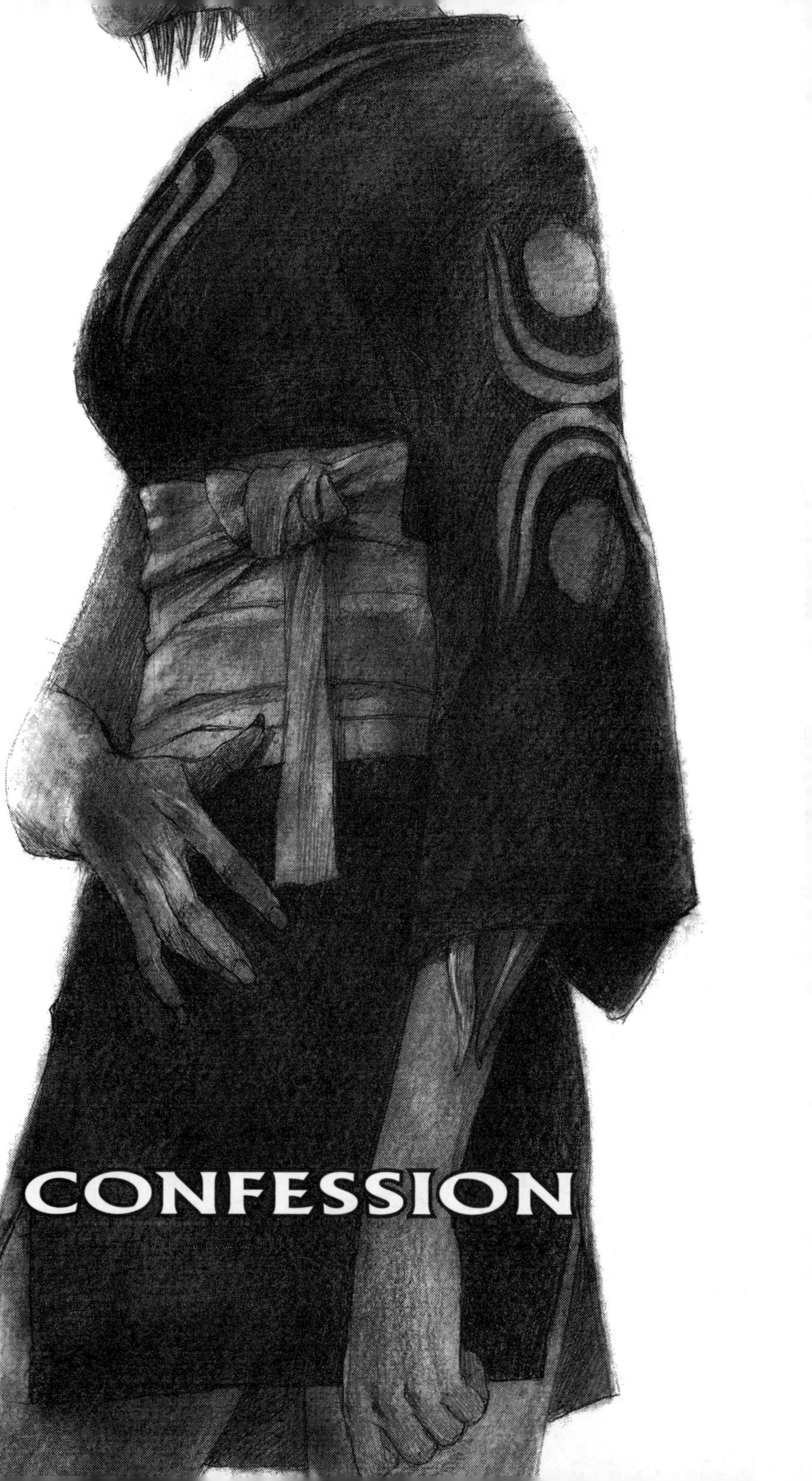
CONFESSION

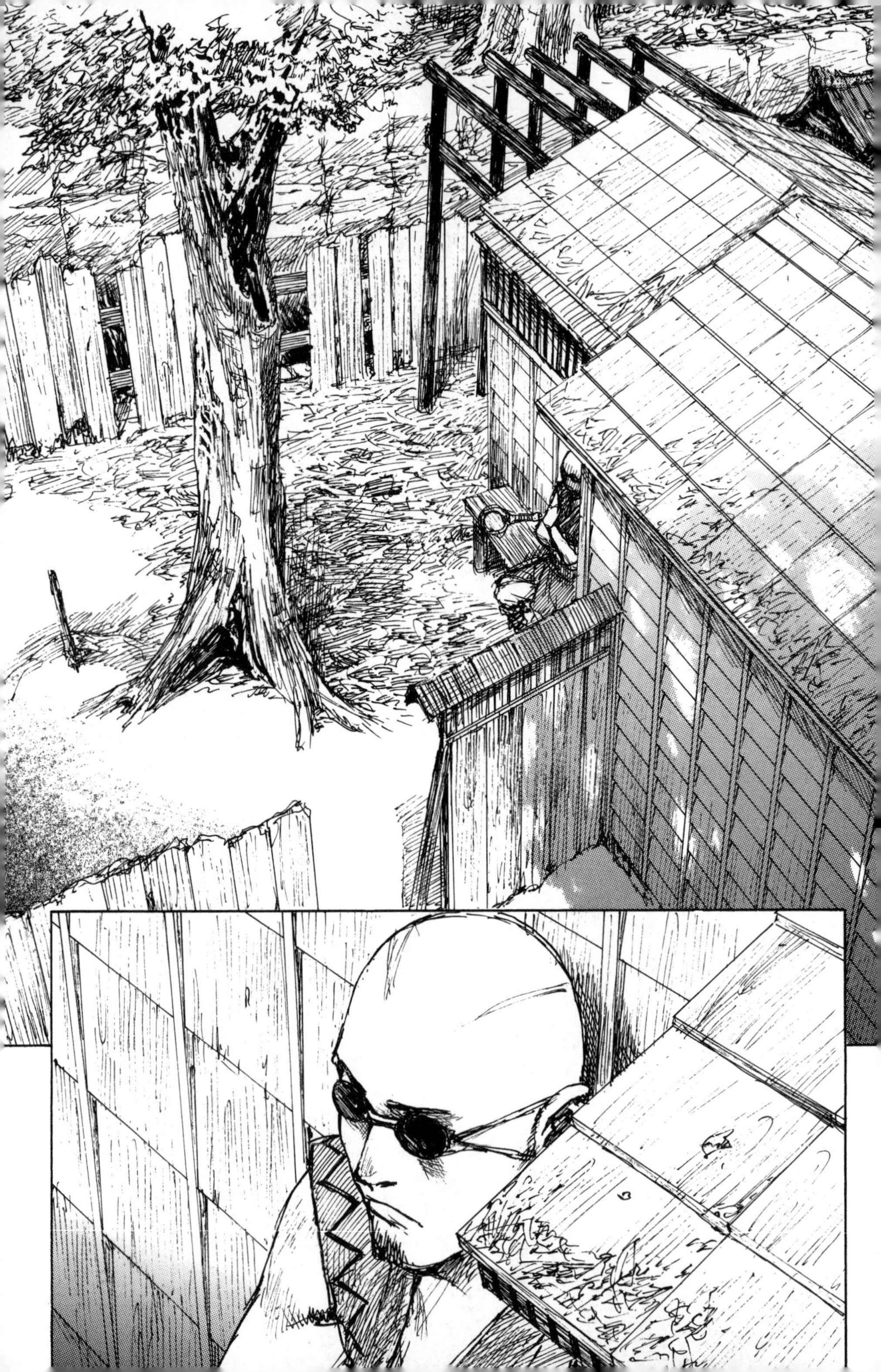

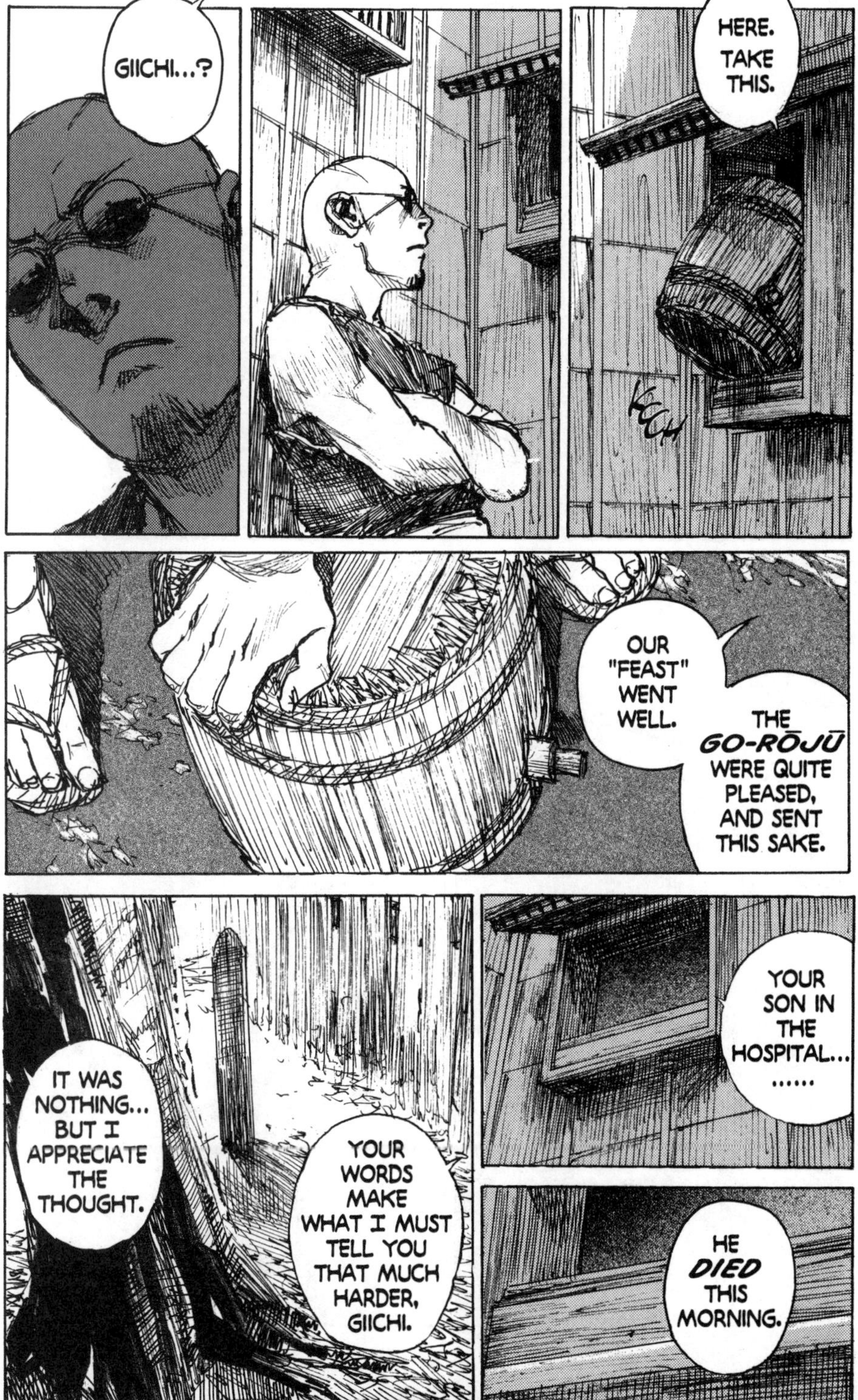
GIICHI...?
HERE. TAKE THIS.
KECH
OUR "FEAST" WENT WELL.
THE *GO-RŌJŪ* WERE QUITE PLEASED, AND SENT THIS SAKE.
IT WAS NOTHING... BUT I APPRECIATE THE THOUGHT.
YOUR WORDS MAKE WHAT I MUST TELL YOU THAT MUCH HARDER, GIICHI.
YOUR SON IN THE HOSPITAL... ......
HE *DIED* THIS MORNING.

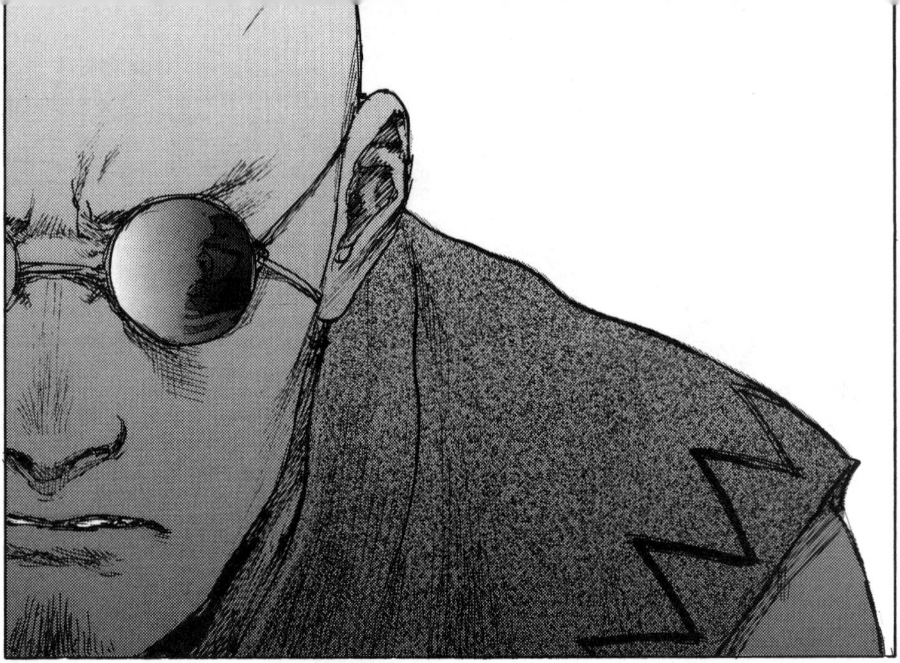

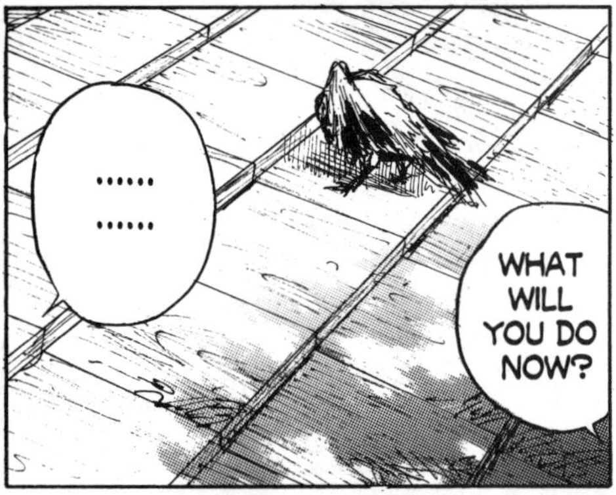
WHAT WILL YOU DO NOW?
......
......

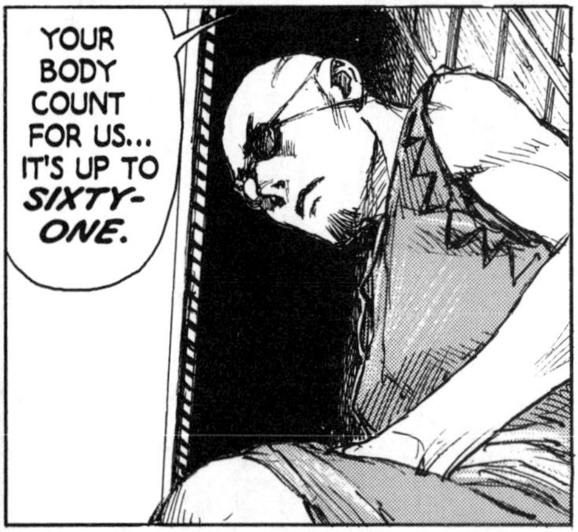
YOUR BODY COUNT FOR US... IT'S UP TO *SIXTY-ONE*.

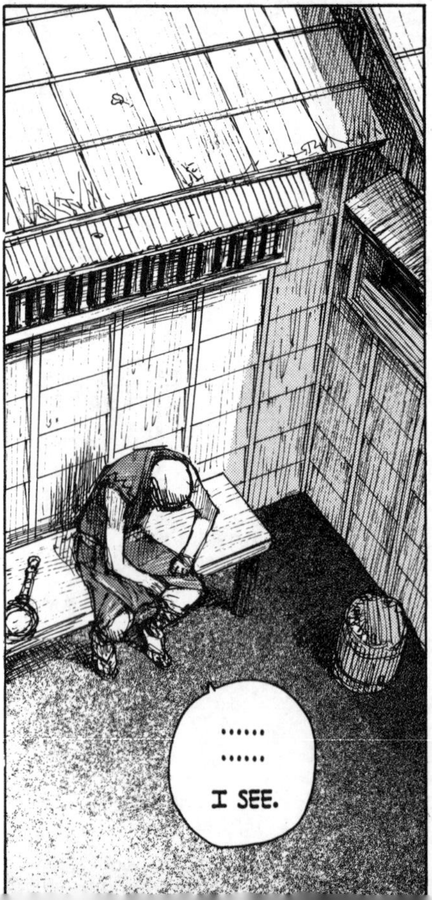
......
......
I SEE.

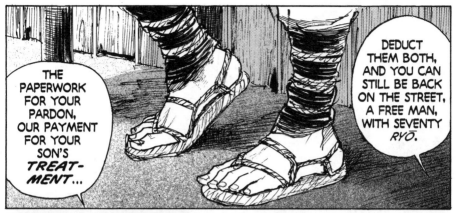

THE PAPERWORK FOR YOUR PARDON, OUR PAYMENT FOR YOUR SON'S *TREAT-MENT*...

DEDUCT THEM BOTH, AND YOU CAN STILL BE BACK ON THE STREET, A FREE MAN, WITH SEVENTY *RYŌ*.

PERHAPS THIS IS NOT THE BEST TIME TO ASK.

WHEN YOU DECIDE WHAT YOU WANT TO DO, COME BY MY COMPOUND.

ANY TIME, OF COURSE.

WAIT, HABAKI.

I ALREADY KNOW HOW I WANT TO USE IT.

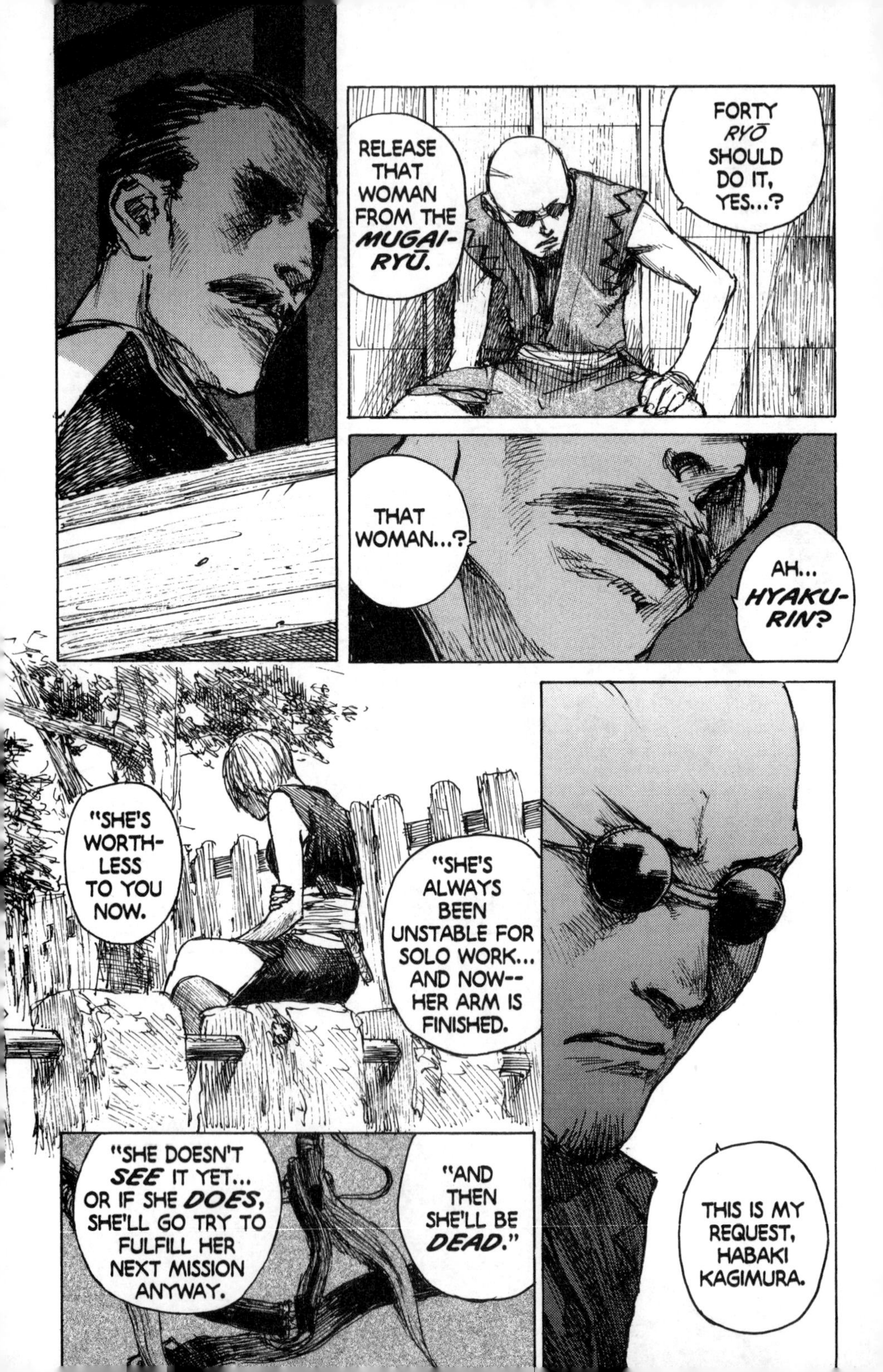
FORTY *RYŌ* SHOULD DO IT, YES...?
RELEASE THAT WOMAN FROM THE ***MUGAI-RYŪ.***
THAT WOMAN...?
AH... ***HYAKU-RIN?***
"SHE'S WORTH-LESS TO YOU NOW.
"SHE'S ALWAYS BEEN UNSTABLE FOR SOLO WORK... AND NOW-- HER ARM IS FINISHED.
"SHE DOESN'T ***SEE*** IT YET... OR IF SHE ***DOES,*** SHE'LL GO TRY TO FULFILL HER NEXT MISSION ANYWAY.
"AND THEN SHE'LL BE ***DEAD.***"
THIS IS MY REQUEST, HABAKI KAGIMURA.

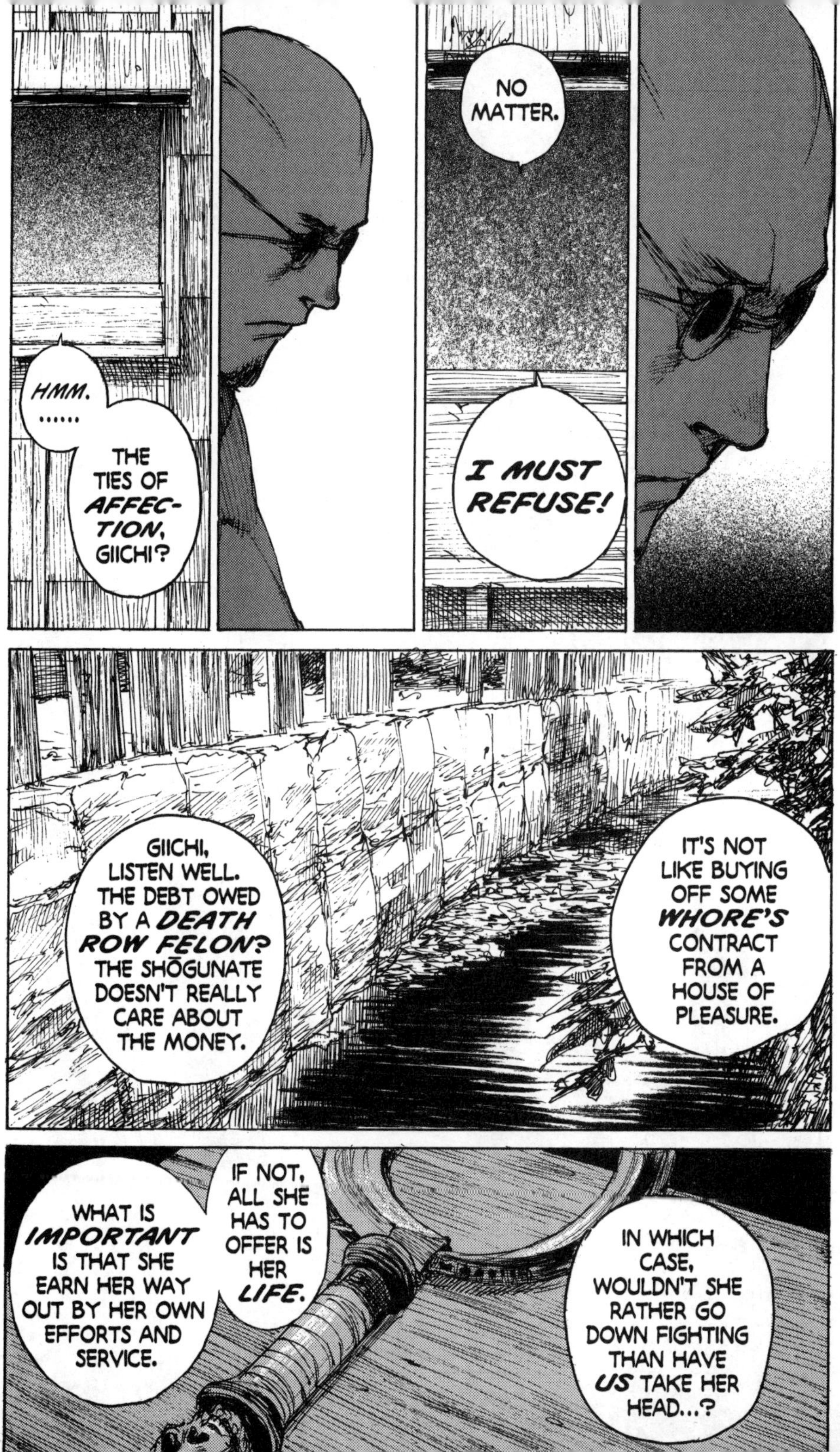
HMM. ......
THE TIES OF AFFECTION, GIICHI?
NO MATTER.
I MUST REFUSE!
GIICHI, LISTEN WELL. THE DEBT OWED BY A DEATH ROW FELON? THE SHŌGUNATE DOESN'T REALLY CARE ABOUT THE MONEY.
IT'S NOT LIKE BUYING OFF SOME WHORE'S CONTRACT FROM A HOUSE OF PLEASURE.
WHAT IS IMPORTANT IS THAT SHE EARN HER WAY OUT BY HER OWN EFFORTS AND SERVICE.
IF NOT, ALL SHE HAS TO OFFER IS HER LIFE.
IN WHICH CASE, WOULDN'T SHE RATHER GO DOWN FIGHTING THAN HAVE US TAKE HER HEAD...?

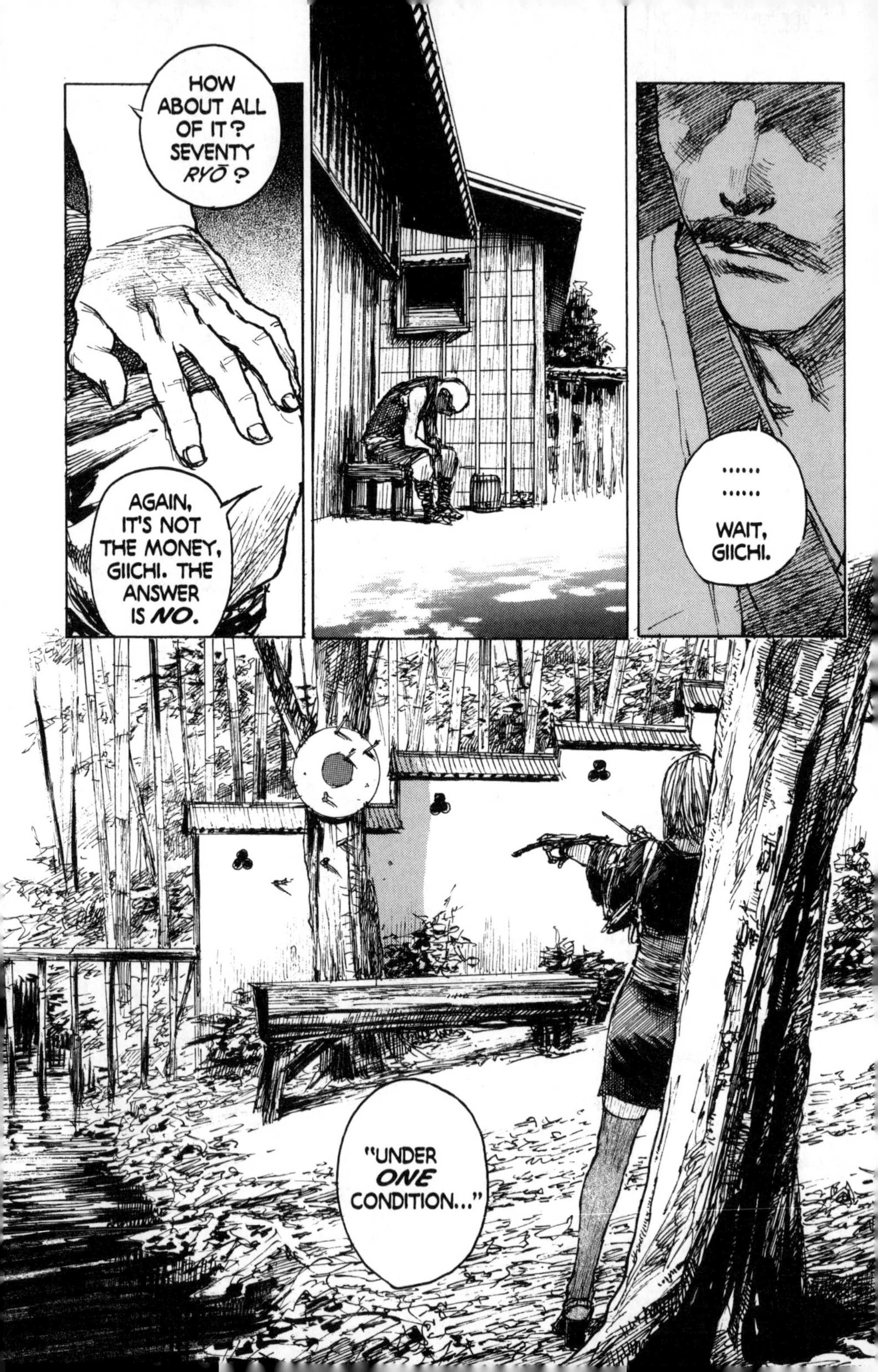
HOW ABOUT ALL OF IT? SEVENTY *RYŌ*?
AGAIN, IT'S NOT THE MONEY, GIICHI. THE ANSWER IS ***NO***.
.... WAIT, GIICHI.
"UNDER ***ONE*** CONDITION..."

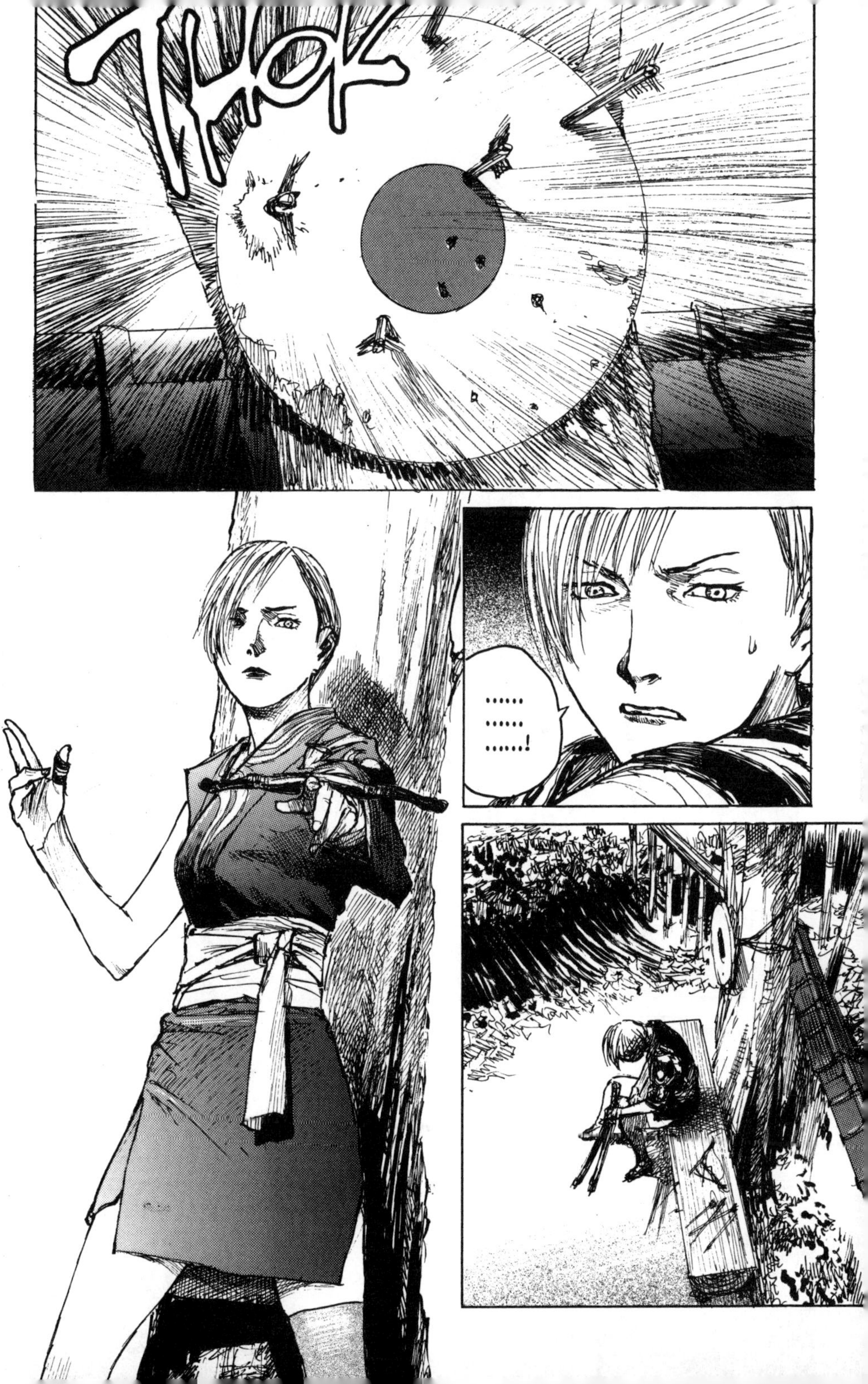
THOCK
......
......
......!

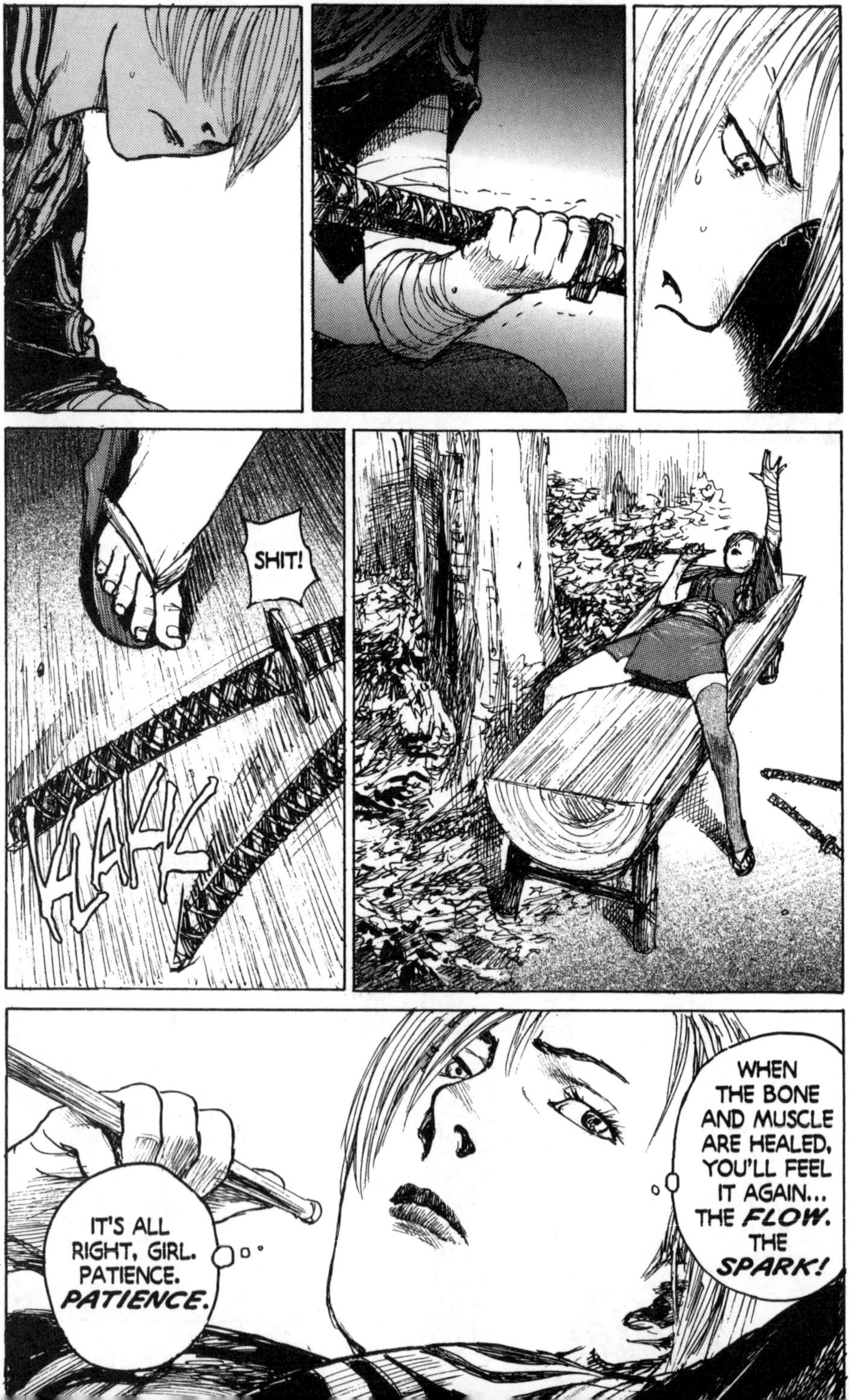
SHIT!
WHEN THE BONE AND MUSCLE ARE HEALED, YOU'LL FEEL IT AGAIN... THE *FLOW*. THE *SPARK!*
IT'S ALL RIGHT, GIRL. PATIENCE. ***PATIENCE.***

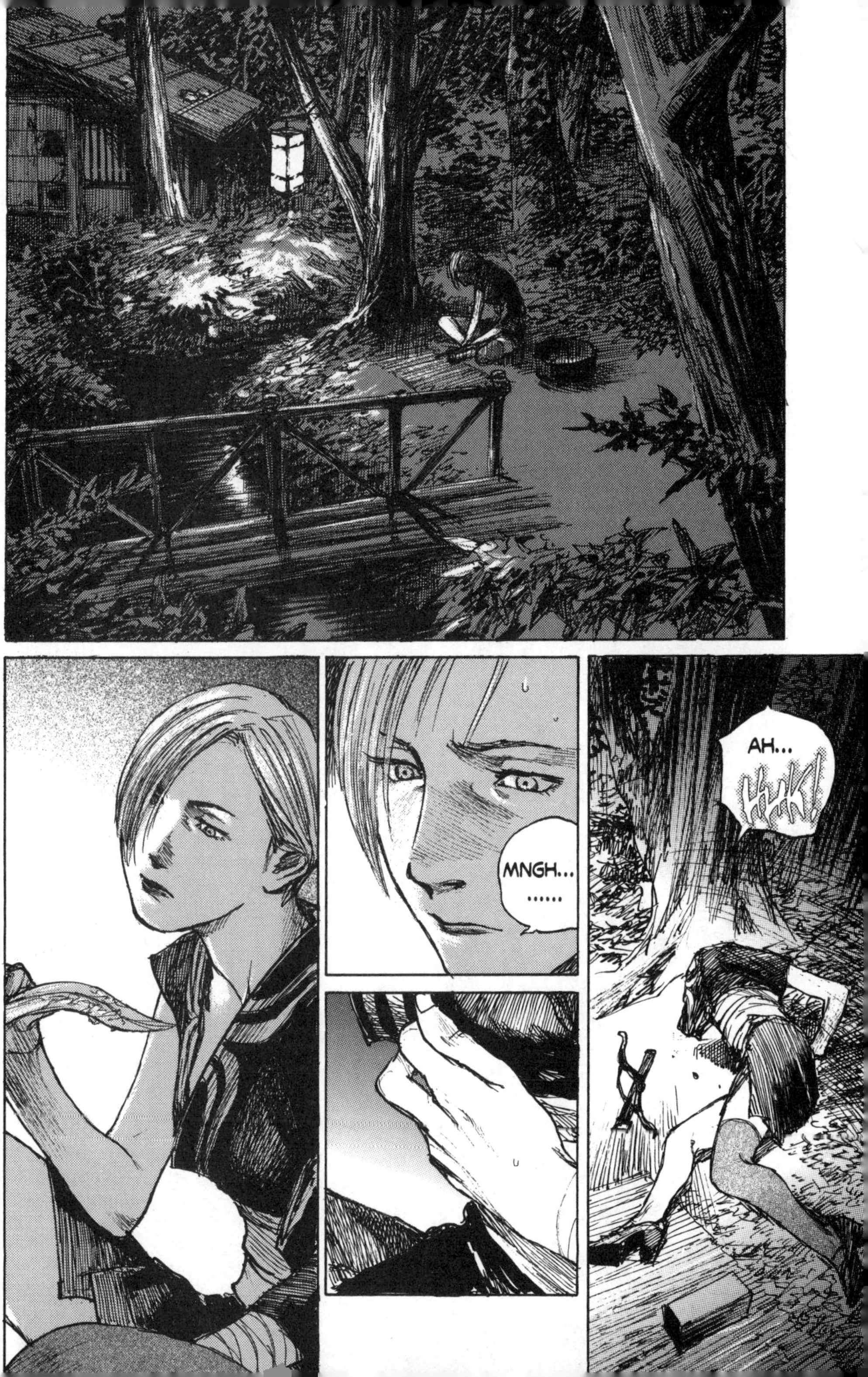
AH...
HUK!
MNGH...
......

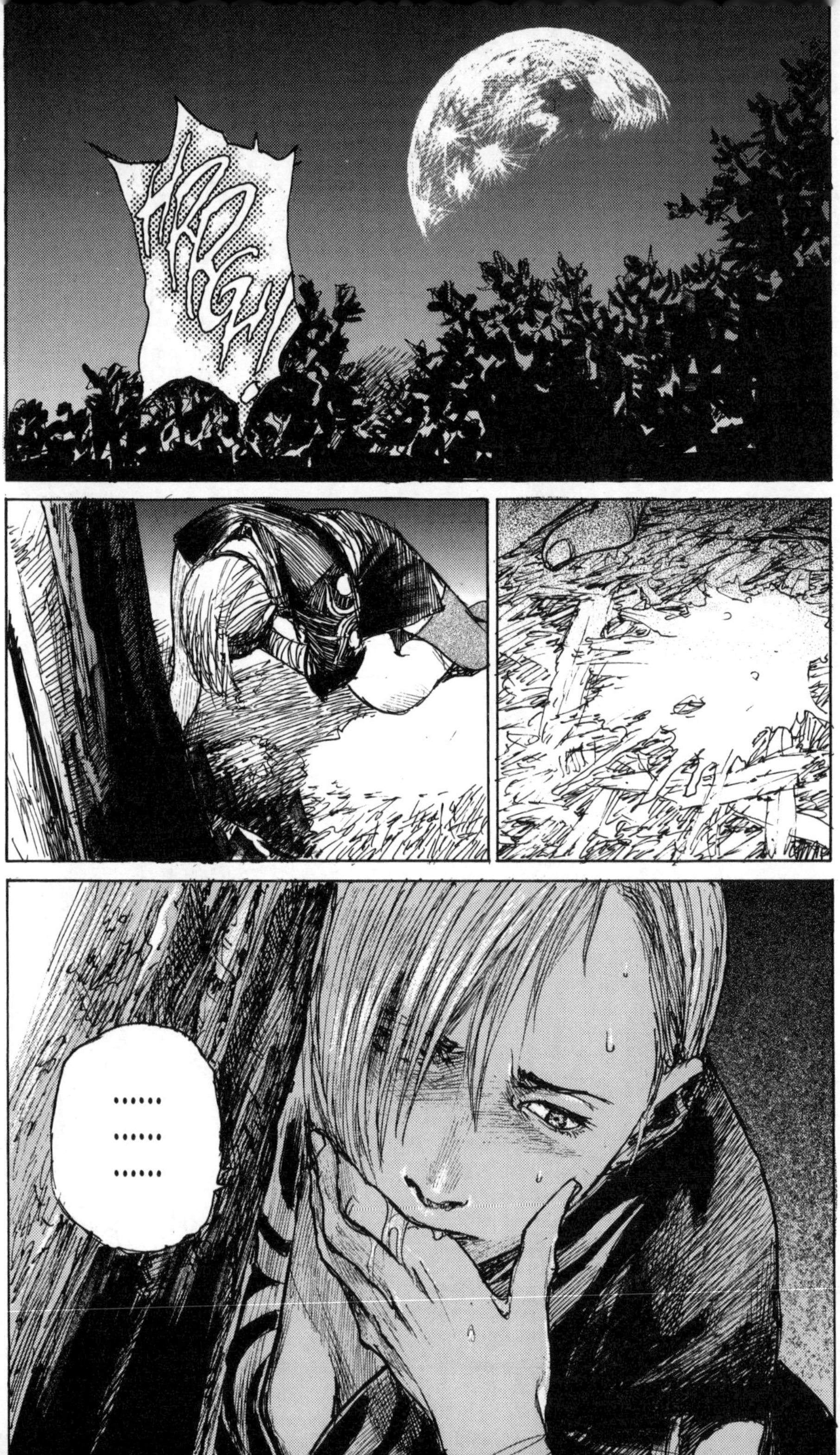
HAAGH!
......
......
......

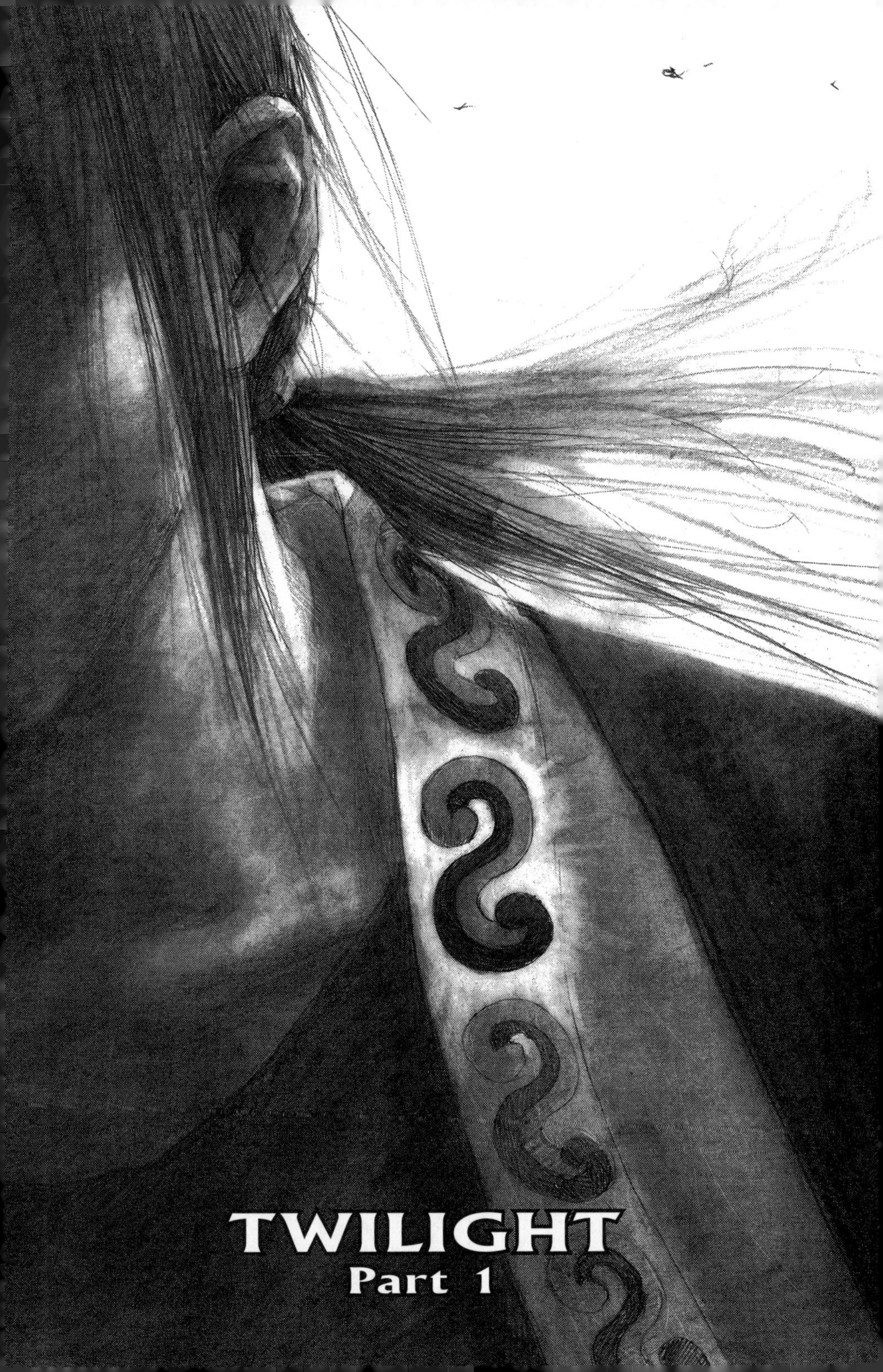
TWILIGHT
Part 1

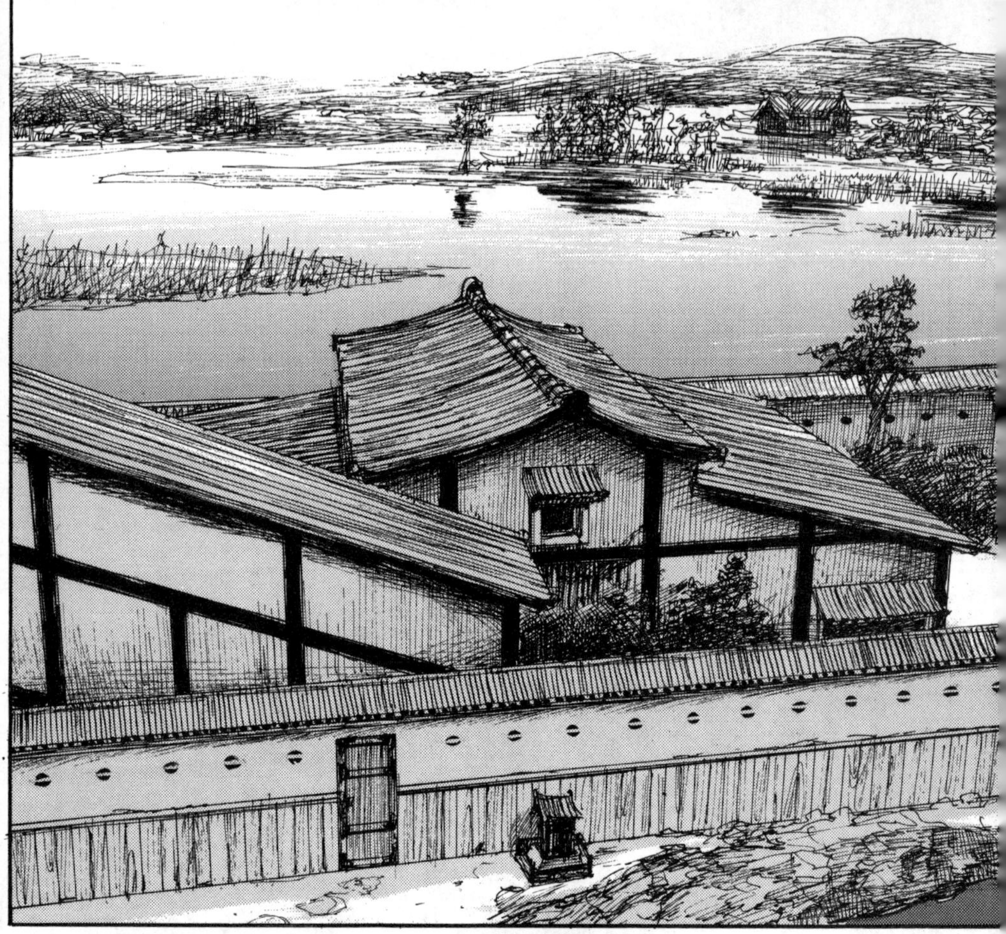

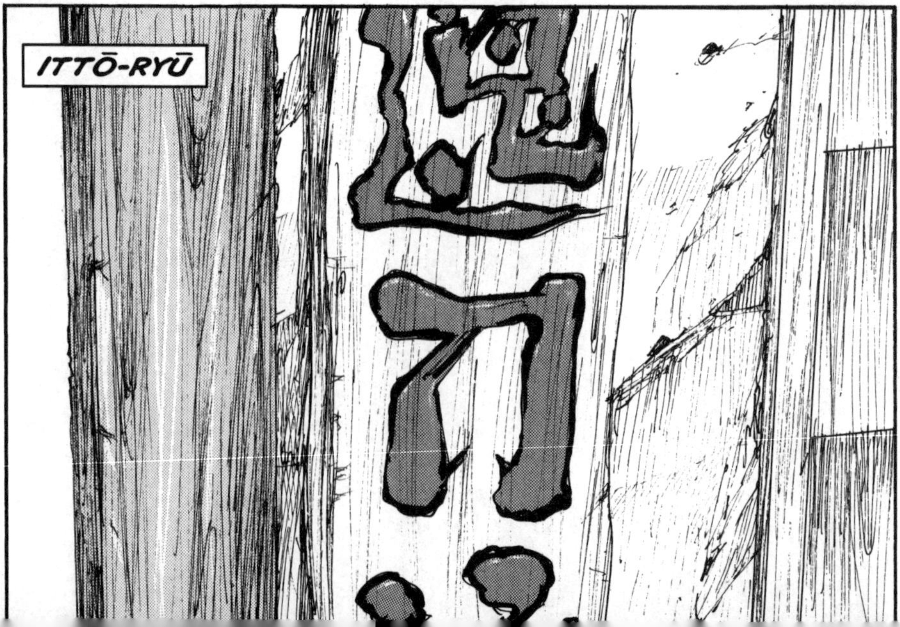
ITTŌ-RYŪ

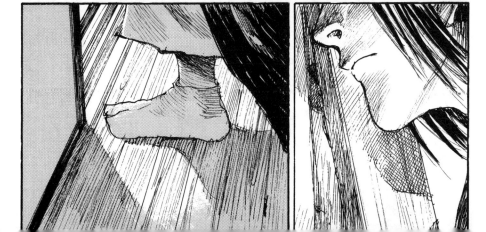

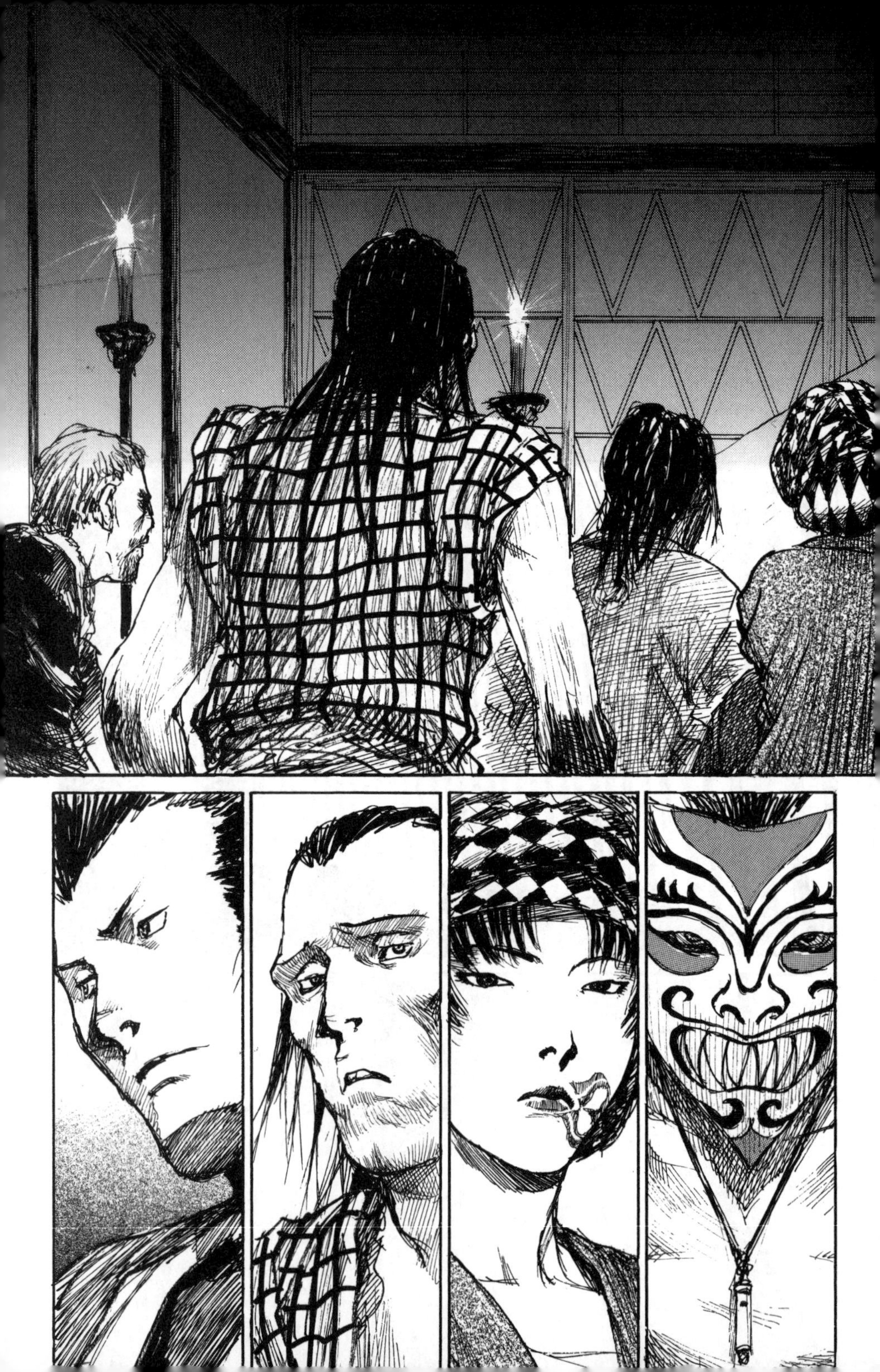

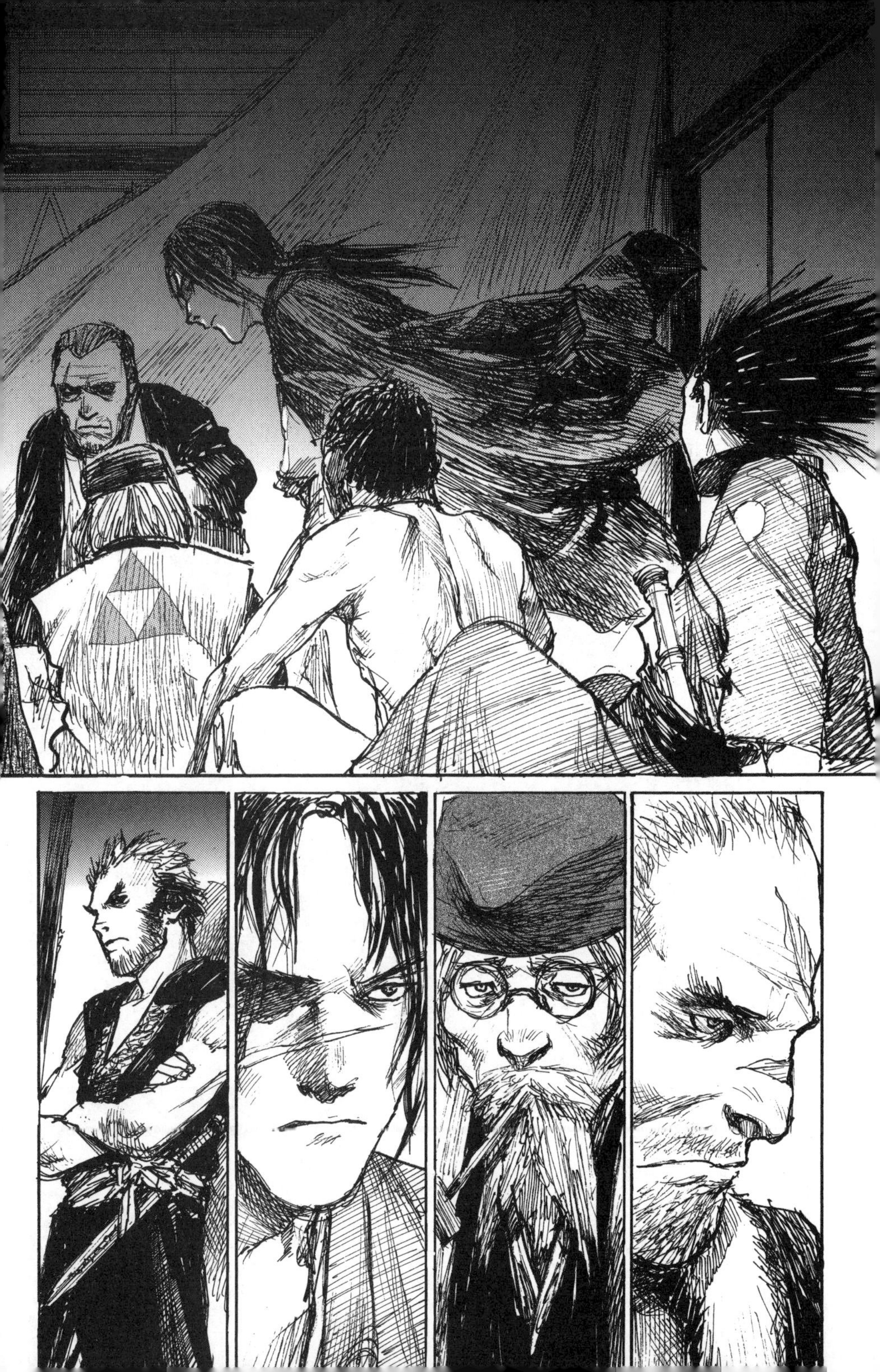

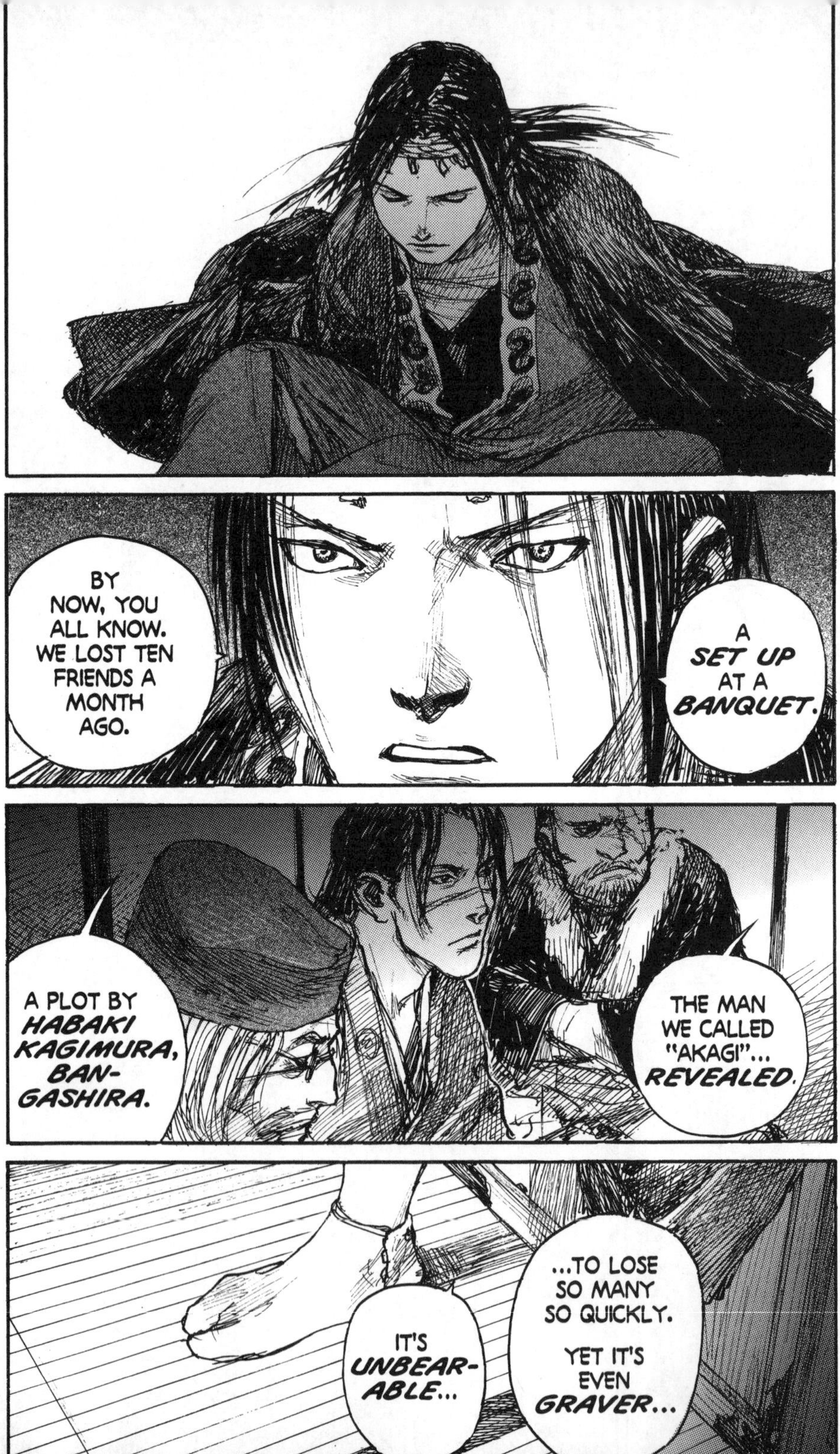
BY NOW, YOU ALL KNOW. WE LOST TEN FRIENDS A MONTH AGO.
A *SET UP* AT A *BANQUET*.
A PLOT BY *HABAKI KAGIMURA, BAN-GASHIRA*.
THE MAN WE CALLED "AKAGI"... *REVEALED*.
IT'S *UNBEARABLE*...
...TO LOSE SO MANY SO QUICKLY.
YET IT'S EVEN *GRAVER*...

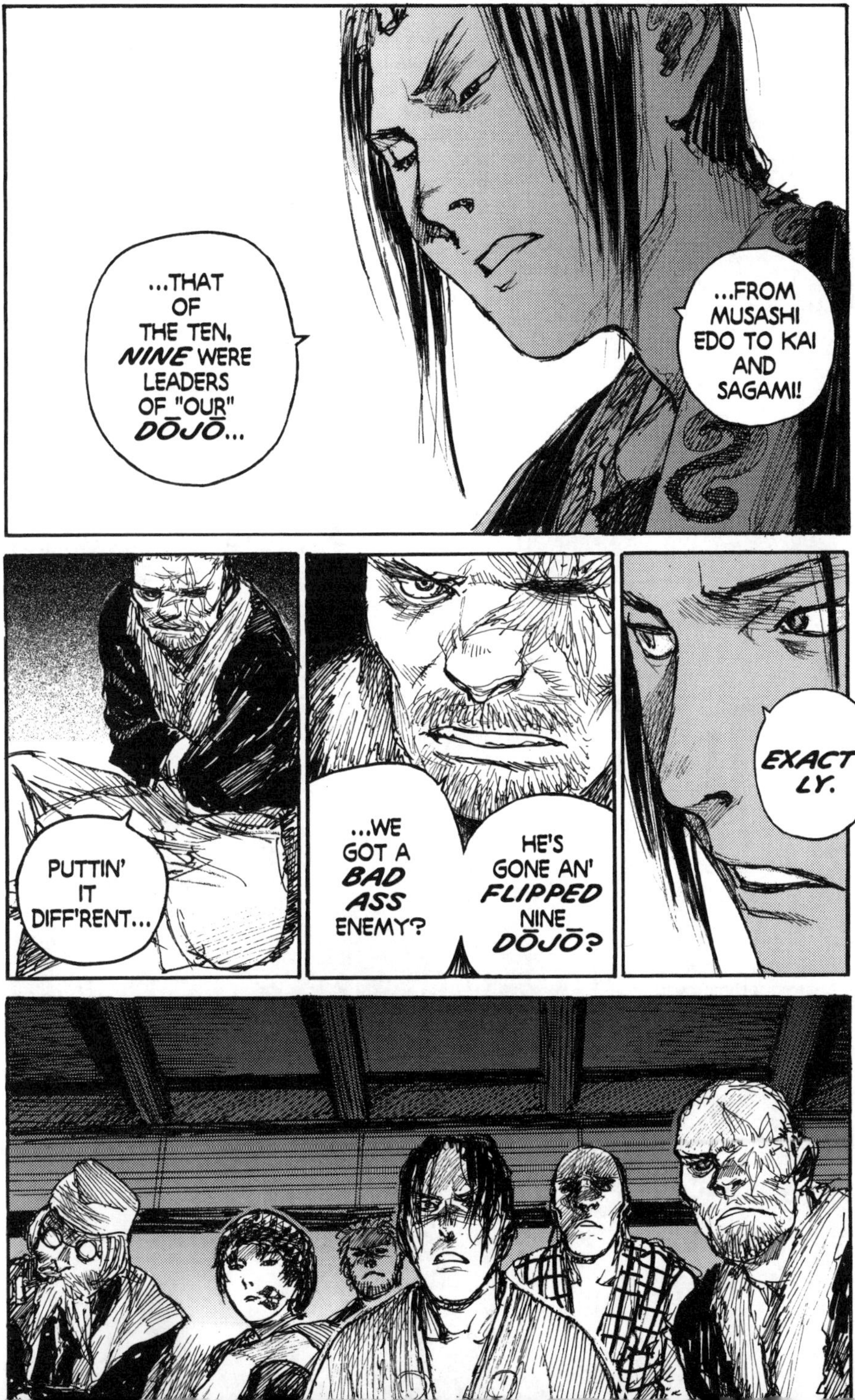
...FROM MUSASHI EDO TO KAI AND SAGAMI!
...THAT OF THE TEN, *NINE* WERE LEADERS OF "OUR" *DŌJŌ*...
EXACT-LY.
HE'S GONE AN' *FLIPPED* NINE *DŌJŌ*?
...WE GOT A *BAD ASS* ENEMY?
PUTTIN' IT DIFF'RENT...

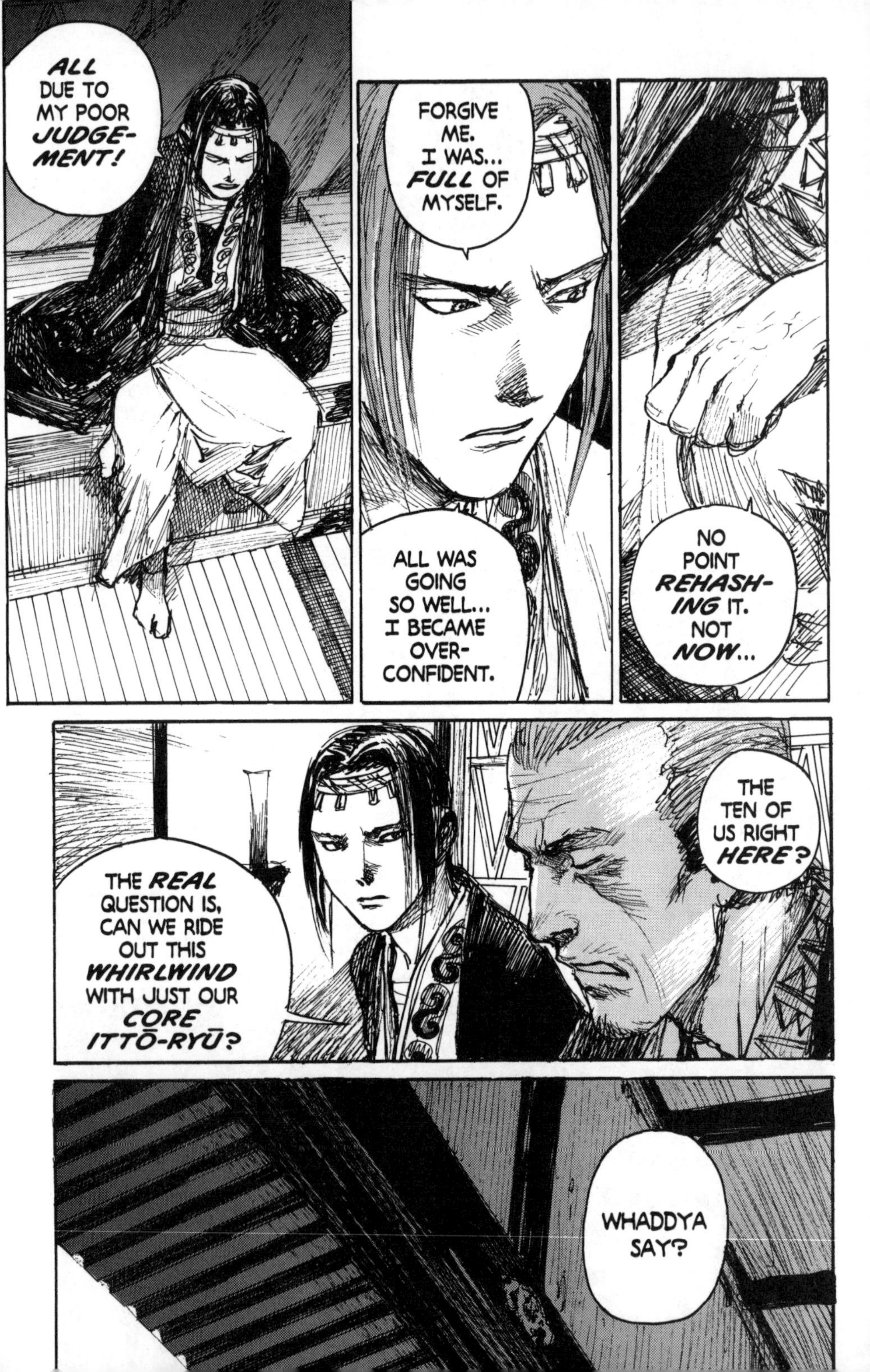
ALL DUE TO MY POOR JUDGEMENT!
FORGIVE ME. I WAS... FULL OF MYSELF.
ALL WAS GOING SO WELL... I BECAME OVERCONFIDENT.
NO POINT REHASHING IT. NOT NOW...
THE REAL QUESTION IS, CAN WE RIDE OUT THIS WHIRLWIND WITH JUST OUR CORE ITTŌ-RYŪ?
THE TEN OF US RIGHT HERE?
WHADDYA SAY?

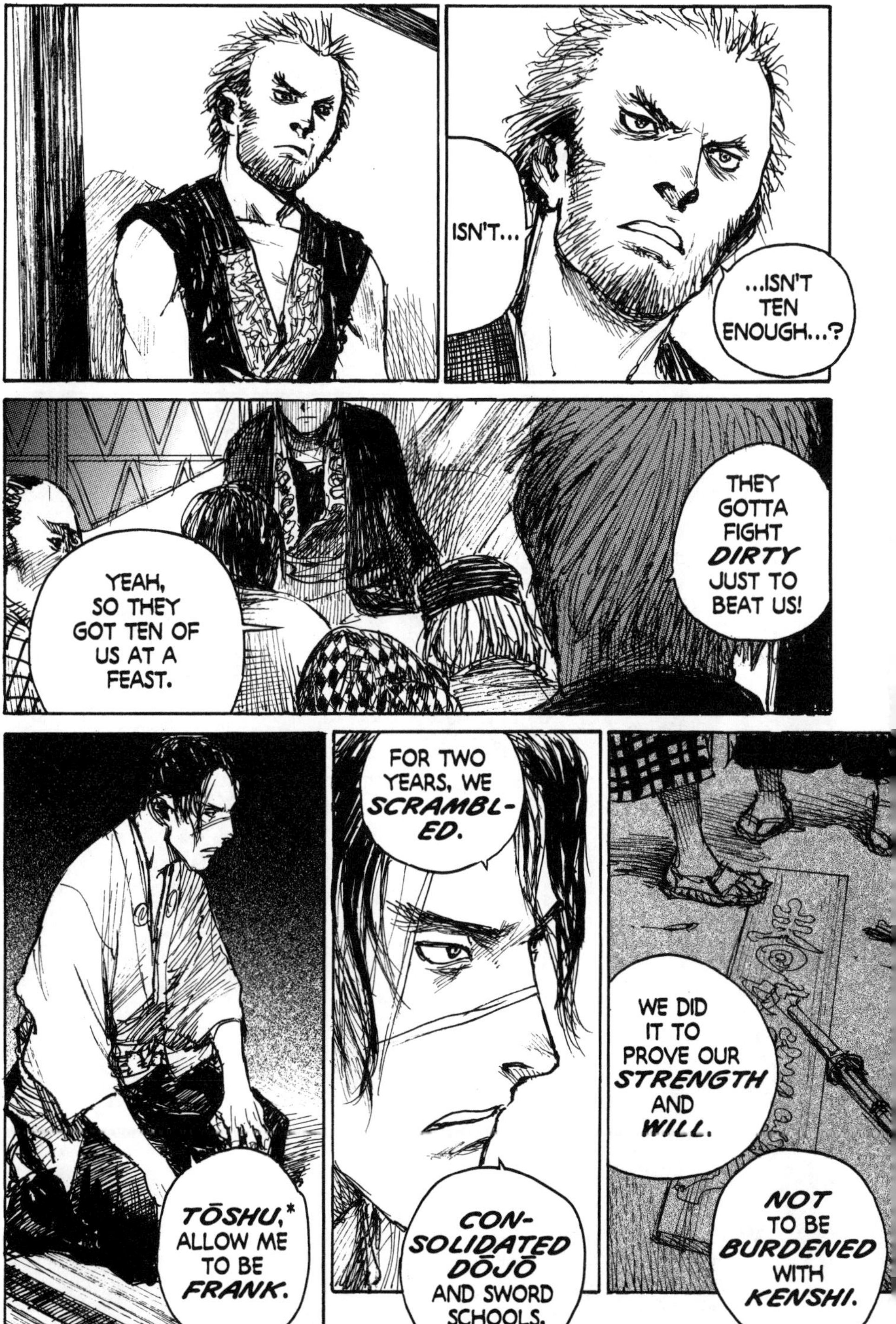
ISN'T...
...ISN'T TEN ENOUGH...?
YEAH, SO THEY GOT TEN OF US AT A FEAST.
THEY GOTTA FIGHT DIRTY JUST TO BEAT US!
TŌSHU,* ALLOW ME TO BE FRANK.
FOR TWO YEARS, WE SCRAMBL-ED.
CON-SOLIDATED DŌJŌ AND SWORD SCHOOLS.
WE DID IT TO PROVE OUR STRENGTH AND WILL.
NOT TO BE BURDENED WITH KENSHI.
*: LEADER.

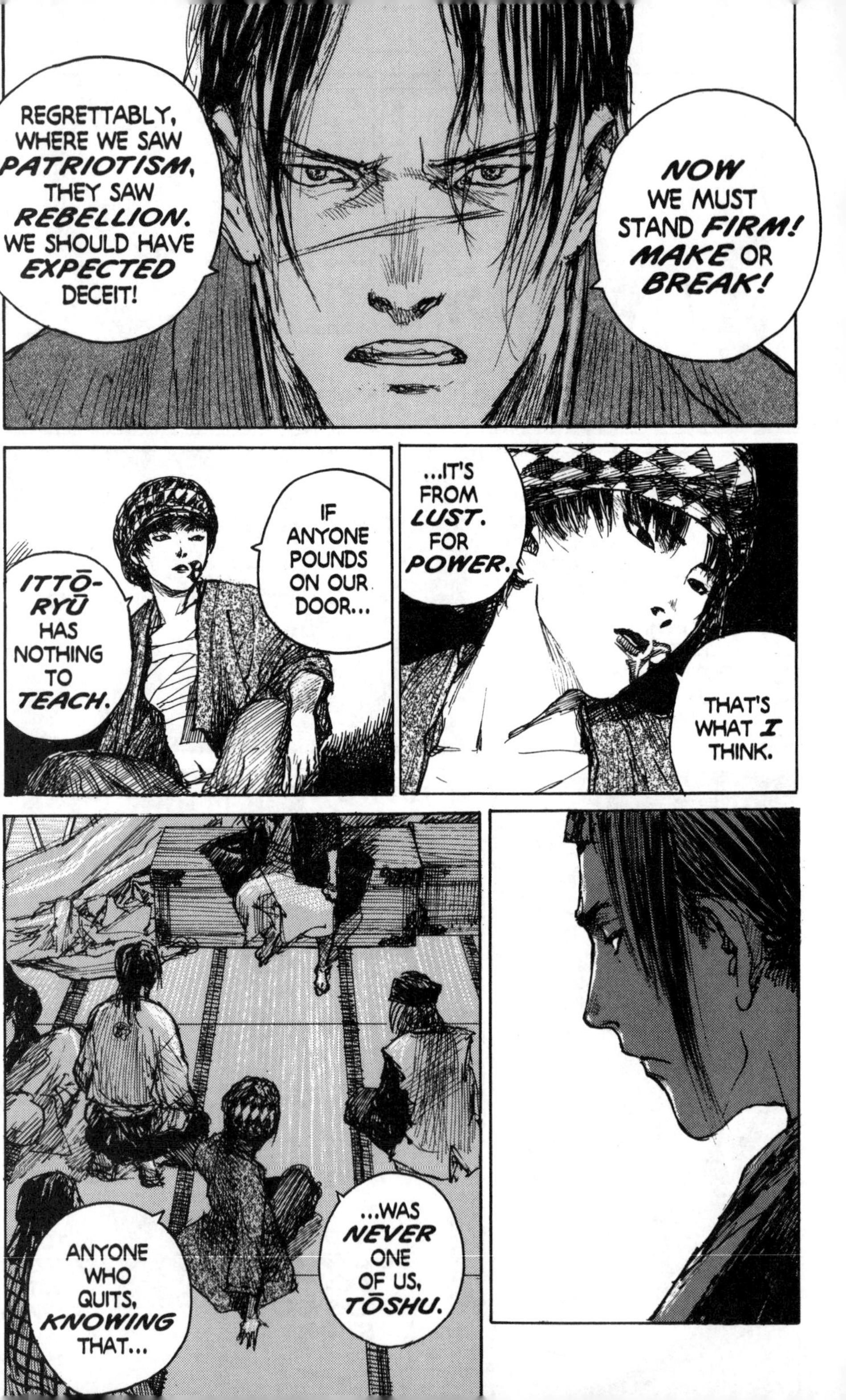
REGRETTABLY, WHERE WE SAW *PATRIOTISM*, THEY SAW *REBELLION*. WE SHOULD HAVE *EXPECTED* DECEIT!
NOW WE MUST STAND *FIRM! MAKE* OR *BREAK!*
IF ANYONE POUNDS ON OUR DOOR...
ITTŌ-RYŪ HAS NOTHING TO *TEACH*.
...IT'S FROM *LUST*. FOR *POWER*.
THAT'S WHAT *I* THINK.
ANYONE WHO QUITS, *KNOWING* THAT...
...WAS *NEVER* ONE OF US, *TŌSHU*.

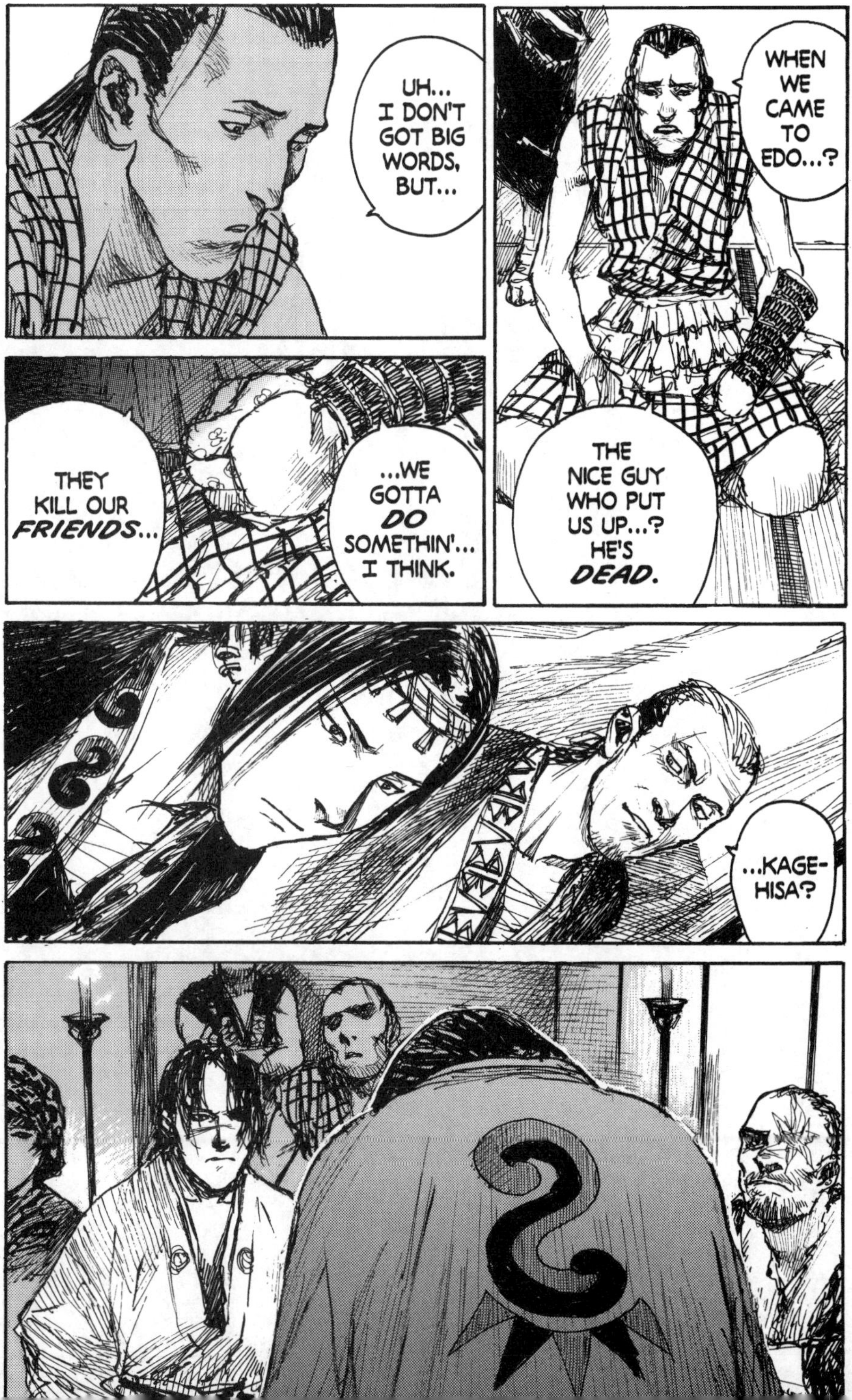
UH... I DON'T GOT BIG WORDS, BUT...
WHEN WE CAME TO EDO...?
THE NICE GUY WHO PUT US UP...? HE'S *DEAD*.
THEY KILL OUR *FRIENDS*...
...WE GOTTA *DO* SOMETHIN'... I THINK.
...KAGE-HISA?

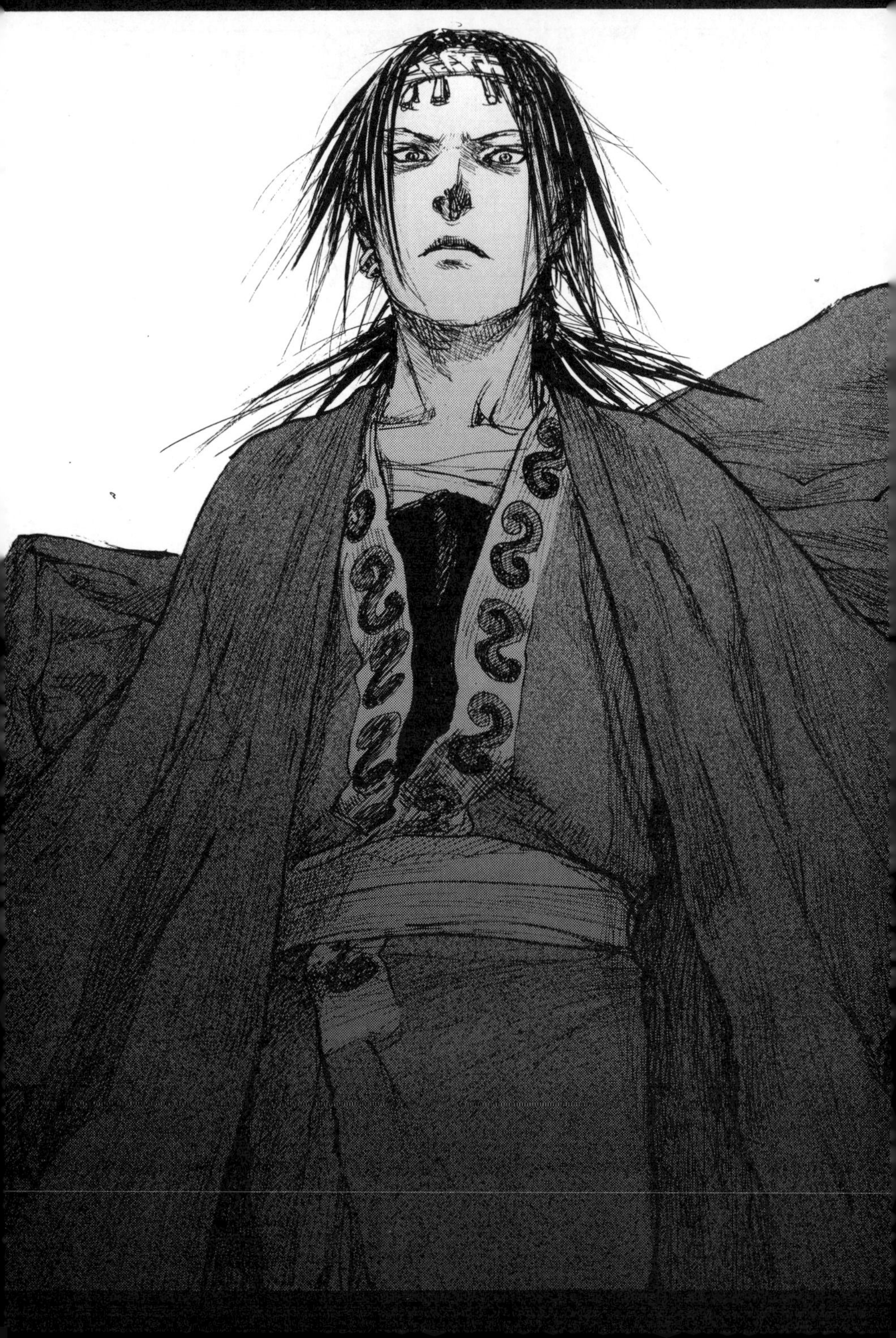

THIS IS OUR LAST STAND!

WE'RE DOGS! PROUD OF OUR FANGS! WE ONCE WISHED TO SERVE OUR MASTER!

BUT IF OUR MASTER HAD GONE SOFT AND DECADENT...?

ALL THE MORE REASON TO KEEP OUR FANGS SHARP!

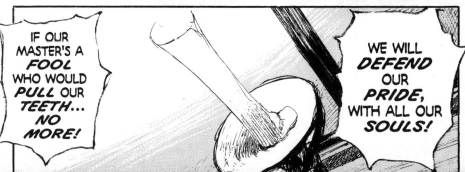

IF OUR MASTER'S A FOOL WHO WOULD PULL OUR TEETH... NO MORE!

WE WILL DEFEND OUR PRIDE, WITH ALL OUR SOULS!

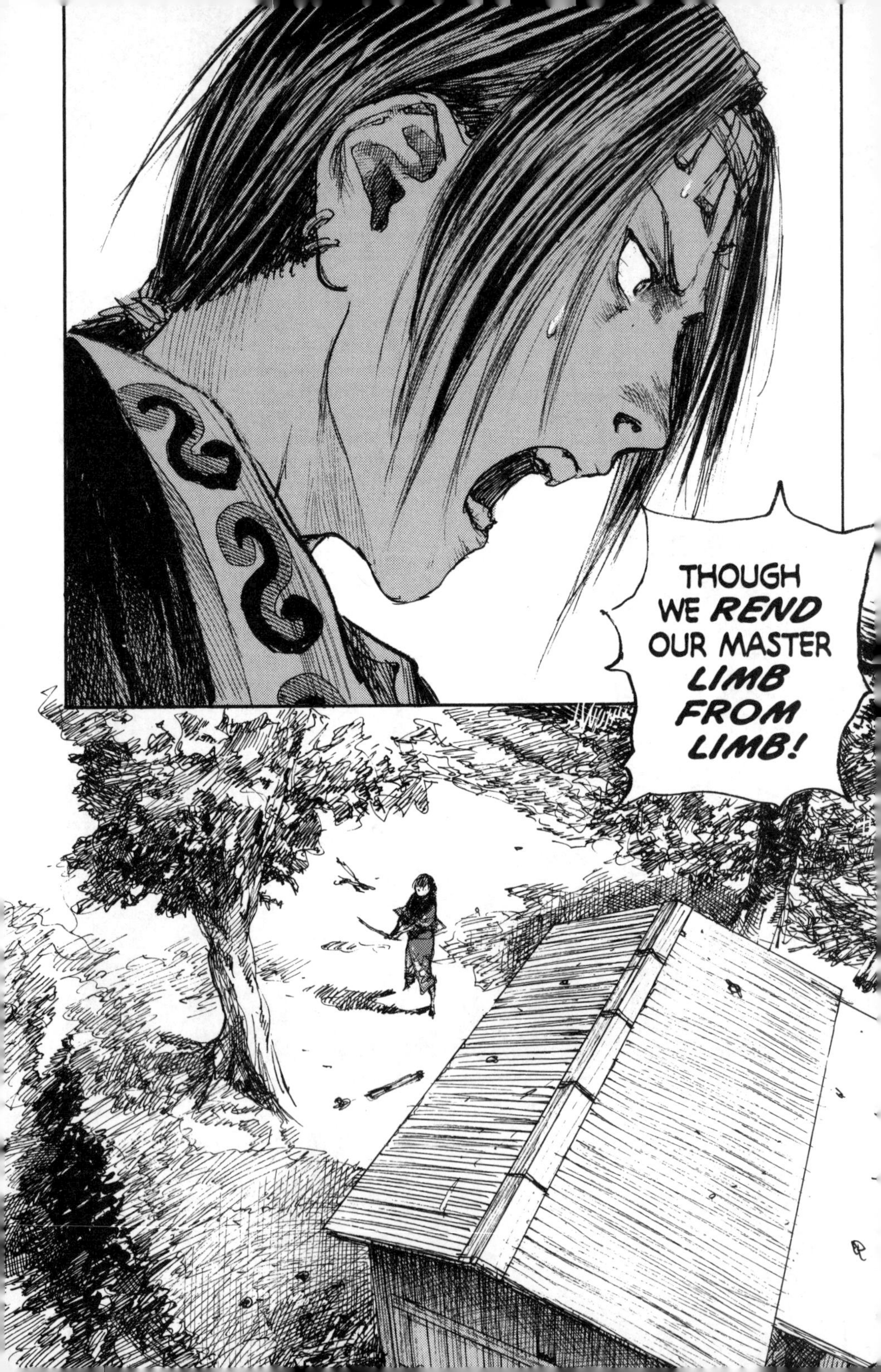
THOUGH WE *REND* OUR MASTER *LIMB FROM LIMB!*

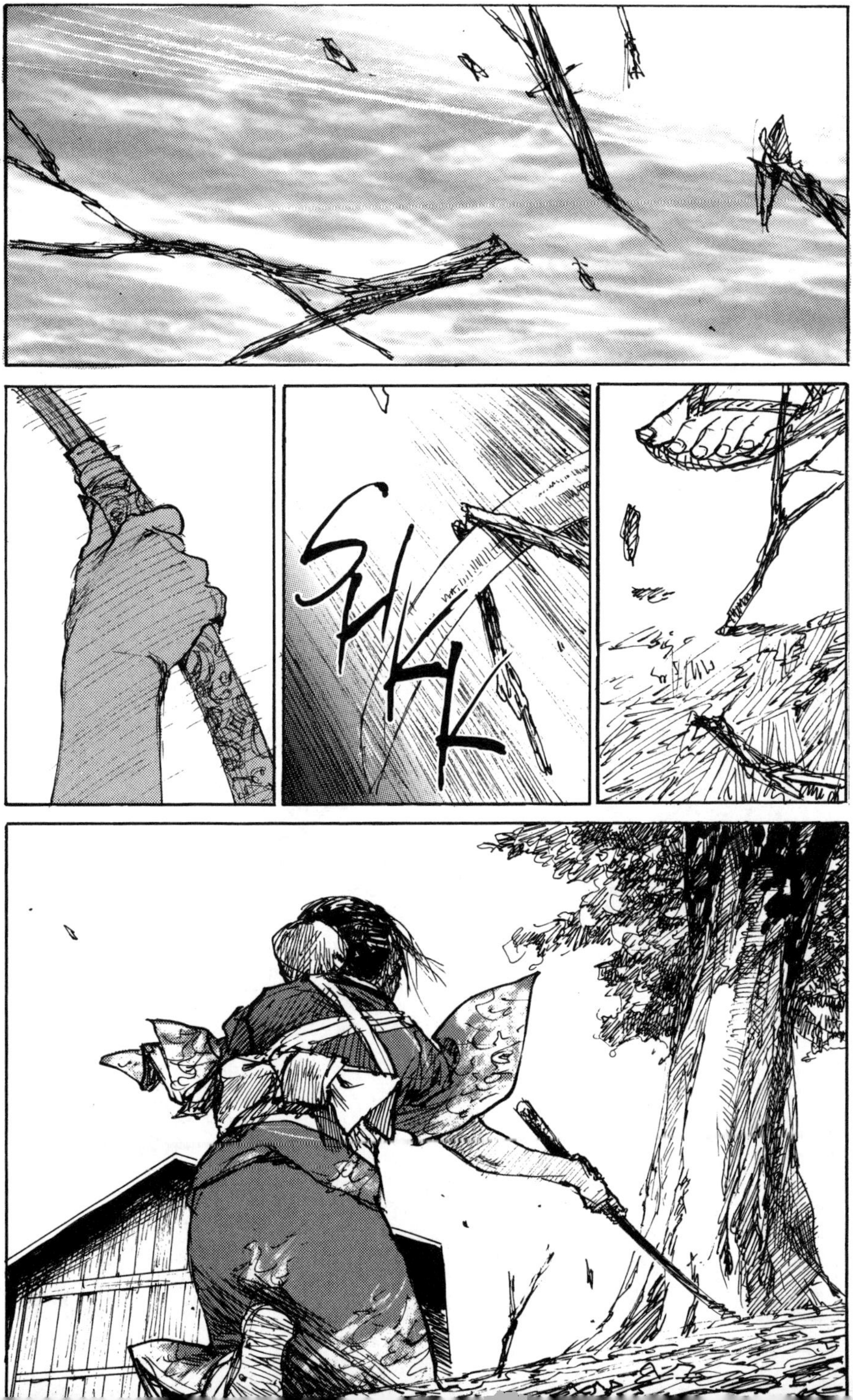
SHKK

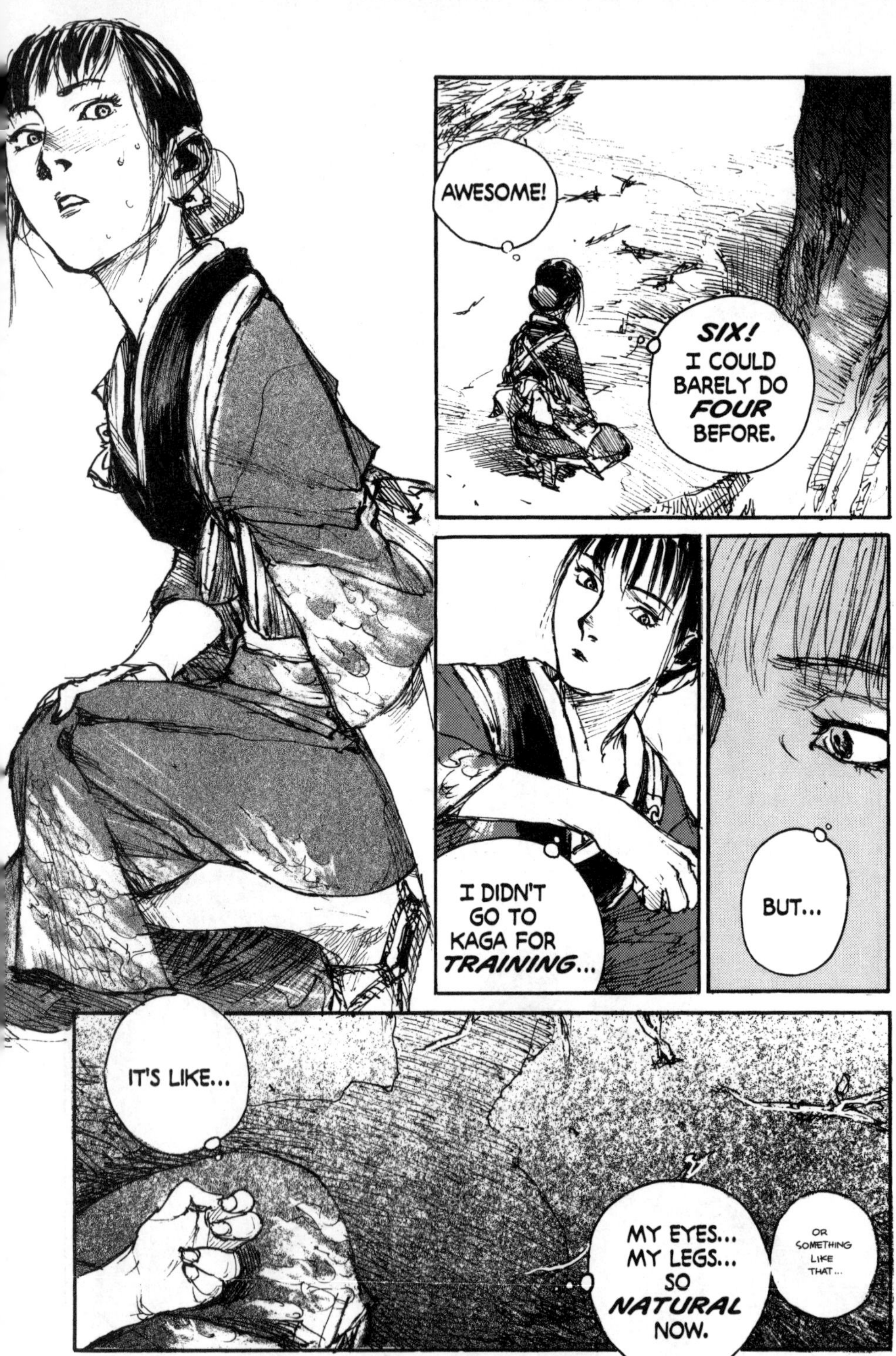
AWESOME!
SIX! I COULD BARELY DO FOUR BEFORE.
I DIDN'T GO TO KAGA FOR TRAINING...
BUT...
IT'S LIKE...
MY EYES... MY LEGS... SO NATURAL NOW.
OR SOMETHING LIKE THAT...

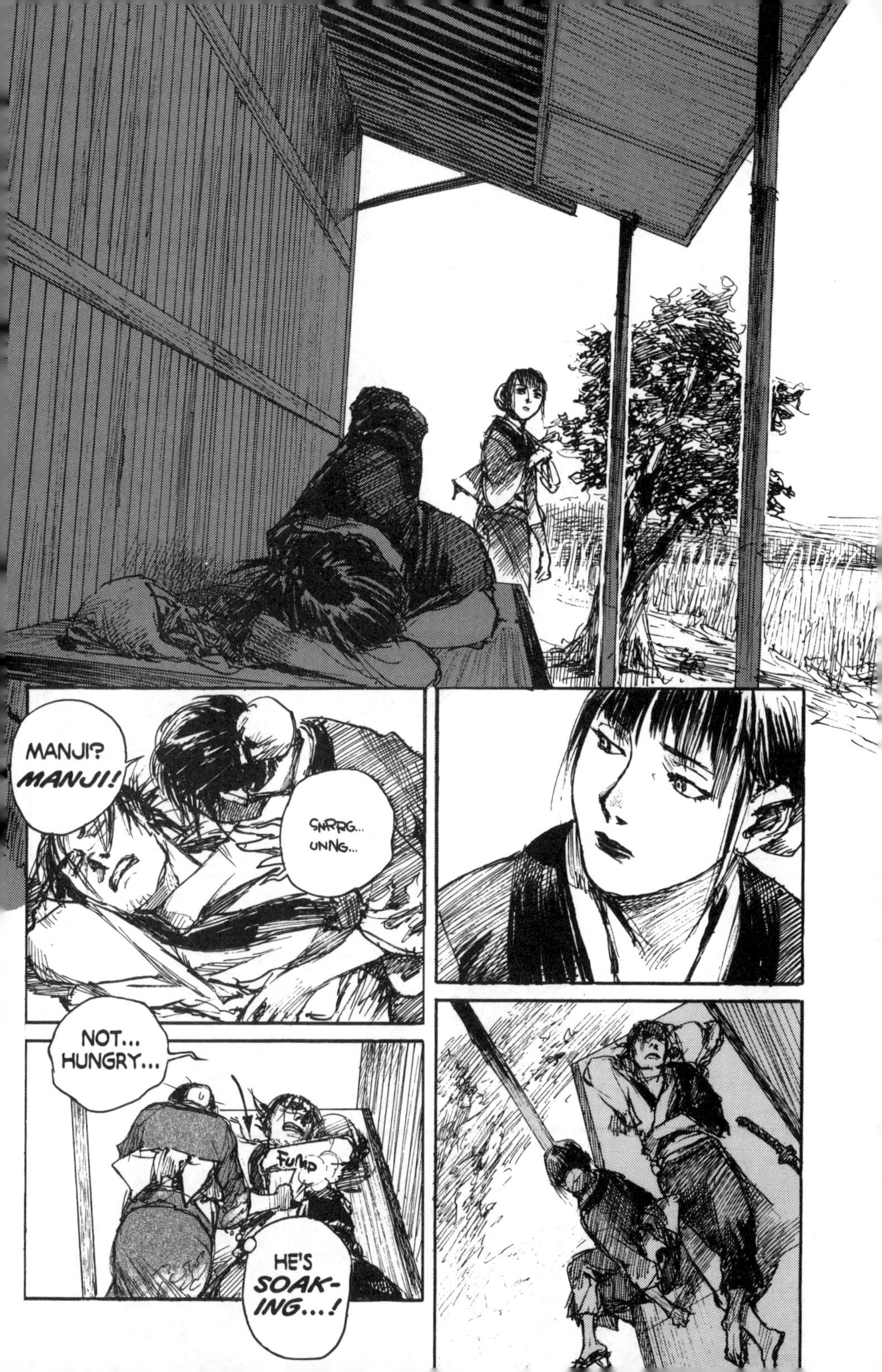
MANJI? MANJI!
SNRRG... UNNG...
NOT... HUNGRY...
FUMP
HE'S SOAK-ING...!

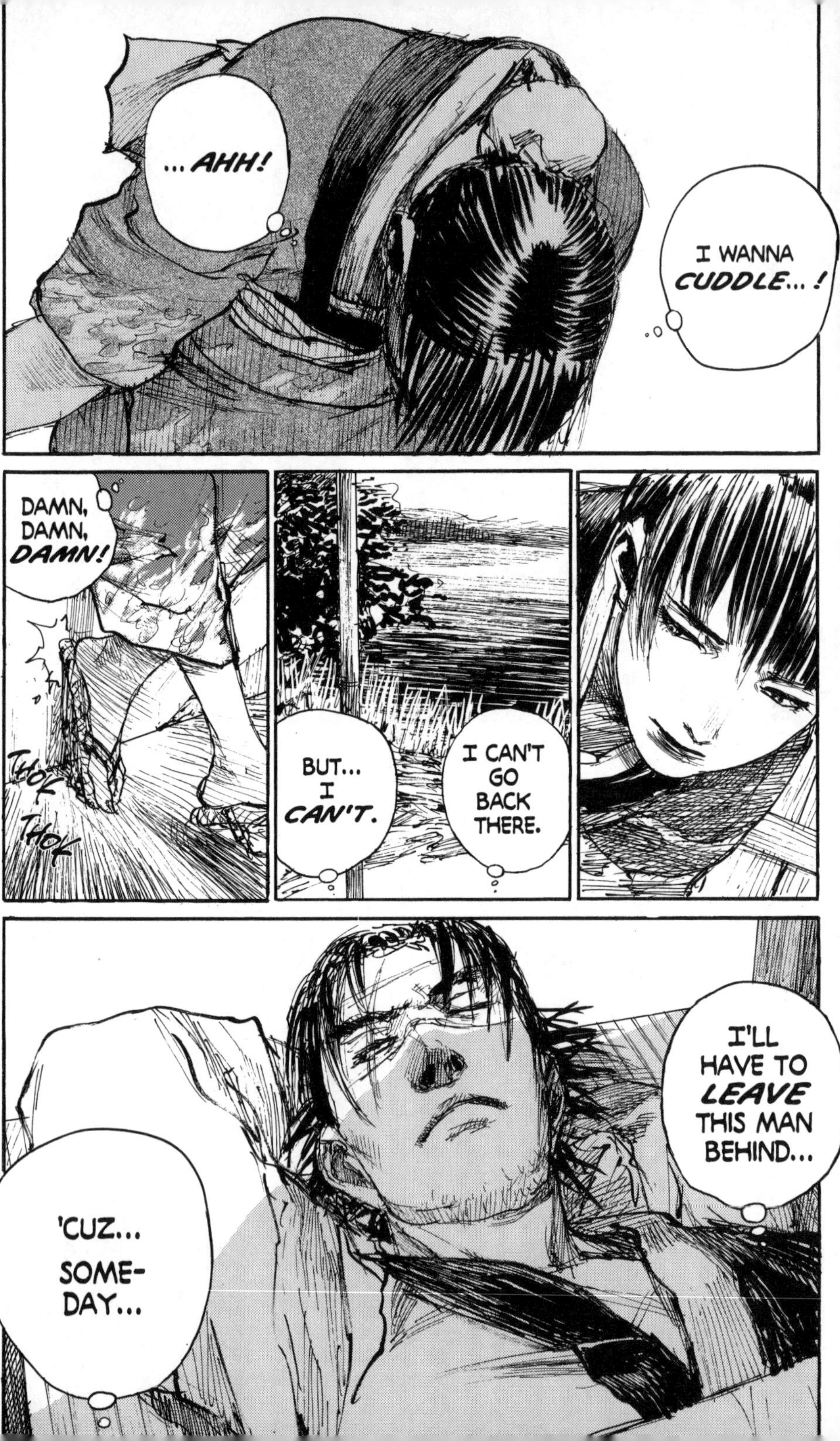

...AHH!
I WANNA CUDDLE...!
I CAN'T GO BACK THERE.
BUT... I CAN'T.
DAMN, DAMN, DAMN!
THOK THOK
I'LL HAVE TO LEAVE THIS MAN BEHIND...
'CUZ... SOME-DAY...

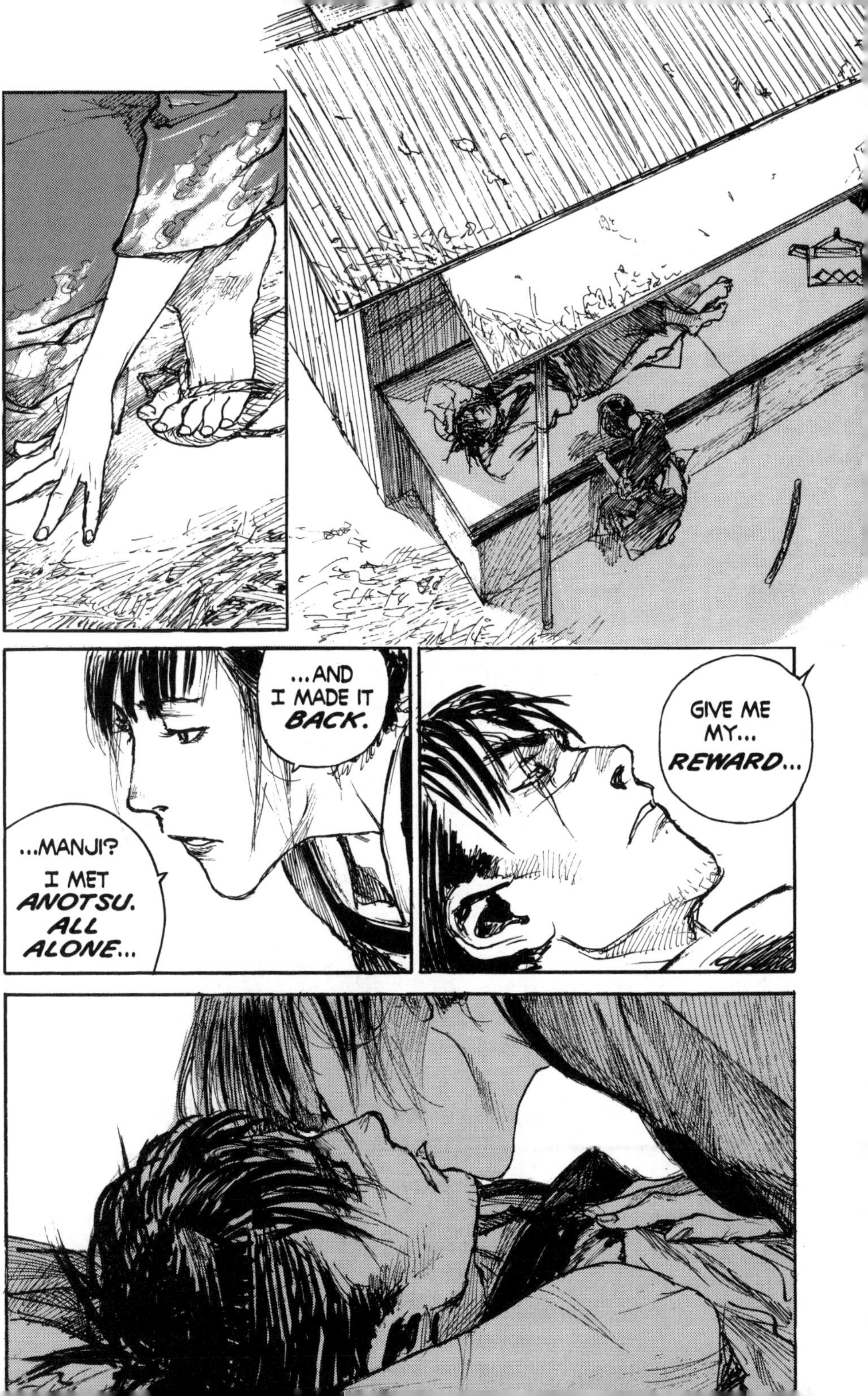
GIVE ME MY... REWARD...
...AND I MADE IT BACK.
...MANJI? I MET ANOTSU. ALL ALONE...

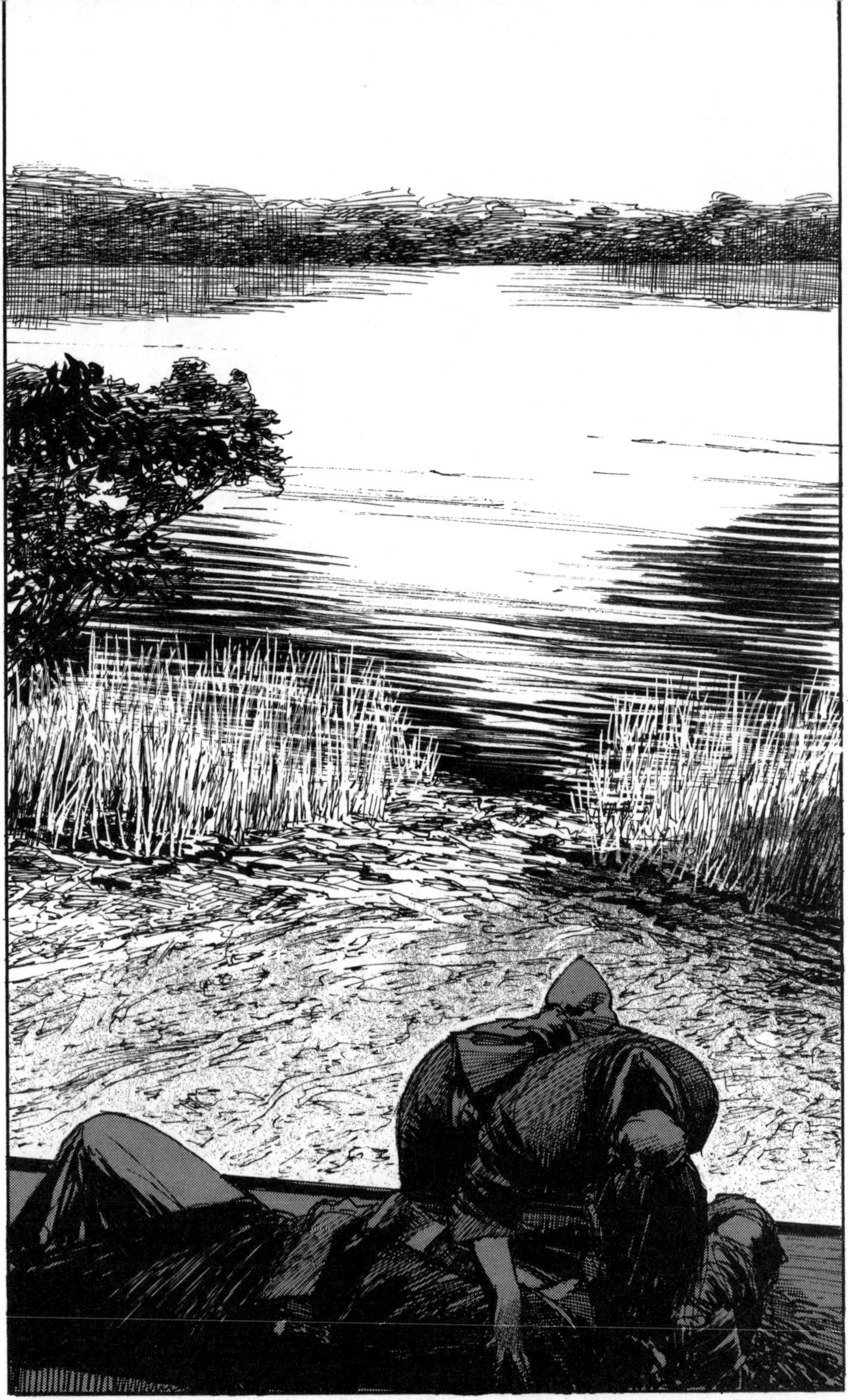

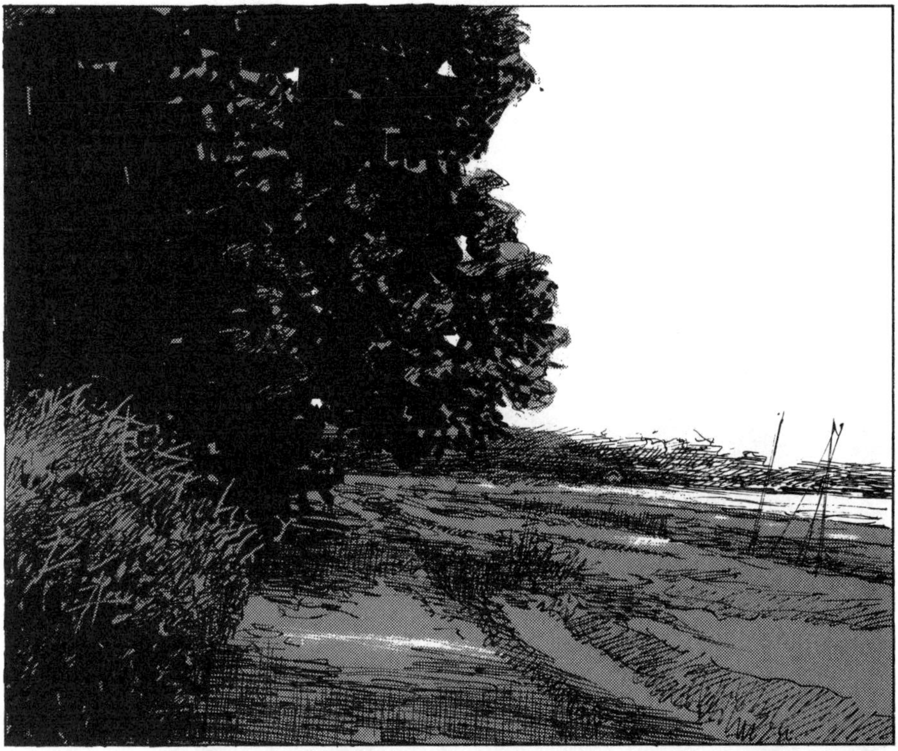
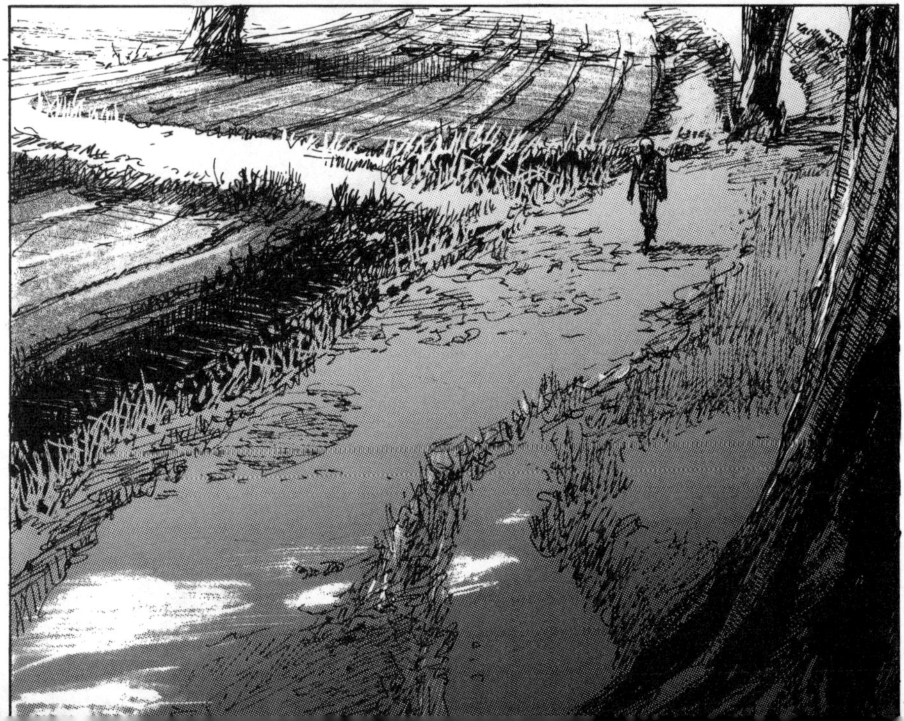

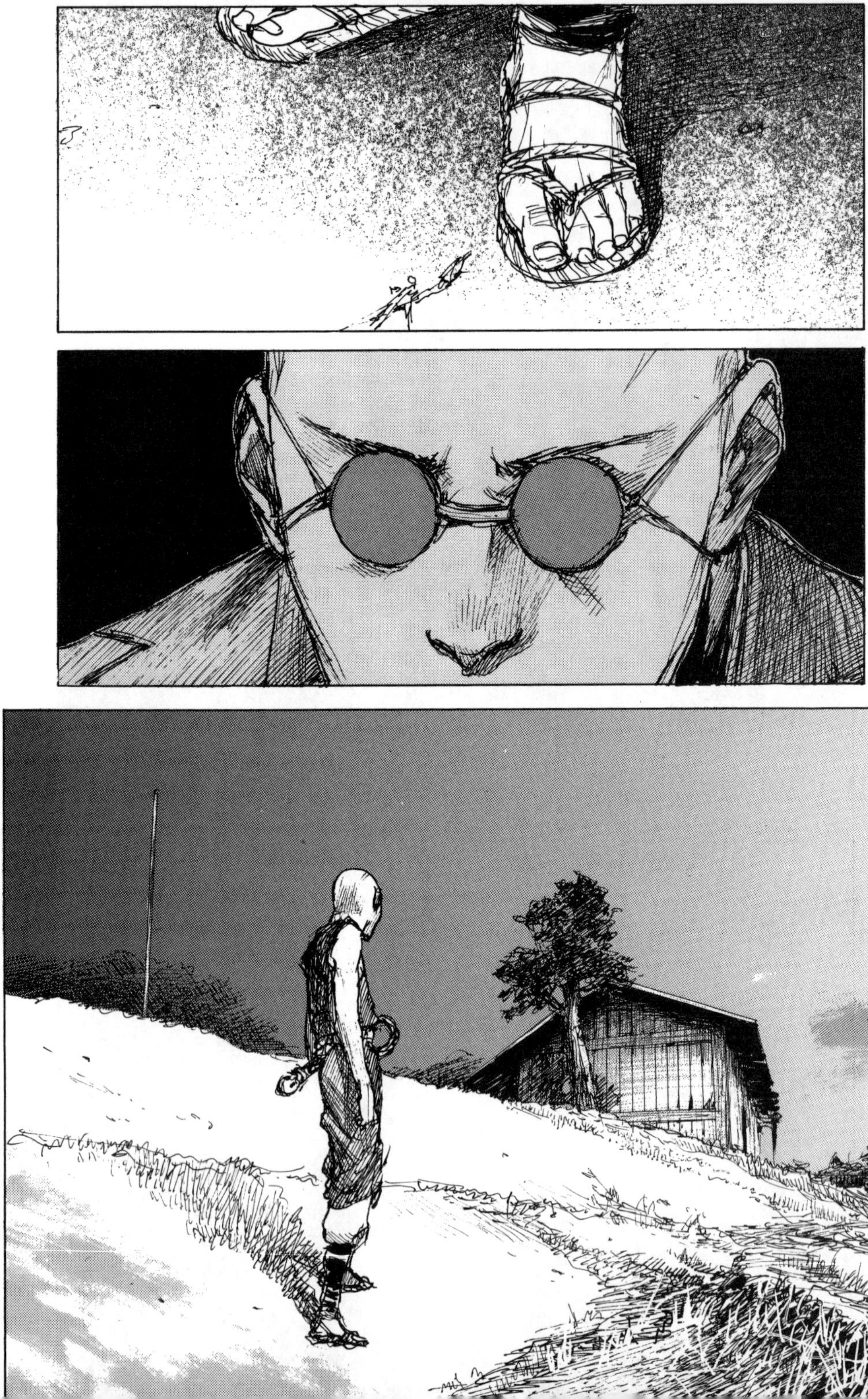

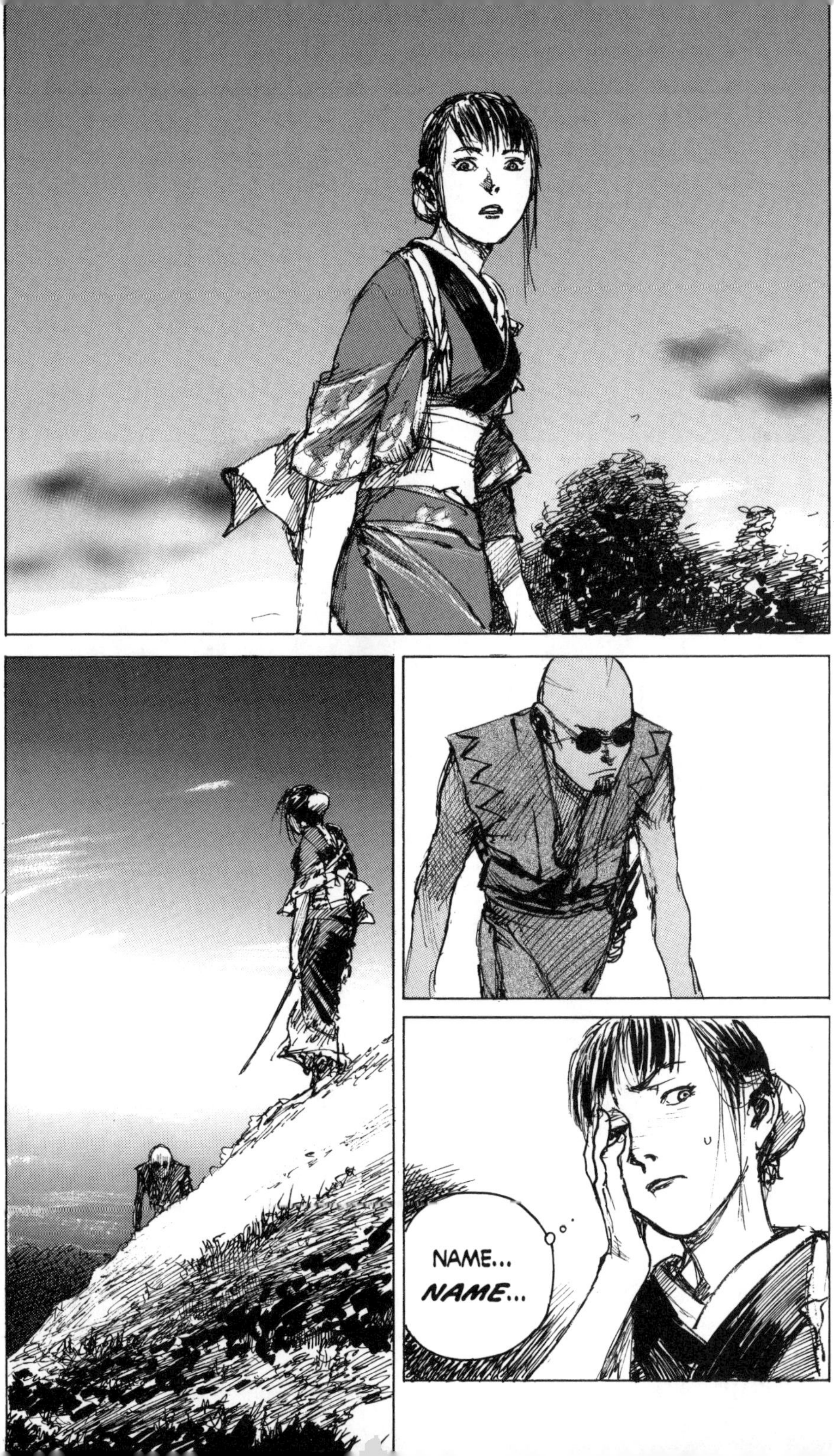
NAME...
NAME...

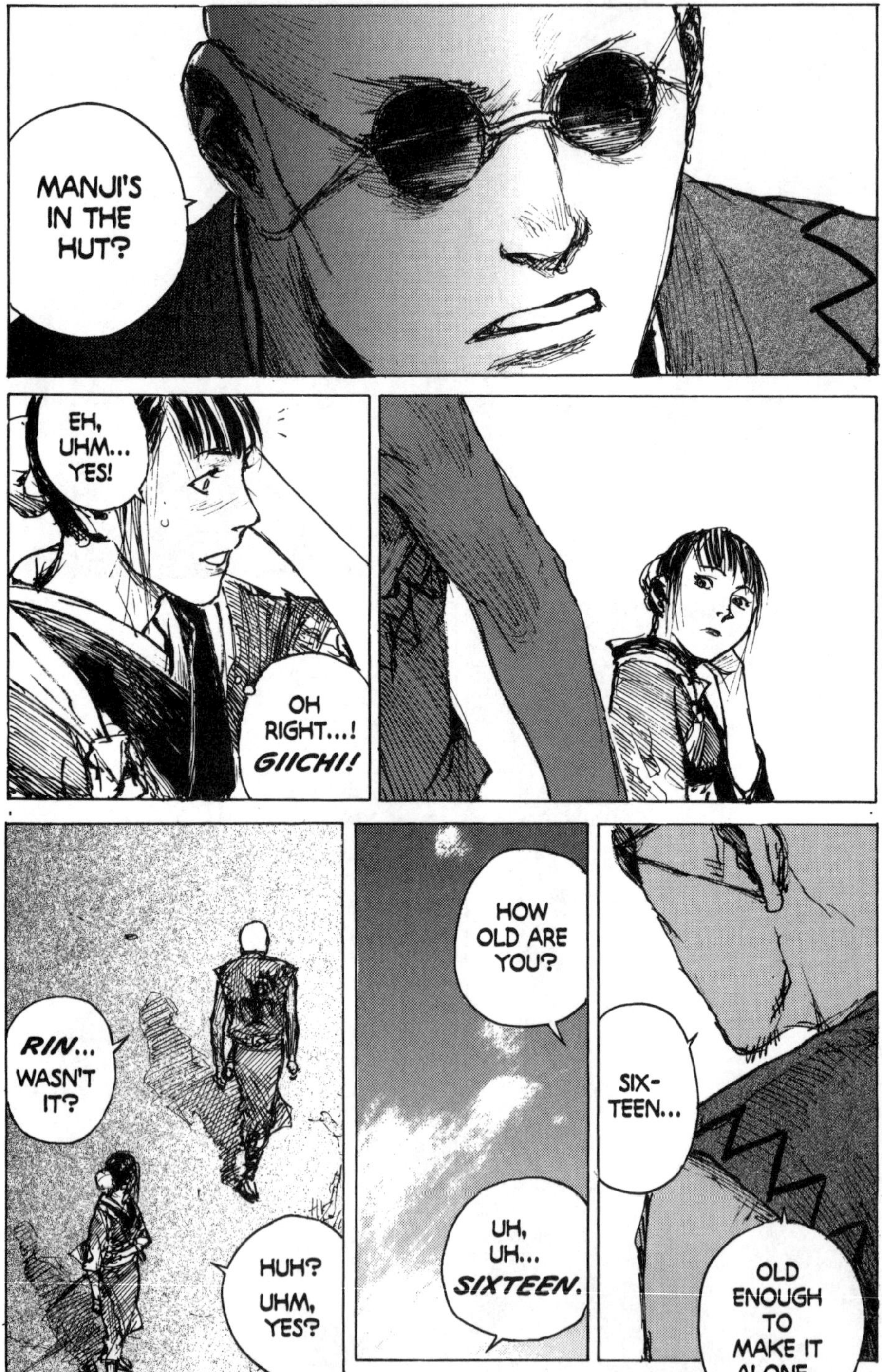
MANJI'S IN THE HUT?
EH, UHM... YES!
OH RIGHT...! GIICHI!
RIN... WASN'T IT?
HUH? UHM, YES?
HOW OLD ARE YOU?
UH, UH... SIXTEEN.
SIX-TEEN...
OLD ENOUGH TO MAKE IT ALONE...

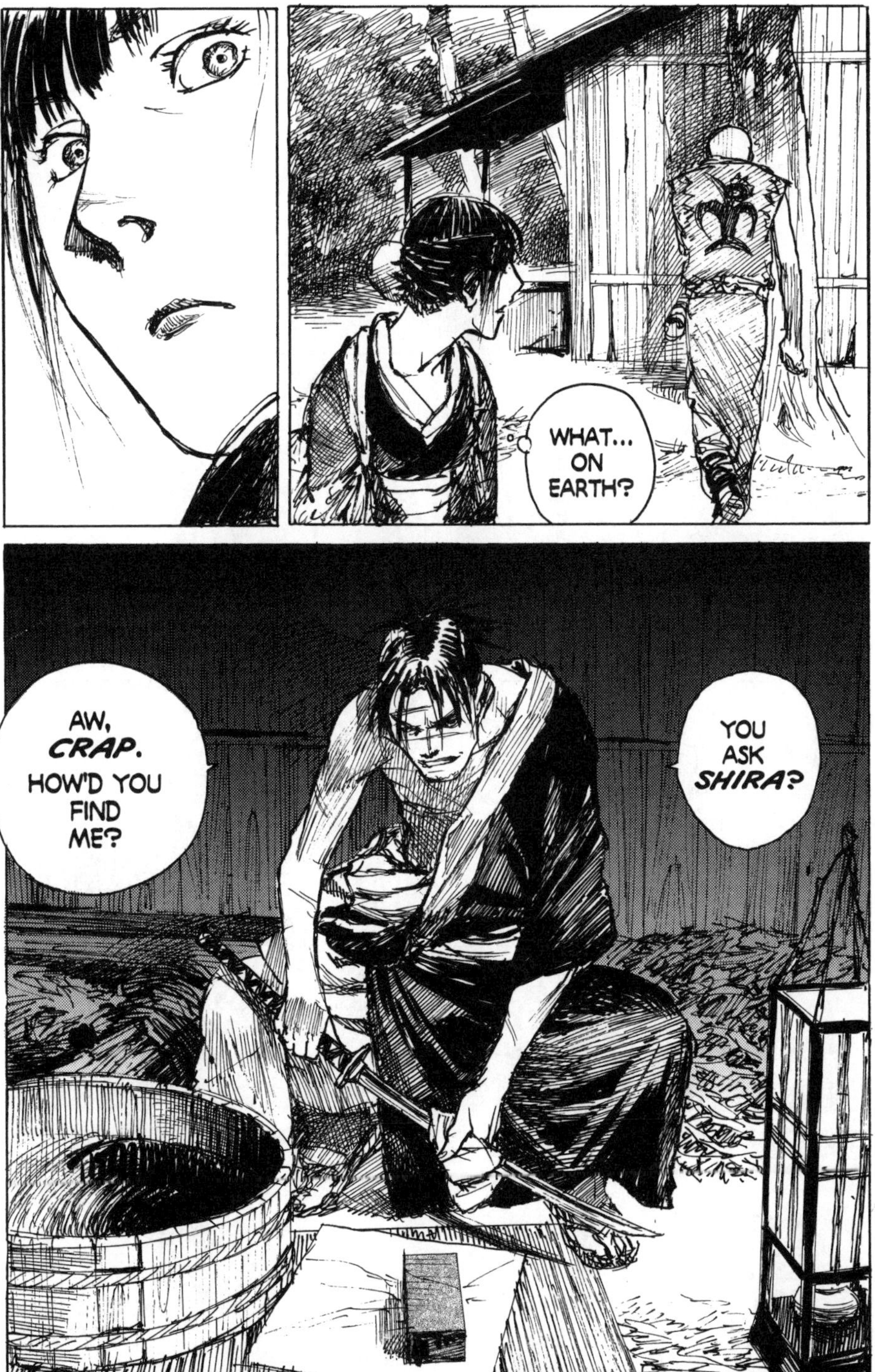
WHAT... ON EARTH?
AW, *CRAP*. HOW'D YOU FIND ME?
YOU ASK *SHIRA*?

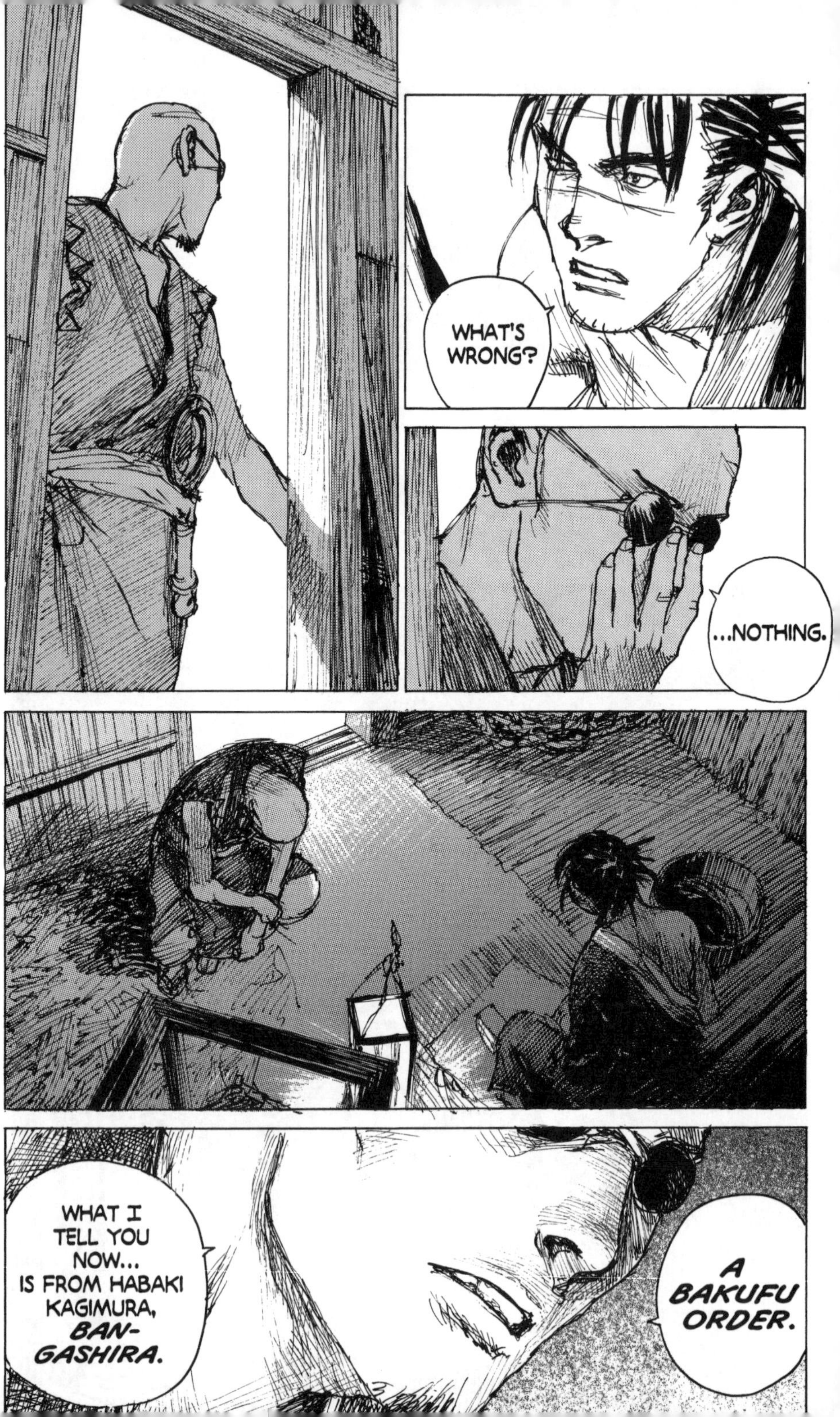
WHAT'S WRONG?
...NOTHING.
WHAT I TELL YOU NOW... IS FROM HABAKI KAGIMURA, ***BAN-GASHIRA.***
A BAKUFU ORDER.

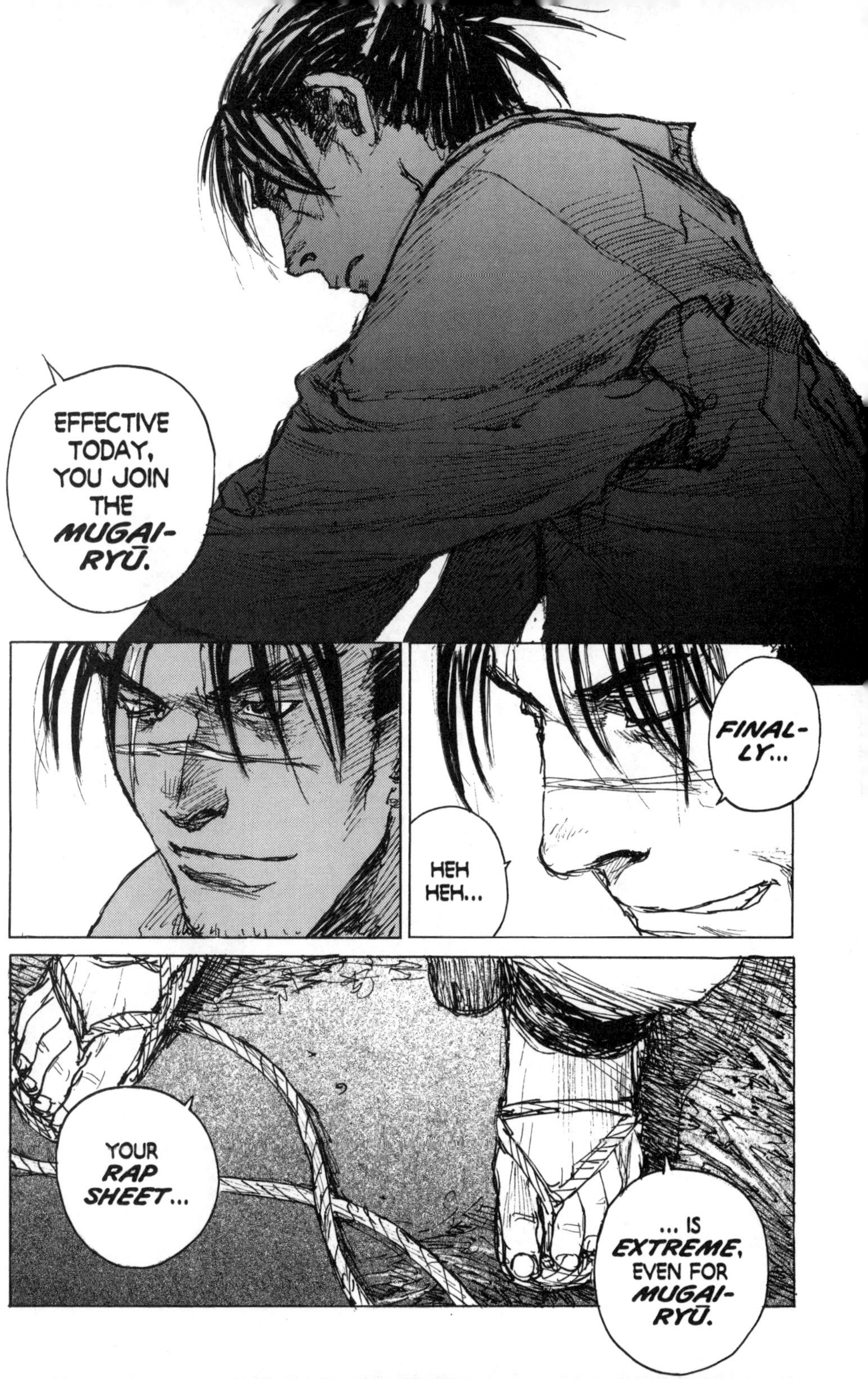
EFFECTIVE TODAY, YOU JOIN THE MUGAI-RYŪ.
FINAL-LY...
HEH HEH...
YOUR RAP SHEET...
... IS EXTREME, EVEN FOR MUGAI-RYŪ.

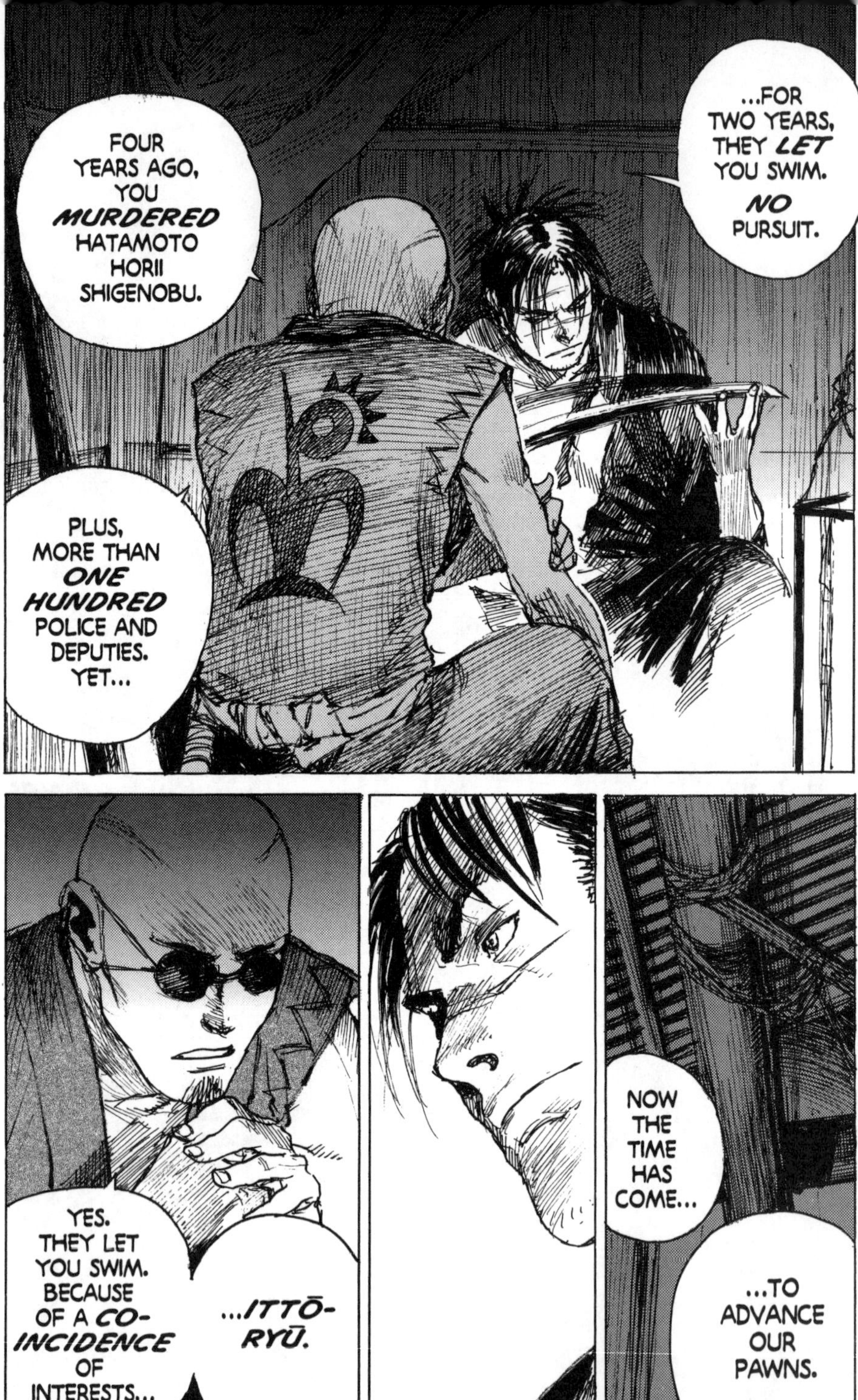
FOUR YEARS AGO, YOU *MURDERED* HATAMOTO HORII SHIGENOBU.
PLUS, MORE THAN *ONE HUNDRED* POLICE AND DEPUTIES. YET...
...FOR TWO YEARS, THEY *LET* YOU SWIM. *NO* PURSUIT.
YES. THEY LET YOU SWIM. BECAUSE OF A *CO-INCIDENCE* OF INTERESTS...
...*ITTŌ-RYŪ*.
NOW THE TIME HAS COME...
...TO ADVANCE OUR PAWNS.

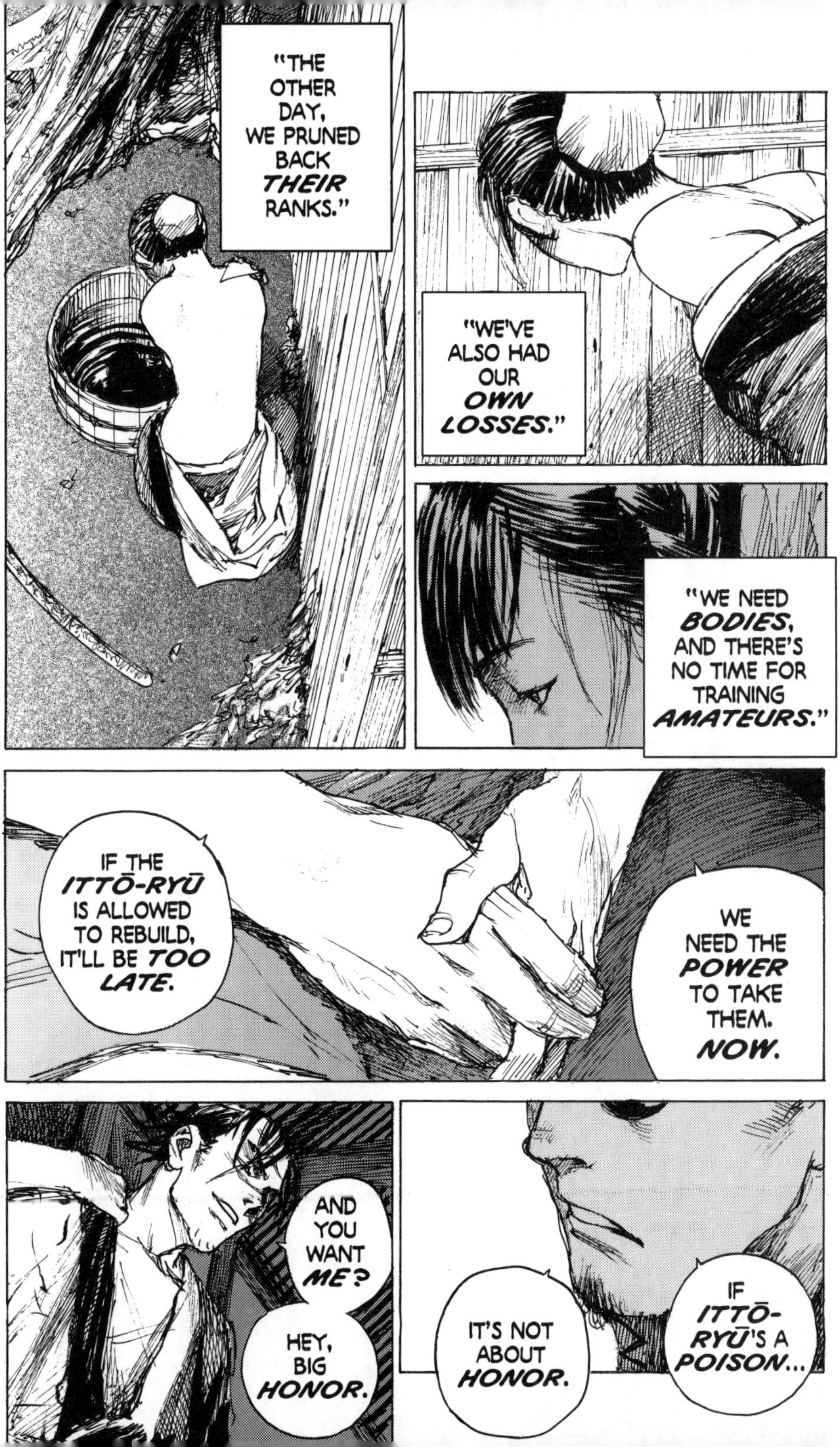
"THE OTHER DAY, WE PRUNED BACK THEIR RANKS."
"WE'VE ALSO HAD OUR OWN LOSSES."
"WE NEED BODIES, AND THERE'S NO TIME FOR TRAINING AMATEURS."
IF THE ITTŌ-RYŪ IS ALLOWED TO REBUILD, IT'LL BE TOO LATE.
WE NEED THE POWER TO TAKE THEM. NOW.
AND YOU WANT ME?
HEY, BIG HONOR.
IT'S NOT ABOUT HONOR.
IF ITTŌ-RYŪ'S A POISON...

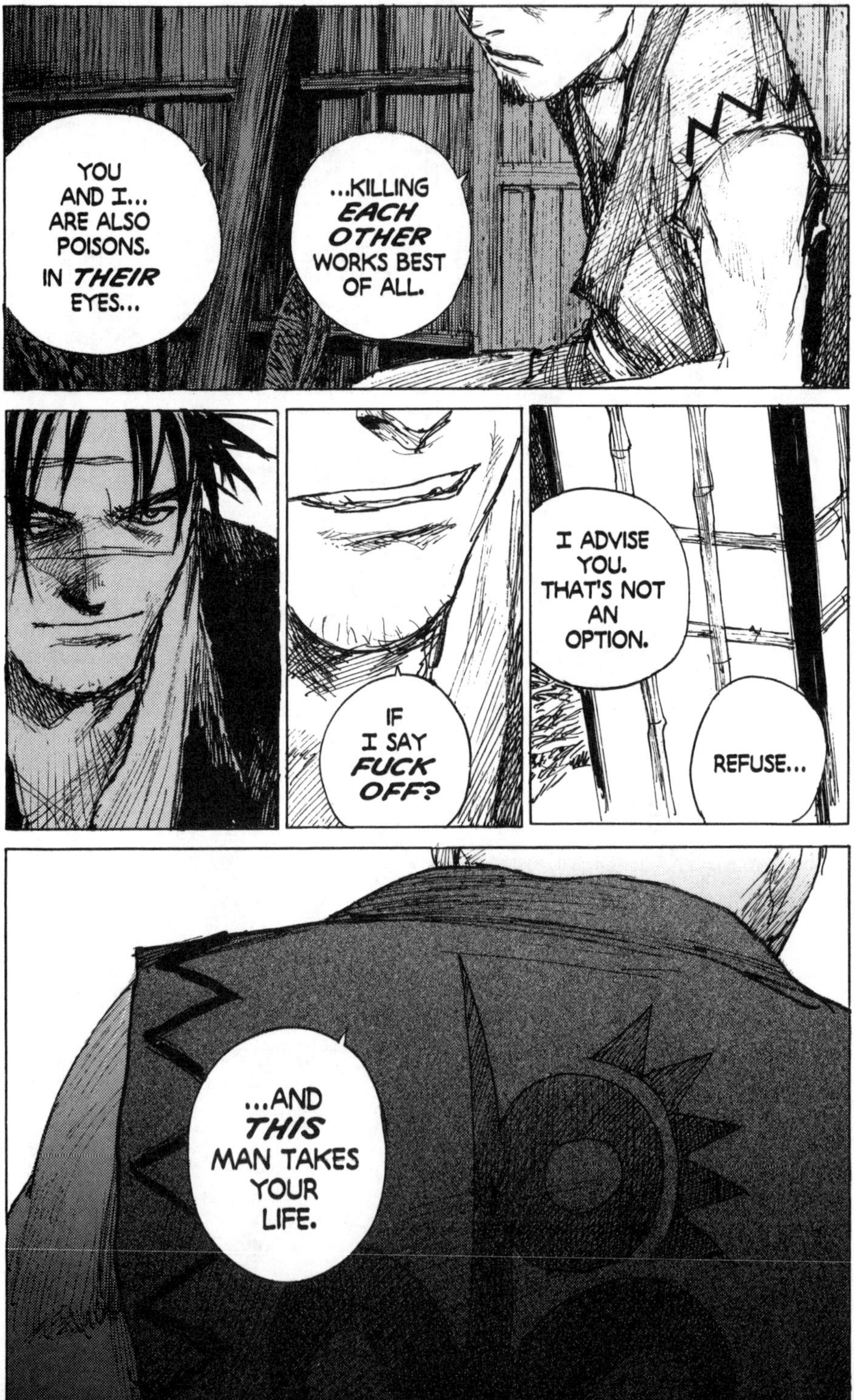
YOU AND I... ARE ALSO POISONS. IN *THEIR* EYES...
...KILLING *EACH OTHER* WORKS BEST OF ALL.
IF I SAY *FUCK OFF?*
I ADVISE YOU. THAT'S NOT AN OPTION.
REFUSE...
...AND *THIS* MAN TAKES YOUR LIFE.

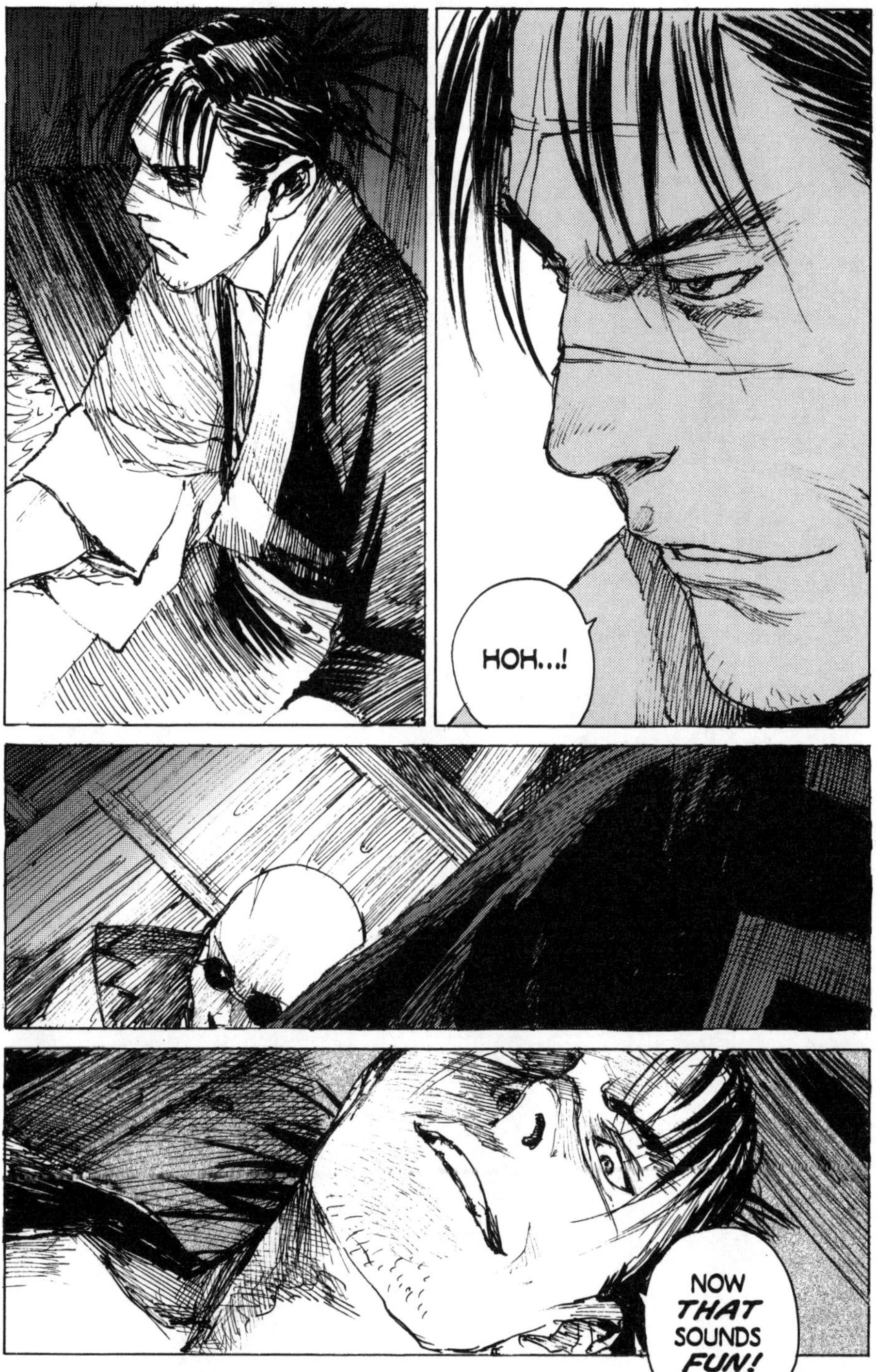
HOH...!
NOW *THAT* SOUNDS *FUN!*

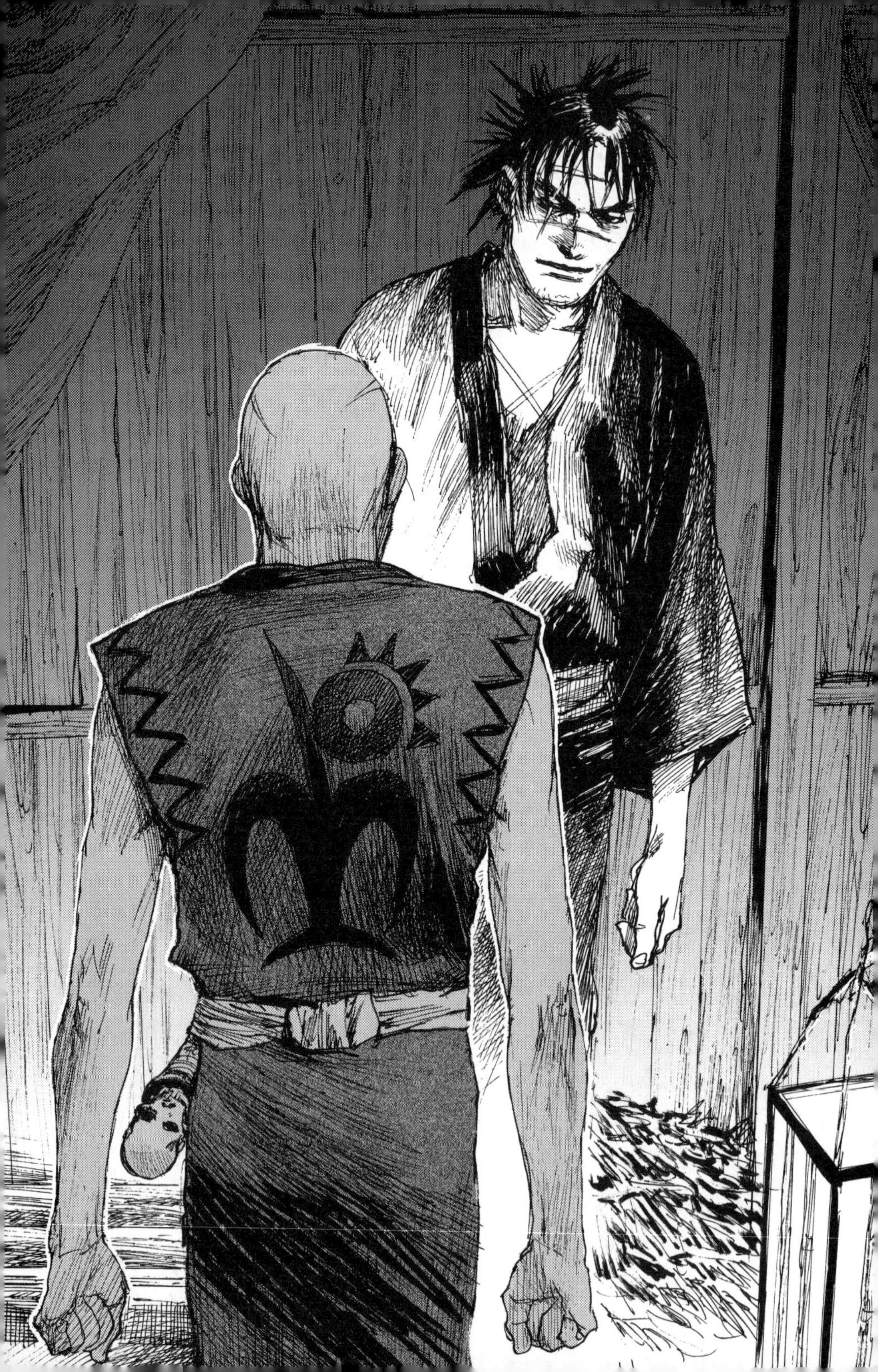

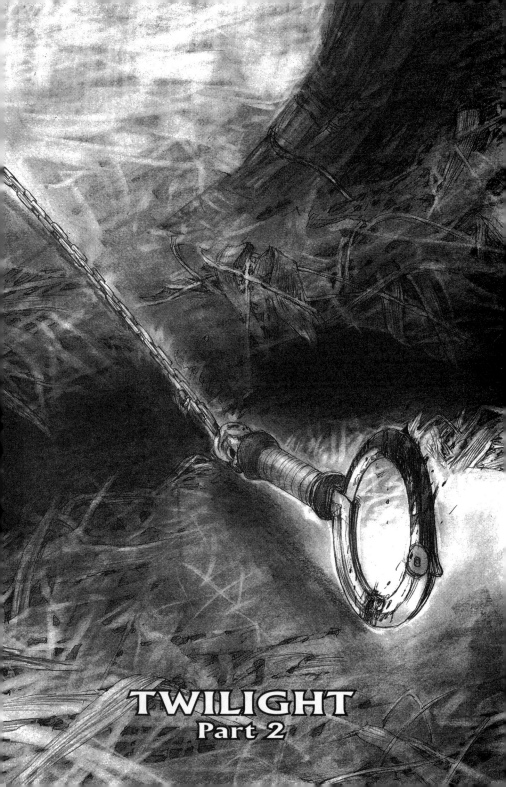

TWILIGHT
Part 2

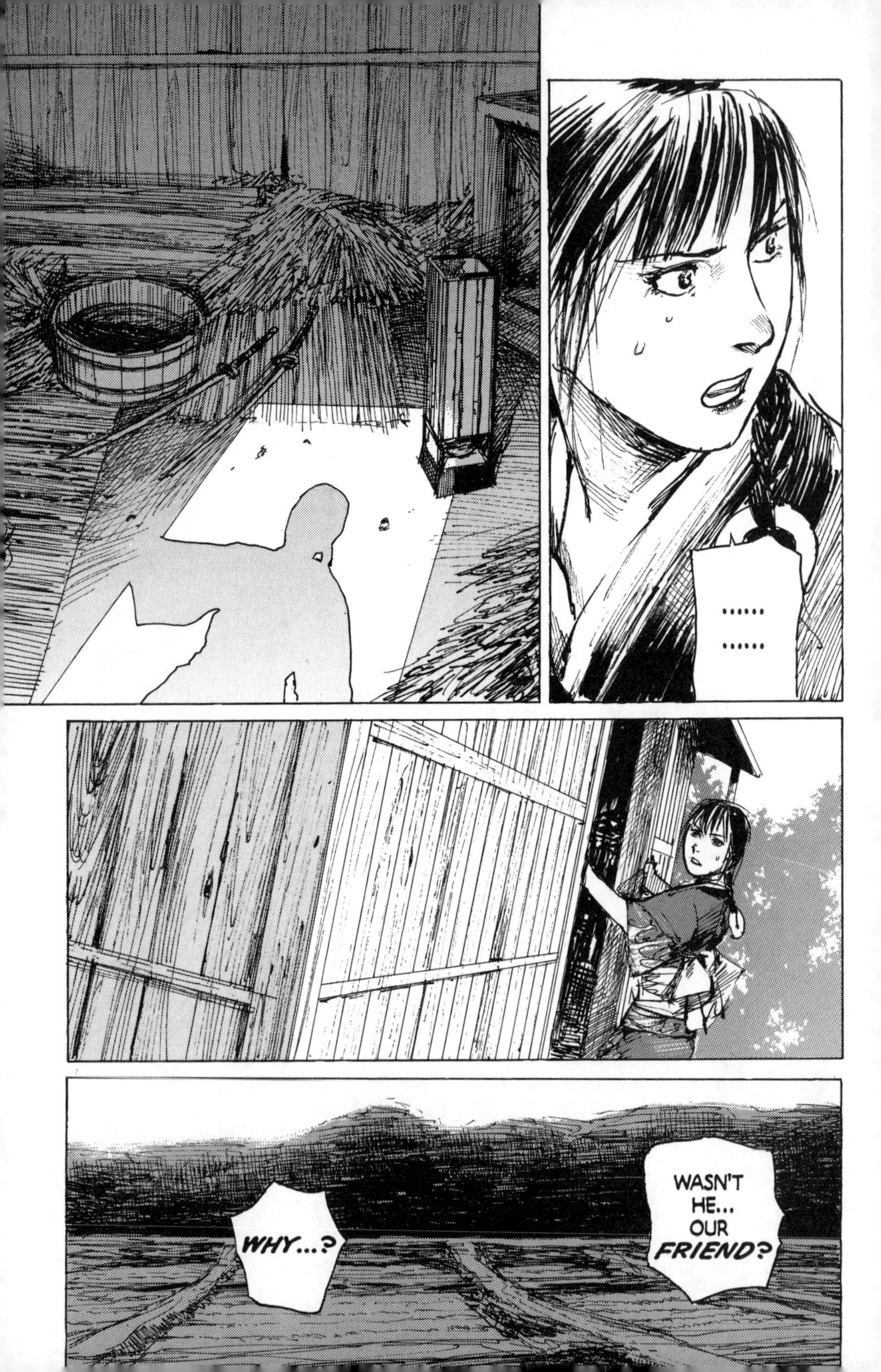
......
......
WASN'T HE... OUR FRIEND?
WHY...?

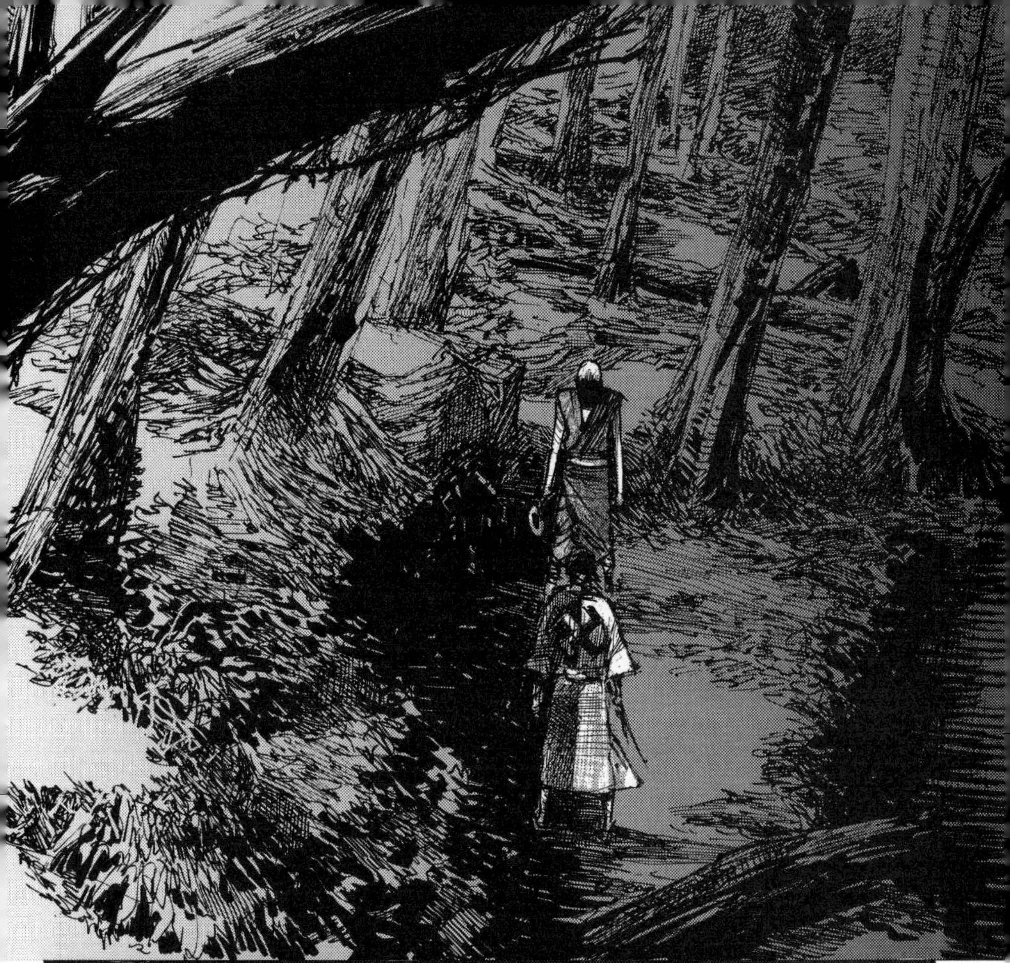
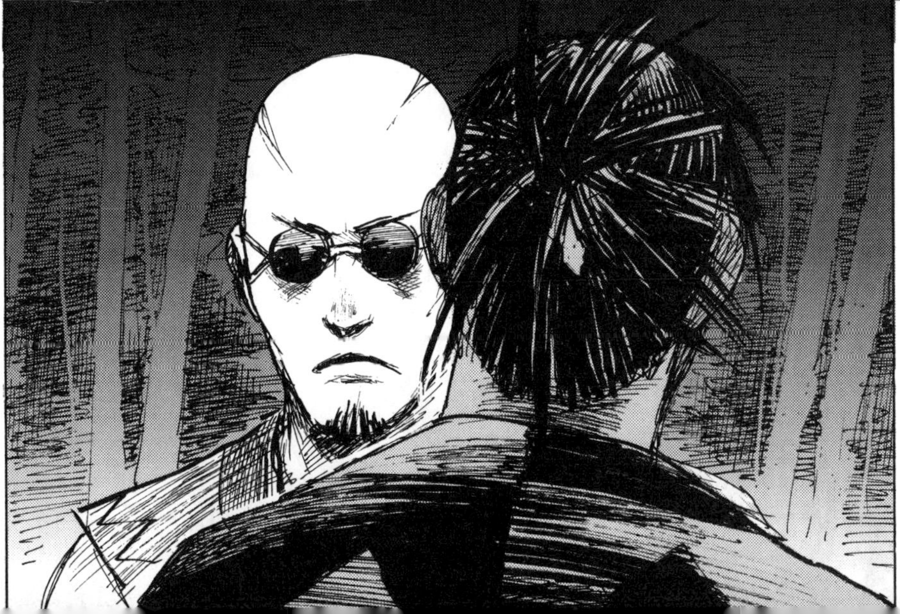

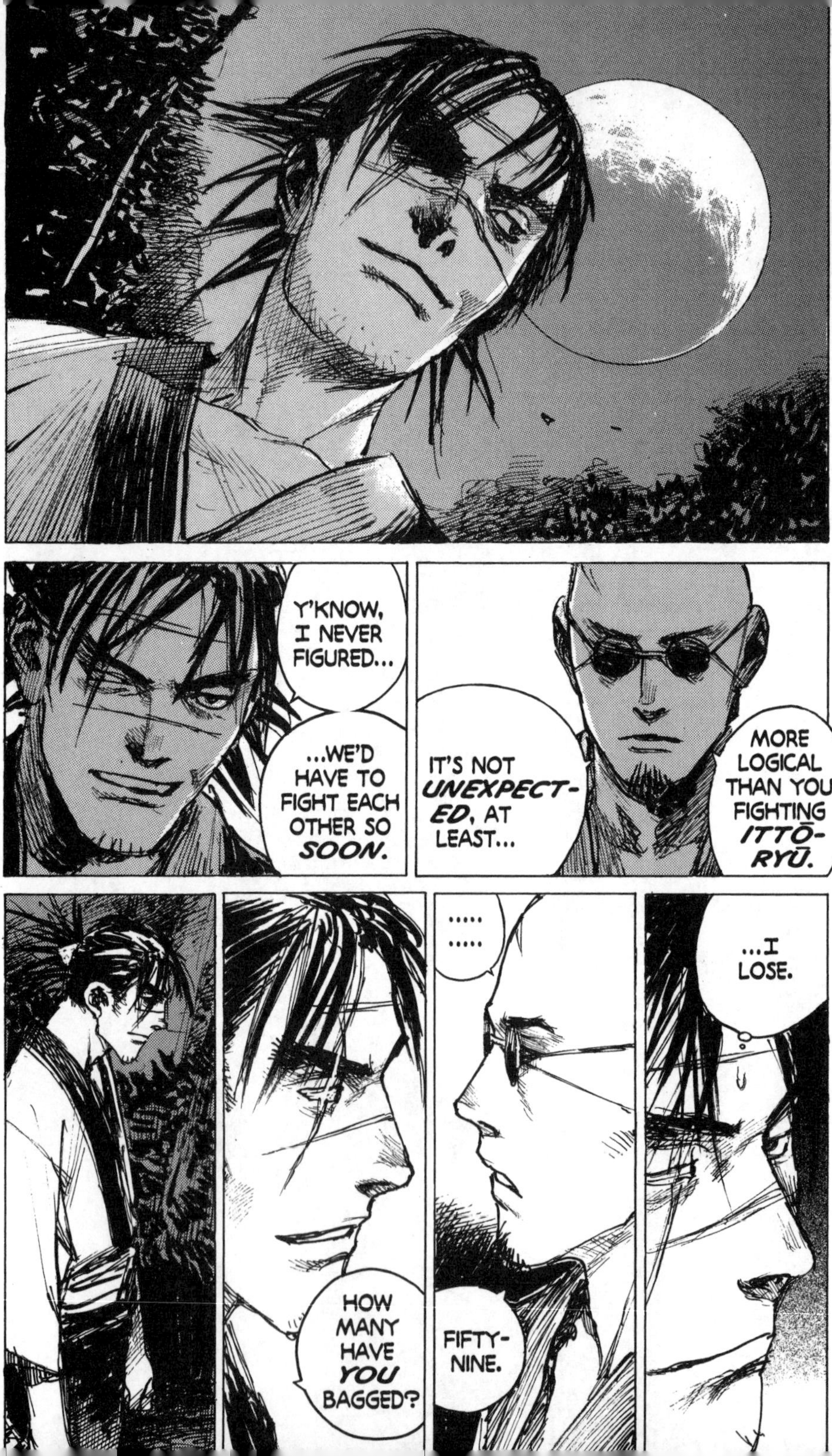
Y'KNOW, I NEVER FIGURED...
...WE'D HAVE TO FIGHT EACH OTHER SO SOON.
IT'S NOT UNEXPECTED, AT LEAST...
MORE LOGICAL THAN YOU FIGHTING ITTŌ-RYŪ.
HOW MANY HAVE YOU BAGGED?
....
FIFTY-NINE.
...I LOSE.

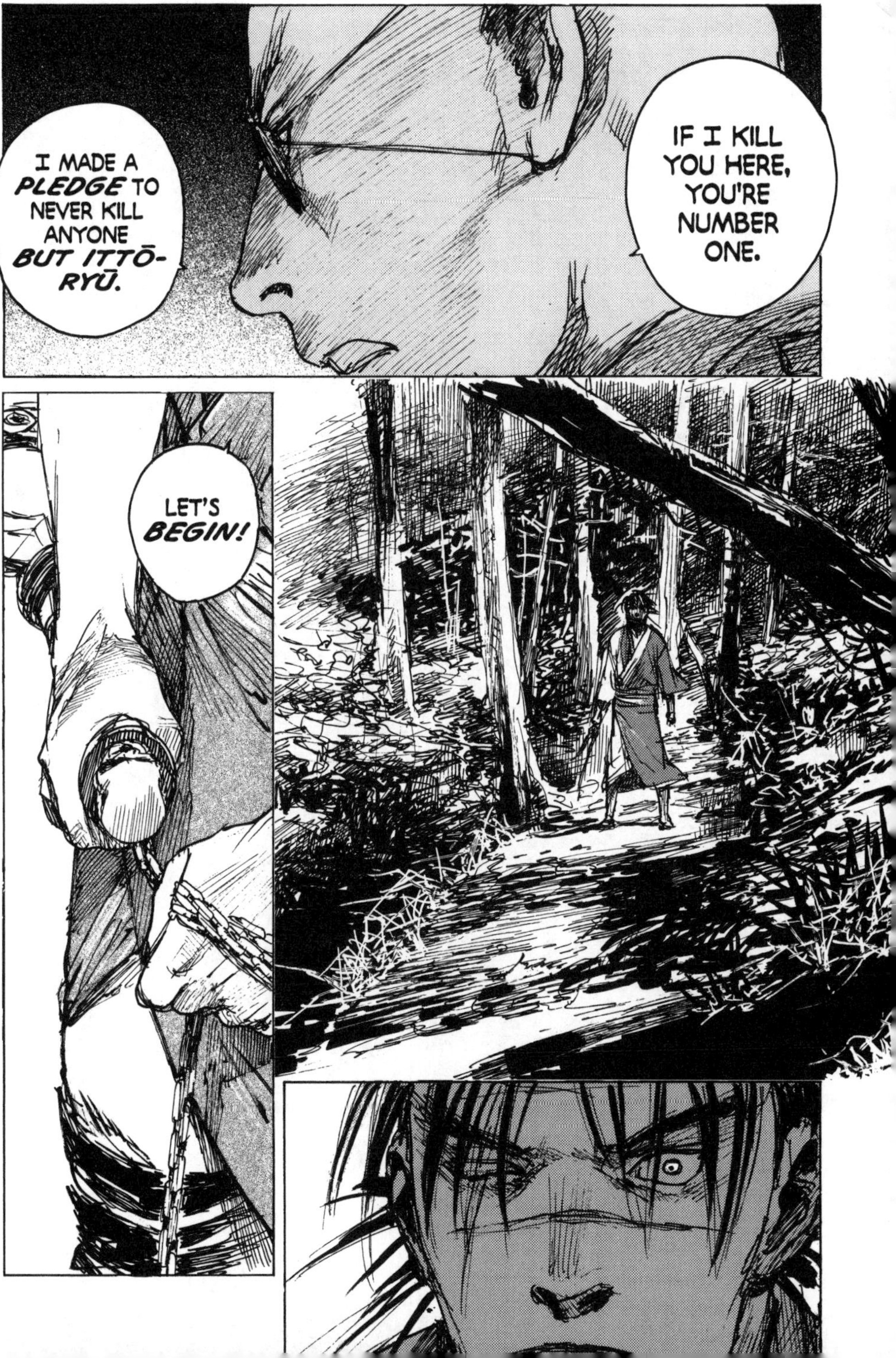
IF I KILL YOU HERE, YOU'RE NUMBER ONE.
I MADE A PLEDGE TO NEVER KILL ANYONE BUT ITTŌ-RYŪ.
LET'S BEGIN!

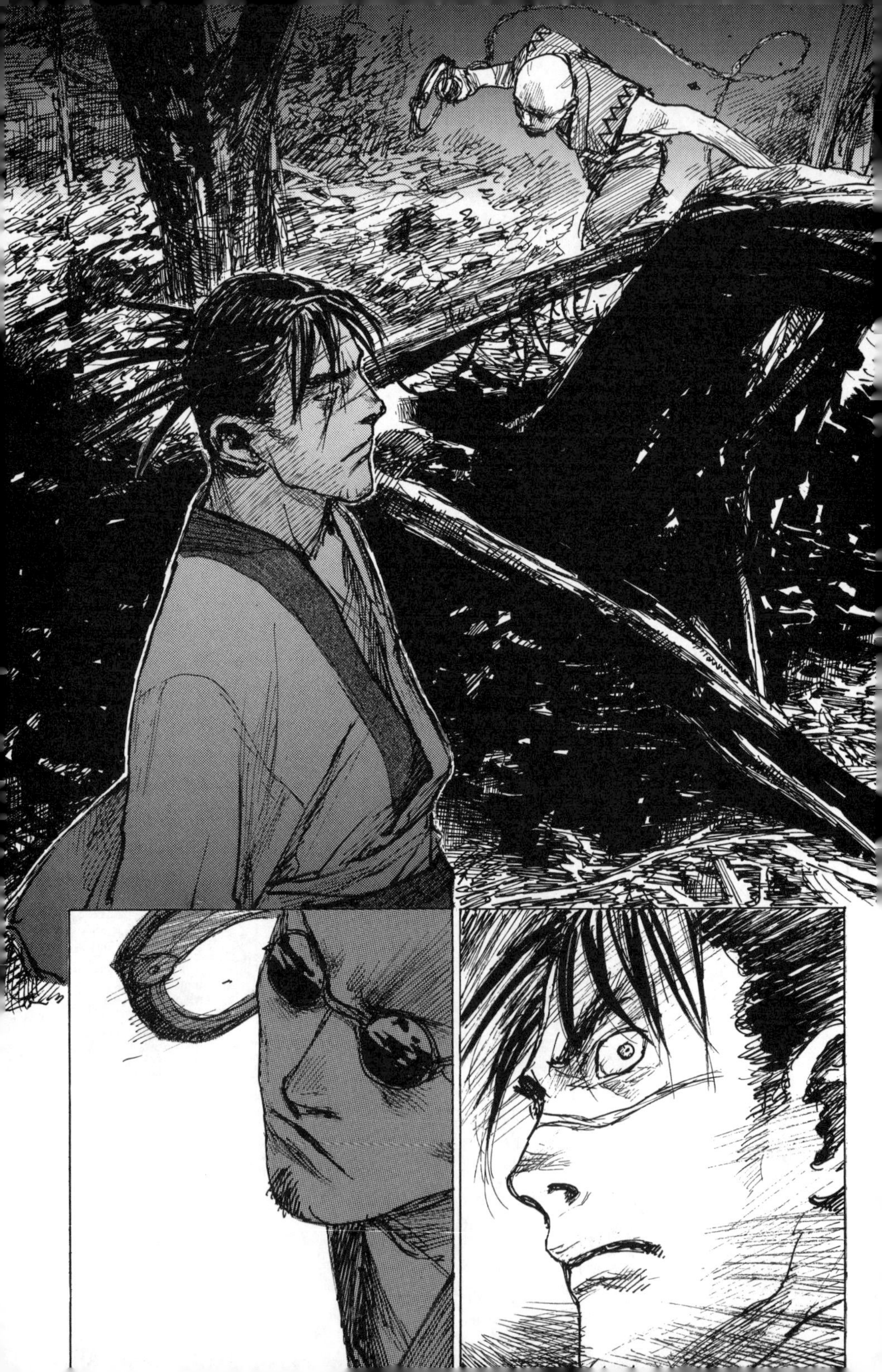

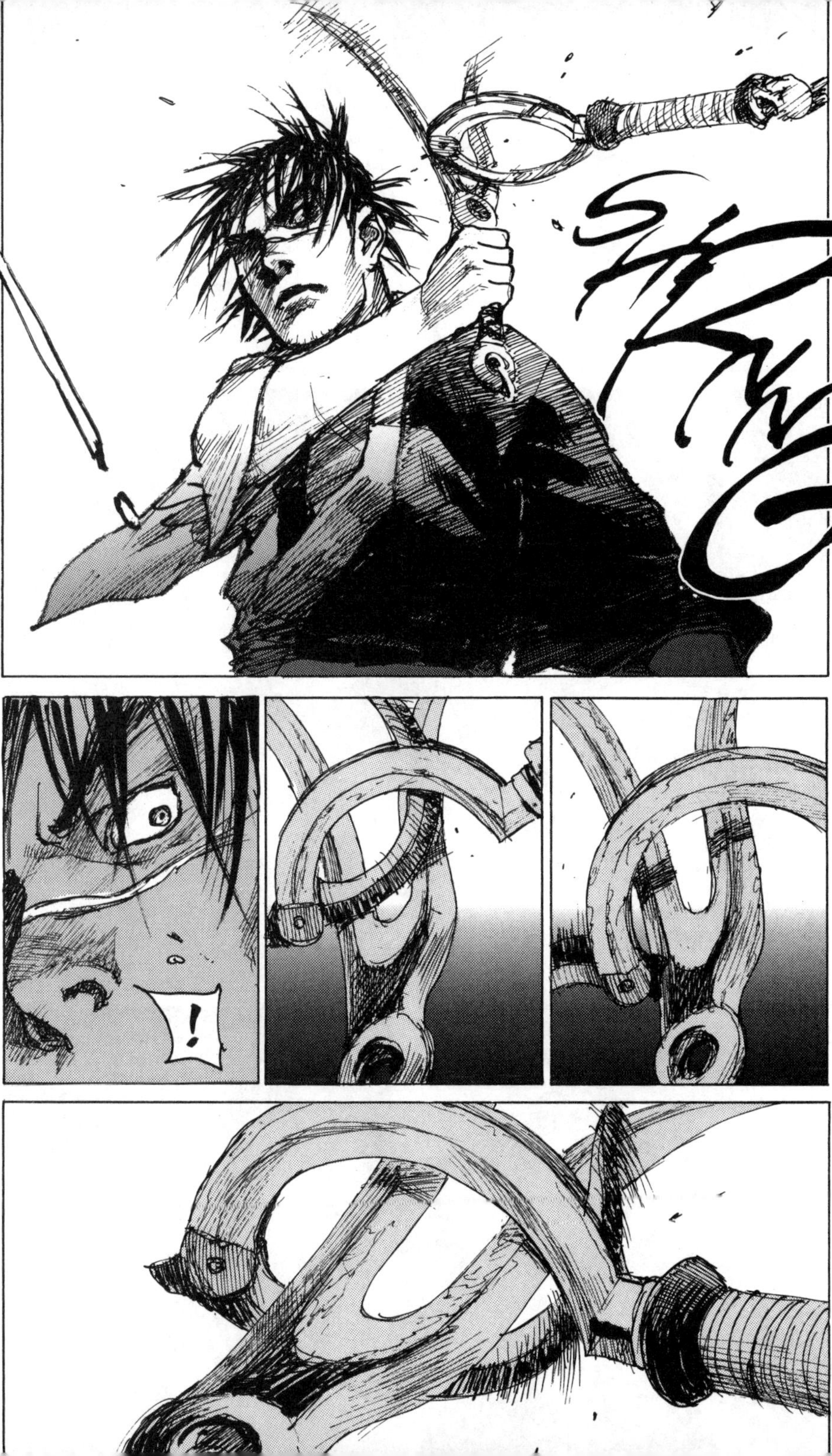
SHING
!

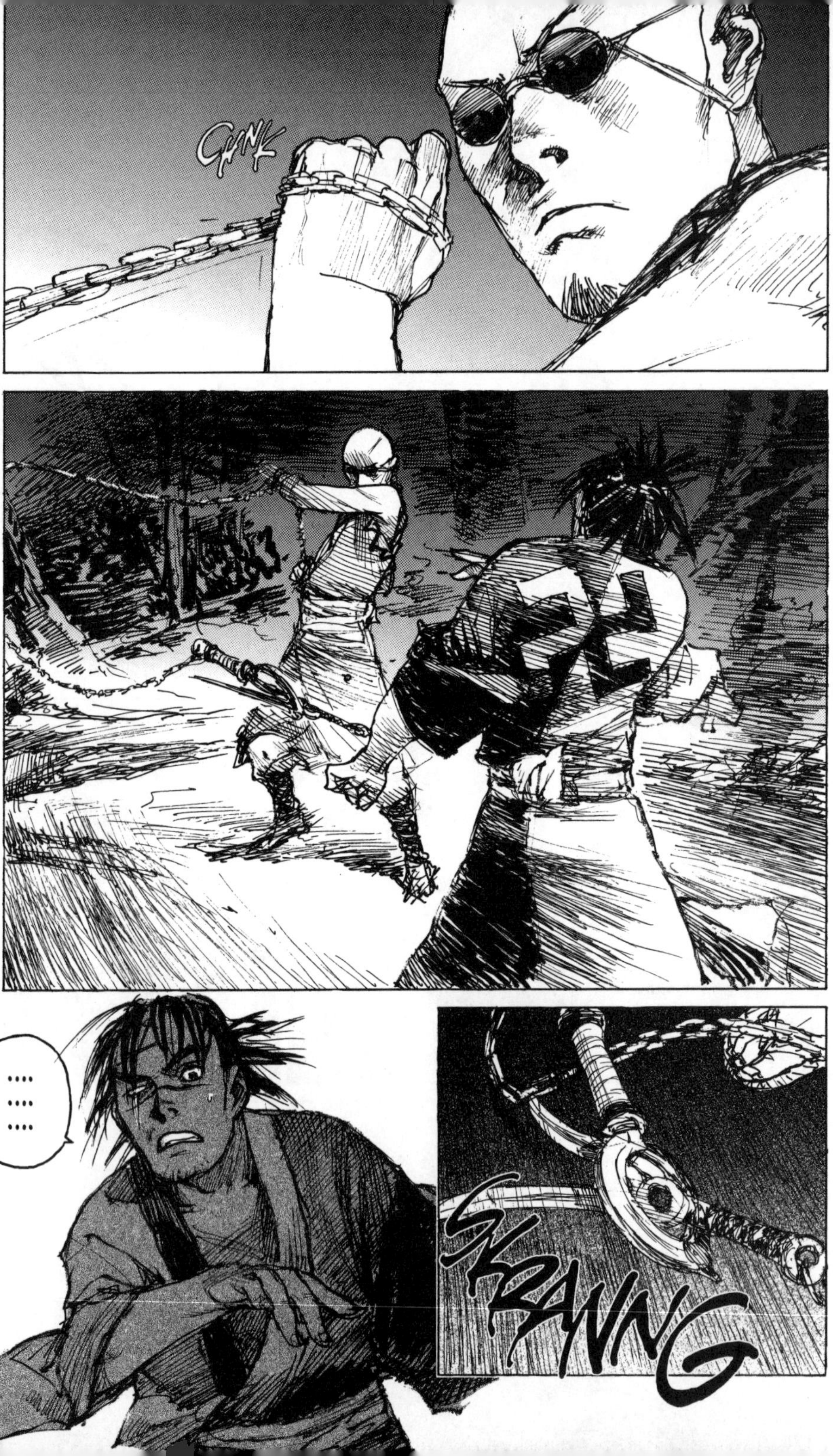
CHNK
SKRANNG
....
....
....

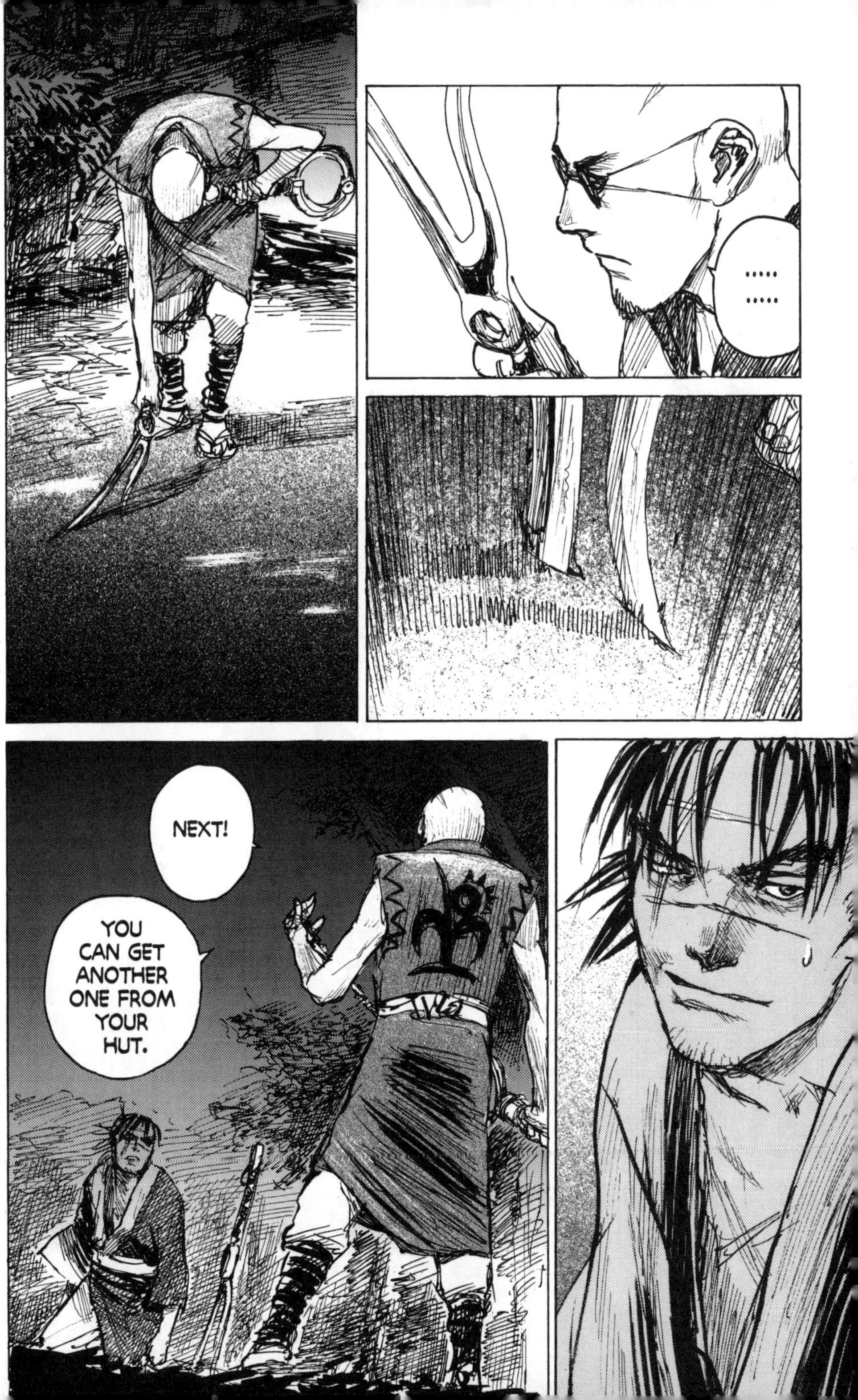
.....
.....
NEXT!
YOU CAN GET ANOTHER ONE FROM YOUR HUT.

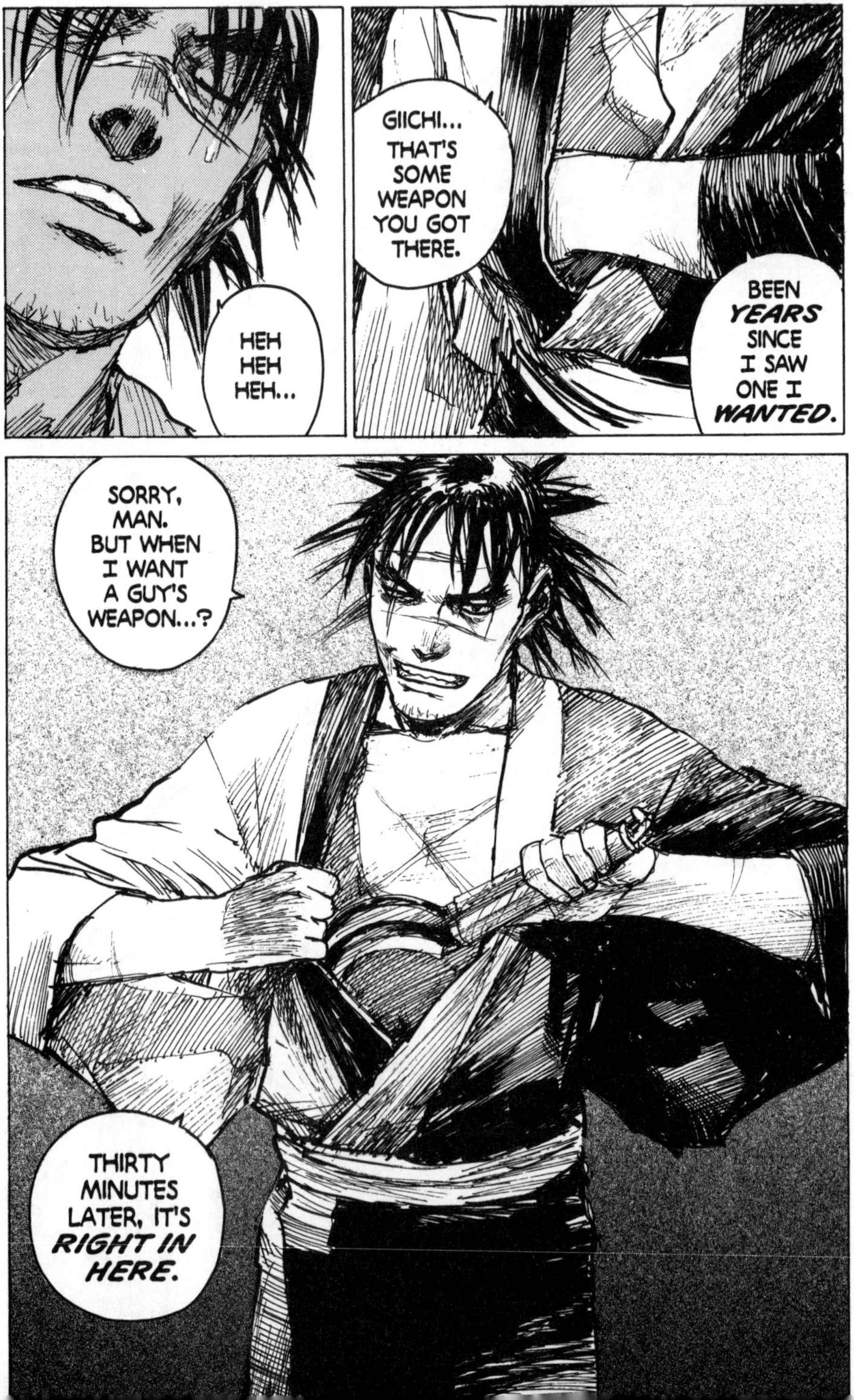
GIICHI... THAT'S SOME WEAPON YOU GOT THERE.
BEEN *YEARS* SINCE I SAW ONE I *WANTED*.
HEH HEH HEH...
SORRY, MAN. BUT WHEN I WANT A GUY'S WEAPON...?
THIRTY MINUTES LATER, IT'S *RIGHT IN HERE*.

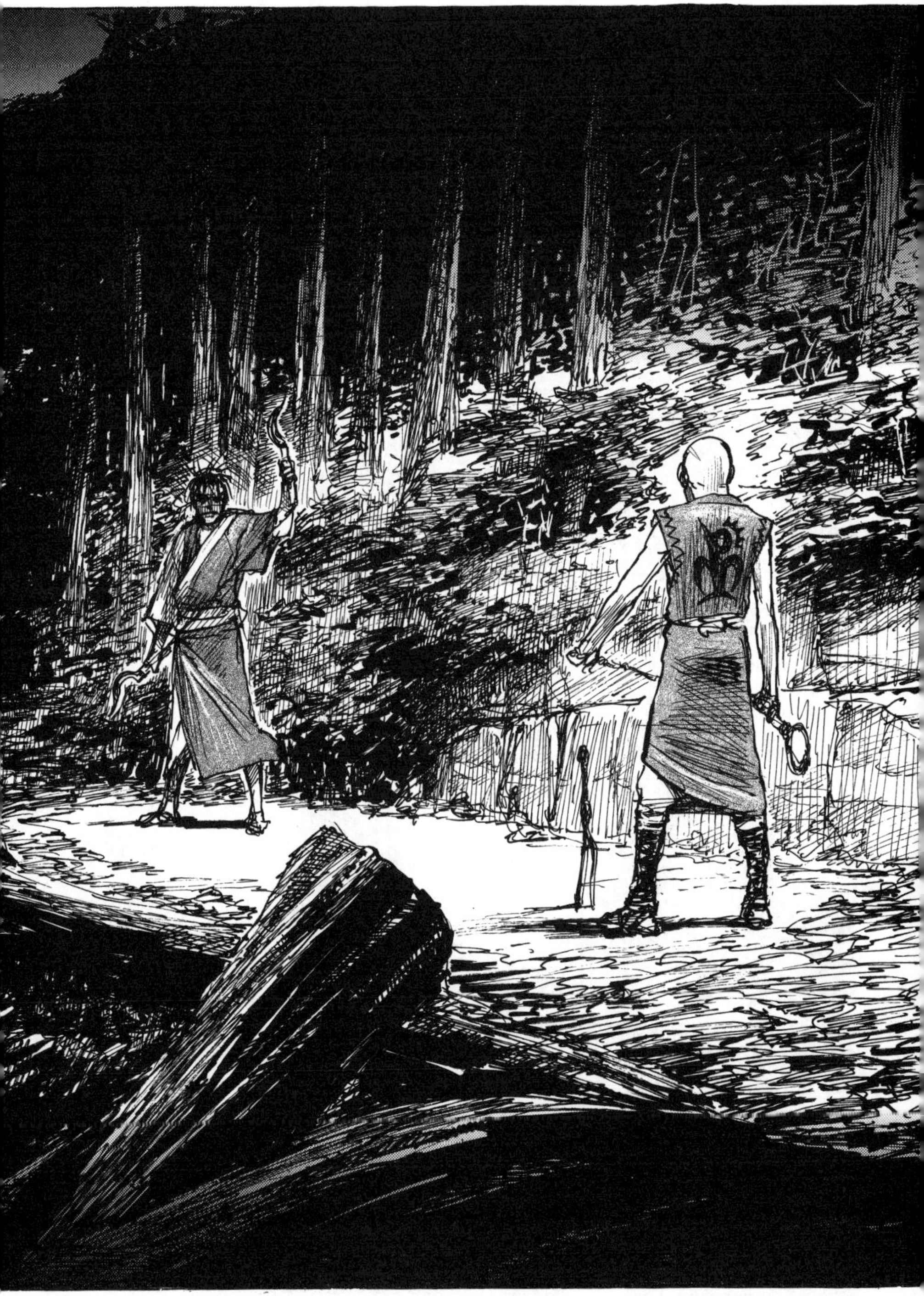

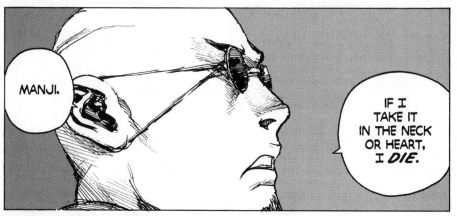

MANJI.

IF I TAKE IT IN THE NECK OR HEART, I *DIE*.

BUT I KNOW YOU'RE BUILT A LITTLE *DIFFERENTLY*.

WHERE IS IT?

WHAT WILL MAKE YOU DIE? I'LL *AIM* FOR IT.

ARE YOU CRAZY?!

YOU THINK I'D TELL YOU *THAT*?!

YOU MIS-UNDERSTAND.

I ASK FOR YOUR SAKE.

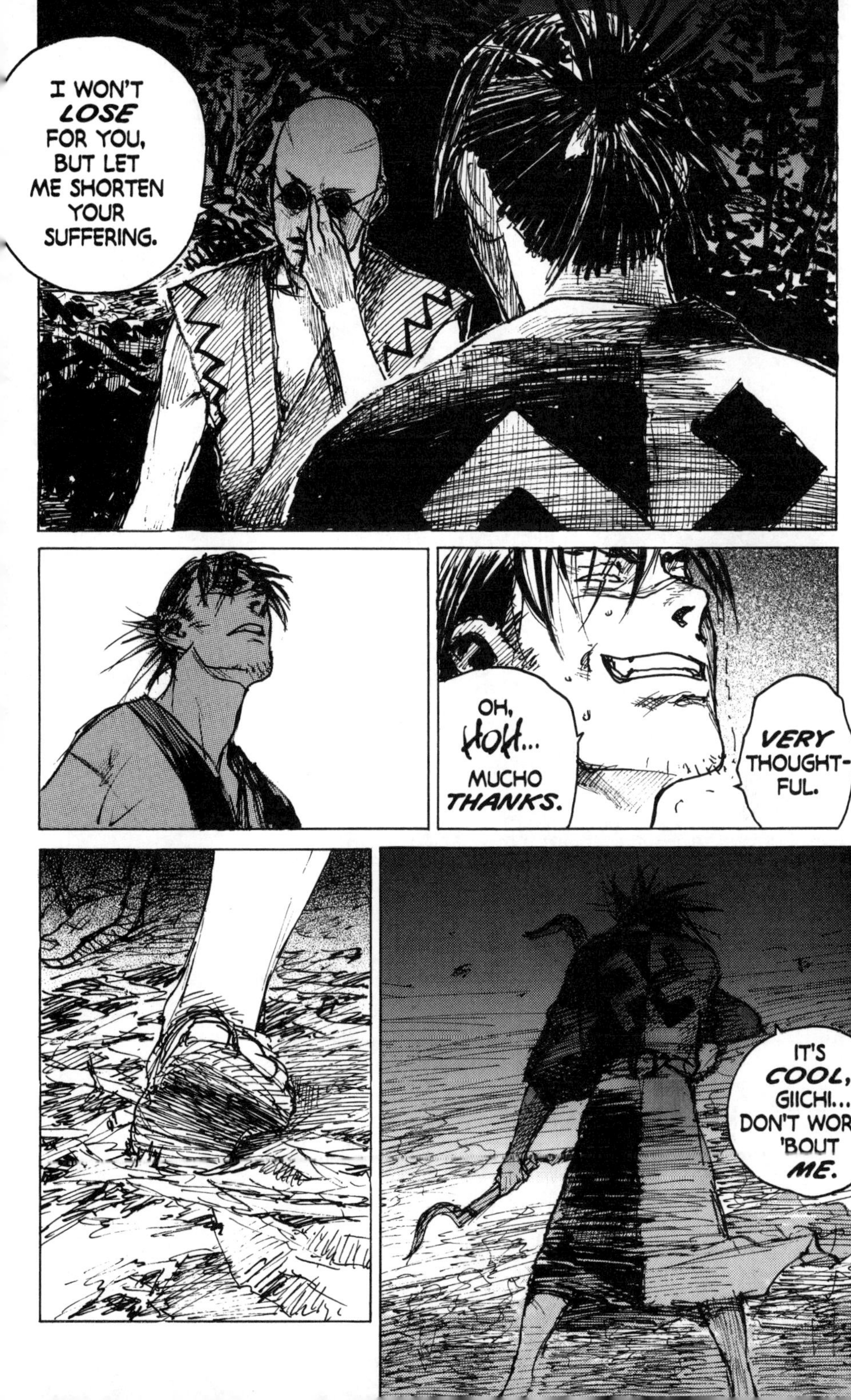
I WON'T *LOSE* FOR YOU, BUT LET ME SHORTEN YOUR SUFFERING.
OH, HOH... MUCHO *THANKS.*
VERY THOUGHT-FUL.
IT'S *COOL,* GIICHI... DON'T WORRY 'BOUT *ME.*

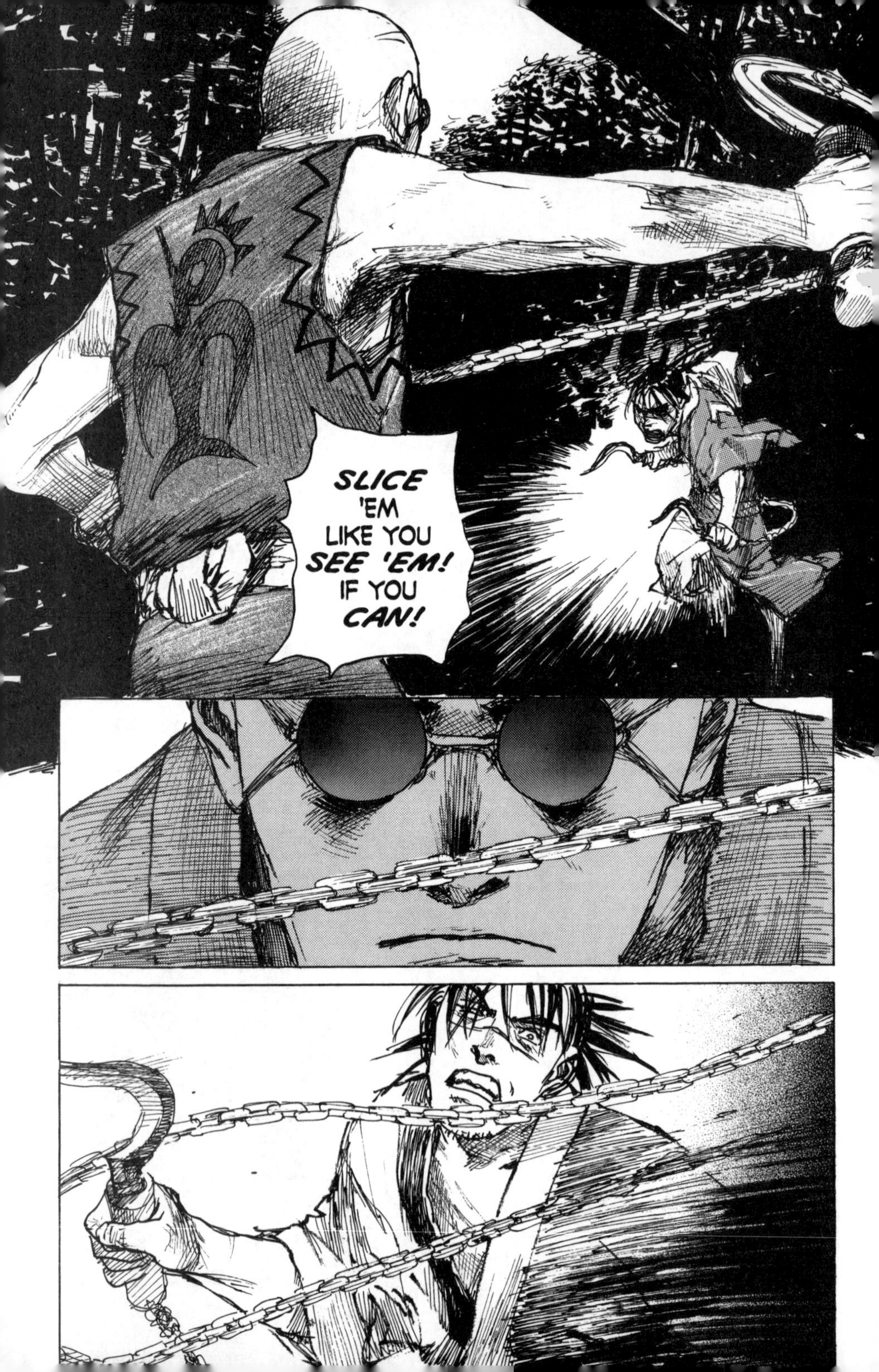
SLICE 'EM LIKE YOU SEE 'EM! IF YOU CAN!

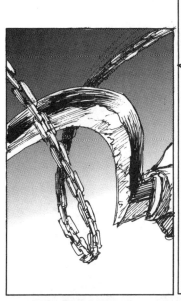

AH...?!

KSHRVNG

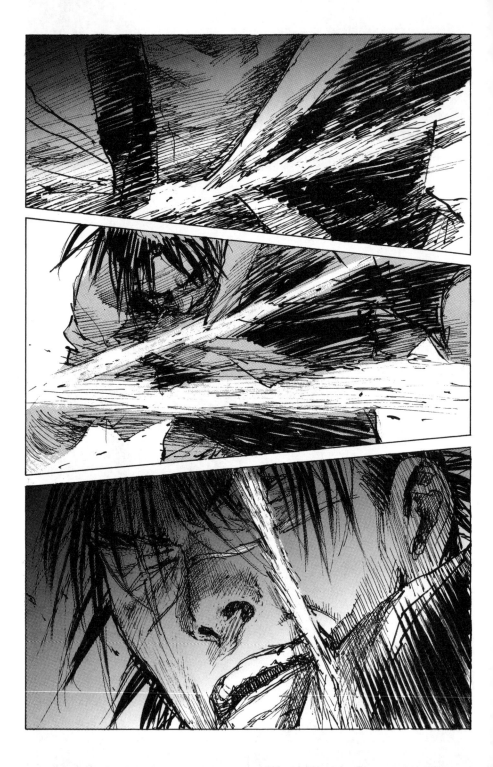

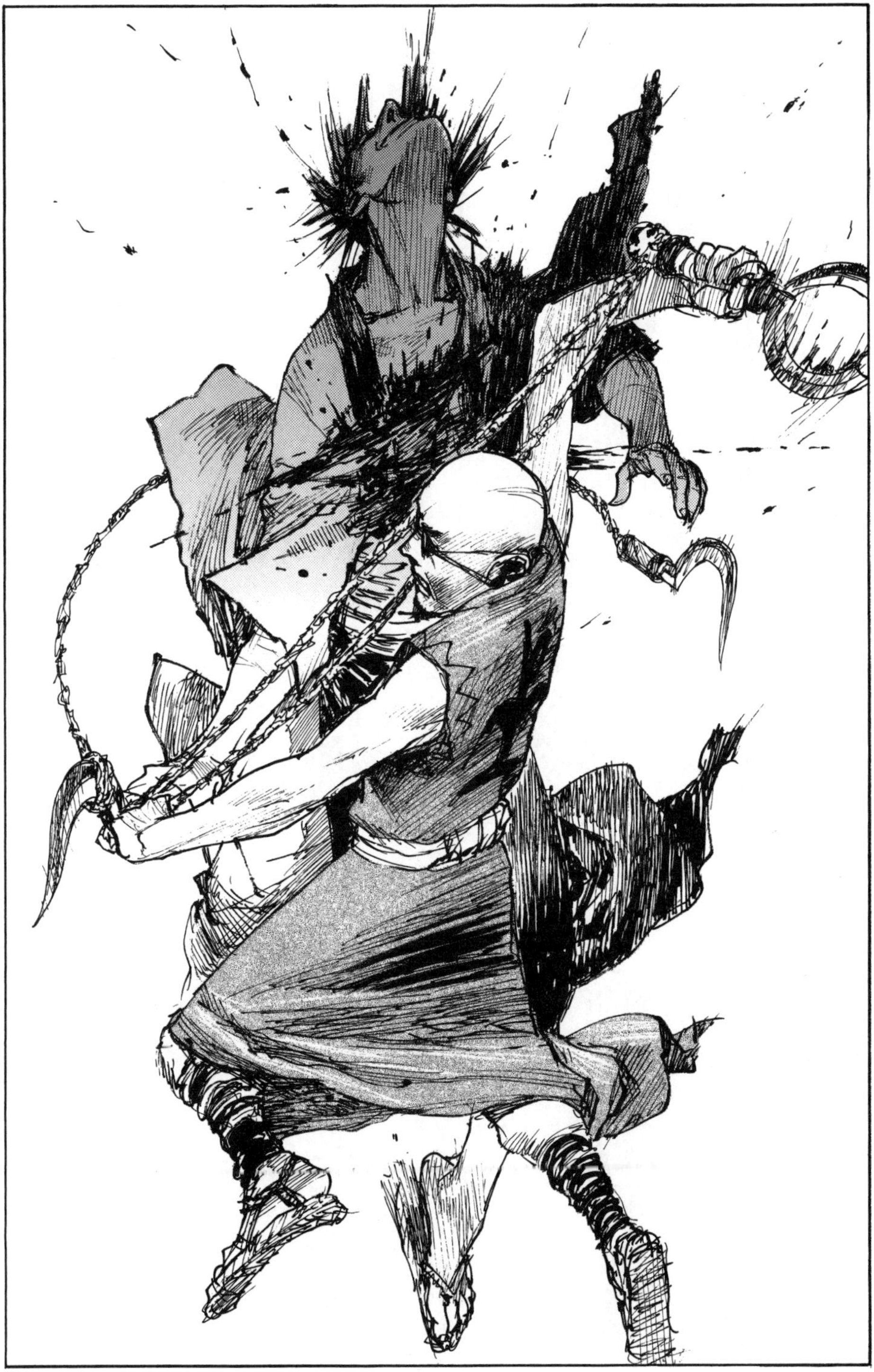

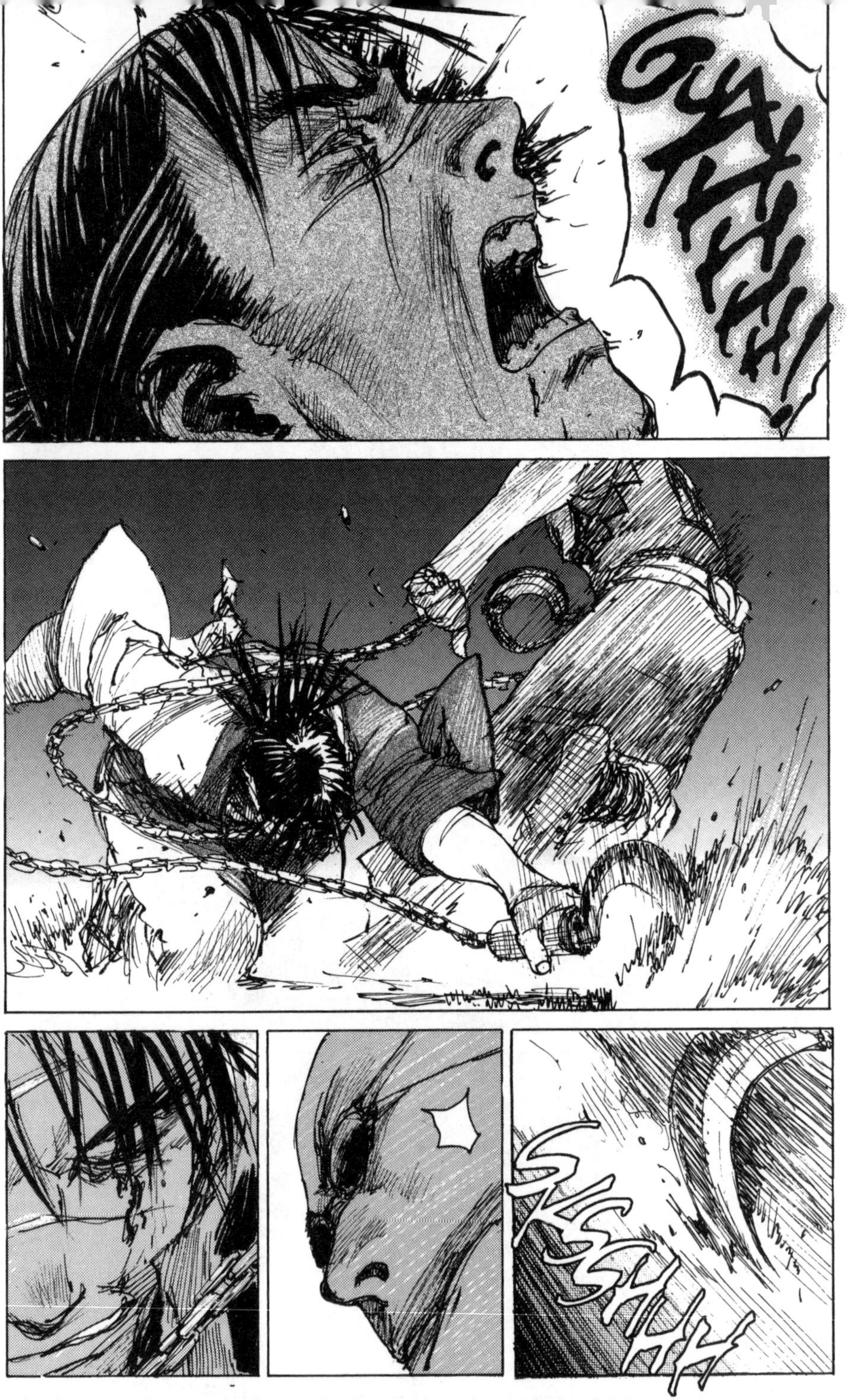
GUAHHHH!!
SKSHHH

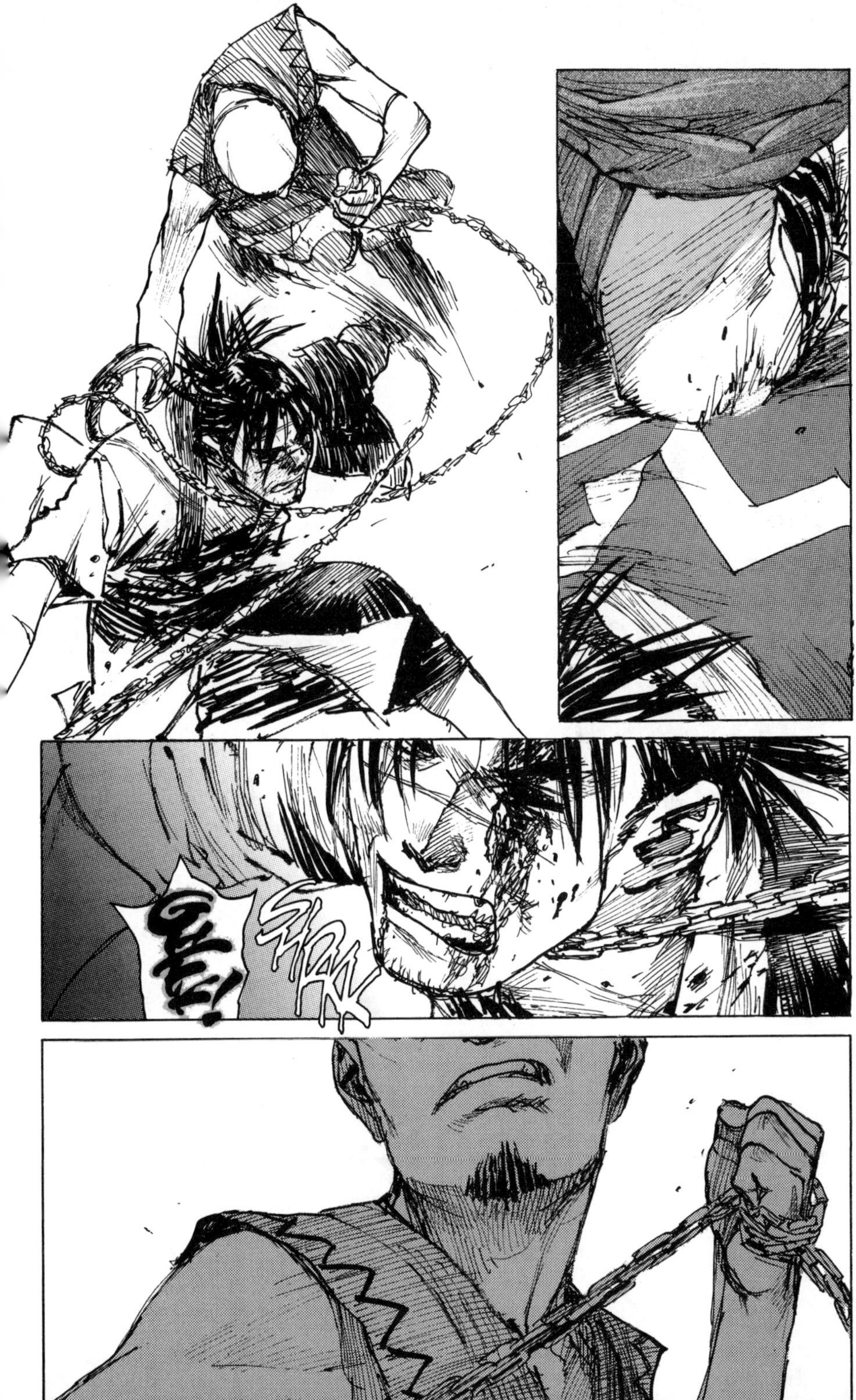
SHAKK
GAHH!

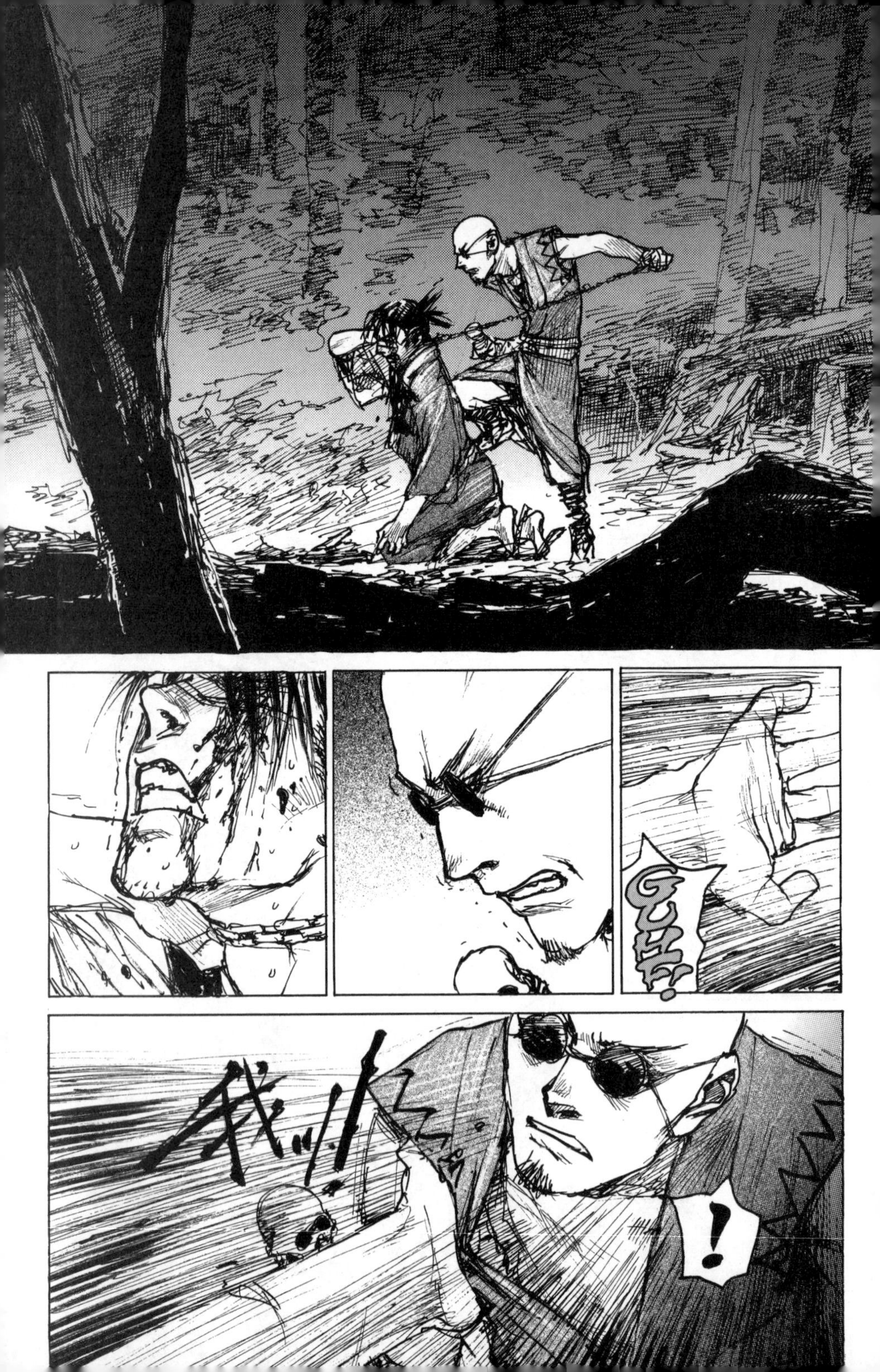
GUH!
!

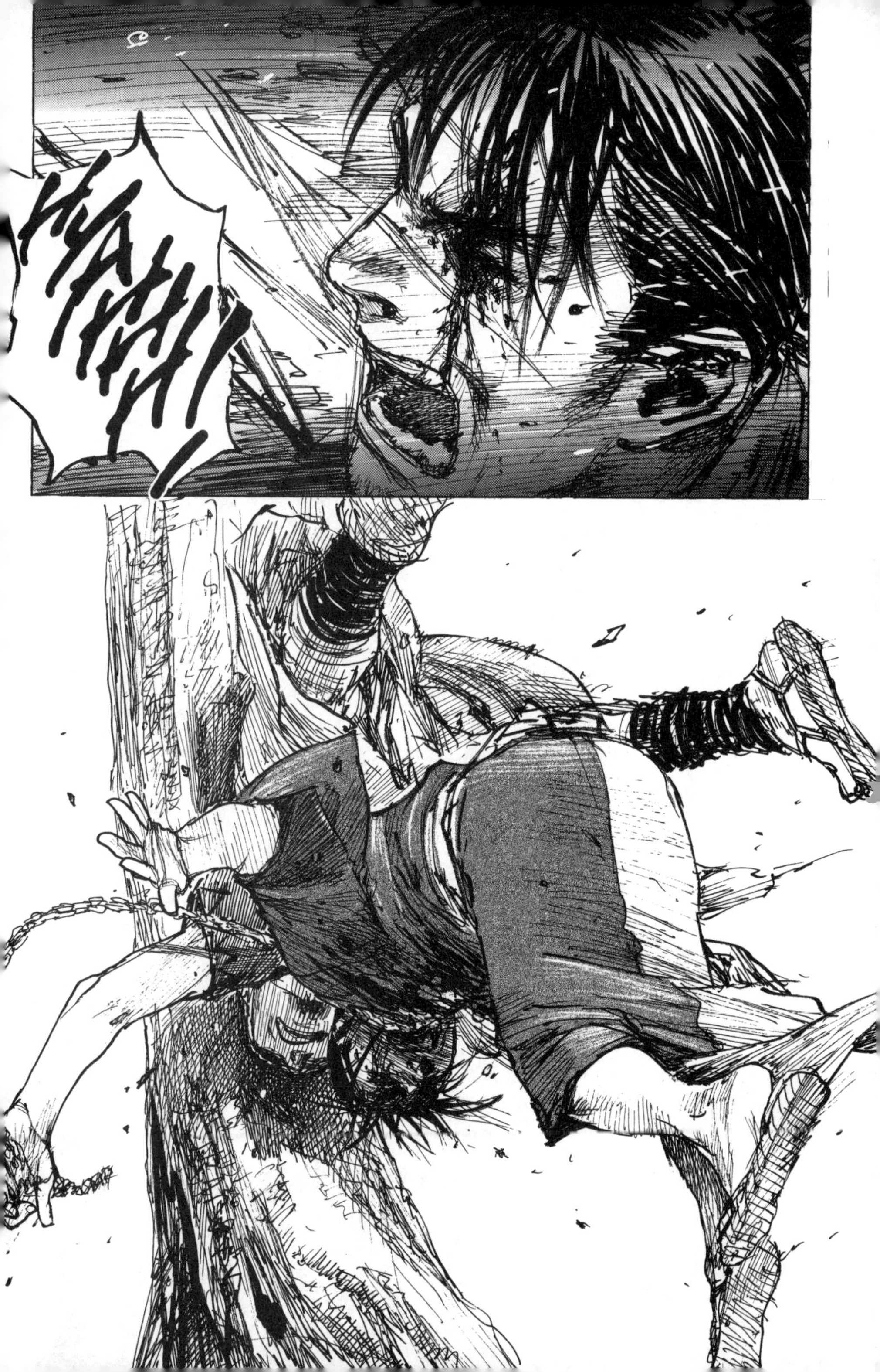
HYAHH!

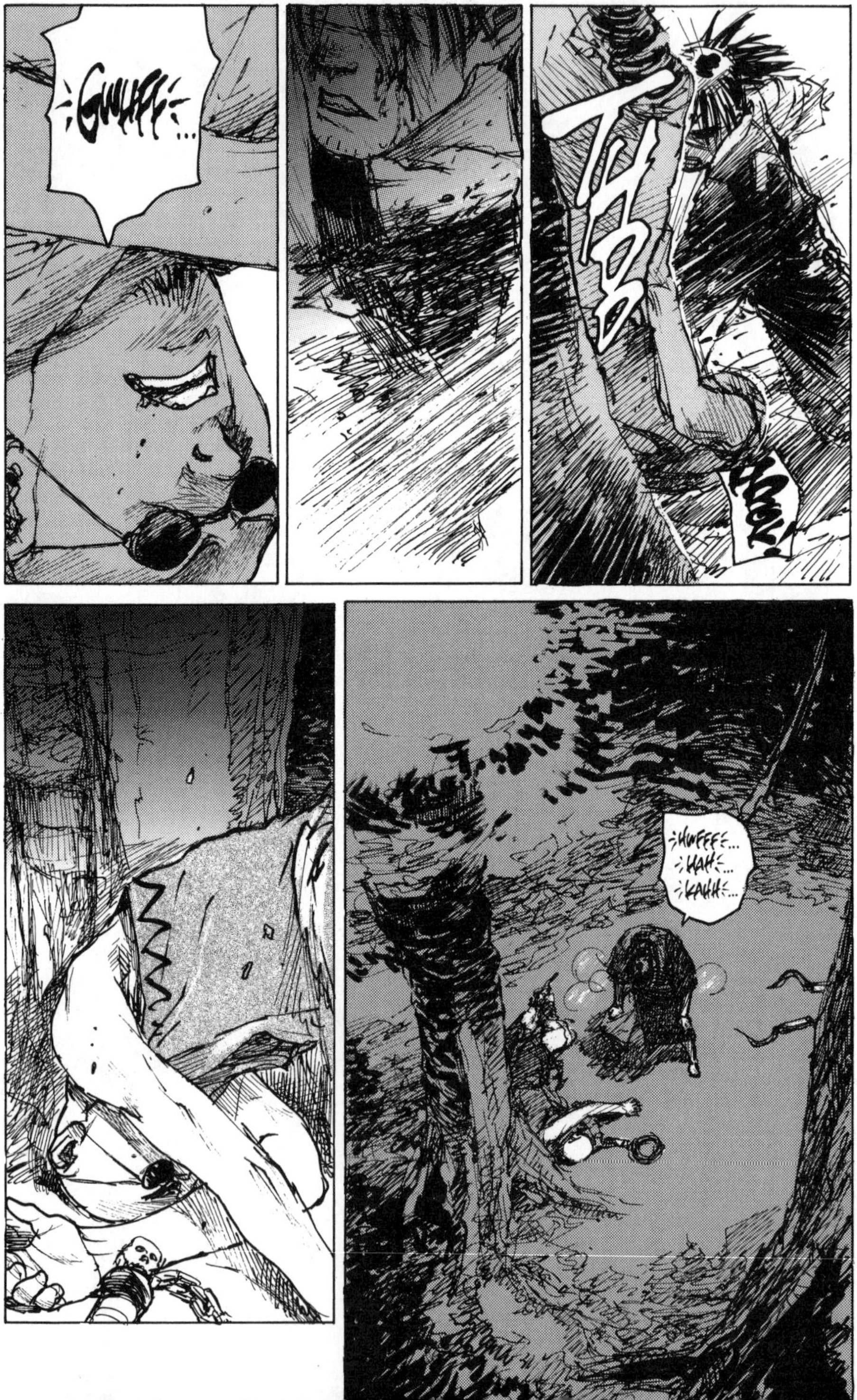
GWUHFF...
HWFFF... HAH... KAHH...

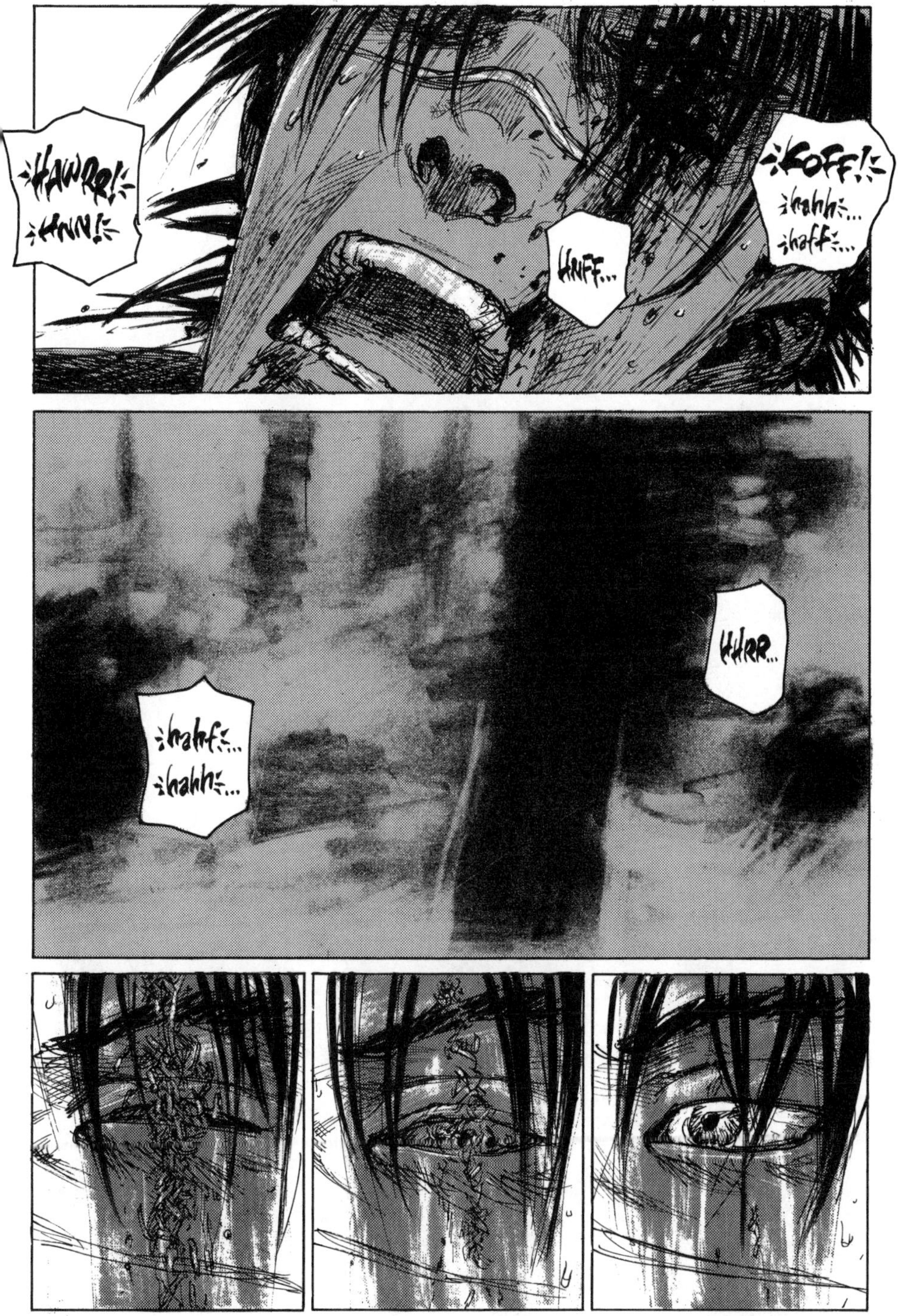
KOFF! hahh... haff...
HNFF...
HAWRR! HNN!
UHRR...
hahf... hahh...

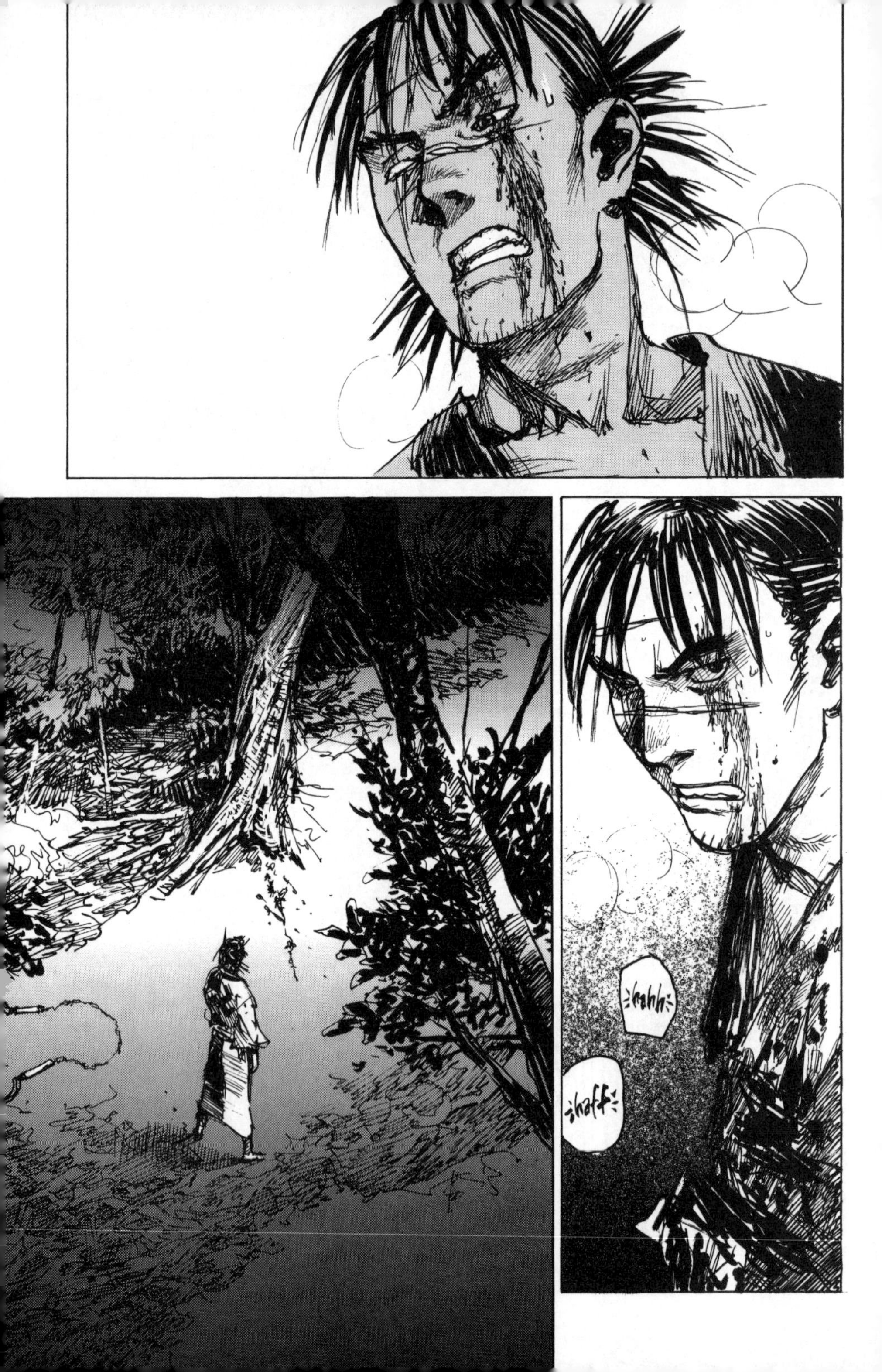
hahh
haff

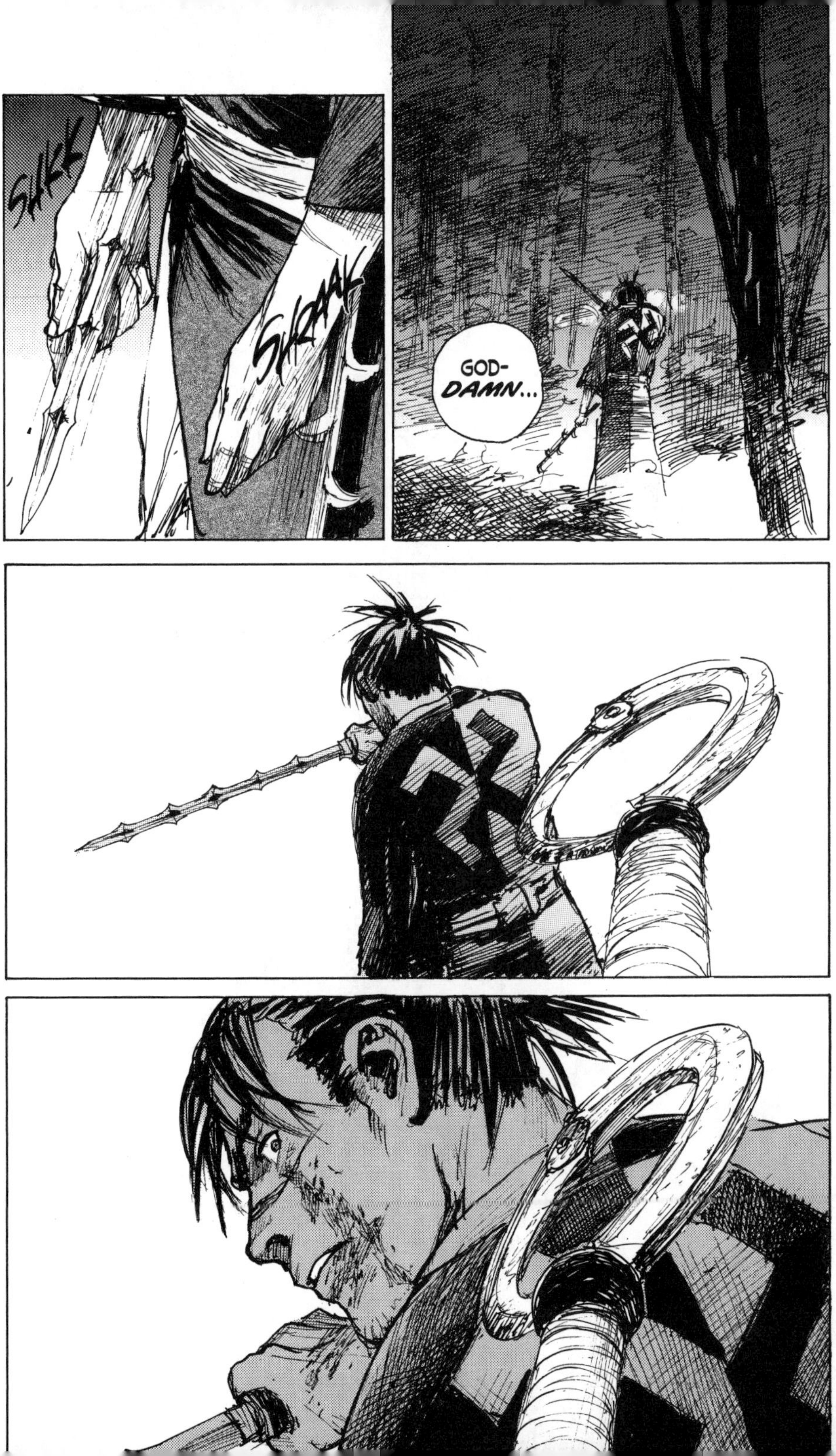
GOD-
DAMN...
SHKK
SHRAAK

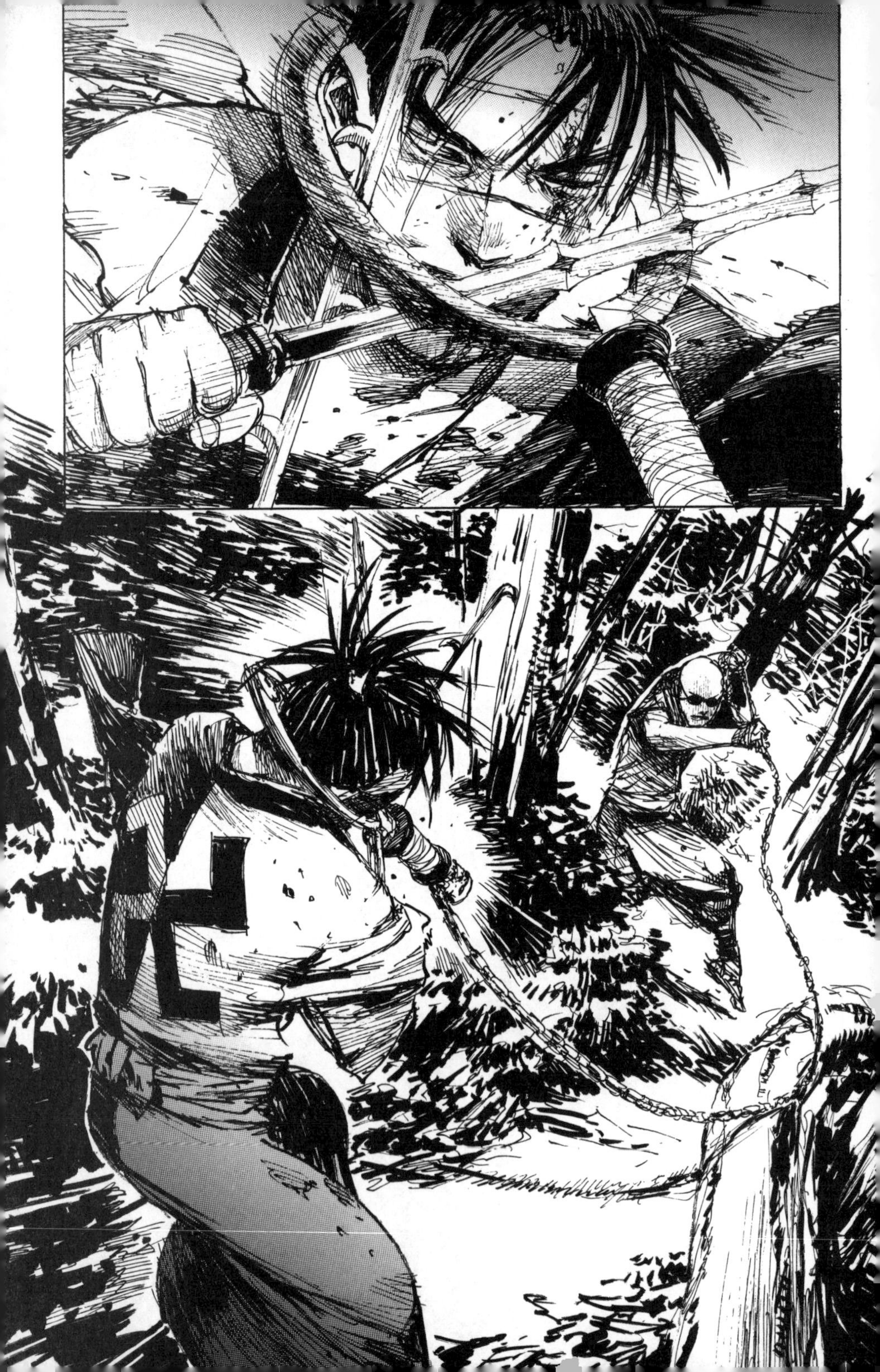

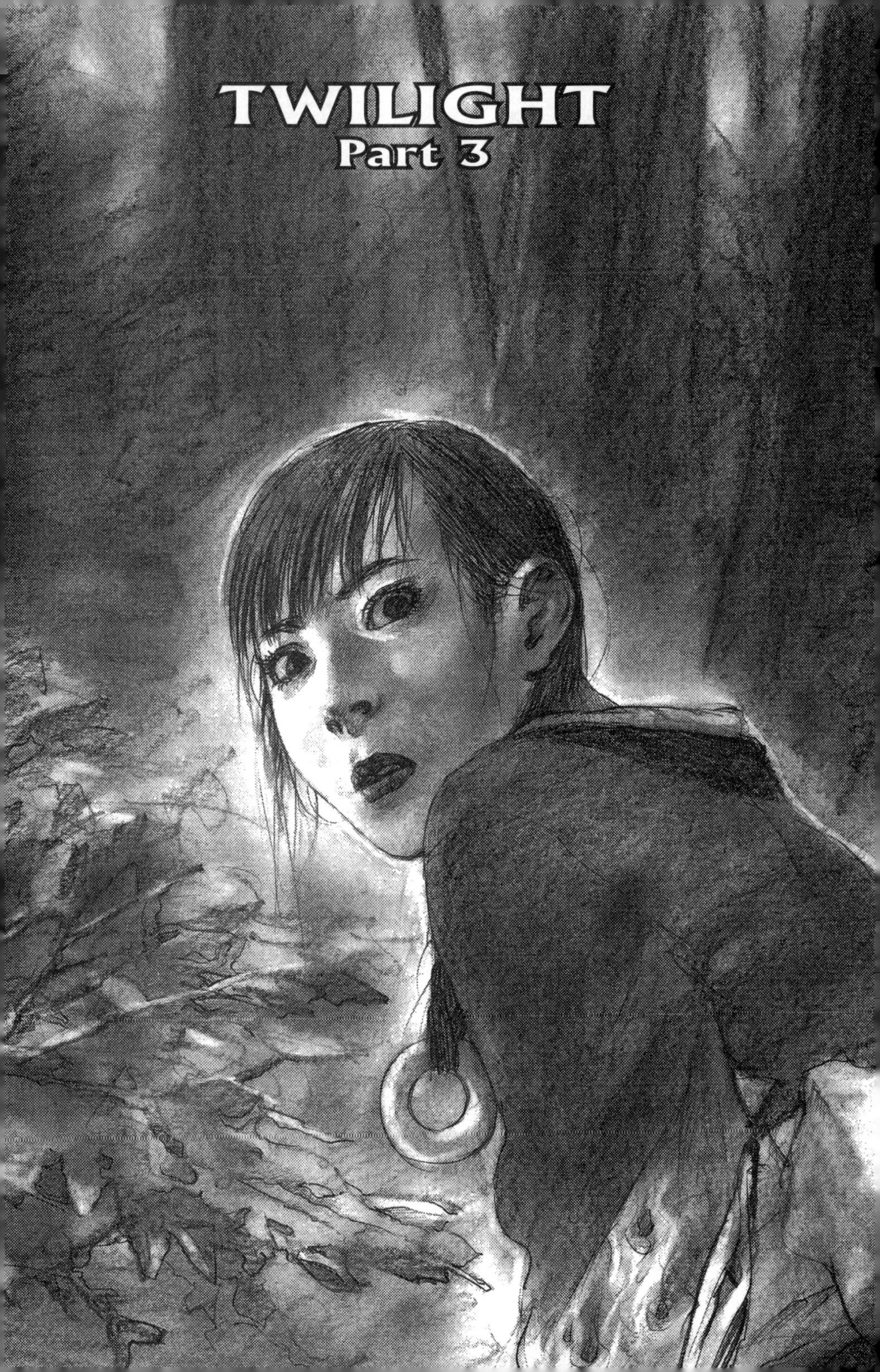
TWILIGHT
Part 3

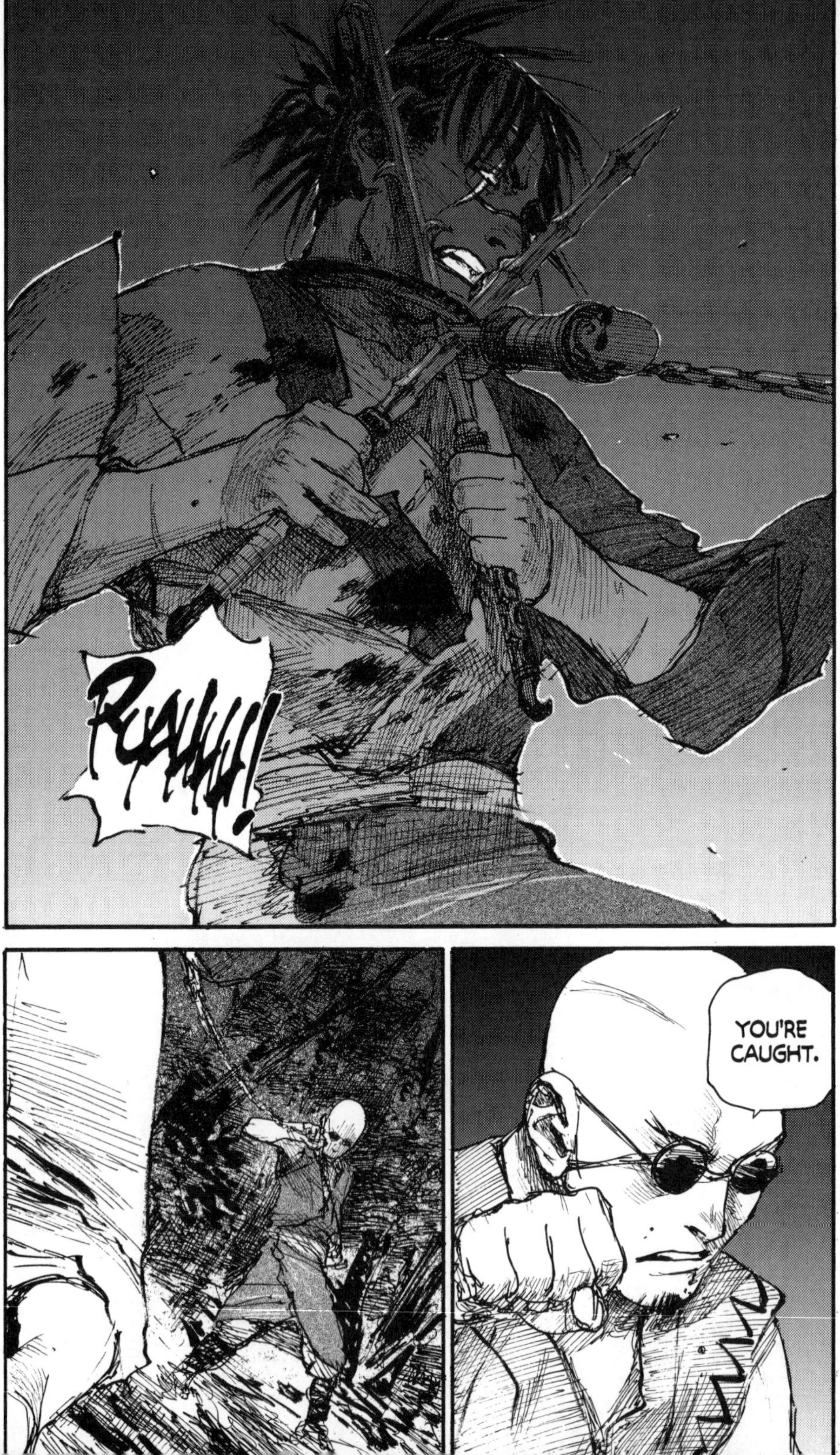
YOU'RE CAUGHT.

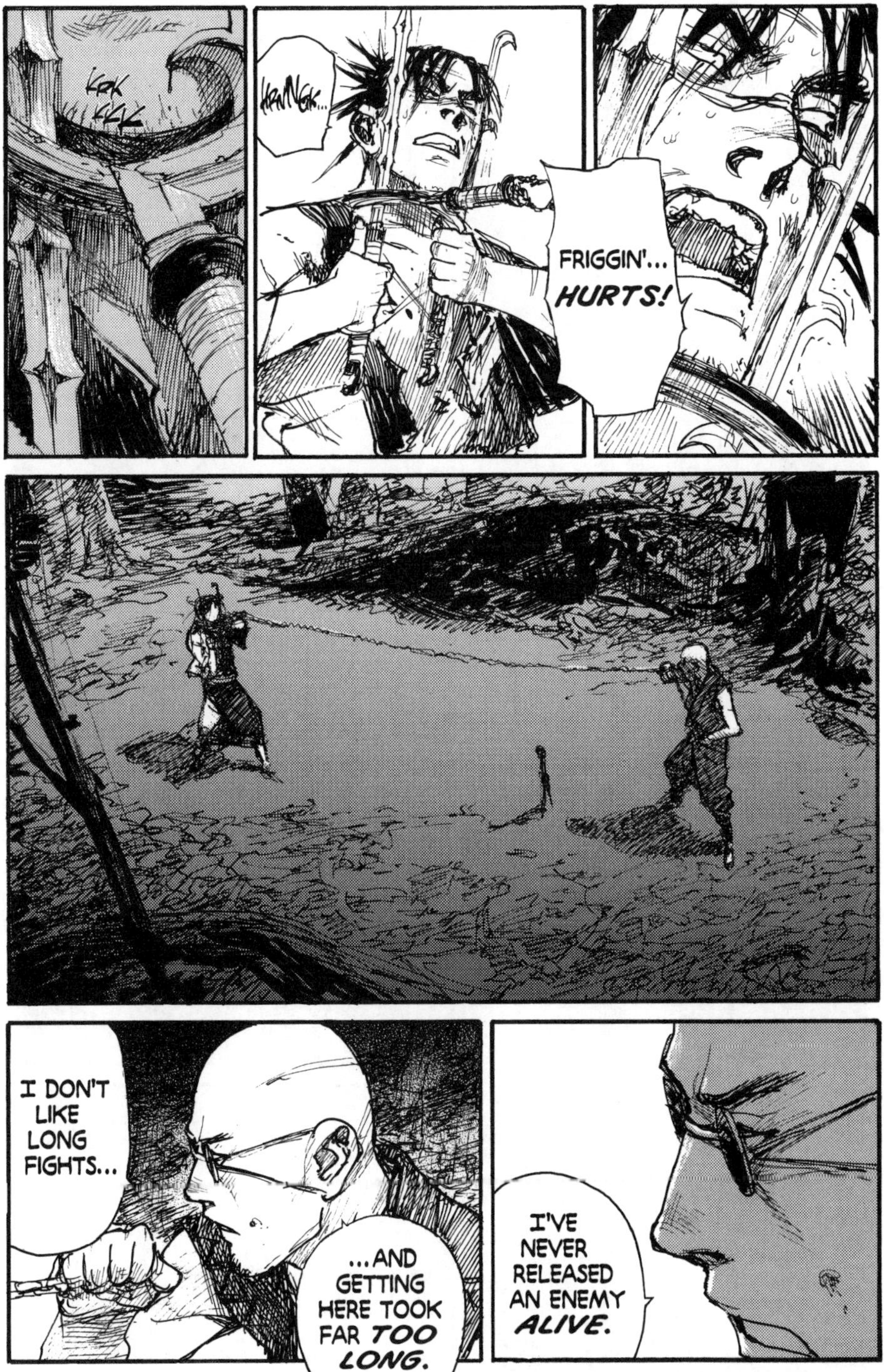
KRK
KLK
HRNNGK...
FRIGGIN'... ***HURTS!***
I DON'T LIKE LONG FIGHTS...
...AND GETTING HERE TOOK FAR ***TOO LONG.***
I'VE NEVER RELEASED AN ENEMY ***ALIVE.***

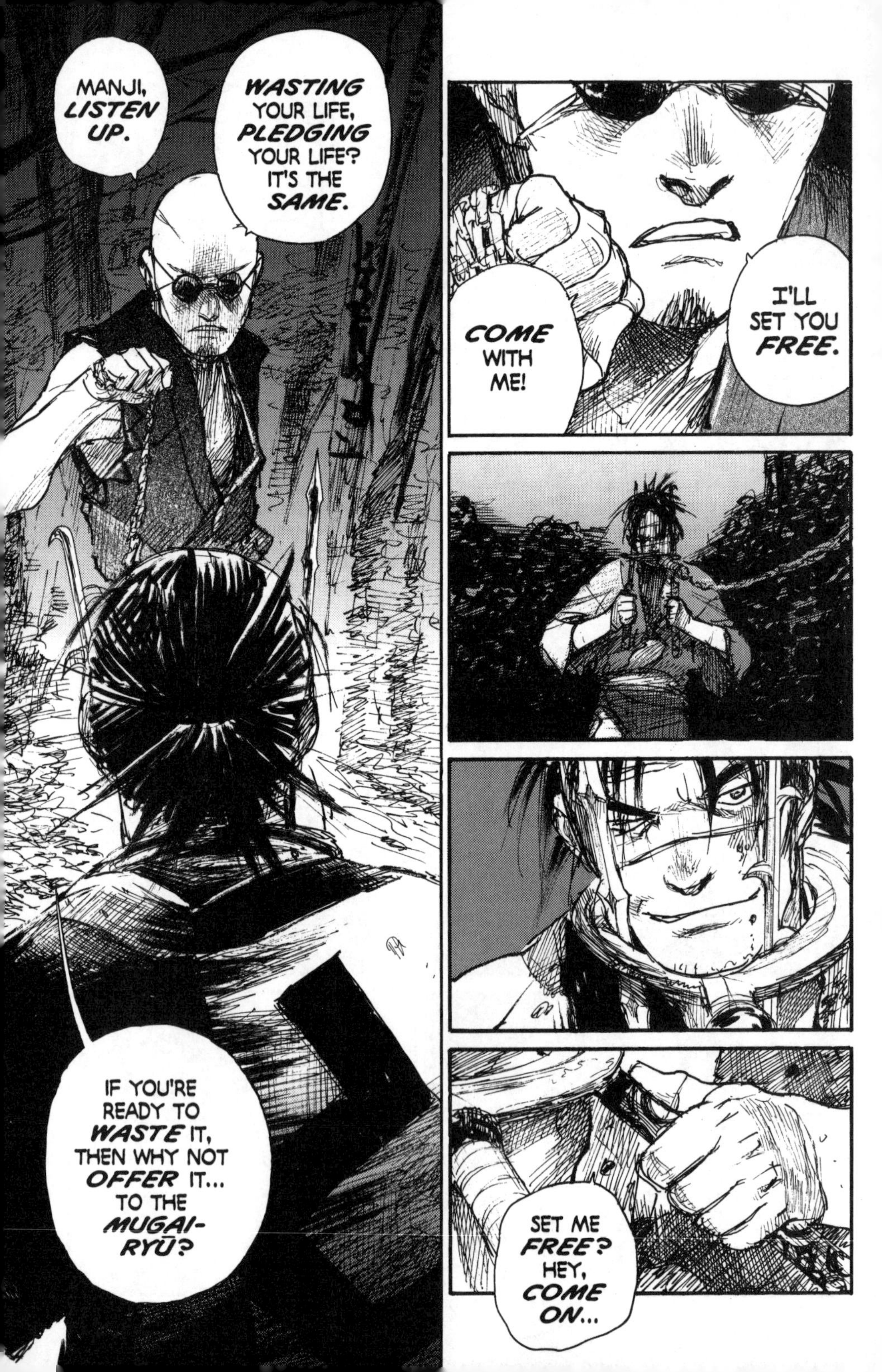

MANJI, LISTEN UP.
WASTING YOUR LIFE, PLEDGING YOUR LIFE? IT'S THE SAME.
IF YOU'RE READY TO WASTE IT, THEN WHY NOT OFFER IT... TO THE MUGAI-RYŪ?
COME WITH ME!
I'LL SET YOU FREE.
SET ME FREE? HEY, COME ON...

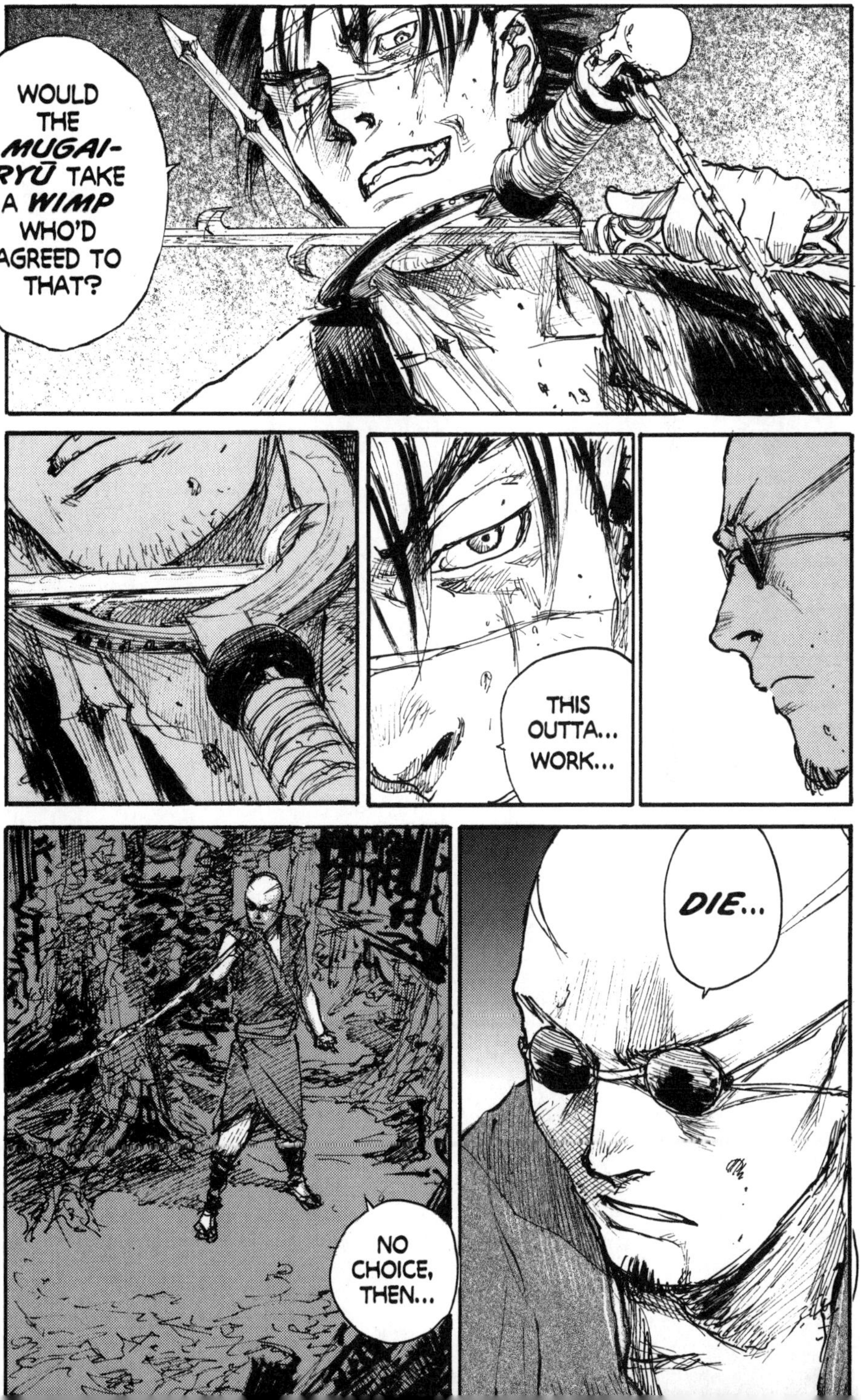
WOULD THE MUGAI-RYŪ TAKE A WIMP WHO'D AGREED TO THAT?
THIS OUTTA... WORK...
DIE...
NO CHOICE, THEN...

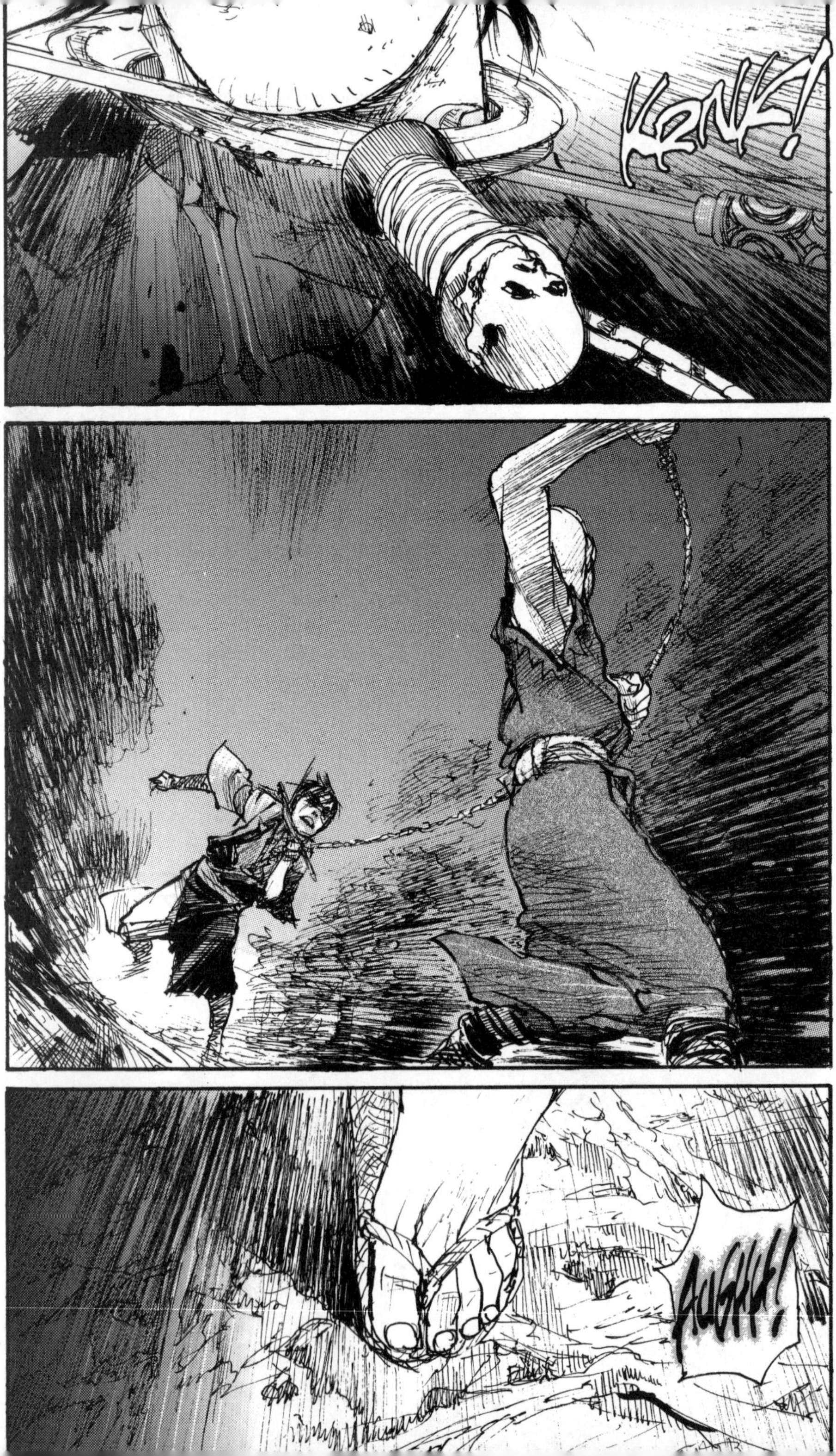
KRNK!
AUGHH!

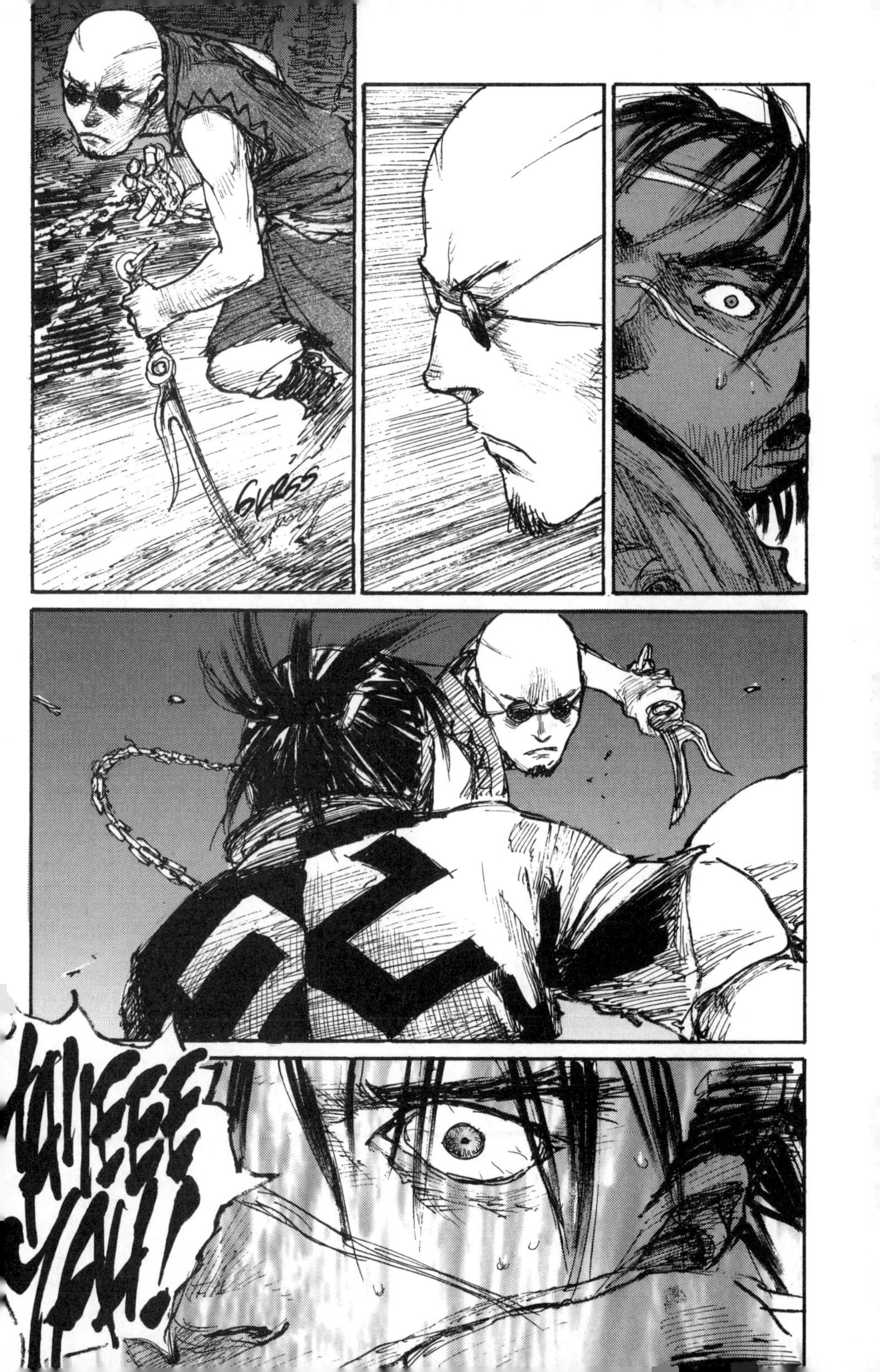
SKRSS
KIEEE YAH!

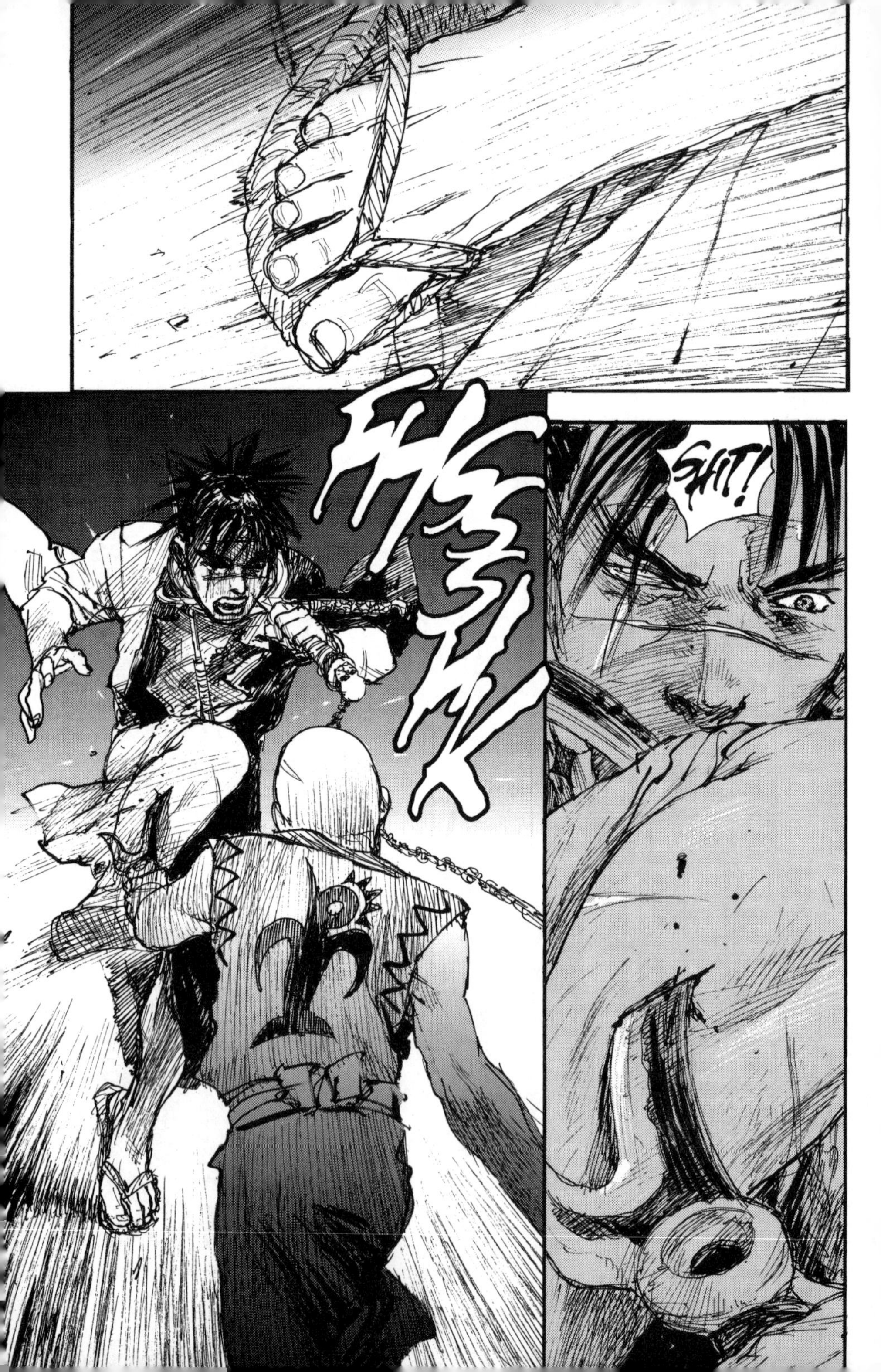

SHIT!

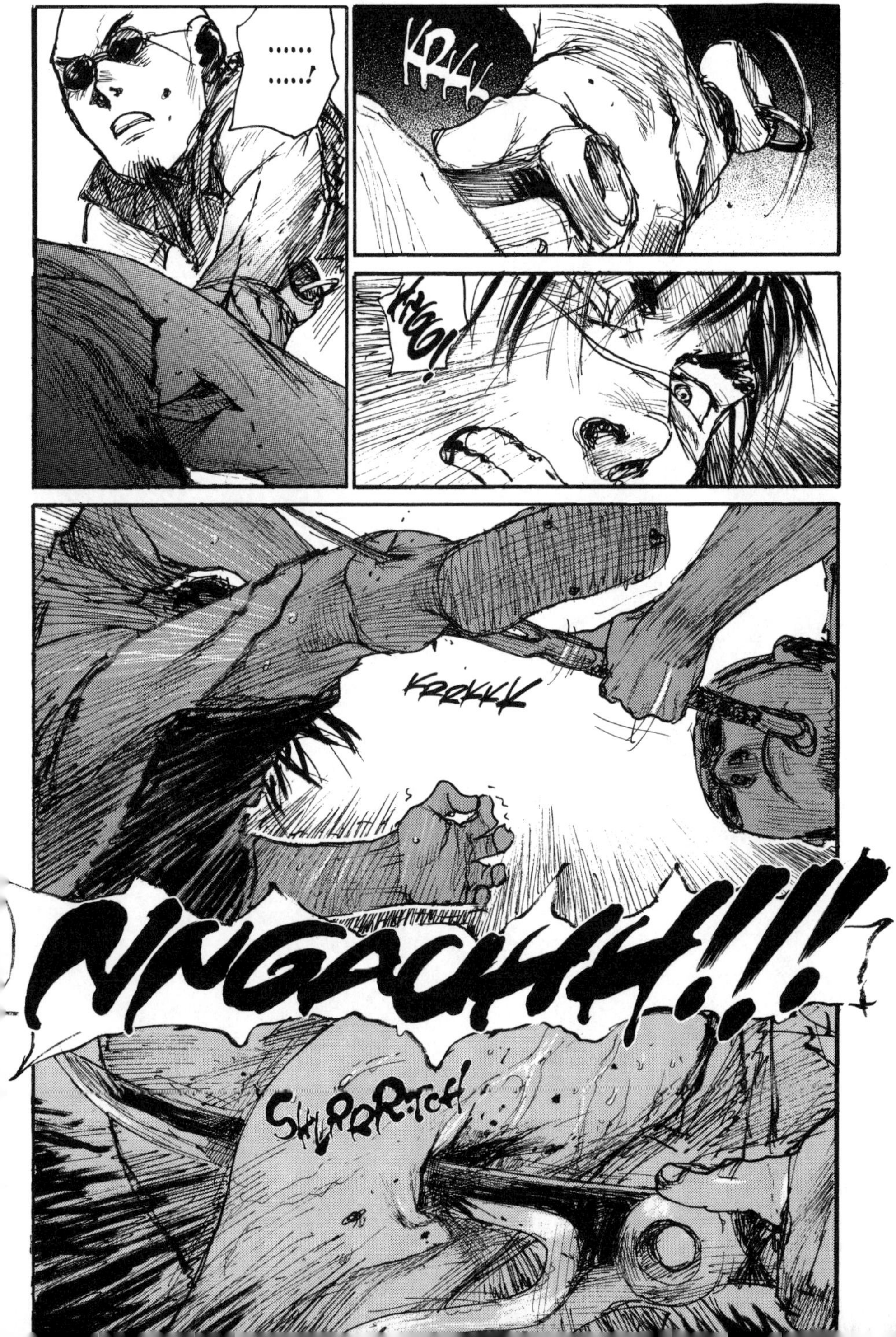
KRUK
KHOO!
......
......!
KRRKKK
NNGAHHH!!!
SKLRRRTCH!

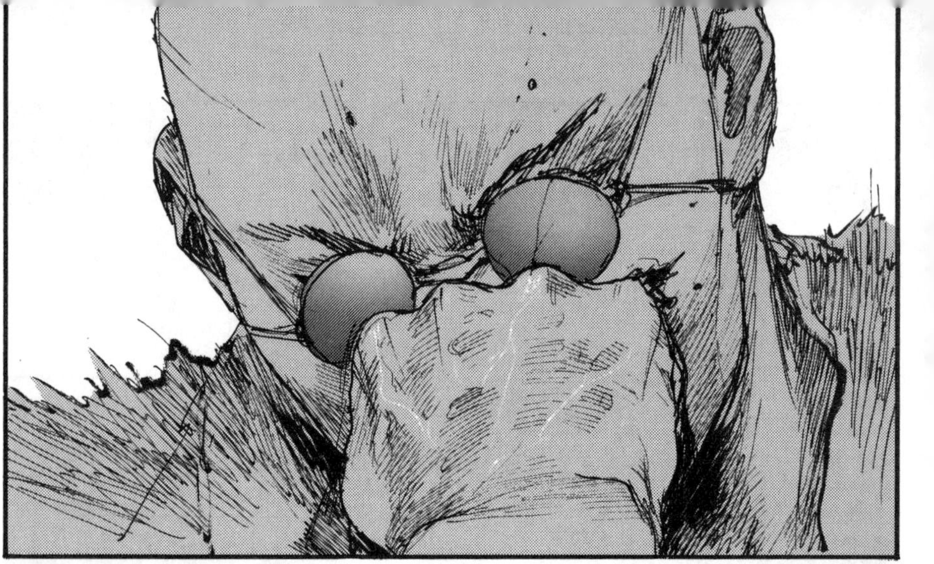
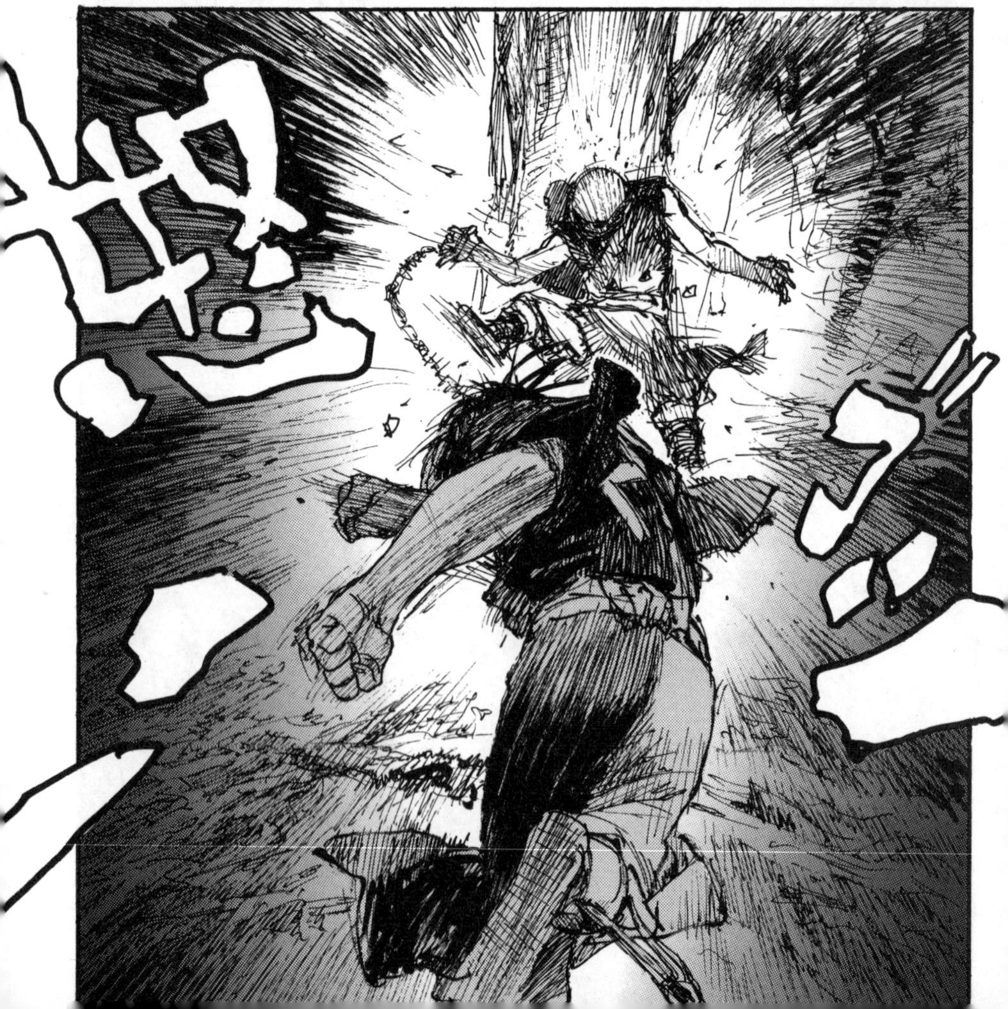

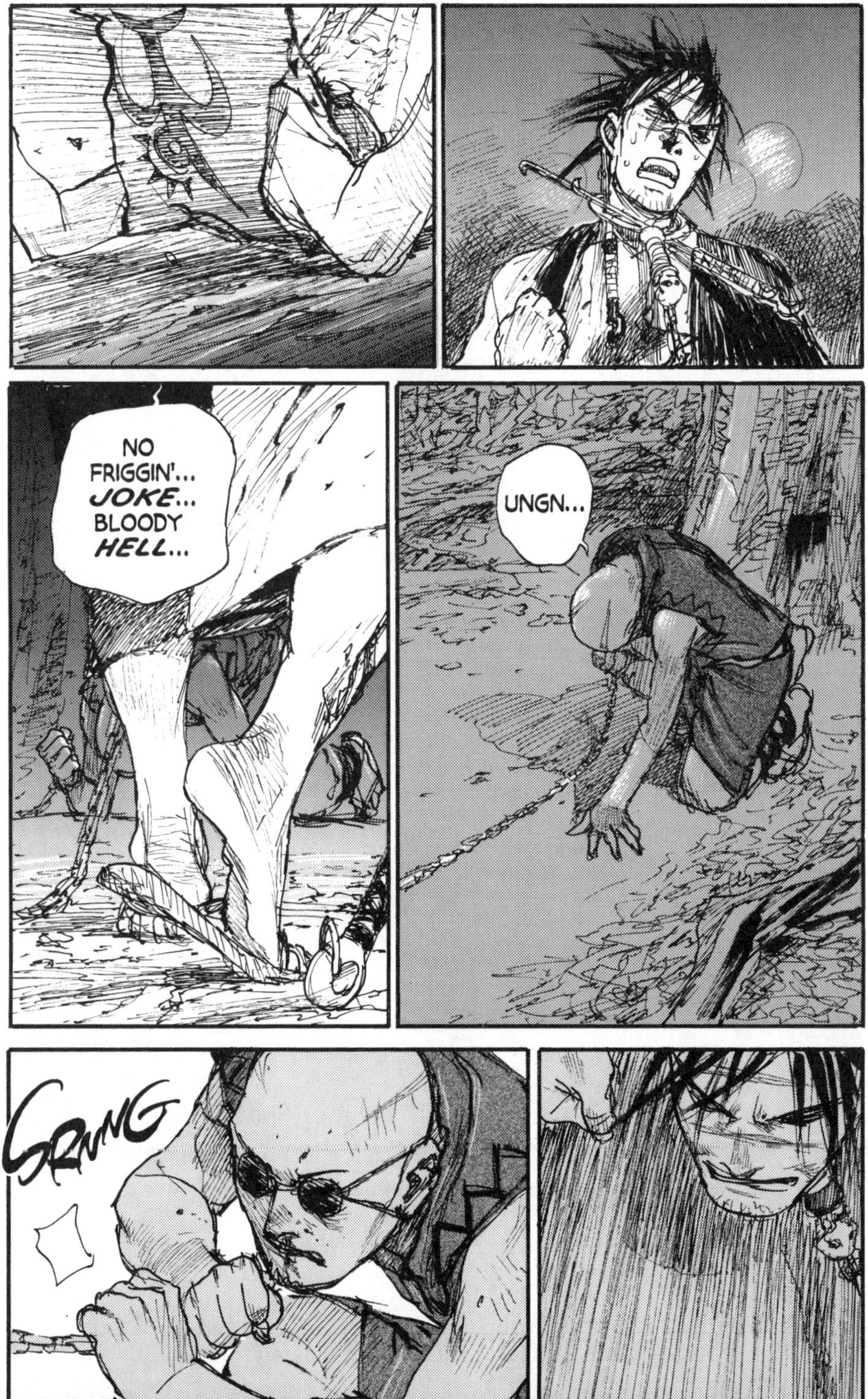
UNGN...
NO FRIGGIN'... JOKE... BLOODY HELL...
GRNNG

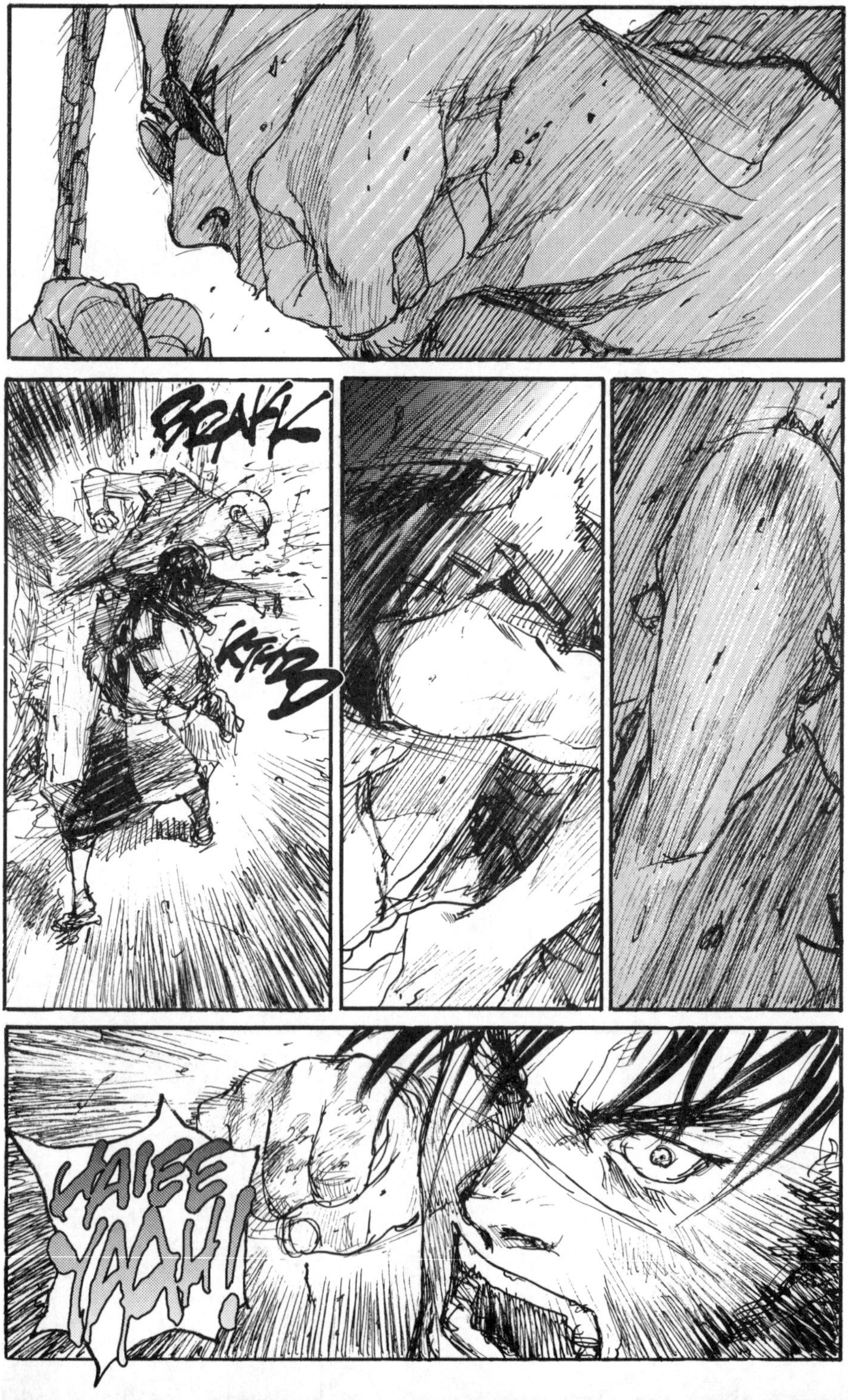
BRAKK
KTHUD
WAIEE YAAH!

FWAP

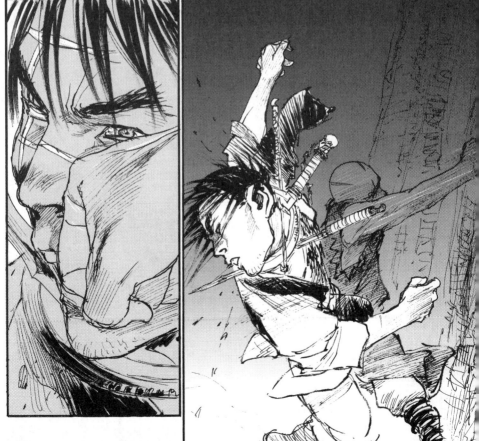

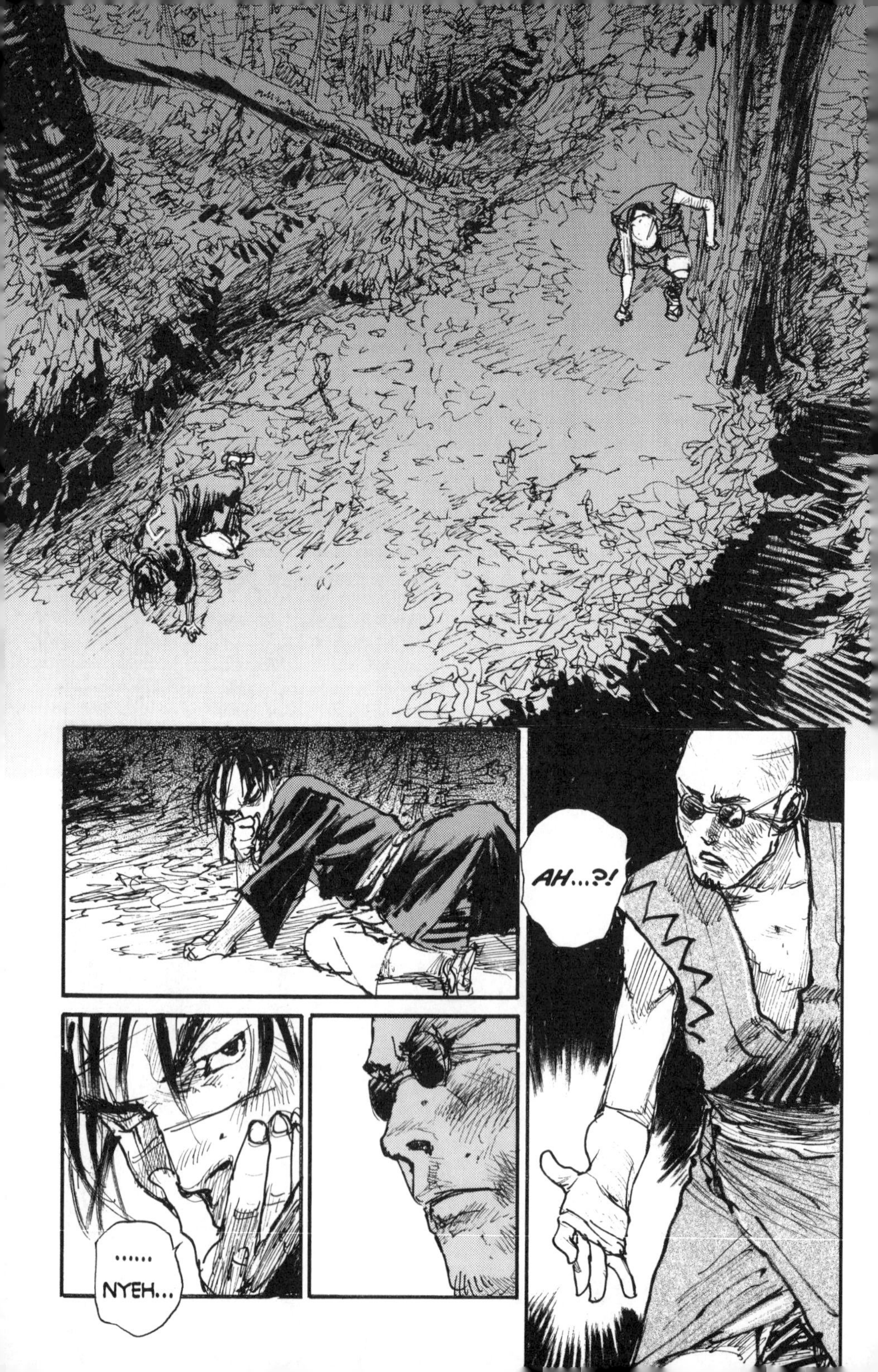
AH...?!
......
NYEH...

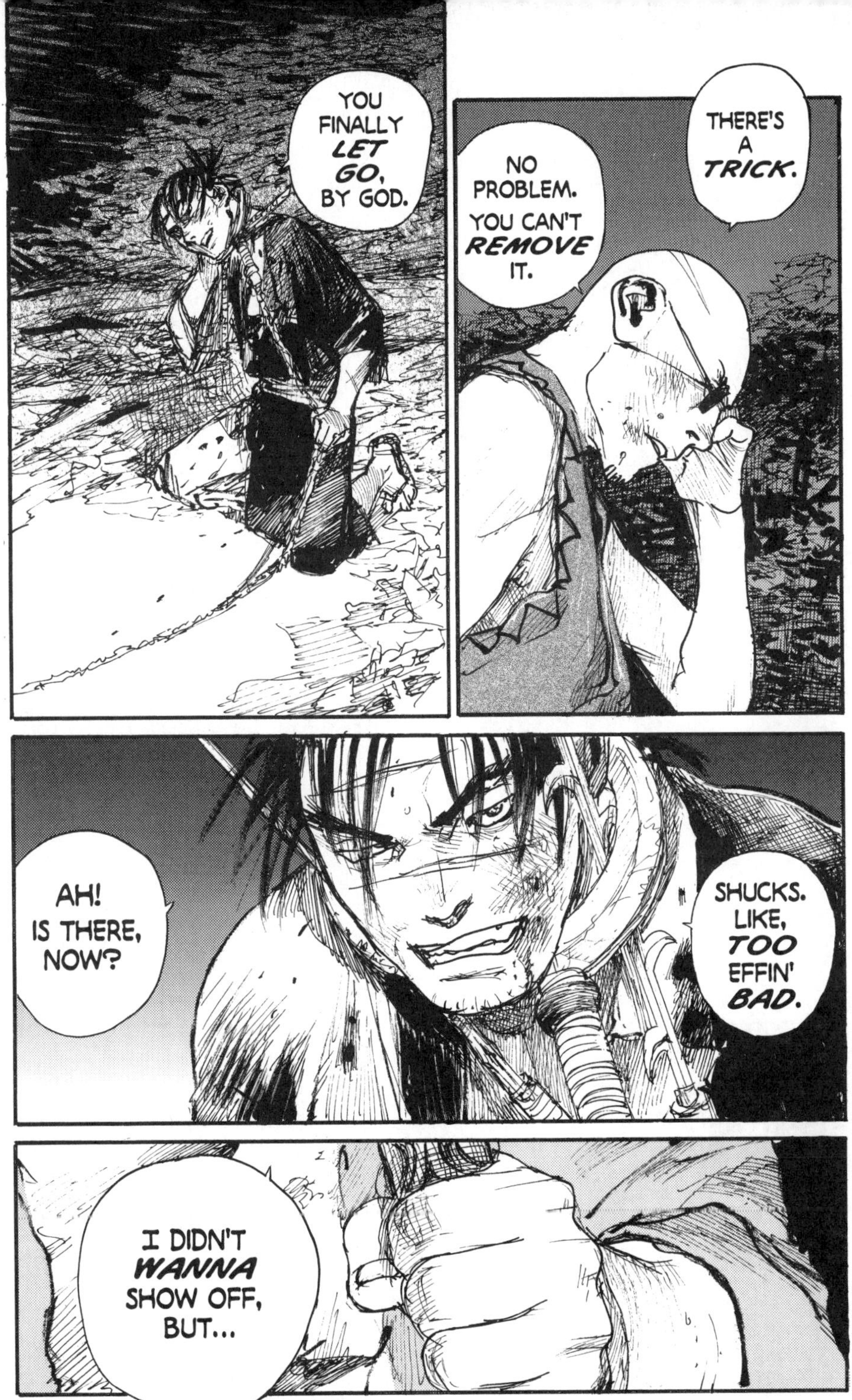
YOU FINALLY LET GO, BY GOD.
NO PROBLEM. YOU CAN'T REMOVE IT.
THERE'S A TRICK.
AH! IS THERE, NOW?
SHUCKS. LIKE, TOO EFFIN' BAD.
I DIDN'T WANNA SHOW OFF, BUT...

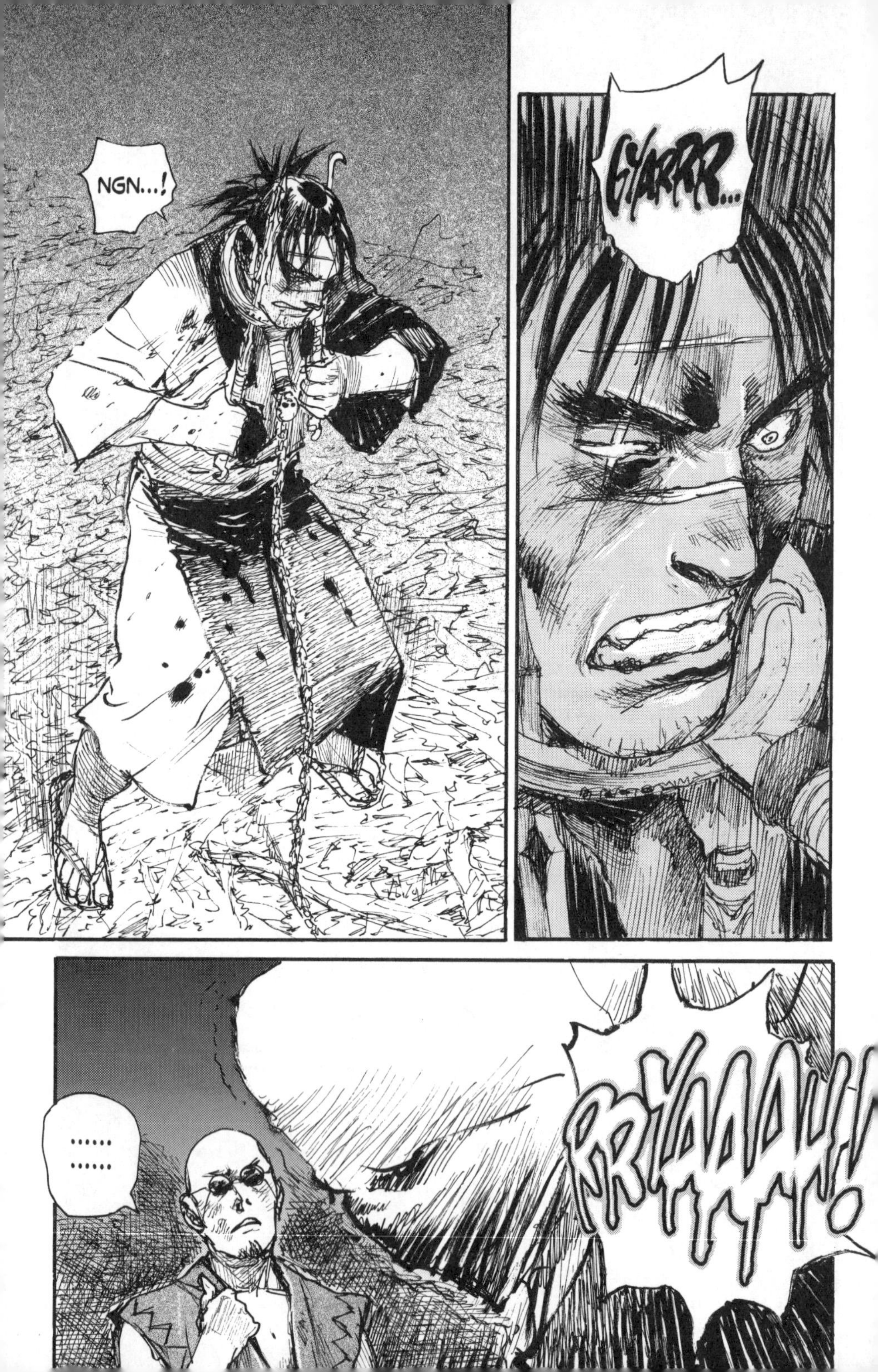
GYARRR...
NGN...!
RRYAAAUU!
......
......

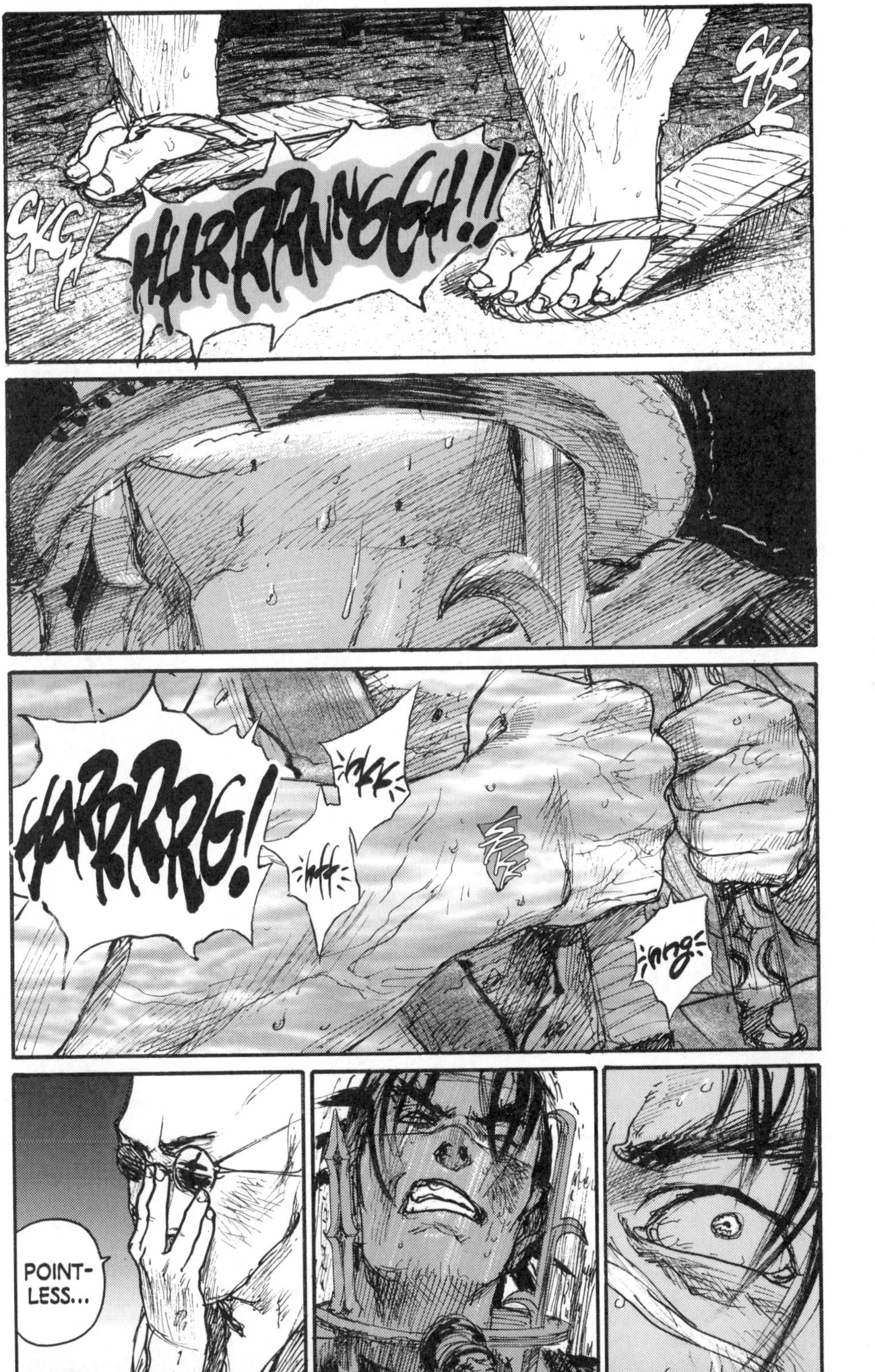
SHRK
SKGH
HURRRNNGGH!!
HARRRRG!
KK
KHH
SKK
NNG
POINT-LESS...

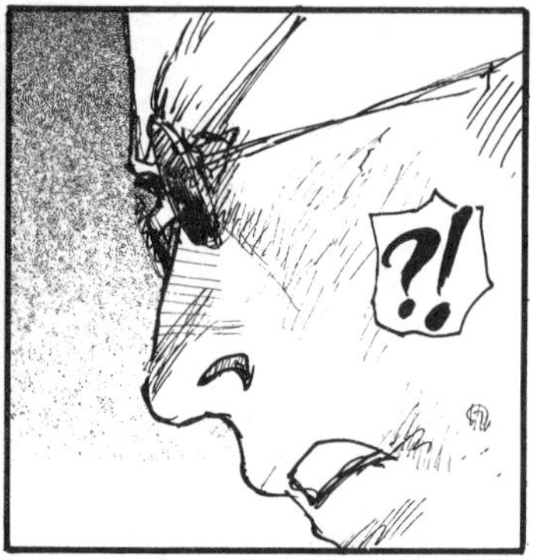
?!
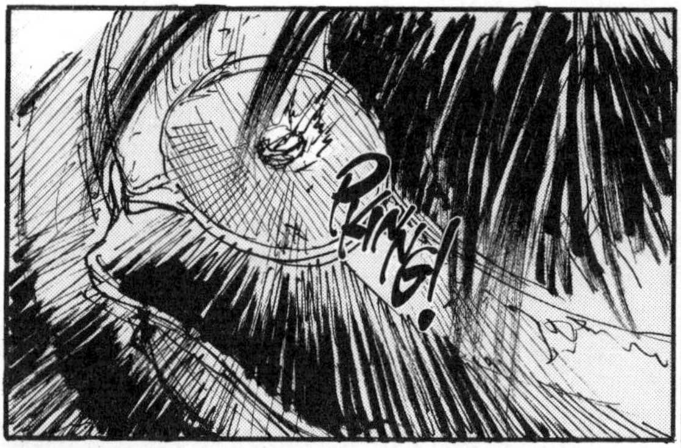
RANG!
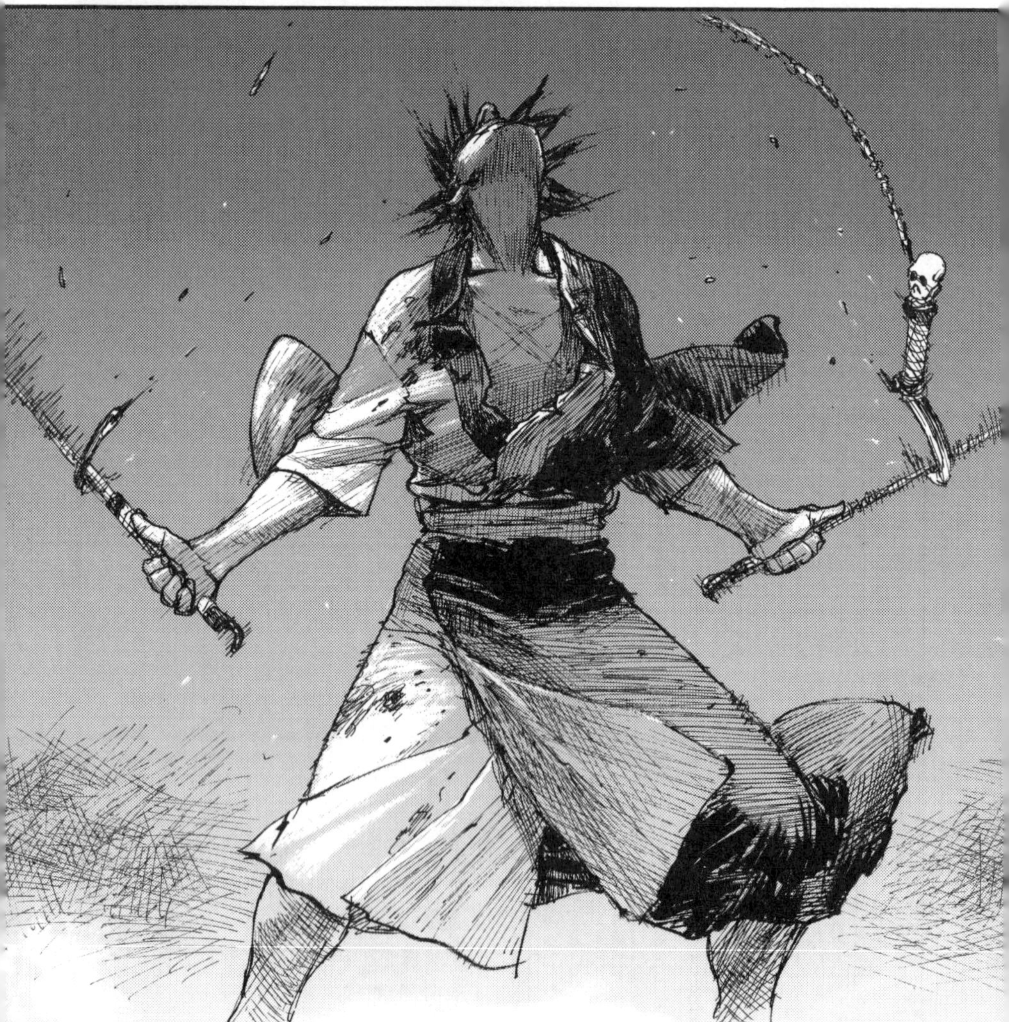

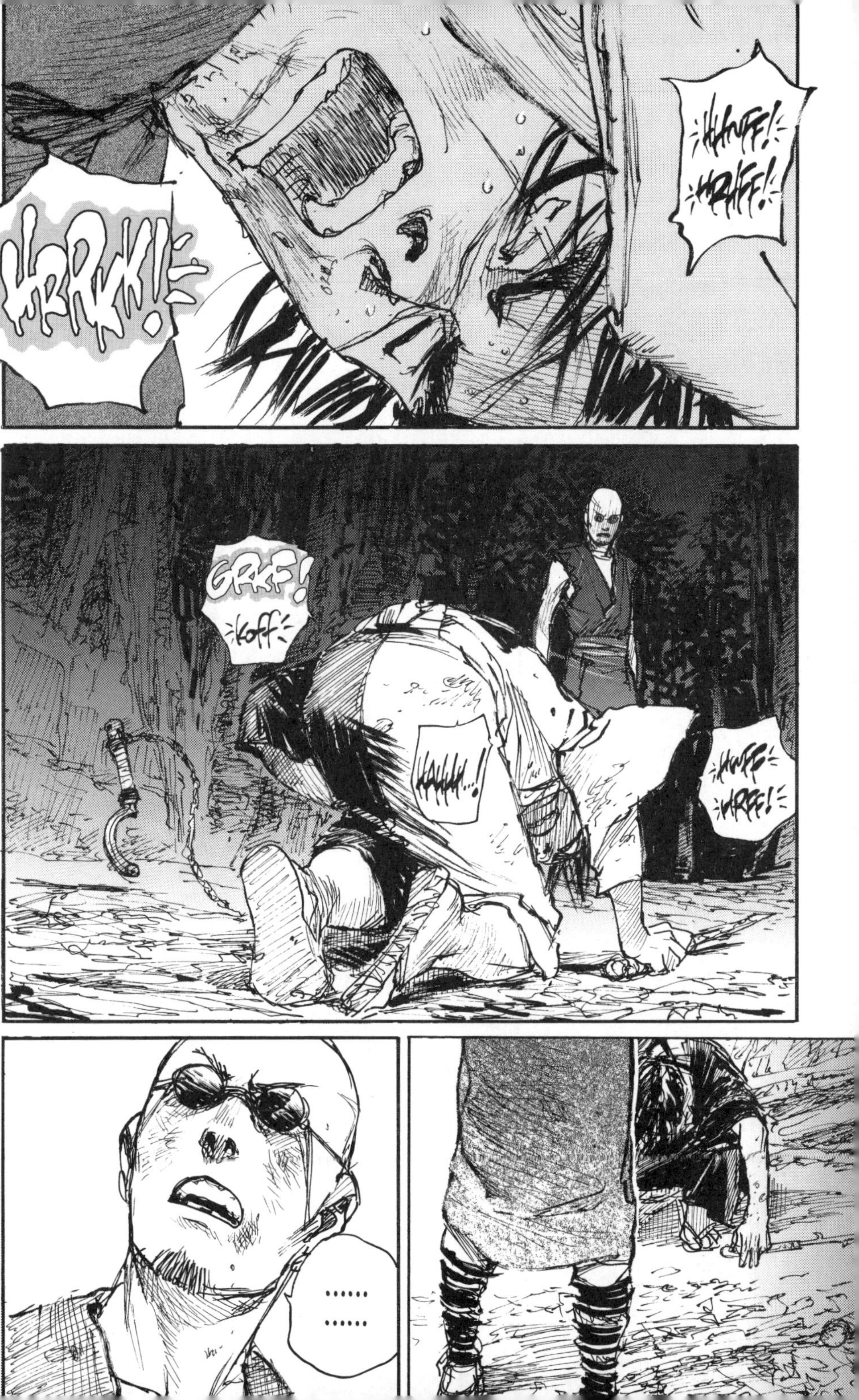
HHAFF! HRHFF!
HRRK!
GRKF! KOFF
HAHH...!
HHAFF HRFF!
......
......

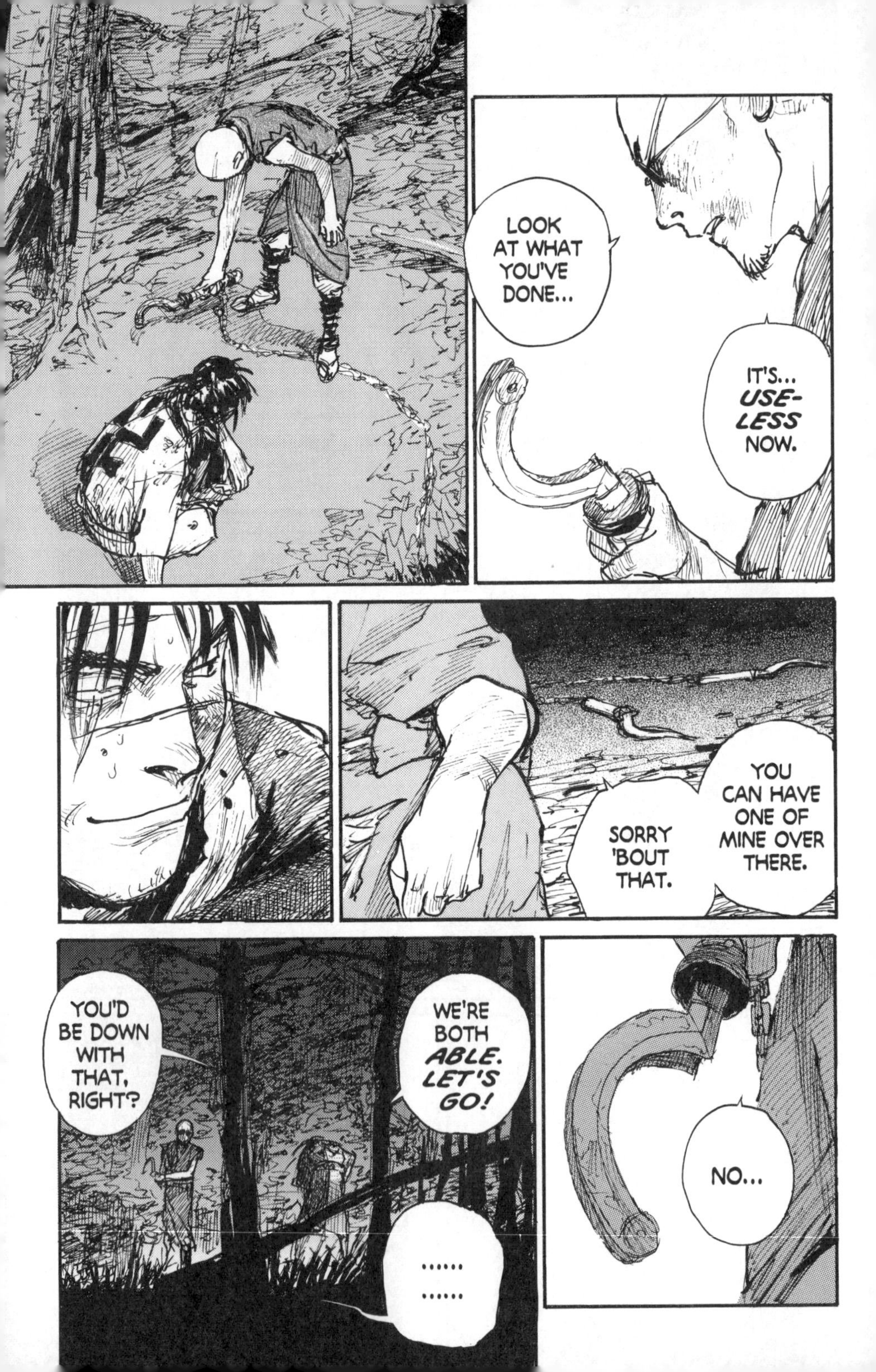
LOOK AT WHAT YOU'VE DONE...
IT'S... *USELESS* NOW.
SORRY 'BOUT THAT.
YOU CAN HAVE ONE OF MINE OVER THERE.
YOU'D BE DOWN WITH THAT, RIGHT?
WE'RE BOTH *ABLE. LET'S GO!*
......
......
NO...

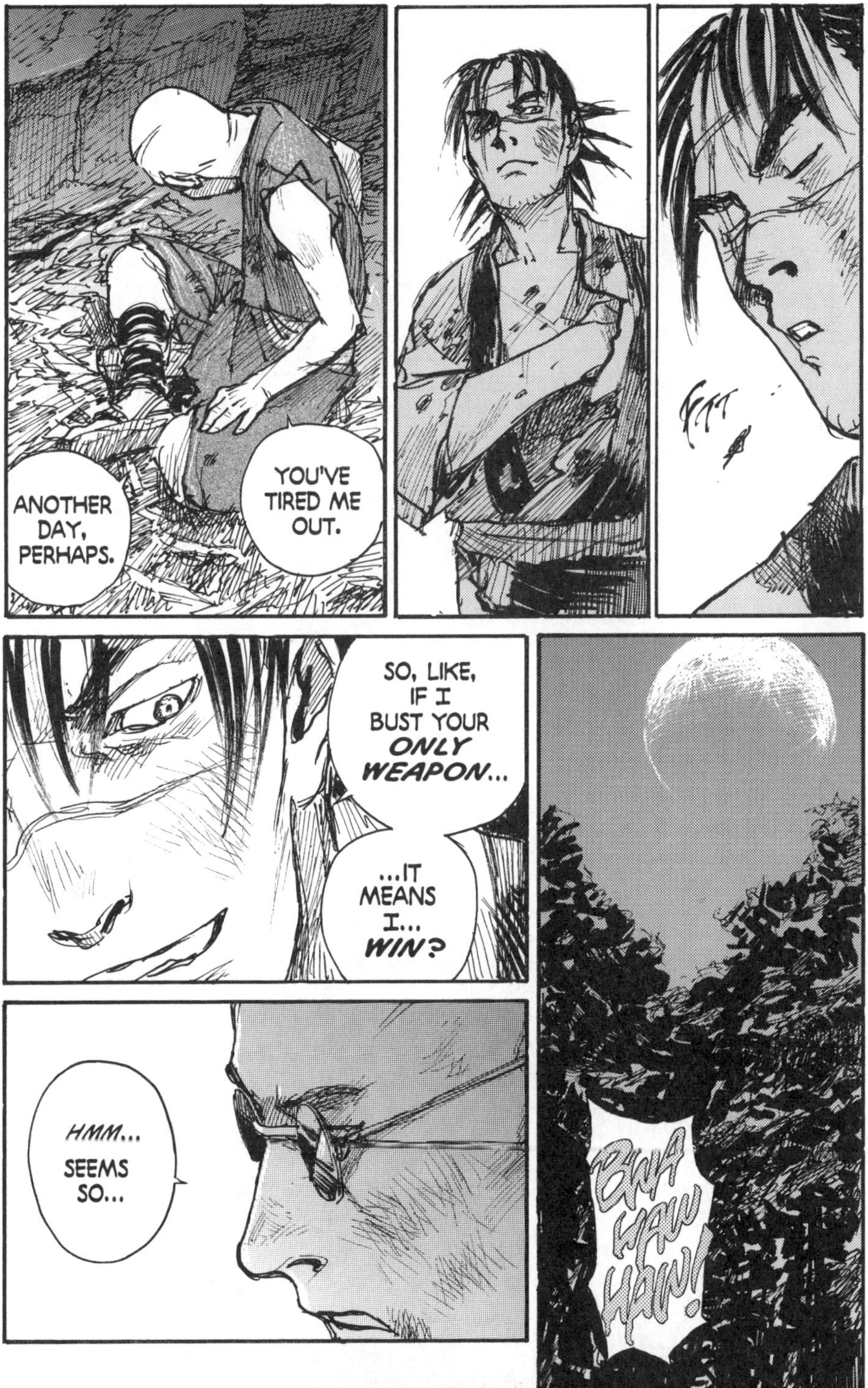
YOU'VE TIRED ME OUT.
ANOTHER DAY, PERHAPS.
FTT
SO, LIKE, IF I BUST YOUR *ONLY WEAPON*...
...IT MEANS I... *WIN?*
HMM... SEEMS SO...
BWA HAW HAW!

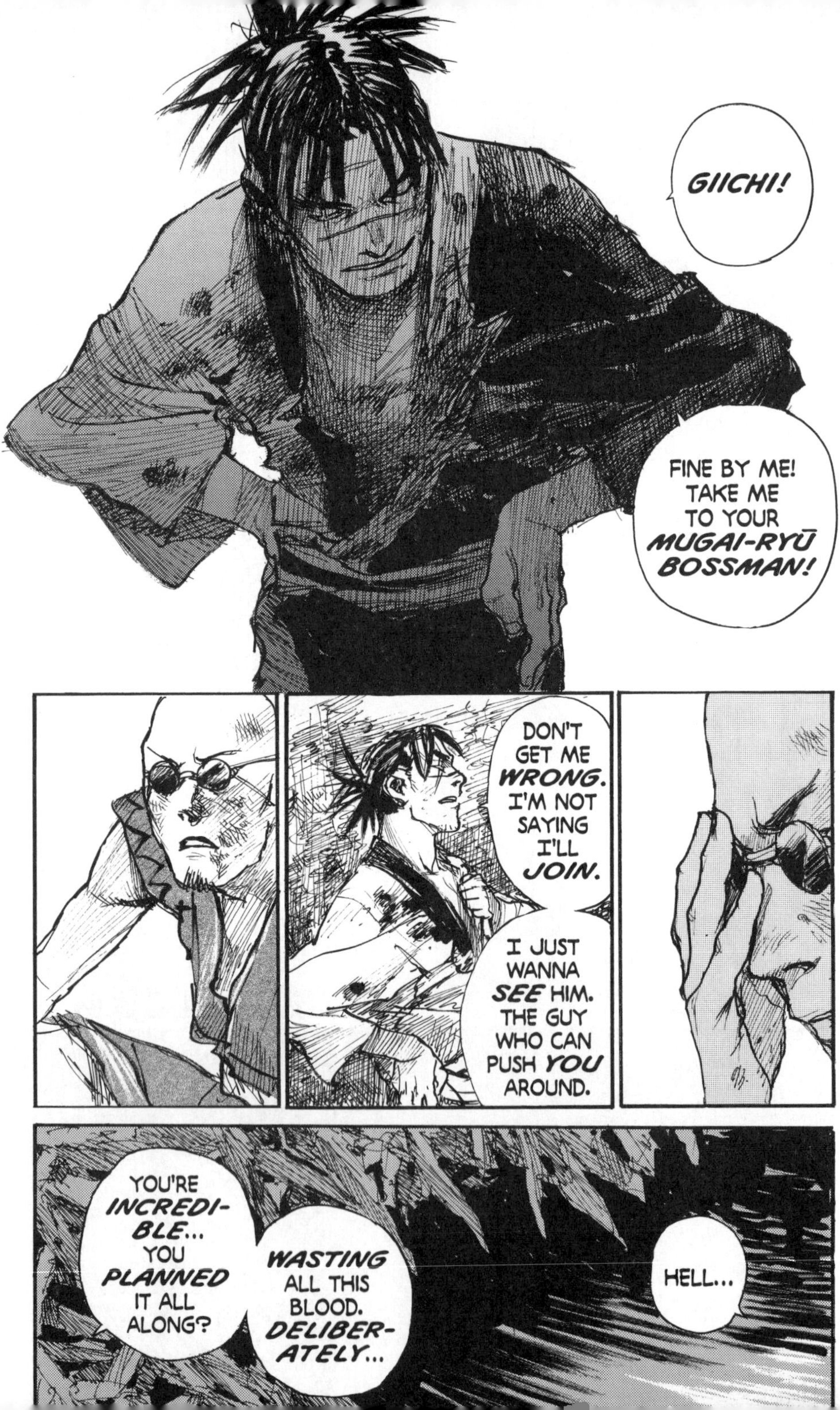
GIICHI!
FINE BY ME! TAKE ME TO YOUR MUGAI-RYŪ BOSSMAN!
DON'T GET ME WRONG. I'M NOT SAYING I'LL JOIN.
I JUST WANNA SEE HIM. THE GUY WHO CAN PUSH YOU AROUND.
HELL...
YOU'RE INCREDI-BLE... YOU PLANNED IT ALL ALONG?
WASTING ALL THIS BLOOD. DELIBER-ATELY...

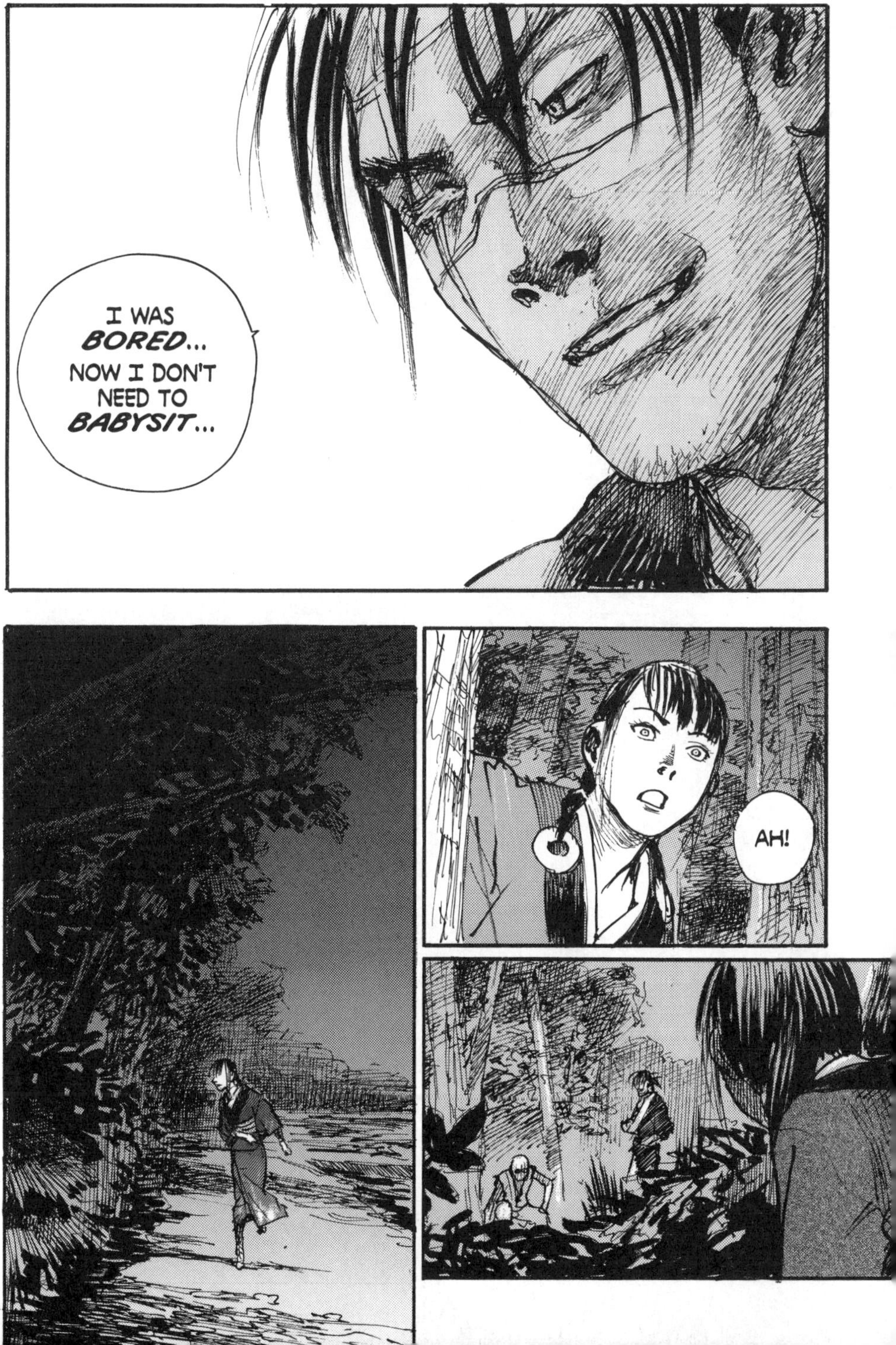
I WAS *BORED*... NOW I DON'T NEED TO *BABYSIT*...
AH!

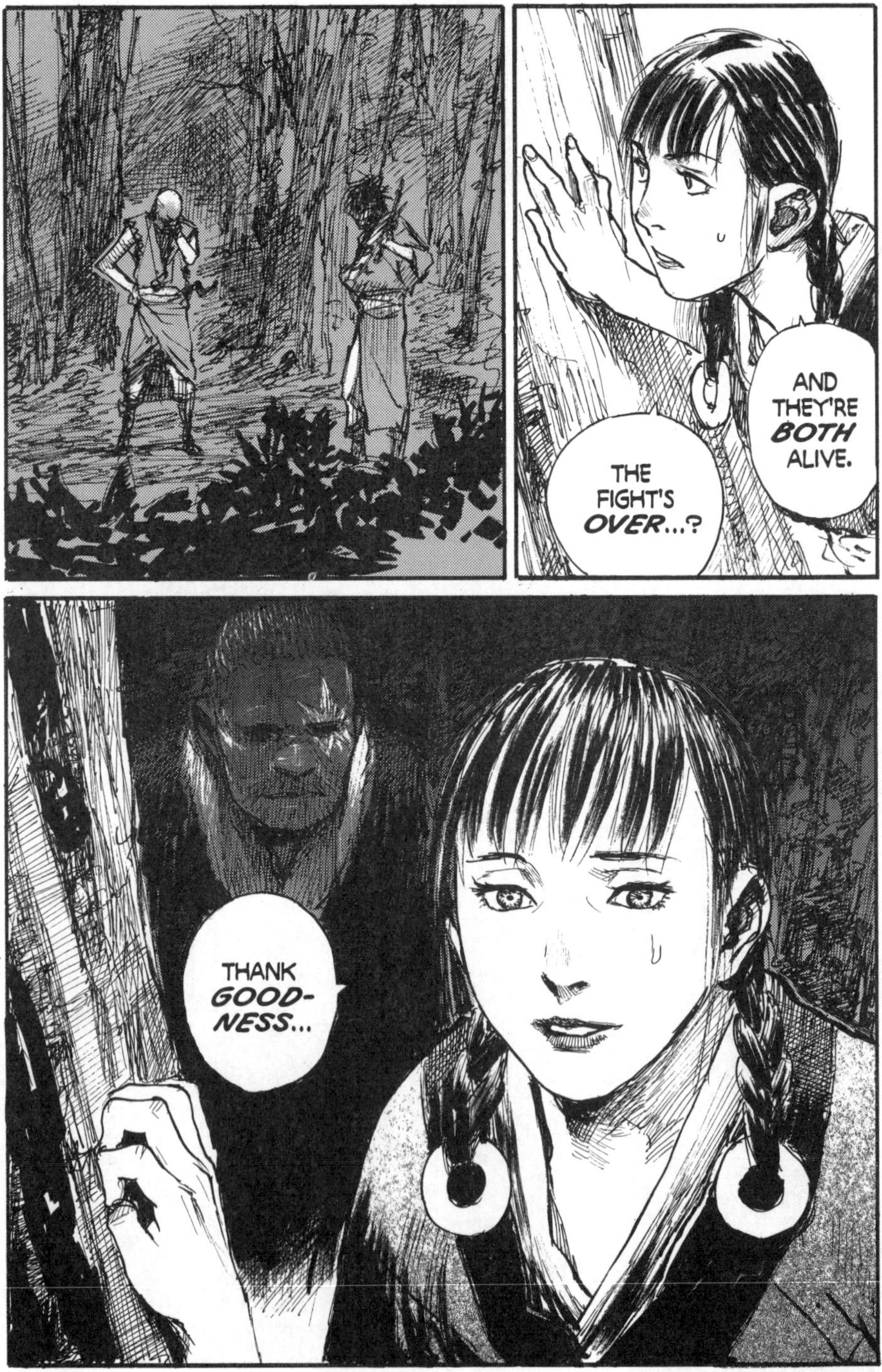
THE FIGHT'S *OVER*...?
AND THEY'RE *BOTH* ALIVE.
THANK *GOOD-NESS*...

TO BE CONTINUED...!

GLOSSARY

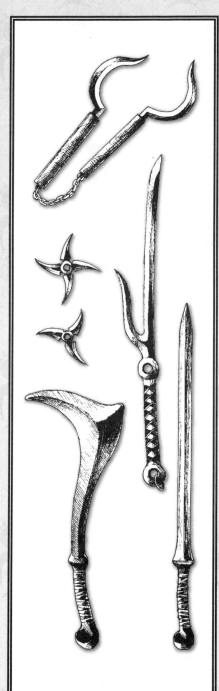

bakufu: the central government; the bureaucracy that grew up around the Tokugawa shoguns. Originally established in Edo, today's Tokyo, by the warlord Tokugawa Ieyasu.

bangashira: head of the *banshū*.

banshū: officers serving under the Shogun, usually assigned to Edo Castle to defend the Shogun himself.

dōjō: a hall for martial arts training; here centers for swordsmanship.

dono: a very polite honorific indicating much respect.

Go-Rōjū: senior councilors to the Shogun, picked from the most trusted *daimyō* (feudal lords).

hakama: outer garment worn by samurai, made of leather or heavy cloth and sometimes dyed with distinctive colors and patterns.

han: a feudal domain.

hara-kiri: ritual suicide by disembowelment.

Ittō-ryū: the radical sword school of Anotsu Kagehisa.

kenshi: a swordsman (or swordswoman), not necessarily born into the samurai caste; a warrior.

ryō: a gold piece.

ryū: a sword school.

Shingyōtō-ryū: a *dōjō* that celebrated older, harsher traditions of combat training.

tsukiyotake: poisonous mushroom unique to Japan.

Hiroaki Samura's Eisner Award-winning manga epic

BLADE
OF THE IMMORTAL

Volume 1: Blood of a Thousand
ISBN-10: 1-56971-239-5
ISBN-13: 978-1-56971-239-9
$14.95
Volume 2: Cry of the Worm
ISBN-10: 1-56971-300-6
ISBN-13: 978-1-56971-300-6
$14.95
Volume 3: Dreamsong
ISBN-10: 1-56971-357-X
ISBN-13: 978-1-56971-357-0
$14.95
Volume 4: On Silent Wings
ISBN-10: 1-56971-412-6
ISBN-13: 978-1-56971-412-6
$14.95
Volume 5: On Silent Wings II
ISBN-10: 1-56971-444-4
ISBN-13: 978-1-56971-444-7
$14.95
Volume 6: Dark Shadows
ISBN-10: 1-56971-469-X
ISBN-13: 978-1-56971-469-0
$14.95
Volume 7: Heart of Darkness
ISBN-10: 1-56971-531-9
ISBN-13: 978-1-56971-531-4
$16.95
Volume 8: The Gathering
ISBN-10: 1-56971-546-7
ISBN-13: 978-1-56971-546-8
$15.95
Volume 9: The Gathering II
ISBN-10: 1-56971-560-2
ISBN-13: 978-1-56971-560-4
$15.95

Volume 10: Secrets
ISBN-10: 1-56971-746-X
ISBN-13: 978-1-56971-746-2
$16.95
Volume 11: Beasts
ISBN-10: 1-56971-741-9
ISBN-13: 978-1-56971-741-7
$14.95
Volume 12: Autumn Frost
ISBN-10: 1-56971-991-8
ISBN-13: 978-1-56971-991-6
$16.95
Volume 13: Mirror of the Soul
ISBN-10: 1-59307-218-X
ISBN-13: 978-1-59307-218-6
$17.95
Volume 14: Last Blood
ISBN-10: 1-59307-321-6
ISBN-13: 978-1-59307-321-3
$17.95

Volume 15: Trickster
ISBN-10: 1-59307-468-9
ISBN-13: 978-1-59307-468-5
$16.95
Volume 16: Shortcut
ISBN-10: 1-59307-723-8
ISBN-13: 978-1-59307-723-5
$16.95

AVAILABLE AT YOUR LOCAL COMICS SHOP OR BOOKSTORE • To find a comics shop in your area, call 1-888-266-4226
For more information or to order direct visit darkhorse.com or call 1-800-862-0052 Mon.-Fri. 9 A.M. to 5 P.M. Pacific Time.
*Prices and availability subject to change without notice

darkhorse.com